The *Essential* Handbook of Offender Assessment and Treatment

Edited by
Clive R. Hollin
Division of Forensic Mental Health,
University of Leicester, Leicester, UK

WILEY

Copyright © 2004   John Wiley & Sons Ltd, The Atrium, Southern Gate, Chichester,
West Sussex PO19 8SQ, England

Telephone (+44) 1243 779777

The chapters in this volume were originally published in the *Handbook of Offender Assessment and Treatment* edited by Clive R. Hollin. Copyright © 2001 by John Wiley & Sons, Ltd.

Email (for orders and customer service enquiries): cs-books@wiley.co.uk
Visit our Home Page on www.wileyeurope.com or www.wiley.com

Reprinted June 2004

Other Wiley Editorial Offices

John Wiley & Sons Inc., 111 River Street, Hoboken, NJ 07030, USA

Jossey-Bass, 989 Market Street, San Francisco, CA 94103-1741, USA

Wiley-VCH Verlag GmbH, Boschstr. 12, D-69469 Weinheim, Germany

John Wiley & Sons Australia Ltd, 33 Park Road, Milton, Queensland 4064, Australia

John Wiley & Sons (Asia) Pte Ltd, 2 Clementi Loop #02-01, Jin Xing Distripark, Singapore 129809

John Wiley & Sons Canada Ltd, 22 Worcester Road, Etobicoke, Ontario, Canada M9W 1L1

Wiley also publishes its books in a variety of electronic formats. Some content that appears in print may not be available in electronic books.

Library of Congress Cataloging-in-Publication Data

The essential handbook of offender assessment and treatment / edited by Clive R. Hollin.
      p.   cm.
Based on Handbook of offender assessment and treatment: New York : Wiley, 2001.
Includes bibliographical references and index.
      ISBN 0-470-85436-7 (Paper : alk. paper)
   1. Prisoners—Mental health services—Handbooks, manuals, etc.   I. Hollin, Clive R.
II. Handbook of offender assessment and treatment.
      RC451.4.P68E875 2003
      364.3—dc21

                                                                                      2003013115

British Library Cataloguing in Publication Data
A catalogue record for this book is available from the British Library

ISBN 0-470-85436-7

Typeset in 10/12pt Times by SNP Best-set Typesetter Ltd., Hong Kong
Printed and bound in Great Britain by TJ International Ltd, Padstow, Cornwall
This book is printed on acid-free paper responsibly manufactured from sustainable forestry in which at least two trees are planted for each one used for paper production.

The *Essential* Handbook of
...ssment
...atment

For Paul and Jane, *Essentially*

Contents

About the Editor

Clive Hollin is Professor of Criminological Psychology in the Department of Psychiatry, Division of Forensic Mental Health, at The University of Leicester based in the Academic Unit at Arnold Lodge Regional Secure Unit. Alongside his academic appointments he has worked as a prison psychologist, as Director of Rehabilitation in the Youth Treatment Service, as a Consultant Forensic Psychologist at Rampton Hospital, and currently at Arnold Lodge RSU. His main research interest lies in the interface between psychology and criminology, particularly with reference to the management and treatment of offenders. He has published widely in the field of criminological psychology, including the best-selling text *Psychology and Crime: An Introduction to Criminological Psychology*, and is co-editor of the journal *Psychology, Crime, & Law*. Professor Hollin works as a consultant and researcher with several practice agencies, including the Prison and Probation Services, on the design, implementation, and evaluation of programmes to reduce offending. He is the 1998 recipient of the Senior Career Award for Distinguished Contribution to the Field of Criminological and Legal Psychology, presented by the Division of Criminological and Legal Psychology of The British Psychological Society.

List of Contributors

Gerard Bailes, *Psychology Department, Norvic Clinic, Norwich N17 0HT, UK.*

Laura Black, *Psychology Department, The State Hospital, Carstairs, Lanarkshire, UK.*

R. Karl Hanson, *Corrections Research Department of the Solicitor General of Canada, 40 Laurier Avenue West, Ottawa, Ontario, Canada K1A OP8.*

Scott W. Henggeler, *Family Services Research Center, Department of Psychiatry and Behavioral Sciences, Medical University of South Carolina, Charleston, SC 29425-9742, USA.*

Sheilagh Hodgins, *Department of Forensic Mental Science, Institute of Psychiatry, DeCrespigny Park, London SE5 8AF, UK.*

Clive R. Hollin, *Division of Forensic Mental Health, University of Leicester, Arnold Lodge, Leicester LE5 OLE, UK.*

Stephen M. Hudson, Late of the *Department of Psychology, University of Canterbury, Christchurch, New Zealand.*

Thomas R. Keenan, *Department of Psychology, University of Canterbury, Christchurch, New Zealand.*

David J. Kolko, *University of Pittsburgh Medical Center, Western Psychiatric Institute and Clinic, 3811 O'Hara Street, Pittsburgh, PA 15213-2593, USA.*

David LeMarquand, *Research Unit on Children's Psychosocial Maladjustment, Université de Montréal, 750 E. Gouvin Blvd, Montréal, Québec, Canada H2C 1A6.*

William L. Marshall, *Department of Psychology, Queen's University, Kingston, Ontario, Canada K7L 3N6.*

James McGuire, *Department of Clinical Psychology, University of Liverpool, The Whelan Building, Liverpool L69 3GB, UK.*

Mary McMurran, *School of Psychology, Cardiff University, Cardiff CF1 3YG, UK.*

Michael A. Milan, *Department of Psychology, Georgia State University, Atlanta, GA 30303-3083, USA.*

Raymond W. Novaco, *Psychology and Social Behavior, School of Social Ecology, University of California, Irvine, CA 92717-5150, USA.*

Emma J. Palmer, *Division of Forensic Mental Health, University of Leicester, Leicester LE5 OLE, UK.*

Devon L. L. Polaschek, *School of Psychology, Victoria University of Wellington, Wellington, New Zealand.*

Frank J. Porporino, *T³ Associates, 159 Gilmour Street, Ottawa, Ontario, Canada K2P ON8.*

Mark Ramm, *Psychology Department, The State Hospital, Carstairs, Lanarkshire, UK.*

Nikki Reynolds, *Department of Corrections Psychological Service, PO Box 5443, Lambton Quay, Wellington, New Zealand.*

David Robinson, *T³ Associates, 159 Gilmour Street, Ottawa, Ontario, Canada K2P ON8.*

Sonja K. Schoenwald, *Family Services Research Center, Department of Psychiatry and Behavioral Sciences, Medical University of South Carolina, Charleston, SC 29425-9742, USA.*

Cynthia Cupit Swenson, *Family Services Research Center, Department of Psychiatry and Behavioral Sciences, Medical University of South Carolina, Charleston, SC 29425-9742, USA.*

Richard E. Tremblay, *Research Unit on Children's Psychosocial Maladjustment, Université de Montréal, 750 E. Gouvin Blvd, Montréal, Québec, Canada H2C 1A6.*

Tony Ward, *Department of Criminology, University of Melbourne, Victoria 3010, Australia.*

Christopher D. Webster, *University of Toronto, Simon Fraser University, and Earlscourt Child and Family Centre, 130 George Street, Toronto, Ontario, Canada M5S 1A1.*

Preface

The hardback version of the *Handbook of Offender Assessment and Treatment* is a bit of a marathon effort, coming in at over 600 pages of accumulated wisdom presented by, as one reviewer put it, "the great and the good of contemporary forensic psychology". My thoughts in putting together the original version were along the lines of producing a compendium of knowledge, written by some of the leading figures in the field, that would provide a comprehensive source for academics, students and practitioners. On reflection, I'm reasonably satisfied that the published text was line in with my thinking: while there are always things that might have been done differently, the book is pretty much as I'd hoped it would be.

After the hardback, of course, comes the paperback. In discussing the possibilities with Vivien Ward at Wiley, we came up with the notion of the essential handbook. Rather than reproducing a full-length paperback version of the hardback, the idea was to distil the absolutely essential chapters to produce a leaner and fitter version of the original. This plan was easier to concoct than to put into action as it quickly became evident that all the chapters were essential! After much angst, it was decided to have an explicit focus on the major offender groups, narrowing down the text to those chapters that are absolutely essential to the assessment and treatment of those groups. In practice, this meant rearranging the structure of the original text and making some hard choices about what to include and what to omit.

I should state explicitly that the decision on which chapters to include and omit was made solely on the basis of what fitted best into the configuration of this text. There were no value or quality judgements made about the chapters in the original text, it was all down to subject matter. The authors of the chapters included here were given the opportunity to make minor changes to their chapters, but what is published here is to all intents and purposes what was in the original.

I hope the *Essential* Handbook becomes essential reading, but even more I hope that readers who pick up the *Essential* Handbook will be stimulated to go to the hardback version, where even more of the great and the good are waiting to be read.

Clive Hollin
Leicester

Foreword

In the last 20 years, there has been a renaissance of rehabilitation – and about time too! The arguments in the 1970s that "nothing works" had very damaging effects: governments focussed on retributive sentencing and cut back on efforts to change offenders. Happily, as Clive Hollin points out, these dark ages are now past and the focus nowadays is on "What Works?" Governments profess commitment to "evidence-based practice" and the evidence clearly shows that it is possible to prevent offending and to rehabilitate (or at least improve) offenders.

I am delighted to welcome this compact Handbook, which contains a mine of useful and up-to-date information about the assessment and treatment of offenders. It is amazing how much valuable knowledge can be packed into such a short book! Partly this is because the contributors include such a dazzling array of leading experts in the field, from several different countries. Hence, the coverage is impressively international.

Risk assessment has become an increasingly important topic in forensic psychology in the last decade. In Part I, Webster and Bailes describe some of the most important violence prediction instruments, including VRAG, HCR-20 and SARA, and Karl Hanson reviews risk assessment instruments for sex offenders. It seems clear that the next generation of risk assessment instruments should focus on dynamic risk factors so that they can be used to assess the effects of interventions.

Part II contains several illuminating reviews of treatment methods, including the famous and widely-used "Reasoning and Rehabilitation" programme (Robinson and Porporino), social skills training (Hollin and Palmer), anger management (Novaco, Ramm and Black), family-based treatments (Swenson, Henggeler and Schoenwald) and school-based treatments (Le Marquand and Tremblay). Michael Milan's chapter provides a useful historical perspective in reviewing some of the early pioneering work on behaviour modification in corrections. These chapters describe not only the treatments but also outcome evaluations, and some chapters contain very helpful and detailed summary tables. Evaluations containing cost-benefit analyses are particularly impressive to government policy-makers.

Part III reviews types of offenders, including sex offenders against women (Marshall) and against children (Ward, Hudson and Keenan), firesetters (Kolko), violent offenders (Polaschek and Reynolds), property offenders (McGuire), offenders with personality disorders (McMurran) and with major mental disorders (Hodgins). These chapters provide information about many types of treatments, including cognitive-behavioural methods, aggression replacement therapy, dialectical behaviour therapy, and therapeutic communities. They also describe assessment techniques and outcome evaluations. While it is rather invidious to pick out any one chapter for special comment, I thought that David Kolko's coverage of prevalence and recidivism, descriptive and clinical characteristics, assessment of children and incidents, risk factors, prevention, treatment, outcome studies, programme development and dissemination, and future directions was particularly comprehensive and compelling. If you want to find out all you need to know about young arsonists, read this chapter!

The whole book can be confidently recommended to anyone who wishes to obtain the most valid and valuable modern information about offender assessment and treatment from leading international experts. Any reader will learn a great deal, as I did. Clive Hollin should be warmly commended for assembling such an important collection of chapters by such leading international scholars within such a concise and accessible framework. This book should be essential reading for forensic psychologists and others concerned with offender assessment and treatment.

David P. Farrington
Professor of Psychological Criminology
Cambridge University

Chapter 1

To Treat or Not to Treat? An Historical Perspective

Clive R. Hollin
University of Leicester, Leicester, UK

INTRODUCTION

> We are passing from the sphere of history to the sphere of the present and partly to the sphere of the future (Vladimir I. Lenin, *What is to be Done?*).

There is, it seems, one statistic that can be predicted with a high degree of accuracy: each year crime figures are released; each year the number of recorded crimes will have increased compared with previous years. In England and Wales, for example, if we look back over the past few decades, the number of recorded crimes has inexorably risen, hitting milestone after milestone with monotonous regularity. In the 1950s there were 500 000 recorded crimes, a figure that steadily rose, million by million, over the following decades. Thus, the Home Office Statistical Bulletin dated 24 September 1996, notes that: "5.1 million offences were recorded by the police in the twelve months to June 1996, an increase of 0.4 per cent from the previous twelve months" (p. 1).

Now, there are many reasons to be cautious about crime figures, official or otherwise (Bottomley & Pease, 1986; Coleman & Moynihan, 1996), but the point to be made is that crime is a significant issue in contemporary society. The significance of crime is at least fourfold: first, there are victims who suffer personal harm or corporate loss; second, there are offenders and their families who may lead impoverished and unhappy lives; third, there is the cost to the public purse in running the criminal justice system and offering health care for victims; fourth, there are the general costs of insurance, repairs, and replacement of lost goods.

There is nothing new about crime. Throughout history all societies have experienced the unwanted effects and costs of crime. It is therefore reasonable to

---

The Essential *Handbook of Offender Assessment and Treatment.* Edited by C. R. Hollin.

assume that crime will always be part of our society; crime is not going to disappear from our everyday lives. If we accept this assumption, and it is one that is difficult to resist, then the crime problem can be seen as a management problem: as a society, how are we best to contain and reduce the harm and the costs of crime?

The quotation at the head of this chapter offers a structure within which the question of management of crime can be considered. In seeking to understand the current moral, philosophical, legal, political, and practical complexities associated with the treatment of offenders, we need to consider first the sphere of history.

THE SPHERE OF HISTORY

If we look to the sphere of history in western society, it is plain that for many centuries the solution to the crime management problem lay in the hands of the rich and powerful. It was royalty, landowners, judges and the like who, in arbitrary fashion, dispensed penalties for crime. Inevitably, the punishments for crime were severe, typically involving public humiliation, mutilation, burning, and execution: in England in the mid-1800s there were more than 100 offences that were punishable by the death penalty. The beginnings of the changes that heralded the development of the current legal system took place in the mid-1700s with the advent of classical theory.

Classical Theory

The roots of classical theory as an influence in law are traced in many texts (e.g. Roshier, 1989; Russell, 1961; Siegal, 1986) to the influence of two key figures: the Italian nobleman and economist, Cesare Beccaria (b. 1738), and the British philosopher, Jeremy Bentham (b. 1748). At a time when punishment for crime was inevitably severe in the extreme, both Beccaria and Bentham argued the case for the principle of *utility*.

The principle of utility, in which Beccaria's economic influence is clear, has its basis in a hedonistic view of human behaviour. The assumption underpinning this theoretical position is that our actions are intended to avoid pain and gain pleasure. It follows that crimes are committed when the criminal judges, making a rational choice of their own free will, that he or she is able to act in a criminal manner, avoiding pain and gaining reward. A system of criminal law, therefore, must aim to make the individual's interests the same as those of society at large; that is, neither the individual nor other members of society will want a crime to be committed. Thus, criminal law must seek to prevent crime by deterring both the individual and society from committing criminal acts by ensuring that the pain of sanctions outweighs the pleasure of a successful crime. Indeed, Bentham held that punishment should seek to achieve four outcomes:

1. To prevent crime.
2. If prevention is not achieved, then to convince a criminal to commit a less serious crime.
3. To reduce the harm inflicted during a crime.
4. To prevent crime as cheaply as possible.

The practical implications of a utilitarian philosophy were to affect profoundly the legal system across nineteenth-century Europe. Contrary to the belief of the day, utilitarianism argued that excessive punishment is both unnecessary and counter-productive in terms of preventing crime. The level of punishment, it is argued, should be in proportion to the severity of the crime. The reasoning behind this position is plain. If all crimes carry an equally harsh penalty, then there can be no selective, differential effect of punishment. For example, if child abuse and murder were both punishable by the death penalty, then logically the child abuser would have little reason not to kill their victim to prevent disclosure of the abuse. In other words, matching the crime to the punishment creates the possibility that punishment can act as a deterrent to criminal acts.

Thus, classical theory offers an explanation for criminal behaviour, and proposes a system based on punishment by which crime can be controlled. There are two key assumptions inherent within classical theory: first, that we exercise free will in making choices about our actions; second, that we act in a rational manner in making those choices.

The legacy of classical theory is clearly seen in the modern day legal systems of Europe and the United States. The principle of *mens rea*, guilty intent, lies close to the concept of free will. The dispensation by contemporary courts of punishments that seek to fit the crime, thereby acting as a deterrent to further offending, clearly owes much to utilitarian thinking. Thus, classical theory, utilitarianism, and crime prevention through punishment are powerful historical factors in shaping the way society both conceptualizes crime and develops strategies to manage the problems presented by criminal behaviour.

The most obvious challenge to the assumptions inherent in classical theory arose as the new discipline of Psychology began to take shape.

Psychological Theory and Crime

A traditional starting place in the history of theoretical developments within mainstream psychology is, of course, the psychoanalytic theory developed by Sigmund Freud. Tracing the broad historical lineage of psychology after Freud and psychodynamic theory, we see the influence of Ivan Pavlov and B. F. Skinner in the development of learning theory; Raymond B. Cattell and Hans Eysenck in the articulation of personality theory; the movement from traditional learning theories to social learning and cognitive–behavioural theory, perhaps best typified by the work of Julian Rotter and Albert Bandura; and, most recently, the advent of cognitive psychology as seen in the writings of John Anderson and Ulric Neisser.

Now, the point to make about most of these theories is that they seek to offer accounts of human action that are not always compatible with classical theory. To take the obvious and extreme example, B. F. Skinner's radical behaviourism seeks to account for human behaviour in terms of a genotype–environment interaction and has no time for the ghost in the machine of free will.

As psychological theories unfolded, there were two further important developments: first, theories became the basis of therapies; second, the theories began to be applied to the phenomenon of criminal behaviour. Thus, to follow the broad theories outlined above, we can chart the unfolding of therapies within the tradition of psychoanalysis and psychodynamic psychotherapy; then behaviour modification, behaviour therapy, and cognitive–behaviour therapy; and, most recently, cognitive therapy. Of course, there are many variations on themes and the distinctions often become blurred in practice, but most psychologists would, I think, recognise these broad churches of therapy.

The application of psychological theories to offer an account of criminal behaviour similarly follows an historical route that closely tracks theoretical development. Psychodynamically orientated accounts of criminal behaviour are to be seen, for example, in Alexander's use of the concept of the reality principle to explain criminal behaviour (Alexander & Healy, 1935; Alexander & Staub, 1931). Similarly, Healy and Bronner (1936) applied the psychoanalytic concept of sublimation to offer an account of criminal behaviour. Most famously, and perhaps most influentially, John Bowlby's writings on material deprivation and delinquency are a clear attempt to apply psychodynamic thought to explain offending (Bowlby, 1944, 1946).

The influence of learning theory is clearly to be seen in Differential Association Theory (Sutherland, 1947), and in Differential Reinforcement Theory (Jeffery, 1965). Bandura (1973) applied his own social learning theory to aggressive behaviour, while Ronald Akers uses social learning theory in its fullest sense to develop a theory of crime (Akers, 1977; Akers, Krohn, Lanza-Kaduce & Radosevich, 1979). The application of personality theory is clearly seen in two traditions: Eysenck most famously developed the theme of personality and crime (Eysenck, 1977), while Blackburn's experimental and theoretical work clearly makes a major contribution within this approach (Blackburn, 1968, 1986).

The impact of cognitive psychology is seen in two conceptually distinct research camps. The first approach is to be found in studies that are concerned with social cognition and social information processing in offenders. A body of evidence has accrued on the relationship between social cognition, such as empathy, social problem solving, moral reasoning and social perception, and offending (Ross & Fabiano, 1985). Similarly, Kenneth Dodge has developed a comprehensive model of social information processing as applied to understanding delinquent behaviour (e.g. Crick & Dodge, 1994). Allied to this approach is the influential research by Raymond Novaco on the role of anger in violent crime (e.g. Novaco, 1994). Dodge's work is concerned with the interaction between socio-cognitive development and the aetiology of child and adolescent problems, including delinquent behaviour. The exploration of the overlap between this work and the findings of the longitudinal research, as exemplified by the highly influential work of David Farrington (e.g. Farrington, 1995), is a project waiting to be completed.

The second cognitive approach, portraying the offender as a rational decision-maker (e.g. Cornish & Clarke, 1986), is interesting for two reasons. First, this approach applies a particular branch of cognitive research, decision-making, to understanding criminal behaviour. Second, the view of the offender as a *rational* decision-maker stands comparison with the classical view of the offender acting of their own free will. Indeed, the whole approach of rational decision-making has been seen as heralding the advent of neo-classical criminological theory.

Applying Theory: The Rise of Rehabilitation Through Treatment

Not content with the development of psychological explanations of criminal behaviour, psychologists were eager to turn theory into practice. As the development of treatment methods followed theoretical advances in psychology, so a succession of therapeutic approaches was applied to work with offenders. For example, working within a psychoanalytic tradition, August Aichhorn (1925–1955) articulated a theory of latent delinquency. Working from this position, in which delinquent behaviour is seen as the product of a failure in psychological development, Aichhorn developed therapeutic methods to work with young offenders. Throughout the years up to the 1970s, treatment with offenders was dominated by methods following psychodynamic principles, with counselling and group therapy particularly widely applied. In addition, educational programmes proved popular during that period, a trend still evident today (e.g. Schweinhart, Barnes, & Weikart, 1993).

While treatment within a psychodynamic tradition continues today (e.g. Cordess & Cox, 1996), the decades since the 1970s, 1980s, and 1990s have seen an upsurge in offender treatment programmes based on behavioural and cognitive–behavioural principles (e.g. Hollin, 1990; McGuire, 1995; Nietzel, 1979; Ross & Fabiano, 1985). Thus, certainly by the late 1950s and into the 1960s, a position had been reached in which psychological theories had been applied to criminal behaviour, and associated treatments were relatively widely used for a range of offender groups.

Conflict Between Criminal Justice and Treatment

It is during the 1960s that the first contemporary signs of unease can be detected. As Jeffery (1960) notes, there are three apparent assumptions inherent within a treatment philosophy; that is, *determinism*, *differentiation*, and *pathology*. Each of these three assumptions sets advocates of treatment in potential conflict with a criminal justice system that is configured on principles stemming from classical theory.

First, determinism holds that factors outside of the individual's control—be they biological, psychological, social factors, or, more likely, some combination of all three—bring about the individual's behaviour. Second, the logical conclusion from a deterministic position is that criminals are different from non-criminals. The origin of this differentiation may be biological, psychological, or social, but the position remains that criminals are in some way different from people who are not criminals. Third, the notion of pathology, the logical next step from differentiation, is that the difference between criminals and non-criminals is one of abnormality. The cause of the abnormality may be individual to the offender (i.e. biological or psychological) or social through learning from an abnormal environment. Thus, we arrive at a position in which the offender is portrayed as a victim of circumstance, with some level of individual or social "wrongness" or abnormality as the root cause of their behaviour. Of course, it is easy to close the loop in arguing that some form of intervention, be it treatment or welfare, is needed to "cure" the offender of their crimes.

Now, clearly there are cases where the legal system makes due allowances, as, for example, with mentally disordered offenders, but in the main, determinism, differentiation, and pathology stand in direct conflict with a system based on the notion of free will (Alper, 1998). A deterministic position, in which the individual is compelled to offend by forces beyond their control, does not accord with rational hedonism as the basis for a criminal justice system.

Throughout the 1950s and 1960s an uneasy truce existed between advocates of treatment and the criminal justice system. Social and probation workers would plead their clients' cases, typically on grounds of personal or social mitigation, and the courts would consider a just verdict. However, it is clear that from a philosophical standpoint, rehabilitation and deterrence make uneasy companions.

The tensions between psychological models of offending, rehabilitation through treatment, and the theoretical underpinnings of criminal justice can be seen elsewhere in the system. As the academic study of crime grew, it became evident that criminology, with its academic base in sociology, was not going to accept easily the imposition of psychology and its attendant theories.

Conflict between Criminology and Psychology

It is difficult to unravel the history of criminology with the myriad of twists and turns that characterize its development as an academic discipline both in Britain and the United States (Tierney, 1996). With its roots in early psychiatric research in prisons, much of it government funded, the first studies in criminology were steeped in a positivist tradition, searching for the essential determinants of crime and the differences between criminals and non-criminals (e.g. Burt, 1925). However, by the 1950s an identifiable sociological criminology had begun to emerge. The forerunner of this sociological tradition in criminology is generally acknowledged to be the Chicago School and its famous studies, conducted through the 1920s, 1930s, and 1940s, showing the relationship between social organization (within the city of Chicago) and the incidence of crime (e.g. Shaw, 1930; Shaw & McKay, 1942). The American sociological criminology developed with, for example, the formulation of strain theory (Merton, 1938), Cohen's (1955) theory of delinquent subcultures, and social control theory (Hirschi, 1969). With the possible exception of Sutherland's differential association theory (Sutherland, 1939), criminology in the United States became predominantly a matter of sociological concern.

In Britain there was some criminological research in the American sociological tradition, as seen in the work of Morris (1957), Willmott (1966), and Downes (1966). However, the late 1960s and 1970s were to see a remarkable intellectual contribution by British criminologists. With its roots in deviancy theory, labelling theory, and European philosophy, the publication in 1973 of *The New Criminology* by Taylor, Walton, and Young marked the real impact of left-wing political analysis in mainstream criminology. While of immense theoretical significance, the new criminology was outright in its rejection of psychological theory and research in the criminological arena.

Since the 1970s, it appears that sociological criminology has become increasingly fragmented with the advent of left realism, critical criminology, feminist criminology, neo-classical theory, and even neo-positivism (Tierney, 1996). However, it is the 1970s that is the key period as we move from the sphere of the past to the sphere of the present.

Just Desserts and Marx: The Fall of Rehabilitation

While the offender treatment ideal flourished throughout the 1950s and 1960s, the fall was waiting to happen. Like a gunshot precipitating an avalanche, the publication in 1974 of Robert Martinson's paper, "What Works? Questions and Answers About Prison Reform", heralded a rush of those eager to disavow rehabilitation. Who were these opponents of rehabilitation? Cullen and Gendreau (1989) offer an analysis of the political and academic forces that very quickly quelled the rehabilitative ideal.

The marked political shift to the right in both the United States and Britain resolved the conflict between rehabilitation and the criminal justice system. Rehabilitation had been shown not to work and the return to a criminal justice philosophy based on force of punishment and just desserts quickly followed. (Martinson's later paper, published in 1979, in which he recanted many of the views expressed in his 1974 paper had little impact.) In England and Wales, for example, the 1979 May Report on the prison service asserted that the rhetoric of training and treatment had had its day and prisons should aim no higher than humane containment. The message that "nothing works" was also in accord with the dominant criminological theories of the mid-1970s, which, as noted above, were heavily based on political analysis and rejected the need for theories of crime that included individual factors. Thus, academic opposition to the over-throw of the rehabilitative ideal was, at best, fragmentary and, at worst, destructive (Andrews & Wormith, 1989).

As the message that "nothing works" continued to hit home during the 1980s, there were three significant strands of development. First, it was clear that any proponents of treatment (e.g. Gendreau & Ross, 1979, 1987) would be working against the ethos of the day. The 1980s became a time for the implementation of harsh measures, such as prison regimes given to boot camps and "short sharp shocks", to punish offenders harshly and deter them from a life of crime. Second, government funding shifted away from rehabilitation and into situational crime prevention. With its roots in a view of offenders as hedonistic rational decision-makers (Cornish & Clarke, 1986), this approach was in accord with classical theory and so attracted considerable government patronage. The legacy of situational crime prevention is to be seen in the plethora of alarms, security devices, video cameras, and electronic tagging of offenders that have rapidly become part of everyday life. Third, the research base in support of the effectiveness of treatment was subjected to intense academic criticism. While all research can be criticized, the thesis has been advanced that the real intention of the adverse academic criticism was to destroy the knowledge that human scientists could bring to explaining crime (Andrews & Bonta, 1998; Andrews & Wormith, 1989).

As events unfolded, the 1980s became a low point for those holding to the rehabilitative ideal: all notions of rehabilitation of offenders, including treatment, were looked on with scepticism and disfavour. The fall from grace was at its nadir.

THE SPHERE OF THE PRESENT

If the 1980s saw the fall of the rehabilitative ideal, then the early 1990s witnessed a spectacular resurrection, certainly in Canada and Britain and also in parts of the United States. The resurrection of treatment as an option within the criminal justice system can be directly traced to the impact of a string of meta-analytic studies of the effects of offender treatment published towards the end of the 1980s and into the 1990s (Andrews et al., 1990; Antonowicz & Ross, 1994; Cleland, Pearson, Lipton & Yee, 1997; Garrett, 1985; Gottschalk, Davidson, Gensheimer, & Mayer, 1987a, Gottschalk, Davidson, Mayer, & Gensheimer, 1987b; Izzo & Ross, 1990; Lipsey, 1992; Lösel & Köferl, 1989; Pearson, Lipton, & Cleland, 1997; Redondo, Garrido, Anguera, & Luque, 1996; Redondo, Sànchez-Meca & Garrido, 1999; Whitehead & Lab, 1989); with several syntheses also available (Gendreau, 1996; Gendreau & Andrews, 1990; Hollin, 1993, 1994, 1999; Lipsey, 1995; Lipsey & Wilson, 1998; Lösel, 1995a, 1995b, 1996; McGuire & Priestley, 1995). The message emerging from these studies was that treatment with offenders can have a small but significant effect in terms of reducing re-offending. Further, when certain treatment factors are combined, the meta-analyses suggest that this small effect can be considerably enhanced. It has therefore proved possible to describe the characteristics of "high-impact" programmes for offenders. Briefly, high-impact programmes would have the following character- istics: theoretically, they would espouse a cognitive–behavioural perspective; they would focus on the offence behaviour of high-risk offenders; the treatment would be delivered using a structured programme with defined aims and objectives; the treatment would be delivered by highly trained practitioners; and organizations would support, manage, and evaluate the programmes to ensure high treatment integrity (Hollin, 1995; Hollin, Epps, & Kendrick, 1995).

Research findings need a voice if they are to reach policy makers and practi- tioners: the development of the "what works" agenda, first by a small group of psychologists and probation officers, then by increasingly large numbers from several professions and service agencies, has provided the necessary impetus for a real movement to be evident (McGuire, 1995). Now, it would be wrong to assume that the case for treatment is proven: it is evident that a great deal more work needs to be carried out on the effectiveness of treatment. In particular, the outcome evidence from current treatment programmes configured according to "what works" principles will prove critical over the coming years.

THE SPHERE OF THE FUTURE

The resurrection of offender treatment raises some interesting possibilities in both the short and long term. In the short term it might be predicted that service agencies will focus on four interrelated aspects of treatment delivery. First, there will be a continued and growing interest in cognitive–behavioural theory and practice. Second, considerably more attention will be paid to practitioner train- ing in order to ensure high-quality delivery of treatment programmes. Third, the issue of treatment integrity will assume greater importance, with more attention being paid to the management, supervision, and support of practitioners deliv- ering treatment. Finally, in an era of evidence-based practice, service agencies will develop ever more sophisticated systems of monitoring and evaluating the effects of treatment.

Looking to the longer term, the predictions might be more speculative but some interesting possibilities arise. In terms of treatment content, it is likely that programmes will become ever more complex, seeking to attend to a range of criminogenic needs. This, in turn, raises questions about the configuration of service agencies: will it be tenable to have separate, dislocated agencies—say at different stages of sentence, or in custody versus community—when the aim should be coherent, sustained treatment? Further, recent evidence (e.g. Lipton, 1998) suggests that there are strong grounds, in terms of reducing recidivism, for increasing the application of "Concept Therapeutic Communities" and Milieu Therapies with offender groups.

For academics and researchers there are many issues awaiting debate. While recent attention has focused on the practical implications of "what works", the theoretical interpretation of the research base (mainly the meta-analyses) remains largely unattempted. It is also important that thought is given to the prevailing belief, discussed above, that "treatment equals pathology". There urgently needs to be some conceptual reworking of this issue in order to move the field forward. However, it is the findings of the eventual long-term recidivism studies from the current "what works" programmes that will undoubtably have the greatest impact over the next generation. It might also be hoped that there might be a rapprochement between psychology and criminology, so that both sides can constructively engage in the study and prevention of criminal behaviour.

Finally, in the long long term, might there be a paradigm shift in the criminal justice system so that classical theory is replaced by a theory more sympathetic to a human science, rather than economic, view of human behaviour? Might such a change herald the replacement of punishment by a more constructive approach to managing the problem of crime? Time, as they say, will tell.

REFERENCES

Aichhorn, A. (1955). *Wayward youth* (Trans.). New York: Meridian Books. (Original work published 1925).

Akers, R. L. (1977). *Deviant behavior: A social learning approach* (2nd ed). Belmont, CA: Wadsworth.

Akers, R. L., Krohn, M. D., Lanza-Kaduce, L., & Radosevich, M. (1979). Social learning and deviant behavior: A specific test of a general theory. *American Sociological Review*, *44*, 636–655.

Alexander, F., & Healy, W. (1935). *Roots of crime*. New York: Knopf.

Alexander, F., & Staub, H. (1931). *The criminal, the judge and the public*. New York: Macmillan.

Alper, J. S. (1998). Genes, free will, and criminal responsibility. *Social Science and Medicine*, *46*, 1599–1611.

Andrews, D. A., & Bonta, J. (1998). *The psychology of criminal conduct* (2nd ed). Cincinnati, OH: Anderson.

Andrews, D. A., & Wormith, J. S. (1989). Personality and crime: Knowledge destruction and construction in criminology. *Justice Quarterly*, *6*, 289–309.

Andrews, D. A., Zinger, I., Hoge, R. D., Bonta, J., Gendreau, P., & Cullen, F. T. (1990). Does correctional treatment work? A clinically relevant and informed meta-analysis. *Criminology*, *28*, 369–404.

Antonowicz, D. H., & Ross, R. R. (1994). Essential components of successful rehabilitation programs for offenders. *International Journal of Offender Therapy and Comparative Criminology*, *38*, 97–104.

Bandura, A. (1973). *Aggression: A social learning analysis*. Englewood Cliffs, NJ: Prentice-Hall.

Blackburn, R. (1968). Personality in relation to extreme aggression in psychiatric offenders. *British Journal of Psychiatry*, *114*, 821–828.

Blackburn, R. (1986). Patterns of personality deviation among violent offenders. *British Journal of Criminology*, *26*, 254–269.

Bottomley, K., & Pease, K. (1986). *Crime and punishment: Interpreting the data*. Milton Keynes, UK: Open University Press.

Bowlby, J. (1944). Forty-four juvenile thieves. *International Journal of Psychoanalysis*, *25*, 1–57.

Bowlby, J. (1946). *Forty-four juvenile thieves: Their characters and home-life*. London: Baillière, Tindall & Cox.

Burt, C. (1925). *The young delinquent*. London: University of London Press.

Cleland, C. M., Pearson, F. S., Lipton, D. S., & Yee, D. (1997, November). *Does age make a difference? A meta-analytic approach to reductions in criminal offending for juveniles and adults*. Paper presented at the annual meeting of The American Society of Criminology, San Diego, CA.

Cohen, A. K. (1955). *Delinquent boys*. London: Free Press.

Coleman, C., & Moynihan, J. (1996). *Understanding crime data: Haunted by the dark figure*. Milton Keynes, UK: Open University Press.

Cordess, C., & Cox, M. (1996). *Forensic psychotherapy: Crime, psychodynamics and the offender patient*. London: Jessica Kingsley.

Cornish, D. B., & Clarke, R. V. G. (Eds.) (1986). *The reasoning criminal: Rational choice perspectives on crime*. New York: Springer-Verlag.

Crick, N. R., & Dodge, K. A. (1994). A review and reformulation of social information-processing mechanisms in children's social adjustment. *Psychological Bulletin, 115*, 74–101.

Cullen, F. T., & Gendreau, P. (1989). The effectiveness of correctional rehabilitation: Reconsidering the "nothing works" debate. In L. Goodstein & D. L. MacKenzie (Eds.), *The American prison: Issues in research and policy*. New York: Plenum.

Downes, D. (1966). *The delinquent solution*. London: Routledge & Kegan Paul.

Eysenck, H. J. (1977). *Crime and personality* (3rd ed.). London: Routledge & Kegan Paul.

Farrington, D. P. (1995). The development of offending and antisocial behaviour from childhood: Key findings from the Cambridge Study in Delinquent Development. *Journal of Child Psychology and Psychiatry, 36*, 929–964.

Garrett, C. J. (1985). Effects of residential treatment of adjudicated delinquents: A meta-analysis. *Journal of Research in Crime and Delinquency, 22*, 287–308.

Gendreau, P. (1996). Offender rehabilitation: What we know and what needs to be done. *Criminal Justice and Behavior, 23*, 144–161.

Gendreau, P., & Andrews, D. A. (1990). What the meta-analyses of the offender treatment literature tells us about "what works". *Canadian Journal of Criminology, 32*, 173–184.

Gendreau, P., & Ross, R. R. (1979). Effective correctional treatment: Bibliotherapy for cynics. *Crime and Delinquency, 25*, 463–489.

Gendreau, P., & Ross, R. R. (1987). Revivification of rehabilitation: Evidence from the 1980s. *Justice Quarterly, 4*, 349–408.

Gottschalk, R., Davidson II, W. S., Gensheimer, L. K., & Mayer, J. (1987a). Community-based interventions. In H. C. Quay (Ed.), *Handbook of juvenile delinquency*. New York: Wiley.

Gottschalk, R., Davidson II, W. S., Mayer, J., & Gensheimer, L. K. (1987b). Behavioural approaches with juvenile offenders: A meta-analysis of long-term treatment efficacy. In E. K. Morris & C. J. Braukmann (Eds.), *Behavioral approaches to crime and delinquency*. New York: Plenum.

Healy, W., & Bronner, A. F. (1936). *New light on delinquency and its treatment*. New Haven, CN: Yale University Press.

Hirschi, T. (1969). *Causes of delinquency*. Berkeley, CA: University of California Press.

Hollin, C. R. (1990). *Cognitive–behavioral interventions with young offenders*. Elmsford, NY: Pergamon Press.

Hollin, C. R. (1993). Advances in the psychological treatment of criminal behaviour. *Criminal Behaviour and Mental Health, 3*, 42–57.

Hollin, C. R. (1994). Designing effective rehabilitation programmes for young offenders. *Psychology, Crime, & Law, 1*, 193–199.

Hollin, C. R. (1995). The meaning and implications of "programme integrity". In J. McGuire (Ed.), *What works: Reducing reoffending—guidelines from research and practice*. Chichester, UK: Wiley.

Hollin, C. R. (1999). Treatment programmes for offenders: Meta-analysis, "what works", and beyond. *International Review of Psychiatry and Law 22*, 361–372.

Hollin, C. R., Epps, K., & Kendrick, D. (1995). *Managing behavioural treatment: Policy and practice with delinquent adolescents*. London: Routledge.

Home Office Statistical Bulletin. (1996, September 24). *Notifiable offences: England and wales, July 1995 to June 1996*. London: Home Office, Information and Publications Group.

Izzo, R. L., & Ross, R. R. (1990). Meta-analysis of rehabilitation programs for juvenile delinquents: A brief report. *Criminal Justice and Behavior, 17*, 134–142.

Jeffery, C. R. (1960). The historical development of criminology. In H. Mannheim (Ed.), *Pioneers in criminology*. London: Stevens.

Jeffery, C. R. (1965). Criminal behavior and learning theory. *Journal of Criminal Law, Criminology and Police Science, 56*, 294–300.

Lipsey, M. W. (1992). Juvenile delinquency treatment: A meta-analytic inquiry into the variability of effects. In T. D. Cook, H. Cooper, D. S. Cordray, H. Hartmann, L. V. Hedges, R. J. Light, T. A. Louis, & F. Mosteller (Eds.), *Meta-analysis for explanation: A casebook*. New York: Russell Sage Foundation.

Lipsey, M. W. (1995). What do we learn from 400 studies on the effectiveness of treatment with juvenile delinquents? In J. McGuire (Ed.), *What works: Reducing reoffending—guidelines from research and practice*. Chichester, UK: Wiley.

Lipsey, M. W., & Wilson, D. B. (1998). Effective intervention for serious juvenile offenders. In R. Loeber & D. Farrington (Eds.), *Serious & violent juvenile offenders: Risk factors and successful interventions*. Thousand Oaks, CA: Sage.

Lipton, D. S. (1998). Therapeutic community treatment programming in corrections. *Psychology, Crime, & Law, 4*, 213–263.

Lösel, F. (1995a). The efficacy of correctional treatment: A review and synthesis of meta-evaluations. In J. McGuire (Ed.), *What works: Reducing reoffending—guidelines from research and practice*. Chichester, UK: Wiley.

Lösel, F. (1995b). Increasing consensus in the evaluation of offender rehabilitation? Lessons from recent research syntheses. *Psychology, Crime, & Law, 2*, 19–39.

Lösel, F. (1996). Working with young offenders: The impact of the meta-analyses. In C. R. Hollin & K. Howells (Eds.), *Clinical approaches to working with young offenders*. Chichester, UK: Wiley.

Lösel, F., & Köferl, P. (1989). Evaluation research on correctional treatment in West Germany: A meta-analysis. In H. Wegener, F. Lösel, & J. Haison (Eds.), *Criminal behaviour and the justice system: Psychological perspectives*. New York: Springer-Verlag.

Martinson, R. (1974). What works? Questions and answers about prison reform. *The Public Interest, 35*, 22–54.

Martinson, R. (1979). New findings, new views: A note of caution regarding sentencing reform. *Hofstra Law Review, 7*, 243–258.

McGuire, J. (Ed.) (1995). *What works: Reducing reoffending—guidelines from research and practice*. Chichester, UK: Wiley.

McGuire, J., & Priestley, P. (1995). Reviewing "what works": Past, present and future. In J. McGuire (Ed.), *What works: Reducing reoffending—guidelines from research and practice*. Chichester, UK: Wiley.

Merton, R. K. (1938). Social structure and anomie. In C. Lemert (Ed.), *Social theory: The multicultural readings*. Boulder, CO: Westview Press.

Morris, T. P. (1957). *The criminal area: A study in social ecology*. London: Routledge & Kegan Paul.

Nietzel, M. T. (1979). *Crime and its modification: A social learning perspective*. Oxford: Pergamon Press.

Novaco, R. W. (1994). Anger as a risk factor for violence among the mentally disordered. In J. Monahan & H. J. Steadman (Eds.), *Violence and mental disorder: Developments in risk assessment*. Chicago, IL: University of Chicago Press.

Pearson, F. S., Lipton, D. S., & Cleland, C. M. (1997, November). *Rehabilitative programs in adult corrections: CDATE meta-analyses*. Paper presented at the annual meeting of The American Society of Criminology, San Diego, CA.

Redondo, S., Garrido, V., Anguera, T., & Luque, E. (1996). Correctional programmes in Europe: A pilot study for a meta-evaluation. In G. Davies, S. Lloyd-Bostock, & C. Wilson (Eds.), *Psychology, law, and criminal justice: International developments in research and practice*. Berlin, Germany: Walter de Gruyter.

Redondo. S., Sànchez-Meca, J., & Garrido, V. (1999). The influence of treatment programmes on the recidivism of juvenile and adult offenders: An European meta-analytic review. *Psychology, Crime, & Law, 5*, 251–278.

Roshier, B. (1989). *Controlling crime: The classical perspective in criminology*. Milton Keynes, UK: Open University Press.

Ross, R. R., & Fabiano, E. A. (1985). *Time to think: A cognitive model of delinquency prevention and offender rehabilitation*. Johnson City, TN: Institute of Social Sciences and Arts.

Russell, B. (1961). *A history of western philosophy* (2nd ed.). London: Allen & Unwin.

Schweinhart, L. L., Barnes, H. V., & Weikart, D. P. (1993). *Significant benefits: The High Scope/Perry preschool study through age 27*. Ypsilanti, MI: High/Scope Press.

Shaw, C. R. (1930). *The jack-roller: A delinquent boy's own story*. Chicago, IL: Chicago University Press.

Shaw, C. R., & McKay, H. D. (1942). *Juvenile delinquency in urban areas*. Chicago, IL: Chicago University Press.

Siegal, L. J. (1986). *Criminology* (2nd ed.). St. Paul, MN: West.

Sutherland, E. H. (1939). *Principles of criminology*. Philadelphia, PA: Lippincott.

Sutherland, E. H. (1947). *Principles of criminology* (4th ed.). Philadelphia, PA: Lippincott.

Taylor, I., Walton, P., & Young, J. (1973). *The new criminology: For a social theory of deviance*. London: Routledge & Kegan Paul.

Tierney, J. (1996). *Criminology: Theory & context*. Hemel Hempstead, UK: Prentice-Hall/Harvester Wheatsheaf.

Whitehead, J. T., & Lab, S. P. (1989). A meta-analysis of juvenile correctional treatment. *Journal of Research in Crime and Delinquency, 26*, 276–295.

Willmott, P. (1966). *Adolescent boys of East London*. London: Routledge & Kegan Paul.

Part I

Risk Assessment

Chapter 2

Assessing Violence Risk in Mentally and Personality Disordered Individuals

Christopher D. Webster
*University of Toronto, Toronto, Simon Fraser University,
Vancouver, and Earlscourt Child and Family Centre,
Toronto, Canada
and*
Gerard Bailes
Norvic Clinic, Norwich, UK

INTRODUCTION

Questions surrounding the prediction of dangerousness seem to change each decade or so. Also, the language in which those questions are framed alters subtly with the accumulation of scientific knowledge, altered professional practice, and changing political and legal realities.

THE 1950s, 1960s, 1970s

In the 1950s, dangerousness had not surfaced as a topic of much interest in forensic psychology and psychiatry. It was generally assumed by judges and administrators that mental health and correctional professionals knew which individuals were apt to be dangerous and which ones were not. The 1960s brought about a sudden change in outlook. This was largely due to the inspired study of Steadman and Cocozza (1974). As many readers will know, these investigators had the wit to take advantage of a "naturally occurring experiment". This exper-

The Essential Handbook of Offender Assessment and Treatment. Edited by C. R. Hollin.
© 2004 John Wiley & Sons Ltd.

iment centred on the case of Johnny Baxstrom. Baxstrom had been confined in New York's Dannemora State Hospital for the criminally insane. Toward the end of his detainment he was civilly committed because authorities were unwilling to release him. Baxstrom contested this added confinement, eventually to the United States Supreme Court. There it was decided that, indeed, Baxstrom had been improperly held. The court ordered his release and took the extraordinary step of requiring a further 966 persons released outright or removed to conditions of lowered security. In this way, the better part of 1000 persons, most or all of whom had been detained on the grounds that they represented a danger to the public, were abruptly reclassified with many eventually reaching the community.

Ninety-eight patients were followed in the community for two to three years. Few of these individuals had further contact with the law (about 20% were arrested) and even fewer were involved in violent acts (2%). This finding suggested very strongly that violence had been over-predicted, at least in that particular institution. Attention became focused on the "false positive problem", the idea that clinicians had too often perceived "dangerousness" where it did not exist. That such over-prediction of dangerousness occurred in the Baxstrom patients was recognized by Steadman and Cocozza as being at least partly due to low overall rates of violence during the follow-up period. It was generally thought at the time that predicting future violence was an almost impossible task because of the difficulty of forecasting events with a low frequency of occurrence.

The Steadman and Cocozza (1974) book, called, aptly enough, *Careers of the Criminally Insane*, excited considerable interest upon its publication. It was also received with scepticism in some quarters. Yet its main conclusion was amply reinforced just five years later in a 1979 parallel case in Pennsylvania (Dixon v. Attorney General of the Commonwealth of Pennsylvania). Again, there was a court-ordered release of a large cohort of persons earlier deemed to have committed violent acts due to mental illness. The patients were followed by another pair of investigators, Thornberry and Jacoby (1979). Exactly the same major finding emerged from the study; very few former patients acted violently during the four-year follow-up. There was again, then, the general conclusion that violence had been over-predicted. Some influential authorities began publishing articles during the period with titles like "flipping coins in the courtroom" (Ennis & Litwack, 1974). There were suggestions that forensic psychiatrists and psychologists would be best advised to get out of the business of predicting violence (e.g. as described by Stone, 1985).

THE 1980s

The late 1970s and early 1980s initiated a different line of thought. The distinguished American psychologist, the late Saleem Shah, began to note in places as prominent as the *American Psychologist* (1978) that mental health professionals were more or less obliged to render opinions about dangerousness at many junctures in general psychiatric, forensic psychiatric, and correctional systems. He also expressed the view that it was unlikely that clinicians are uniformly poor at predicting future violence. In his own words: "To say something is difficult to do (namely, to achieve high levels of accuracy in predicting events with very low base rates) is *not* the same as asserting that the task is impossible and simply cannot be done" (1981, p. 161, parentheses and emphasis in original). Shah also made the vital point that individual assessors tend to have little or no idea as to the relative accuracy of their predictions.

Doubtless influenced to some extent by Shah, Monahan published in 1981 his book called *Predicting Violent Behavior: An Assessment of Clinical Techniques*. This text was influential at the time and has remained so. Aside from a compelling summary of the literature then extant, Monahan organized his text largely around the distinction between actuarial and clinical prediction. This distinction, explored early by Meehl (1954), enabled Monahan to stress the importance of both kinds of variables. His point was that it makes sense to ground predictions of violence in easy-to-establish background "static", demographic-type factors. It was, even at that time, apparent that certain actuarial variables like past crime— particularly violent crime—age, sex, socioeconomic status, and alcohol or drug abuse have at least some demonstrable link to subsequent dangerous acts. Moreover, certain variables like family, employment, peer relations, availability of victims, and availability of weapons, could be presumed to have associations with future violence risk. In his book Monahan viewed mental illness as a *non-correlate* of violence. As noted later in this chapter, this particular observation later required another look. What is perhaps most surprising is that the text as a whole has worn so well over the years. It has provided a blueprint for much of the research conducted over the better part of the last two decades.

In this text, and in subsequent articles (1984, 1988), Monahan called for prediction-outcome studies conducted over relatively short periods. This so-called "second generation" research placed insistence on clearly defined predictor and outcome measures. Studies began to appear suggesting that, high though the false positive problem might remain, there was at least some possibility of showing sustainable correspondences between prediction and outcome (e.g. Convit, Jaeger, Lin, Meisner, & Volavka, 1998; Sepejak, Menzies, Webster, & Jensen, 1983).

How is predictive power shown when it comes to gauging the accuracy of violence forecasts? As explained by Monahan in 1981, the most usual way of going about the task is to place individuals following evaluation in one of two categories; dangerous or not dangerous. Similarly, at eventual outcome days, weeks, months, or even years later, persons are again grouped into two categories; those known not to have behaved violently and those known to have committed harm. This gives rise to a 2 × 2 contingency table under which there are two ways of being correct and two ways of being wrong. It is possible to predict that the person will be danger-free over the study period and be correct in that assertion (true negative); it is possible to predict a non-violent outcome and be wrong in that forecast (false negative); it is possible, as was found in the aftermaths of Baxstrom and Dixon, to predict violence but not find it at follow-up (false positive); and, finally, it is possible to predict violence and have that prediction confirmed (true positive). This scheme for organizing data, though not without its limitations (Hart, Webster, & Menzies, 1993), can be quite useful. Through the use of the basic chi-square statistic, it is easy to determine whether the scores distributed across the four cells depart from chance. This way it can be shown, for example, whether or not particular variables like previous violence, age at time of offence, and global clinical opinion about dangerousness yield "statistically significant" effects (e.g. Sepejak et al., 1983).

Helpful though chi-square and related statistics may be to those with a statistical bent, it soon becomes apparent that the effects of a false negative error are markedly different from those of a false positive error (Walker, 1991). In the former case, some bureaucrat, some judge, or some mental health professional stands a chance of being held accountable for an "error". As a result of miscategorization, there is now a victim. In the latter case, improper classification results in the undue detention of the individual. Small wonder then that there is a tendency for clinicians and administrators, in their understandable reluctance to be stuck with false negative errors, to drive up the level of false positives in a corresponding way. There is one other point about the 2×2 table which merits note. It is that in the usual course of events, persons viewed during assessment as dangerous tend to be confined—that is, the prediction is not tested. A related matter is that even if the individual is free to act violently during the follow-up period, and does in fact do so, there is a good chance that such violence, unless extremely serious, may remain unreported. So what would actually be a true positive if the full facts were known can enter the data analysis as a false positive.

The yes/no characteristic of the chi-square table can be overcome with use of correlation coefficients according to which a *range* of predictor scores can be associated with a *range* of outcome scores. A correlation coefficient yields a maximum correspondence of +1.0 (or −1.0). A correlation of zero implies no correspondence whatever between prediction and outcome. At least in theory it ought to be possible to build a prediction instrument which would show a close to +1.0 correlation between prediction and outcome. In the late 1970s, early 1980s, one of us (CDW), with others, attempted to elucidate a couple of dozen factors which might conceivably link prediction to outcome (Menzies, Webster, & Sepejak, 1985a). Such factors were organized into a scheme called the Dangerous Behaviour Rating Scheme (DBRS). Typical items in this device were called "anger", "rage", "hostility", "manipulative", and "violence increased under alcohol". When forensic psychiatric patients were followed first after two years and later after six (Menzies, Webster, McMain, Staley, & Scaglione, 1994), correlations between DBRS scores at assessment and follow-up tended to be of the order of +0.24. This led us to conclude that it was more or less impossible to break a "sound barrier" of around 0.40 (Menzies, Webster, & Sepejak, 1985b). The DBRS itself, though yielding statistically significant chi-squares and correlations, did not, as we had hoped, yield strength much, if any, more impressive than a handful of easy-to-obtain and score demographic variables (see Menzies & Webster, 1995).

These findings of our own in the mid 1980s seemed fairly consistent with those of other investigators active at the time. Generally, overall prediction-outcome correlations were unimpressive, with a preponderance of false positives. One result of the DBRS venture did, though, catch our attention. This was that, as Shah (1981) had previously suggested, individual clinicians varied markedly in their ability to forecast violence. Some performed at chance levels, others were able to yield positive correlations of around +0.25 or even +0.35, and a few even yielded negative correlations. When we published our results in 1985 we stressed the limited validity of the DBRS. To our surprise, we were deluged with requests for the manual on which the scale was based. Practising clinicians seemed undaunted by its lack of demonstrated reliability and validity. This taught us that, although the DBRS was not "it", there would potentially be acceptance of an instrument that was reasonably succinct and acceptably grounded in clinical and research practice.

THE 1990s

It was the realization that there is a demand for practical down-to-earth instruments that began to lead us and others in a new direction starting in the early 1990s. In 1994 we published *The Violence Prediction Scheme* (Webster, Harris, Rice, Cormier, & Quinsey). This short book was written explicitly for use by mental health and correctional professionals. It was based on an earlier work by Harris, Rice and Quinsey (1993). These authors, based at the maximum-secure "Oak Ridge" Division of the Penetanguishene Mental Centre in Ontario, Canada, published data on some 600 men, all of whom had previously committed at least one serious violent offence. Using statistical techniques more sophisticated than those mentioned above in this chapter, they were able to pool the effects of several actuarial variables (i.e. through discriminant function analysis). The men in this study had been released for seven years and the investigators had been able to determine which men had failed violently during follow-up and which ones had not. Harris et al. had no difficulty in this important study in showing that it was possible to break the +0.40 "sound barrier" referred to earlier.

The overall prediction scores in the "Oak Ridge" population were derived retrospectively from files kept at the hospital. These scores were organized by the researchers, on the basis of comprehensive statistical analysis, into a device named the Violence Risk Appraised Guide (VRAG). All 12 items individually correlated with the outcome measure ("failed violently" over seven and later 10 years vs. "did not fail violently"). The 12 items in the VRAG listed here in terms of strength of correlations against outcome were as follows:

1. Psychopathy Checklist Score
2. Elementary School Maladjustment
3. DSM-III Diagnosis of Personality Disorder
4. Age at Index Offence

5. Separated from Parents under Age 16
6. Failure on Prior Conditional Release
7. Non-violent Offence History
8. Never Married
9. DSM-III Diagnosis of Schizophrenia
10. Victim Injury
11. Alcohol Abuse
12. Female Victim in Index Offence.

The correlations between combined predictor variables and outcome scores across the whole population were +0.45 (ranging up to +0.53 in one subsample).

An impressive part of the write-up of the Harris et al. (1993) study was the use of a histogram depicting the main results. Supported by the main statistical analyses, the authors chose to plot on the ordinate the probability of violent failure. On the abscissa they showed VRAG scores divided into nine equal-sized bins. The result is a visually pleasing correspondence with the bars running from low left to high right. Though not quite as "tight", a second plot based on only seven variables yielded the same basic pattern. These seven variables were included based merely on their ease of scoring (e.g. age at index offence, never married). This observation is reminiscent of that by Menzies et al. (1994) mentioned earlier (i.e. that a few actuarial variables do possess surprising predictive power).

A little attention needs now to be focused on the single most powerful predictor isolated by Harris et al. (1993), psychopathy. Psychopathy as indexed by Hare's Psychopathy Checklist—Revised—PCL—R (1991) can be measured according to 20 items, each scored on a 0 (absent), 1 (possibly present), or 2 (definitely present) scale. The items, as many readers will know, are:

1. Glibness/superficial charm
2. Grandiose sense of self-worth
3. Need for stimulation/proneness to boredom
4. Pathological lying
5. Conning/manipulative
6. Lack of remorse or guilt
7. Shallow affect
8. Callous/lack of empathy
9. Parasitic lifestyle
10. Poor behavioural controls
11. Promiscuous sexual behaviour
12. Early behaviour problems
13. Lack of realistic long-term goals
14. Impulsivity
15. Irresponsibility
16. Failure to accept responsibility for actions
17. Many short-term marital relationships

18. Juvenile delinquency
19. Revocation of conditional release and
20. Criminal versatility.

Statistical analyses based on the PCL—R data show consistently that psychopathy is actually a composite of two factors: one centring on affective/interpersonal considerations and the other dealing with impulsivity, irresponsibility, unstable lifestyle, and persistent violation of social norms. Other studies have shown that the PCL—R, or its more recent short adaptation (Hart, Hare, & Forth, 1994; Hart, Cox, & Hare, 1995), links as well, or better than, any other single predictor of violence yet isolated (e.g. Hill, Rogers, & Bickford, 1996). With its careful description, its "manualization' (Kazdin, 1997), and a body of knowledge to support it, psychopathy at least for the moment would seem to be the 'flagship' variable in the area of violence risk prediction. It is worth noting that the construct was not originally intended by Hare to become a prediction device. It is also worth noting that, interesting and helpful though the device may have become in the area of risk prediction, it is easily subject to misuses of various kinds (Hare, 1998). For example, although the device likely taps the kinds of variables of interest to decision-makers faced with making parole release recommendations, there can be a regrettable tendency to consider an exceptionally low or exceptionally high psychopathy score to be *all* that is needed. As well, it may even be that the use of the term "checklist" leads administrators and even professionals to think that the scale can be used rapidly and without the required extensive training. Hare has himself recently remarked that the notion of psychopathy is more complex than it looks and that, originally based in clinical observation (Cleckley, 1941), its assessment requires a substantial degree of clinical sophistication and training (Hare, 1998).

There are other points to be noted about the critically important work of Harris et al. (see Quinsey, Harris, Rice, & Cormier, 1998; Rice, 1997). One is that childhood variables turn out to be quite powerful. Early childhood maladjustment is a key factor (see Hodgins, 1994), as is separation from parents before the age of 16 years. Another point is that schizophrenia shows a *negative* correlation with violent failure during follow-up. It is worth stressing that the Harris et al. findings likely have applicability to *men* destined for corrections as well as mental hospitalization. This is because their population included not just men sent to Oak Ridge for treatment but also men who were sent there for evaluation before being routed to correctional interventions. It may well be found, as was the case with the PCL—R, that the VRAG has applicability well beyond men found not guilty by reason of insanity. It is the kind of device, given its already strong support, that will merit close study with other groups into the future. The question of "How well can dangerousness be predicted?" dissolves into another question, "How well able is the VRAG able to predict violence in this or that context?" Such questions can be answered with relative ease given the existence of the requisite detailed coding manual (Cormier, 1994).

Another study of the same vintage as that by Harris et al. is that by Lidz, Mulvey, and Gardner (1993). This was based on a general psychiatric population. It is a thorough and important study. The outcome measures were particularly strong, based as they were in part on information about violence provided by friends and relatives ("collaterals"). The study is among a few to show that global clinical opinion about the likelihood of future violence can be valid. Yet, what was surprising about the outcome of this study was that predictions made on behalf of women were on the whole largely inaccurate. Since in this conventional psychiatric sample women made up about half the population, the effectiveness of successful predictions made about men was greatly attenuated by the unsuccessful ones about women. The difficulty was that the assessors markedly underestimated the base rate of violence in these woman (i.e. they made far too many false negative errors).

The year 1994 not only saw the publication of the *Violence Prediction Scheme* but, importantly, it was also marked by the publication of *Violence and Mental Disorder: Developments in Risk Assessment* by Monahan and Steadman. This is an edited volume containing much hitherto unpublished data and commentary. Of special importance perhaps is preliminary material from the MacArthur risk assessment project. This is a multi-site study using prediction and outcome data (see Steadman et al., 1994). As well, there is in the book ample evidence to suggest that Monahan's (1981) earlier assertion about mental disorder being a *non*-correlate of violence is incorrect (see also Monahan, 1992). It is now more accurate to say that mental disorder has a low to moderate association with violence; one, though, which is substantially less than that between alcohol and drug abuse and violence.

In early 1995, one of us (CDW) joined with others to produce a broad-spectrum, workable manual for the assessment of risk of violence (Webster, Eaves, Douglas, & Wintrup, 1995). In so doing, we took a leaf from Robert Hare's book by opting for 20 items scored simply as 0, 1 or 2. The rationale was straightforward: 20 is a seemingly reasonable number of items for clinicians completing busy assessment schedules. And a three-point scoring system does not oblige colleagues to make distinctions which might be altogether too fine (e.g. our experience with the DBRS, based on a 5-point system, was not entirely satisfactory). The scheme has become known as the "HCR-20". There are 10 "historical" (H) items (influenced to some extent by the VRAG), five current clinical items and five future-oriented risk items. A modified version of the scheme was published two years later (Webster, Douglas, Eaves, & Hart, 1997a, 1997b). Items in the scheme are currently labelled as follows: H1, Previous violence; H2, Young age at first violent incident; H3, Relationship instability; H4, Employment problems; H5, Substance use problems; H6, Major mental illness; H7, Psychopathy; H8, Early maladjustment; H9, Personality disorder; H10, Prior supervision failure; C1, Lack of insight; C2, Negative attitudes; C3, Active symptoms of mental illness; C4, Impulsivity; C5, Unresponsive to treatment; R1, Plans lack feasibility; R2, Exposure to destabilizers; R3, Lack of personal support; R4, Non-compliance with remediation attempts; and R5, Stress. Such limited data supporting the validity of the HCR-20 as are available are listed in the manual. Much of what has so far been reported is of a retrospective nature (e.g. Douglas & Webster, 1999; Belfrage, 1998).

Although as yet in its infancy, the HCR-20 has attracted notice (e.g. Borum, 1996). It may well turn out that, aside from the value of the scheme itself, the HCR-20's main benefit derives from the effort to draw together the results of scientific investigations, on the one hand, with the actualities of clinical practice, on the other. As was said in the manual, "The challenge in what remains of the 1990s is to integrate the almost separate worlds of research on the prediction of violence and the clinical practice of assessment. At present the two worlds scarcely intersect" (Webster et al., 1997b, p. 1). Certainly, it is anticipated that the scheme will require revision from time to time. It has to be seen as a starting place for research, not an end in itself (though see Douglas, 1998). As was true of the DBRS a decade or more earlier, there has been a considerable demand for the manual. It has also been observed that some colleagues have found the device useful not so much as an assessment scheme in itself, but as a means of measuring the effects of interventions and treatments over weeks and months.

Emboldened to some extent by the "success" of the HCR-20, we have developed other similar scales to examine specific topics like spousal assault (Kropp, Hart, Webster, & Eaves, 1995; Kropp & Hart, 1997), sex offending (Boer, Wilson, Gauthier, & Hart, 1997; Boer, Hart, Kropp & Webster, 1998) and the potential of correctional inmates to attempt suicide (Polvi, 1997). Impulsivity seems a central feature of many persons with mental or personality disorder. That, at any rate, is an impression gleaned from the content of the American Psychiatric Associations's *Diagnostic and Statistical Manual* (APA, 1994). For that reason, we have also proposed a 20-item scheme for measuring clinical impulsivity (Webster & Jackson, 1997). Indeed, with reference to the so-called Impulsivity Checklist (ICL), we opted quite deliberately to define the construct based largely on *clinical* experience. Just as Hare relied on Cleckley's *Mask of Sanity* (1941) as a starting point, we chose to depend upon Harold Wishnie's 1977 book *The Impulsive Personality: Understanding People with Destructive Character Disorders*. In the most general way, we have found it instructive to rely upon well-expressed clinical opinion as we have tried to place metrics on the variables of seeming greatest interest. To us it seems vital that, as the next important step, there be a renewal of emphasis on establishing scientist–practitioner models (Webster & Cox, 1997). At present there seems a regrettable tendency for researchers to talk one language and clinicians another. Researchers are often insensitive or unknowledgeable about clinical realities and clinicians too often are ill-informed about the results of dependable, informative, research studies.

The rise in importance of psychopathy as a construct over the past 10 or 15 years is a good case in point. Psychopathy is a clinical notion, or actually a pair of notions. Hare has found a convenient, scientifically sound, way of making these notions intelligible and useful to clinicians. Recently, as noted above, we have made a similar attempt with psychopathy's sister concept, impulsivity (Webster & Jackson, 1997). But there must be many other constructs, all used daily (but mostly in different ways) by clinicians. It seems to us self-evident that the accuracy of risk evaluations will not improve very greatly until more attention is paid to the definition of terms. Just as had been mistakenly assumed that there was a low "sound barrier" for prediction–outcome correlations in this type of work, it may well be that with continued emphasis on the definition of terms and the logic of prediction (Jackson, 1997) much greater accuracy can be obtained than now seems possible. In saying this, we recognize that in the future it may prove expedient to find altogether new types of prediction model (e.g. Marks-Tarlow, 1993).

Quite aside from the importance of being able to demonstrate greater prediction accuracy than is currently possible, increased attention must surely now be focused on how best to encourage true collaboration between clinicians and researchers (Polvi & Webster, 1997). Perfect prediction schemes are not going to fly from the brows of researchers or from clinicians. In this respect, the gradual evolution of devices designed to predict critically important human behaviours may follow exactly the same pattern as is found in applied engineering tasks. The process ought to be the same. Consider, for example, the task of creating a device to clean institutional walls and floors. First, the task must be defined. Then an idea, likely involving chemicals, pumps, nozzles, and sprays must be sketched on a drawing board (the initial design phase). Then, with plans in hand, the task is moved to the machine shop where a prototype is fabricated (the working model phase). The model must then be applied to the task proper (the trial phase). Since it is unlikely that the new device will perform in a completely satisfactory way during initial testing, it is almost certain that there will have to be a return to the design and prototype phases. Actual full-scale production of the cleaning device will be at some considerable remove from the initial concept. Only rarely are short-cuts available. As we have evolved Version 2 of the HCR-20 from Version 1, we have been surprised at the effort required to revisit the design, model, and trial phases.

Recently, we set ourselves the challenge of creating a 20-item scheme for assessing violence potential in children under 12. The need for such a device seemed self-evident. And it was not as if prominent researchers had done no work in the area (e.g. Eron, 1997; Farrington, 1997). At a routine clinical level we were already using at the Earlscourt Child and Family Centre in Toronto, a 50-item yes/no checklist (yet with no attempt at reliability or validity checking). It took some time to isolate 20 factors on the basis of the published literature, the underdeveloped prototype checklist, and the opinions of colleagues who work daily with under-12 children and their families. Our eventual list of six Family (F) items, 12 Child (C) items and two Amenability (A) items is as follows: F1, Household circumstances; F2, Caregiver continuity; F3, Supports; F4, Stressors; F5, Parenting style; F6, Antisocial values and conduct; C1, Developmental problems; C2, Onset of behavioural difficulties; C3, Trauma; C4, Impulsivity; C5, Likeability; C6, Peer socialization; C7, School functioning; C8, Structured community activities; C9, Police contact; C10, Antisocial attitudes; C11, Antisocial behaviour; C12, Coping ability; A1, Family responsivity; and A2, Child treatability.

As we developed the items and corresponding descriptions, we came to the realization that different versions would have to be created for boys and girls. After identifying and defining in a draft manual the seemingly most essential 20 items, we tried them out on 21 consecutive cases (prototype test). Round-table discussion among all participants resulted in the dropping of some items, the addition of others, and the reworking of many others (back to the drawing board). Further testing followed in the clinic and production of the so-called Early Assessment of Risk List—Boys' Version (EARL-20B) has now taken place (Augimeri, Webster, Koegl, & Levene, 1998). No one claims for this more than a starting point for much needed research. Yet, in our view, the "two worlds phenomenon" means that, regrettably, the task often does not get started, let alone finished.

Our general point, then, is that there has been a marked shift in outlook with respect to risk prediction over the past two decades. Although some still argue strenuously that mental health and correctional researchers do more harm than good with their attempts to improve precision in decision making (e.g. Mathiesen, 1998), the general current view from experienced and thoughtful psychiatrists and psychologists is that it is well within our grasp to assess and manage violence risk at standards appreciably higher than those presently in routine use (see Monahan, 1996; Snowden, 1997).

REFERENCES

American Psychiatric Association (1994). *Diagnostic and statistical manual of mental disorders* (4th ed.). Washington, DC: Author.

Augimeri, L., Webster, C. D., Koegl, C., & Levene, K. (1998). The early assessment of risk list for boys' (EARL-20B) (Version 1, Consultation edition). Toronto, Canada: Earlscourt Child and Family Centre.

Belfrage, H. (1998). Implementing the HCR-20 scheme for risk assessment in a forensic psychiatric hospital: Integrating research and clinical practice. *Journal of Forensic Psychiatry, 9*, 328–338.

Boer, D. P., Hart, S. D., Kropp, P. R., & Webster, C. D. (1998). *The SVR-20 manual*. Vancouver, Canada: Family Violence Institute.

Boer, D. P., Wilson, R. J., Gauthier, C. M., & Hart, S. D. (1997). Assessing risk for sexual violence: Guidelines for clinical practice. In C. D. Webster & M. A. Jackson (Eds.), *Impulsivity: Theory, assessment, and treatment* (pp. 326–342). New York: Guilford.

Borum, R. (1996). Improving the clinical practice of violence risk assessment: Technology, guidelines, and training. *American Psychologist, 51*, 945–956.

Cleckley, H. (1941). *The mask of sanity*. St. Louis, MO: Mosby.

Convit, A., Jaeger, J., Lin, S. P., Meisner, M., & Volavka, J. (1988). Predicting assaultiveness in psychiatric inpatients: A pilot study. *Hospital and Community Psychiatry, 39*, 429–434.

Cormier, C. (1994). *Offender psycho-social assessment manual correctional model*. Penetanguishene, Ontario, Canada: Ontario Mental Health Centre.

Douglas, K. (1998, March). The HCR-20 violence risk assessment scheme: A summary of research findings. Paper presented at the biennial meeting of the American Psychology-Law Society, Redondo Beach, CA.

Douglas, K. S., & Webster, C. D. (1999). The HCR-20 violence risk assessment scheme:

Concurrent validity in a sample of incarcerated offenders. *Criminal Justice and Behavior, 26*, 3–19.

Ennis, B. J., & Litwack, T. R. (1974). Psychiatry and the presumption of expertise: Flipping coins in the courtroom. *California Law Review, 62*, 693–752.

Eron, L. D. (1997). The development of antisocial behavior from a learning perspective. In D. M. Stoff, J. Breiling, & J. D. Maser, *Handbook of antisocial behavior* (pp. 140–147). New York: Wiley.

Farrington, D. P. (1997). A critical analysis of research on the development of antisocial behavior from birth to adulthood. In D. M. Stoff, J. Breiling, & J. D. Maser (Eds.), *Handbook of antisocial behavior* (pp. 234–240) New York: Wiley.

Hare, R. D. (1991). *Manual for the Hare Psychopathy Checklist—Revised.* Toronto, Canada: Multi-Health Systems.

Hare, R. D. (1998). The Hare PCL—R: Some issues concerning its use and misuse. *Legal and Criminological Psychology, 3*, 99–119.

Harris, G. T., Rice, M. E., & Quinsey, V. L. (1993). Violent recidivism of mentally disordered offenders: The development of a statistical prediction instrument. *Criminal Justice and Behavior, 20*, 315–355.

Hart, S. D., Cox, D., & Hare, R. D. (1995). *Manual for the screening version of the Hare Psychopathy Checklist—Revised (PCL: SV).* Toronto, Canada: Multi-Health Systems.

Hart, S. D., Hare, R. D., & Forth, A. E. (1994). Psychopathy as a risk marker for violence: Development and validation of a screening version of the Revised Psychopathy Checklist. In J. Monahan & H. J. Steadman (Eds.), *Violence and mental disorder: Developments in risk assessment* (pp. 81–97). Chicago, IL: University of Chicago Press.

Hart, S. D., Webster, C. D., & Menzies, R. J. (1993). A note on portraying the accuracy of violence predictions. *Law and Human Behavior, 17*, 695–700.

Hill, C. D., Rogers, R., & Bickford, M. E. (1996). Predicting aggressive and socially disruptive behavior in a maximum security forensic hospital. *Journal of Forensic Sciences, 41*, 56–69.

Hodgins, S. (1994). Status at age 30 of children with conduct problems. *Studies on Crime and Crime Prevention, 4*, 41–61.

Jackson, J. (1997). A conceptual model for the study of violence and aggression. In C. C. Webster & M. A. Jackson, *Impulsivity: Theory, assessment and treatment* (pp. 233–247). New York: Guilford.

Kazdin, A. E. (1997). A model for developing effective treatments: Progression and interplay of theory, research, and practice. *Journal of Clinical Child Psychology, 26*, 114–129.

Kropp, P. R., & Hart, S. D. (1997). Assessing risk for violence in wife assaulters: The Spousal Assault Risk Assessment Guide. In C. D. Webster & M. A. Jackson (Eds.), *Impulsivity: Theory, assessment, and treatment* (pp. 302–325). New York: Guilford.

Kropp, P. R., Hart, S. D., Webster, C. D., & Eaves, D. (1995). *Manual for Spousal Assault Risk Assessment Guide* (2nd ed.). Vancouver, Canada: British Columbia Institute on Family Violence.

Lidz, C. W., Mulvey, E. P., & Gardner, W. (1993). The accuracy of predictions of violence to others. *Journal of the American Medical Association, 269*, 1007–1111.

Marks-Tarlow, T. (1993). A new look at impulsivity: Hidden order beneath apparent chaos? In W. G. McCown, J. L. Johnson, & M. B. Shure (Eds.), *The impulsive client: Theory, research and treatment* (pp. 119–138). Washington, DC: American Psychological Association.

Mathiesen, T. (1998). Selective incapacitation revisited. *Law and Human Behavior, 22*, 453–467.

Meehl, P. E. (1954). *Clinical versus statistical prediction.* Minneapolis, MN: University of Minnesota Press.

Menzies, R., & Webster, C. D. (1995). Construction and validation of risk assessments in a six-year follow-up of forensic patients: A tridimensional analysis. *Journal of Consulting and Clinical Psychology, 63*, 766–778.

Menzies, R. J., Webster, C. D., McMain, S., Saley, S., & Scaglione, R. (1994). The dimensions of dangerousness revisited: Assessing forensic predictions about violence. *Law and Human Behavior*, *18*, 1–28.

Menzies, R. J., Webster, C. D., & Sepejak, D. S. (1985a). The dimensions of dangerousness: Evaluating the accuracy of psychometric predictions of violence among forensic patients. *Law and Human Behavior*, *9*, 35–56.

Menzies, R. J., Webster, C. D., & Sepejak, D. S. (1985b). Hitting the forensic sound barrier: Predictions of dangerousness in a pre-trial psychiatric clinic. In C. D. Webster, M. H. Ben-Aron, & S. J. Hucker (Eds.), *Dangerousness: Probability and prediction, psychiatry and public policy* (pp. 115–143). New York: Cambridge University Press.

Monahan, J. (1981). *Predicting violent behavior: An assessment of clinical techniques.* Beverly Hills, CA: Sage.

Monahan, J. (1984). The prediction of violent behavior: Toward a second generation of theory and policy. *American Journal of Psychiatry*, *141*, 10–15.

Monahan, J. (1988). Risk assessment of violence among the mentally disordered: Generating useful knowledge. *International Journal of Law and Psychiatry*, *11*, 249–257.

Monahan, J. (1992). Mental disorder and violent behavior. *American Psychologist*, *47*, 511–521.

Monahan, J. (1996). Violence prediction: The last 20 and the next 20 years. *Criminal Justice and Behavior*, *23*, 107–120.

Monahan, J., & Steadman, H. J. (Eds.) (1994). *Violence and mental disorder: Developments in risk assessment.* Chicago, IL: University of Chicago Press.

Polvi, N. (1997). Assessing risk of suicide in correctional settings. In C. D. Webster & M. A. Jackson (Eds.), *Impulsivity: Theory, assessment and treatment* (pp. 278–301). New York: Guilford.

Polvi, N., & Webster, C. D. (1997). Challenging assessments of dangerousness and risk: The recent research. In J. Ziskin (Ed.), *Coping with psychiatric and psychological testimony* (Supplement to 5th ed., pp. 148–164). Los Angeles, CA: Law and Psychology Press.

Quinsey, V. L., Harris, G. T., Rice, M. E., & Cormier, C. A. (1998). *Violent offenders: Appraising and managing risk.* Washington, DC: American Psychological Association.

Rice, M. E. (1997). Violent offender research and implications for the criminal justice system. *American Psychologist*, *52*, 414–423.

Sepejak, D. S., Menzies, R. J., Webster, C. D., & Jensen, F. A. S. (1983). Clinical predictions of dangerousness: Two-year follow-up of 408 pre-trial forensic cases. *Bulletin of the American Academy of Psychiatry and the Law*, *11*, 171–181.

Shah, S. A. (1978). Dangerousness: A paradigm for exploring some issues in law and psychology. *American Psychologist*, *33*, 224–238.

Shah, S. A. (1981). Dangerousness: Conceptual, prediction, and public policy issues. In J. R. Hays, T. K. Roberts, & K. S. Solway (Eds.), *Violence and the violent individual* (pp. 151–178). New York: SP Medical and Scientific Books.

Snowden, P. (1997). Practical aspects of clinical risk assessment and management. *British Journal of Psychiatry*, *170*, 32–34.

Steadman, H. J., & Cocozza, J. J. (1974). *Careers of the criminally insane: Excessive social control of deviance.* Lexington, MA: Lexington Books.

Steadman, H. J., Monahan, J., Appelbaum, P. S., Grisso, T., Mulvey, E. P., Roth, J. H., Robbins, P. C., & Klassen, D. (1994). Designing a new generation of risk assessment research. In J. Monahan & H. J. Steadman (Eds.), *Violence and mental disorder: Developments in risk assessment* (pp. 297–318). Chicago, IL: University of Chicago Press.

Stone, A. A. (1985). The new legal standard of dangerousness: Fair in theory, unfair in practice. In C. D. Webster, M. H. Ben-Aron, & S. J. Hucker (Eds.), *Dangerousness: Probability and prediction, psychiatry and public policy* (pp. 13–24). New York: Cambridge University Press.

Thornberry, T. P., & Jacoby, J. E. (1979). *The criminally insane: A community follow-up of mentally ill offenders.* Chicago, IL: University of Chicago Press.

Walker, N. (1991). Dangerous mistakes. *British Journal of Psychiatry*, *138*, 752–757.

Webster, C. D., & Cox, D. N. (1997). Integration of nomothetic and ideographic positions in risk assessment: Implications for practice and the education of psychologists and other mental health professionals. *American Psychologist*, *52*, 1245–1246.

Webster, C. D., Douglas, K. S., Eaves, D., & Hart, S. D. (1997a). Predicting violence in mentally and personality disordered individuals. In C. D. Webster & M. A. Jackson (Eds.), *Impulsivity: Theory, assessment, and treatment* (pp. 251–277). New York: Guilford.

Webster, C. D., Douglas, K. S., Eaves, D., & Hart, S. D. (1997b). *HCR-20: Assessing risk for violence, Version 2*. Vancouver, Canada: Mental Health, Law, and Policy Institute, Simon Fraser University.

Webster, C. D., Eaves, D., Douglas, K. S., & Wintrup, A. (1995). *The HCR-20 scheme: The assessment of dangerousness and risk*. Vancouver, Canada: Simon Fraser University and British Columbia Forensic Psychiatric Services Commission.

Webster, C. D., Harris, G. T., Rice, M. E., Cormier, C., & Quinsey, V. L. (1994). *The violence prediction scheme: Assessing dangerousness in high risk men*. Toronto, Canada: University of Toronto, Centre of Criminology.

Webster, C. D., & Jackson, M. (1997). A clinical perspective on impulsivity. In C. D. Webster & M. A. Jackson (Eds.), *Impulsivity: Theory, assessment, and treatment* (pp. 13–31). New York: Guilford.

Wishnie, H. (1977). *The impulsive personality: Understanding people with destructive character disorders*. New York: Plenum.

Chapter 3

Sex Offender Risk Assessment

R. Karl Hanson

Department of the Solicitor General of Canada, Ottawa, Canada

INTRODUCTION

Last year, you saw Mr Smith for three sessions of couples counselling. Mr Smith has just pleaded guilty to his second attempted rape, for which he could face life imprisonment. His lawyer now wants you to testify at his sentencing hearing.

You are working with a mother and her two daughters as part of child protection services. The eldest daughter has recently disclosed being sexually abused by a neighbour. You learn that the mother's new boyfriend was convicted 15 years ago for molesting his step-daughter. You have no power to prevent him from moving in. Should you remove the children from the home?

You are a probation officer with a specialized caseload of 60 sexual offenders. Two of your cases worry you. Yesterday, a 50-year-old repeat child molester began talking openly about his sexual attraction to a particular boy. Today, you learn that a 22-year-old date rapist was evicted from treatment for denying he had done anything wrong. You have the opportunity to make one more home visit this week. Which one would you choose?

The need for accurate risk assessment permeates clinical practice. Given the serious consequences of sexual victimization (Hanson, 1990; Koss, 1993), special care is justified in the evaluation of sexual offenders. Evaluators are most often concerned about new sexual offences, but sexual offenders also have considerable potential for inflicting other forms of damage. Sexual offenders, particularly rapists, are as likely to recidivate with a non-sexual violent offence as with a sexual offence (Hanson & Bussière, 1996, 1998). The predictors of sexual offence recidivism, however, appear to be different from the predictors of violent non-sexual recidivism (Hanson & Bussière, 1998; Hanson, Scott, & Steffy, 1995). Consequently, the careful clinician should evaluate separately the risk for sexual and for non-sexual recidivism. Given that the assessment of general, violent recidi-

The Essential Handbook of Offender Assessment and Treatment. Edited by C. R. Hollin.
© 2004 John Wiley & Sons Ltd.

vism is addressed elsewhere (Bonta, Law, & Hanson, 1998; Quinsey, Harris, Rice, & Cormier, 1998), the present chapter will focus only on assessing the risk for sexual recidivism.

PREDICTORS OF SEXUAL RECIDIVISM

Future behaviour can never be predicted with certainty. Nevertheless, a growing body of research indicates that well-informed evaluators can predict sexual offence recidivism with at least moderate accuracy (Hanson, 1998; Quinsey, Lalumière, Rice, & Harris, 1995). Risk assessments consider two distinct concepts:

1. enduring propensities, or potentials, to reoffend
2. factors that indicate the onset of new offences.

These offence triggers are not random, but can be expected to be organized into predictable patterns (offence cycles), some unique to the individual and some common to most sexual offenders (see Laws, 1989).

Different evaluation questions require the consideration of different types of risk factors. Static, historical variables (e.g. prior offences, childhood maladjustment) can indicate deviant developmental trajectories and, as such, enduring propensities to sexually offend. Evaluating changes in risk levels (e.g. treatment outcome), however, requires the consideration of dynamic, changeable risk factors (e.g. cooperation with supervision, deviant sexual preferences) (Bonta, 1996). Although age is sometimes considered a dynamic factor, the most important dynamic factors are those that respond to treatment. Dynamic factors can be further classified as stable or acute. Stable factors have the potential to change, but typically endure for months or years (e.g. personality disorder), and, as such, represent ongoing risk potential. In contrast, acute factors (e.g. negative mood) may be present for short durations (minutes, days) and can signal the timing of offending. Most risk decisions require consideration of both static and dynamic risk factors.

Follow-up Studies of Sexual Offenders

The strongest evidence for identifying risk factors comes from follow-up studies (Furby, Weinrott, & Blackshaw, 1989). Even the best study, however, is insufficient to establish that a characteristic is (or is not) a risk factor. Knowledge advances through orderly replication (Lakatos, 1970; Schmidt, 1996). When the same factor is identified in many independent studies, evaluators can be reasonably confident that the risk factor is reliable. Consequently, rather than discuss individual follow-up studies in detail, this section relies heavily on our meta-analysis (quantitative summary) of sexual offender recidivism studies (Hanson & Bussière, 1998; for an earlier version see Hanson & Bussière, 1996).

Our meta-analysis examined 61 different follow-up studies including a total of

28 972 sexual offenders. Table 3.1 presents the risk factors that were examined in at least four independent settings and correlated with recidivism at $r = .10$ or greater. Overall, the strongest predictors of sexual offence recidivism were factors related to sexual deviance. Sexual offenders were more likely to recidivate if they had deviant sexual interests, had committed a variety of sexual crimes, had begun offending sexually at an early age, or had targeted boys, strangers, or unrelated victims. Sexual interest in children as measured by phallometric testing (Launay, 1994) was the single strongest predictor of sexual offence recidivism.

After sexual deviance, the next most important predictors were general criminological factors, such as any prior offences, age, and antisocial personality disorder. These factors mark a dimension common to many criminal populations that has been variously referred to as "low self-control" (Gottfredson & Hirschi, 1990), psychopathy (Hare et al., 1990), or lifestyle instability (Cadsky, Hanson, Crawford, & Lalonde, 1996). There is extensive research linking general criminological factors to non-sexual recidivism among both sexual and non-sexual offender populations (Bonta et al., 1998; Gendreau, Little, & Goggin, 1996; Hanson & Bussière, 1998). Although criminal lifestyle is, in itself, only moderately related to sexual offence recidivism, there is some evidence that the combination of deviant sexual preferences and psychopathy places offenders at particularly high risk for committing further sexual offence crimes (Rice & Harris, 1997).

One of the more interesting findings was that offenders who failed to complete treatment were at higher risk than those who completed treatment ($r = .17$). Offenders' verbal reports of treatment motivation had little or no relationship to

Table 3.1 Predictors of sexual offence recidivism from Hanson & Bussière (1998)

Risk factors	Average r	Sample (studies) size
Sexual deviance		
Sexual interest in children as measured by phallometry	0.32	4 853 (7)
Any deviant sexual preference	0.22	570 (5)
Prior sexual offences	0.19	11 294 (29)
Any stranger victims	0.15	465 (4)
Early onset of sex offending	0.12	919 (4)
Any unrelated victims	0.11	6 889 (21)
Any boy victims	0.11	10 294 (19)
Diverse sex crimes	0.10	6 011 (5)
Criminal history/lifestyle		
Antisocial personality disorder/psychopathy	0.14	811 (6)
Any prior offences (non-sexual/any)	0.13	8 683 (20)
Demographic factors		
Age (young)	0.13	6 969 (21)
Single (never married)	0.11	2 850 (8)
Treatment history		
Failure to complete treatment	0.17	806 (6)

recidivism (average $r = .01$ based on three studies), but those offenders who actively engaged in treatment recidivated less often than treatment drop-outs. Such findings have sometimes been attributed to the effectiveness of treatment (e.g. Hall, 1995), but could also indicate that the highest risk offenders fail to complete treatment. In particular, it is well known that antisocial personality, lifestyle instability, and general impulsiveness are reliable predictors of treatment attrition (Cadsky et al., 1996; Wierzbicki & Pekarik, 1993).

Notably absent from the list of risk factors were any measures of subjective distress or general psychological symptoms (e.g. low self-esteem, depression). Overall, the average correlation with recidivism for general psychological variables was virtually zero (average $r = .01$, with 95% confidence interval of $-.02$ to $+.04$) (Hanson & Bussière, 1998). As will be discussed later, this does not mean that subjective distress plays no role in the recidivism process. Mood could be an acute, but not a long-term, risk factor. Because sexual offenders recidivated years after the assessments, rapidly changing factors, such as mood, would not be expected to predict long-term recidivism.

In summary, follow-up studies have identified a number of static (e.g. prior offences) or highly stable factors (e.g. deviant sexual preferences) that can usefully identify an enduring propensity for sexual offending. Much less is known about how changes on risk factors are associated with changes in recidivism risk potential. Early research suggested that decreasing sexual deviance reduced recidivism (Quinsey, Chaplin, & Carrigan, 1980), but with extended follow-up, recidivism was predicted by pre-treatment, not post-treatment, deviance scores (Rice, Quinsey, & Harris, 1991).[1]

Dynamic Risk Factors

If evaluators wish to maintain high levels of certainty, the discussion of dynamic risk would be extremely short: there are no well-established dynamic risk predictors for sexual offence recidivism. Dynamic factors, however, are too important to ignore. Consequently, the next section will provide some discussion of variables that could potentially be useful dynamic risk factors.

My suggestions regarding dynamic risk factors were guided by social cognitive theory (e.g. Bandura, 1977; Fiske & Taylor, 1991) as has been applied to general criminal behaviour (e.g. Andrews & Bonta, 1994) and sexual offending (Johnson & Ward, 1996; Laws, 1989). In this model, recidivistic sexual offenders would be expected to hold deviant schema, or habitual patterns of thought and action, that facilitate their offences. The likelihood that an offender will invoke such schema would increase if the schema were well rehearsed, were triggered by common circumstances, were considered socially acceptable, and were consistent with the offender's personality and values. Each offender's crime cycle

---

[1] In general, the reduced variability in post-treatment scores would be expected to restrict the extent to which they could predict recidivism.

would be somewhat unique. Nevertheless, certain characteristics would be expected to provide fertile ground for the development and maintenance of deviant sexual schema. An outline of some of these potential dynamic risk factors is presented in Table 3.2.

Among the more promising dynamic risk factors are problems with intimacy and attachment (Marshall, 1993; Seidman, Marshall, Hudson, & Robertson, 1994;

Table 3.2 Potential dynamic predictors of sexual offence recidivism

Predictor	Level
Intimacy deficits	low: a stable romantic relationship with an appropriate partner, and several constructive long-term friendships moderate: some intimate relationships, but short-term or unsatisfying high: no intimate relationships, or relationships only with wholly inappropriate partners (e.g. children)
Negative peer influences	low: all significant people are positive influences moderate: a mixture of positive and negative influences high: overtly deviant peer groups (e.g. paedophile exchange members, bike gang)
Attitudes tolerant of sexual assault	low: identifies no situations in which sexual assault is justified. Consistently views sexual offending as wrong moderate: generally disapproves of sexual crimes, but occasionally will express excuses/justifications (e.g. mature child, victim asked for it) high: sees little wrong with sexual offending; able to justify in many situations (e.g. age of consent laws are "arbitary")
Emotional/sexual self-regulation	low: has consistently coped with stressful situations without resorting to sexual fantasies or high-risk behaviour moderate: occasionally lapses into sexual fantasies (deviant or otherwise) and/or high-risk behaviour when stressed high: negative mood/stress consistently trigger sexual imagery, and feels urge to act upon them. Frequently feels sexually frustrated and is unable/unwilling to delay gratification
General self-regulation	low: consistently cooperative with supervision and/or treatment. Avoids high-risk situations, even when it involves personal sacrifices moderate: recognizes need to self-regulate, but little commitment or weak implementation. Attends treatment but not highly motivated. Occasional missed appointments/rescheduling high: disengaged, or overtly manipulative in supervision. Feels no need to change/self-monitor or feels "out of control". Frequent non-attendance or treatment drop-out. Commonly exposed to high-risk situations

Ward, Hudson, & McCormack, 1997). Normative sexuality involves mutually consenting behaviour within a relationship of trust. In contrast, the social interactions connected with sexual offending are, by definition, problematic. The victims are either incapable of mutuality (child molesting), or the contact is overtly hostile (rape), or extremely detached (voyeurism, exhibitionism). Such problems with the initiation and development of sexual relationships has been referred to as courtship disorder (Freund, Seto, & Kuban, 1997) or as heterosexual social skills deficits (McFall, 1990).

Recidivism studies provide some evidence that relationship deficits increase recidivism risk. In general, the closer the pre-existing relationship with the victim, the lower the recidivism rate (incest < acquaintances < strangers) (Hanson & Bussière, 1998). As well, offenders who have never been married/common-law are at increased risk for sexual offence recidivism compared to married offenders. Frisbie's (1969) follow-up study similarly found that "grave difficulties in establishing meaningful relationships with adult females" (p. 163) was one of the most important recidivism risk factors.

Group comparisons between sexual offenders and non-sexual offenders also support the importance of intimacy deficits. In comparison to non-sexual offenders, sexual offenders receive little satisfaction from their intimate relationships (Seidman et al., 1994), lack empathy for women (Hanson, 1997b), and prefer sex in uncommitted relationships (Malamuth, 1998).

A careful examination of the full range of sexual offenders' personal relationships is not only useful for identifying intimacy deficits, but may also reveal direct social support for sexual offending (e.g. paedophile rings; peer support for rape). There is extensive research indicating that having criminal companions is a strong predictor of criminal behaviour (Gendreau et al., 1996). Similarly, there is some evidence that sexual offenders are likely to have friends and relatives who are sexual offenders (Hanson & Scott, 1996). In a recent study of sexual offenders on community supervision (total, $n = 408$), we found that the recidivists were more likely than the non-recidivists to have predominantly negative social influences (43% versus 21%, respectively, Hanson & Harris, 1998, 2000).

Attitudes or values tolerant of sexual assault should also be considered potential dynamic predictors. Among community samples, there is consistent evidence that men who admit to sex offending also endorse "rape myths" or attitudes that condone such behaviour (Dean & Malamuth, 1997; Malamuth, Sockloskie, Koss, & Tanaka, 1991). The research with convicted sexual offender samples has not always been consistent, but there is some evidence that deviant sexual attitudes are common among both child molesters and rapists (Bumby, 1996; Hanson, Gizzarelli, & Scott, 1994). Typically, sexual offenders state that sexual offending is wrong but provide justifications and excuses that mitigate the seriousness of their own crimes. Those rare offenders who directly challenge the morality of existing sexual laws should be considered particularly high risk (e.g. paedophile club members).

According to relapse prevention theory, a common trigger for sexual offending is negative mood or stress (Pithers, Beal, Armstrong, & Petty, 1989). Offenders are considered to cope with stress through sexual fantasies, which may eventually be acted upon. In support of this position, repeated assessments of inpatient sexual offenders has found that deviant sexual fantasies tended to follow stressful events (McKibben, Proulx, & Lusignan, 1994; Proulx, McKibben, & Lusignan, 1996). Cortoni, Heil, and Marshall (1996) similarly found that sexual offenders reported using sexual fantasies (both deviant and non-deviant) as coping mechanisms much more often than did other types of offenders. Given that sexual offenders may feel justified or entitled to act out their sexual feelings with little "courtship" (Freund et al., 1997; Hanson et al., 1994), it is easy to imagine how sexual responses to stress could be an important risk indicator. The overall level of subjective distress does not appear to be important in predicting recidivism (Hanson & Bussière, 1998): what seems more important are the mechanisms used by sex offenders for regulating their emotional and sexual feelings. In particular, sexual offenders should be considered at high risk to reoffend if (a) many circumstances, including negative affect, arouse sexual imagery; and (b) offenders feel deprived or frustrated if they are unable to quickly satisfy their urges.

In addition to problems with emotional/sexual self-regulation discussed above, offenders may also have problems with general self-regulation or self-control strategies. Offenders who are motivated to prevent reoffence and can effectively manage their own behaviour should be able to reduce their recidivism risk. This dimension overlaps with the criminal lifestyle variables previously discussed, but includes additional indicators. In our recent study we found that some of the best predictors of recidivism while on community supervision related to poor self-management strategies. In particular, recidivists, in comparison to non-recidivists, were perceived as failing to acknowledge their own potential for reoffence, exposing themselves to high-risk situations, being unmotivated for treatment, and being uncooperative with community supervision (Hanson & Harris, 2000).

Combining Risk Factors

Since no single factor is sufficient to determine whether offenders will or will not recidivate, evaluators need to consider a range of relevant risk factors. There are three plausible methods by which risk factors can be combined into overall evaluations of risk:

1. empirically guided clinical evaluations
2. pure actuarial predictions, and
3. clinically adjusted actuarial predictions.

The empirically guided clinical evaluation begins with the overall recidivism base rate, and then adjusts the risk level by considering factors that have been empirically associated with recidivism risk. The risk factors to be considered are explicit, but the method for weighing the importance of the risk factors is left to the judgement of the evaluator (e.g. Boer, Wilson, Gauthier, & Hart, 1997).

Actuarial approaches, in contrast, explicitly state not only the variables to be considered, but also the precise procedure through which ratings of these variables will be translated into a risk level. In the pure actuarial approach, risk levels are estimated through mechanical, arithmetic procedures requiring a minimum of judgement. The "adjusted" actuarial approach begins with a pure actuarial prediction, but then raises or lowers the risk level based on consideration of relevant factors that were not included in the actuarial method. As research develops, actuarial methods can be expected to consistently outperform clinical predictions (Grove & Meehl, 1996). With the current state of knowledge, however, both actuarial and guided clinical assessment approaches can be expected to provide risk assessments with moderate levels of accuracy (Hanson, Morton, & Harris, in press).

Actuarial Risk Scales for Sexual Offence Recidivism

The starting point for all risk prediction should be the expected recidivism base rate. The rate at which sexual offenders are reconvicted for sexual offences is much lower than is commonly believed. In our meta-analytic review (Hanson & Bussière, 1998) 13.4% of the sexual offenders recidivated with a sexual offence (n = 23 393; 18.9% for 1839 rapists and 12.7% for 9603 child molesters) during the average four-to-five-year follow-up period. These rates should be considered underestimates since many sexual offences, particularly those against children, are never reported (Bonta & Hanson, 1994). With longer follow-up periods, the rate increases to 35%–45% after 15–25 years (Hanson et al., 1995; Prentky, Lee, & Knight, 1997; Rice & Harris, 1997). The long-term rate for child molesters is similar to that of rapists, although there is a tendency for rapists to recidivate somewhat earlier after release.

Actuarial scales further refine base-rate predictions by estimating the recidivism rates for sub-groups of sexual offenders (e.g. first-time incest offenders, boy-object child molesters with prior sexual offence convictions). Efforts to develop actuarial risk scales for sexual offenders have been the focus of considerable research in recent years.

The most well-established risk scales for sexual offenders are the Rapid Risk Assessment for Sexual Offence Recidivism (RRASOR; Hanson, 1997a); Static-99 (Hanson & Thornton, 2000); the Violence Risk Appraisal Guide (VRAG) and Sex Offender Risk Appraisal Guide (SORAG; Quinsey et al., 1998). Each of these scales has moderate predictive accuracy in predicting sexual recidivism, although the VRAG and SORAG appear better at predicting general violent recidivism than either the Static-99 or RRASOR. The Static-99 and RRASOR, however, have the advantage of being relatively easily scored from commonly available information (official criminal history, victim characteristics, age).

The Minnesota Sexual Offender Screening Tool (SOST; Epperson, Kaul, & Huot, 1995) was the first instrument specifically designed to assess the risk of sexual recidivism. The original version contained 21 items related to sexual and non-sexual criminal history, substance abuse, marital status, and treatment compliance. The revised version, the MinSOST-R, showed moderately high correlations with sexual recidivism in samples from Minnesota (Epperson, Kaul, & Hesselton, 1998), but the results from other jurisdictions has been less encouraging (Barbaree, Seto, Langton, & Peacock, 2001).

The Rapid Risk Assessment for Sexual Offence Recidivism, or RRASOR, was constructed by re-analysing the data from eight different follow-up studies (total sample of 2,604) (Hanson, 1997a). It contains four items: prior sexual offences, age less than 25, any male victims, and any unrelated victims.

David Thornton developed a risk scale for Her Majesty's Prison Service, entitled the Structured Anchored Clinical Judgement (SACJ; Grubin, 1998). The scale categorises offenders into three risk levels (low, medium, high) based on sexual and nonsexual criminal convictions, and the type of victim in the sexual offences (males, strangers). The initial results have been encouraging, although the SACJ has now been largely replaced in the UK by the revised version, entitled Risk Matrix 2000 (David Thornton, personal communication, August 17, 2002).

Each item is worth one point, except for prior sexual offences, which can be worth up to three points. Overall, the RRASOR showed moderate predictive accuracy (average $r = .27$, area under ROC curve = .71), with relatively little variability between the development and validation samples.

Static-99 was developed by combining 10 non-redundant items from the SACJ and RRASOR (Hanson & Thornton, 2000). Static-99 shows slightly better predictive accuracy than the RRASOR, both of which have been examined in more than 15 replication studies, including samples from Canada, the US, the UK, and Sweden (Hanson, Morton, & Harris, in press). Those who score in the lowest Static-99 category show a sexual recidivism rate of about 5% after five years, compared to a rate of about 40% for those in the highest category. A scoring guide is available online (see *www.sgc.gc.ca*; Phenix, Hanson, & Thornton, 2000).

The VRAG and SORAG were both developed of the prediction of general violence (Quinsey et al., 1998). The SORAG, however, was designed specifically to predict violent reoffending among sexual offenders. It contains 14 items, the most heavily weighted items being the Psychopathy Checklist – Revised (Hare et al., 1990) and age at index offence. Direct comparisons between the SORAG and Static-99 have found that they predict sexual recidivism equally well (e.g., Barbaree et al., 2001).

The available research suggests that it is possible to assess an offender's long-term risk potential using brief actuarial scales. The predictive accuracy of these scales is only moderate, however, and none are comprehensive. Consequently, the prudent evaluator would start with the rates estimated by the actuarial scales, and then consider whether important factors have been omitted. Evaluators should be exceedingly cautious, however, about adjusting actuarial predictions given the poor track record of clinical risk evaluation (Grove & Meehl, 1996).

SUMMARY AND CONCLUSIONS

Different risk assessment contexts call for different combinations of static and dynamic risk predictors. The follow-up research has identified a number of reliable risk factors related to sexual deviance, criminal lifestyle, and treatment compliance. Almost all of the identified risk factors are static or highly stable. Such factors are useful for assessing enduring propensities to reoffend, but they cannot be used to assess treatment outcome or monitor risk on community supervision. Although the research support is tentative, there are several factors that may be useful dynamic risk factors, including intimacy and attachment deficits, deviant peer groups, poor emotional/sexual self-regulation, and general self-regulation problems.

All risk evaluations should be grounded in the expected recidivism base rates. Evaluators can then adjust their predictions based on the presence or absence of relevant risk factors. Several actuarial scales have been developed that may be useful for assessing long-term risk potential. There are no validated scales, however, for assessing changes in the risk for sexual offence recidivism. Consequently, the available information is better at identifying high-risk offenders than it is at determining how to intervene, or whether the interventions have been effective.

ACKNOWLEDGEMENTS

The views expressed are those of the author and do not necessarily represent the views of the Ministry of the Solicitor General of Canada. I would like to thank Andrew Harris for comments on an earlier version of this chapter. Correspondence should be addressed to R. Karl Hanson, Corrections Research, Department of the Solicitor General of Canada, 340 Laurier Avenue, West, Ottawa, Ontario, Canada, K1A 0P8, or by e-mail to hansonk@sgc.gc.ca.

REFERENCES

Andrews, D. A., & Bonta, J. (1994). *The psychology of criminal conduct*. Cincinnati, OH: Anderson.

Bandura, A. (1977). *Social learning theory*. Englewood Cliffs, NJ: Prentice-Hall.

Barbaree, H. E., Seto, M. C., Langton, C. M., & Peacock, E. J. (2001). Evaluating the predictive accuracy of six risk assessment instruments for adult sex offenders. *Criminal Justice and Behavior, 28*, 490–521.

Boer, D. P., Wilson, R. J., Gauthier, C. M., & Hart, S. D. (1997). Assessing risk for sexual violence: Guidelines for clinical practice. In C. D. Webster & M. A. Jackson (Eds.), *Impulsivity: Theory, assessment, and treatment* (pp. 326–342). New York: Guilford.

Bonta, J. (1996). Risk–needs assessment and treatment. In A. T. Harland (Ed.), *Choosing correctional options that work* (pp. 18–32). Thousand Oaks, CA: Sage.

Bonta, J., & Hanson, R. K. (1994). *Gauging the risk for violence: Measurement, impact and strategies for change* (User Report No. 1994-09). Ottawa, Canada: Department of the Solicitor General of Canada.

Bonta, J., Law, M., & Hanson, R. K. (1998). The prediction of criminal and violent recidivism among mentally disordered offenders: A meta-analysis. *Psychological Bulletin, 123*, 123–142.

Bumby, K. M. (1996). Assessing the cognitive distortions of child molesters and rapists: Development and validation of the MOLEST and RAPE scales. *Sexual Abuse: A Journal of Research and Treatment, 8*, 37–54.

Cadsky, O., Hanson, R. K., Crawford, M., & Lalonde, C. (1996). Attrition from a male batterer treatment program: Client-treatment congruence and lifestyle instability. *Violence and Victims, 11*, 51–64.

Cortoni, F., Heil, P., & Marshall, W. L. (1996, November). Sex as a coping mechanism and its relationship to loneliness and intimacy deficits in sexual offending. Presentation at the 15th Annual Conference of the Association for the Treatment of Sexual Abusers, Chicago.

Dean, K., & Malamuth, N. M. (1997). Characteristics of men who aggress sexually and of men who imagine aggressing: Risk and moderating variables. *Journal of Personality and Social Psychology, 72*, 449–455.

Epperson, D. L., Kaul, J. D., & Hesselton, D. (1998). *Minnesota Sex Offender Screening Tool – Revised (MnSOST-R): Development, performance, and recommended risk level cut scores.* Iowa State University/Minnesota Department of Corrections.

Epperson, D. L., Kaul, J. D., & Huot, S. J. (1995, October). *Predicting risk for recidivism for incarcerated sex offenders: Updated development on the Sex Offender Screening Tool (SOST).* Poster session presented at the annual conference of the Association for the Treatment of Sexual Abusers, New Orleans, LA.

Fiske, A., & Taylor, S. (1991). *Social cognition* (2nd ed.). New York: McGraw-Hill.

Freund, K., Seto, M. C., & Kuban, M. (1997). Frotteurism and the theory of courtship disorder. In D. R. Laws & W. O'Donohue (Eds.), *Sexual deviance: Theory, assessment, and treatment* (pp. 111–130). New York: Guilford.

Frisbie, L. V. (1969). *Another look at sex offenders in California.* (California Mental Health Research Monograph No. 12). California: State of California Department of Mental Hygiene.

Furby, L., Weinrott, M. R., & Blackshaw, L. (1989). Sex offender recidivism: A review. *Psychological Bulletin, 105*, 3–30.

Gendreau, P., Little, T., & Goggin, C. (1996). A meta-analysis of the predictors of adult offender recidivism: What works! *Criminology, 34*, 575–607.

Gottfredson, M. R., & Hirschi, T. (1990). *A general theory of crime.* Stanford, CA: Stanford University Press.

Grove, W. M., & Meehl, P. E. (1996). Comparative efficiency of informal (subjective, impressionistic) and formal (mechanical, algorithmic) prediction procedures: The clinical–statistical controversy. *Psychology, Public Policy, and Law, 2*, 293–323.

Grubin, D. (1998). *Sex offending against children: Understanding the risk.* Police Research Series Paper 99. London: Home Office.

Hall, G. C. N. (1995). The preliminary development of a theory-based community treatment for sexual offenders. *Professional Psychology: Research and Practice, 26*, 478–483.

Hanson, R. K. (1990). The psychological impact of sexual victimization on women and children. *Annals of Sex Research, 3*, 187–232.

Hanson, R. K. (1997a). *The development of a brief actuarial risk scale for sexual offense recidivism* (User Report No. 1997-04). Ottawa, Canada: Department of the Solicitor General of Canada.

Hanson, R. K. (1997b). Invoking sympathy: Assessment and treatment of empathy deficits among sexual offenders. In B. K. Schwartz & H. R. Cellini (Eds.), *The sex offenders: New insights, treatment innovations and legal developments* (Vol. 2, pp. 1:1–1:12). Kingston, NJ: Civic Research Institute.

Hanson, R. K. (1998). What do we know about sexual offender risk assessment. *Psychology, Public Policy, and Law*, *4*, 50–72.

Hanson, R. K., & Bussière, M. T. (1996). *Predictors of sexual offender recidivism: A meta-analysis* (User Report 96-04). Ottawa, Canada: Department of the Solicitor General of Canada.

Hanson, R. K., & Bussière, M. T. (1998). Predicting relapse: A meta-analysis of sexual offender recidivism studies. *Journal of Consulting and Clinical Psychology*, *66*, 348–362.

Hanson, R. K., Gizzarelli, R., & Scott, H. (1994). The attitudes of incest offenders: Sexual entitlement and acceptance of sex with children. *Criminal Justice and Behavior*, *21*, 187–202.

Hanson, R. K., & Harris, A. J. R. (1998). *Dynamic predictors of sexual recidivism*. (User Report 1998-01). Ottawa, Canada: Department of the Solicitor General of Canada.

Hanson, R. K., & Harris, A. J. R. (2000). Where should we intervene? Dynamic predictors of sex offense recidivism. *Criminal Justice and Behavior*, *27*, 6–35.

Hanson, R. K., Morton, K. E., & Harris, A. J. R. (in press). Sexual offender recidivism risk: What we know and what we need to know. In R. Prentky, E. Janus, & M. Seto (Eds.), *Understanding and managing sexually coercive behaviour*. New York: Annals of the New York Academy of Sciences.

Hanson, R. K., & Scott, H. (1996). Social networks of sexual offenders. *Psychology, Crime, & Law*, *2*, 249–258.

Hanson, R. K., Scott, H., & Steffy, R. A. (1995). A comparison of child molesters and non-sexual criminals: Risk predictors and long-term recidivism. *Journal of Research in Crime and Delinquency*, *32*, 325–337.

Hanson, R. K., & Thornton, D. (2000). Improving risk assessments for sex offenders: A comparison of three actuarial scales. *Law and Human Behavior*, *24*(1), 119–136.

Hare, R. D., Harpur, T. J., Hakstian, A. R., Forth, A. E., Hart, S. D., & Newman, J. P. (1990). The Revised Psychopathy Checklist: Reliability and factor structure. *Psychological Assessment*, *2*, 338–341.

Johnson, L., & Ward, T. (1996). Social cognition and sexual offending: A theoretical framework. *Sexual Abuse: A Journal of Research and Treatment*, *8*, 55–80.

Koss, M. P. (1993). Rape: Scope, impact, interventions, and public policy responses. *American Psychologist*, *48*, 1062–1069.

Lakatos, I. (1970). Falsification and the methodology of scientific research programs. In A. Musgrave & I. Lakatos (Eds.), *Criticism and the growth of knowledge* (pp. 91–195). New York: Cambridge University Press.

Launay, G. (1994). The phallometric assessment of sex offenders: Some professional and research issues. *Criminal Behaviour and Mental Health*, *4*, 48–70.

Laws, D. R. (Eds.) (1989). *Relapse prevention with sexual offenders*. New York: Guilford.

Malamuth, N. M. (1998). An evolutionary-based model integrating research on the characteristics of sexually coercive men. In J. Adair & D. Belanger (Eds.), *Advances in psychological sciences (Vol. 1): Personal, social and developmental aspects*, 151–184. Hove, UK: Psychology Press.

Malamuth, N. M., Sockloskie, R., Koss, M. P., & Tanaka, J. (1991). The characteristics of aggressors against women: Testing a model using a national sample of college students. *Journal of Consulting and Clinical Psychology*, *59*, 670–681.

Marshall, W. L. (1993). The role of attachment, intimacy, and loneliness in the eitology and maintainance of sexual offending. *Sexual and Marital Therapy*, *8*, 109–121.

McFall, R. M. (1990). The enhancement of social skills: An information-processing analysis. In W. L. Marshall, D. R. Laws, & H. E. Barbaree (Eds.), *Handbook of sexual assault: Issues, theories, and the treatment of the offender* (pp. 311–330). New York: Plenum.

McKibben, A., Proulx, J., & Lusignan, R. (1994). Relationships between conflict, affect and deviant sexual behaviors in rapists and child molesters. *Behaviour Research and Therapy*, *32*, 571–575.

Phenix, A., Hanson, R. K., & Thornton, D. (2000). *Coding rules for the Static-99*. Corrections Research: Manuals and Forms. Ottawa: Department of the Solicitor General of Canada.

Pithers, W. D., Beal, L. S., Armstrong, J., & Petty, J. (1989). Identification of risk factors through clinical interviews and analysis of records. In D. R. Laws (Ed.), *Relapse prevention with sex offenders* (pp. 77–87). New York: Guilford.

Prentky, R. A., Lee, A. F. S., & Knight, R. A. (1997). Recidivism rates among child molesters and rapists: A methodological analysis. *Law and Human Behavior, 21*, 635–659.

Proulx, J., McKibben, A., & Lusignan, R. (1996). Relationships between affective components and sexual behaviors in sexual aggressors. *Sexual Abuse: A Journal of Research and Treatment, 8*, 279–289.

Quinsey, V. L., Chaplin, F. C., & Carrigan, W. F. (1980). Biofeedback and signaled punishment in the modification of inappropriate sexual age preferences. *Behavior Therapy, 11*, 567–576.

Quinsey, V. L., Harris, G. T., Rice, M. T., & Cormier, C. A. (1998). *Violent offenders: Appraising and managing risk*. Washington, DC: American Psychological Association.

Quinsey, V. L., Lalumière, M. L., Rice, M. E., & Harris, G. T. (1995). Predicting sexual offenses. In J. C. Campbell (Ed.), *Assessing dangerousness: Violence by sexual offenders, batterers, and child abusers* (pp. 114–137). Thousand Oaks, CA: Sage.

Rice, M. E., & Harris, G. T. (1997). Cross-validation and extension of the Violence Risk Appraisal Guide for child molesters and rapists. *Law and Human Behavior, 21*, 231–241.

Rice, M. E., Quinsey, V. L., & Harris, G. T. (1991). Sexual recidivism among child molesters released from a maximum security psychiatric institution. *Journal of Consulting and Clinical Psychology, 59*, 381–386.

Schmidt, F. L. (1996). Statistical significance testing and cumulative knowledge in psychology: Implications for training of researchers. *Psychological Methods, 1*, 115–129.

Seidman, B. T., Marshall, W. L., Hudson, S. M., & Robertson, P. J. (1994). An examination of intimacy and loneliness in sex offenders. *Journal of Interpersonal Violence, 9*, 518–534.

Ward, T., Hudson, S. M., & McCormack, J. (1997). Attachment style, intimacy deficits, and sexual offending. In B. K. Schwartz & H. R. Cellini (Eds.), *The sex offenders: New insights, treatment innovations and legal developments* (Vol. 2, pp. 2:1–2:14). Kingston, NJ: Civic Research Institute.

Wierzbicki, M., & Pekarik, G. (1993). A meta-analysis of psychotherapy dropout. *Professional Psychology: Research and Practice, 24*, 190–195.

Part II

Approaches to Treatment

Part II

Approaches to Treatment

Chapter 4

Behavioral Approaches to Correctional Management and Rehabilitation

Michael A. Milan
Georgia State University, Atlanta, USA

INTRODUCTION

This chapter will examine the contributions of behavioral principles to the management and rehabilitation of youthful and adult criminal offenders in institutional settings. In addition, the chapter will focus on research with offenders who commit the most typical crimes against property (e.g. burglary, theft) and persons (e.g. robbery, assault), rather than with special management offenders, many of whom are addressed elsewhere in this text. Behaviorists devoted considerable attention to the management and rehabilitation of more typical offenders in institutional settings during the 1960s and 1970s. As Haney and Zimbardo (1998) have noted, the United State's concern about the rehabilitation of the typical offender virtually ended in the 1970s:

> The country moved abruptly from a society that justified putting people in prison on the basis of the belief that their incarceration would somehow facilitate their productive reentry into the free world to one that used imprisonment merely to disable criminal offenders ("incapacitation") or to keep them far away from the rest of society ("containment")... In fact, prison punishment soon came to be thought of as its own reward, serving only the goal of inflicting pain (p. 712).

As a result of this pro-punishment, anti-rehabilitation movement in the United States, correctional rehabilitation research programs not only lost their funding but also lost their welcome in correctional institutions. It should therefore not be

The Essential Handbook of Offender Assessment and Treatment. Edited by C. R. Hollin.
© 2004 John Wiley & Sons Ltd.

surprising that with the exception of the growing body of social skills research (Hollin, 1989) that has been conducted elsewhere and will not be addressed herein, descriptions of original behavioral research and new behavioral programs with the typical offender have all but disappeared from the literature since the 1970s. This chapter therefore describes much of the early history of behavioral approaches to correctional management and rehabilitation, while other chapters address more recent endeavors with other offenders in other settings. The lack of interest in the typical incarcerated offender is doubly unfortunate, for the incarceration of typical offenders is most certainly on the rise in the United States, if not elsewhere, and the history of behavioral programs for those offenders showed much promise for more effective and more humane management and rehabilitation practices.

Offender management practices and rehabilitation programs are equally important aspects of the justice system (Ayllon, Milan, Roberts, & McKee, 1979). Positive management practices are called for to minimize the often painful (Toch, 1992) and potentially harmful (Paulus, 1988; McCorkle, 1992) effects of imprisonment on offenders, thereby reducing the likelihood that offenders are a greater threat to society when they leave the justice system than they were when they entered it. Effective rehabilitation programs are called for to reduce further the likelihood that released offenders will offend again (Milan & Evans, 1987). Behavioral theories of the origins and continuance of criminal behavior provide direction for both management and rehabilitation efforts. Most behaviorists would undoubtedly agree with the long-standing assumption that the principles of behavior that explain non-criminal behavior also explain criminal behavior (e.g. Milan & McKee, 1974). Two influential theories that elaborate upon that general assumption are those of Hans Eysenck, a psychologist, and Ronald Akers, a sociologist, who have sought to understand better how the principles of conditioning and learning act at the individual and group levels to produce criminal behavior.

BEHAVIORAL THEORIES OF CRIME AND DELINQUENCY

Eysenck's explanation of criminal behavior (Eysenck, 1977; Eysenck & Gudjonsson, 1989) is an outgrowth of his more general theory of personality (Eysenck, 1967, 1981) that emphasizes the interaction of biological and environmental determinants of behavior. The theory postulates one general intelligence factor (g) and three temperamental factors: extraversion, neuroticism, and psychoticism. These dimensions are said to have biological bases that are strongly influenced by genetic factors. The extraversion continuum is considered to be a product of central nervous system functioning, particularly the reticular activating system, and is generally characterized by high to low stimulation-seeking, impulsivity, and irritability. The neuroticism continuum is said to reflect peripheral nervous system functioning, most specifically the limbic system, and is typically manifest in high to low negative affectivity such as heightened reactions to need states or stress, anxiety, depression, and hostility. The psychoticism continuum is postulated to be a product of blood chemistry, and is characterized by high to low social insensitivity, indifferent cruelty to others, and disregard of danger to self. The personality factors are not viewed as the causes of personality and behavior, but instead as predisposing factors. It is the interaction of the unique mix of these factors with unique environmental experiences that determines each individual's adaptation to life and the various forms of psychopathology and criminality they may exhibit.

In general, the principles of conditioning and learning explain the contribution of environmental experiences to adjustment. Eysenck emphasizes the role of respondent (or classical) conditioning during the socialization of children in his understanding of criminal behavior, and seeks to explain why individuals do *not* engage in criminal activities rather than why they do. Eysenck postulates that during the socialization process, children develop a "conscience" as a result of the respondent conditioning components of punishment for misbehavior. Eysenck invokes his personality theory to explain why some children are less affected by the socialization process than others. The lower cortical arousal of individuals high on the extraversion dimension is said to reduce the responsivity to punishment, thereby impeding a punitive socialization process and the development of the conscience. Research on conditionability and crime indicates that criminals do indeed condition more slowly than non-criminals (Raine, 1993). The effects of reduced conditionability are compounded for those high on the neuroticism dimension, where heightened responsivity to need states further increases the likelihood that individuals will engage in prohibited behavior, and/or for those high on the psychoticism dimension, where decreased sensitivity to others and danger to self also decrease the likelihood that individuals will refrain from criminal behavior. Eysenck and Gudjonsson (1989) have reported numerous studies in support of the theory. Its implications are clear: positive reinforcement is to be preferred to punishment and deprivation during both socialization and rehabilitation.

Akers' differential association–reinforcement theory of deviant behavior was initially formulated in conjunction with Robert Burgess (Burgess & Akers, 1966) and has evolved in response to the research it has generated (Akers, 1973, 1977, 1985). It serves as a thoroughgoing example of the manner in which the principles of operant conditioning and learning may be applied to the explanation of criminal behavior. The theory itself is a reformulation of Edwin Sutherland's differential association theory of criminal behavior. The seven original assumptions of the theory are.

1. Criminal behavior is learned according to the principles of operant conditioning.
2. Criminal behavior is learned both in non-social situations that are reinforcing or discriminative and through that social interaction in which the

behavior of other persons is reinforcing or discriminative for criminal behavior.

3. The principal part of the learning of criminal behavior occurs in those groups which comprise the individual's major source of reinforcement.

4. The learning of criminal behavior, including specific techniques, attitudes, and avoidance procedures, is a function of the effective and available reinforcers, and the reinforcement contingencies.

5. The specific classes of behavior which are learned and their frequency of occurrence are a function of the reinforcers which are effective and available, and the rules or norms by which those reinforcers are applied.

6. Criminal behavior is a function of norms which are discriminative for criminal behavior, the learning of which takes place when such behavior is more highly reinforced than non-criminal behavior.

7. The strength of criminal behavior is a direct function of the amount, frequency, and probability of reinforcement.

Akers' (1998) most recent formulation of the theory summarizes its assumptions in the following manner. The probability that persons will engage in criminal and deviant behavior is increased and the probability of their conforming to the norm is decreased when they differentially associate with others who commit criminal behavior and espouse definitions favorable to it, are relatively more exposed in-person or symbolically to salient criminal/deviant models, define it as desirable or justified in a situation discriminative for the behavior, and have received in the past and anticipate in the current or future situation relatively greater reward than punishment for the behavior. The theory therefore explains initial criminal acts as a juvenile or an adult, whether they will continue and, if they do, the modification and elaboration of those activities. It has been employed as the basis for the explanation of a range of criminal activities, including professional crime, drug use, white collar crime, prostitution, and violent assault. The theory emphasizes the importance of the initial socialization process by the family during childhood, and the subsequent competition between continuing socialization by the family and socialization by the peer group during adolescence. Finally, the theory also explains the failure of the socialization process in adulthood. A central component of that explanation is either the lack or loss of non-deviant means of obtaining reinforcement. Akers' review of the research bearing upon the theory provides strong support for its explanatory power.

The following overview of behavioral approaches to correctional management and rehabilitation describes representative examples of its use in institutional settings with those individuals for whom socialization by the family and, subsequently, community agencies in the form of primary and secondary prevention efforts (Milan & Long, 1980) have failed. Experimental single case and group studies will be emphasized. A more detailed review of such programs is also available (see Milan, 1987a, 1987b). The work of Eysenck and Akers indicates that resocialization programs should emphasize positive reinforcement, rather than punishment, to instill pro-social behavior, and that they should focus on building social, academic, and vocational skills that enable those individuals to achievement reinforcement without recourse to antisocial behavior.

PROCEDURES TO DECREASE UNDESIRABLE BEHAVIOR

Time-out and response cost appear to be the most widely examined behavioral management procedures for the reduction of undesirable behavior in correctional settings. In the typical time-out procedure, the individual is either removed briefly from a setting in which social and non-social reinforcers are available freely, or the individual remains in a setting from which those reinforcers are removed briefly. The brief nature of time-out distinguishes it from more punitive administrative procedures, such as detention, segregation, and punitive isolation, that are common in correctional settings. Response cost procedures call for individuals to either relinquish reinforcers, such as money or tokens, as a fine, or increase the amount of effort required to earn reinforcers.

Two early studies of the effectiveness of time-out were conducted by Tyler and his colleagues (Burchard & Tyler, 1965; Tyler & Brown, 1967) in one cottage of a training school. The target behaviors consisted of general rule violations and disruptive misbehavior. In the Burchard and Tyler study, the time-out procedure was explored in a single-inmate case study and consisted of 15 minutes in a small time-out room in the corner of the cottage. The authors reported a 63% drop in offenses. Using a reversal design with 15 inmates, Tyler and Brown replicated the effect in a study in which the procedure was supplemented with reinforcement for appropriate behavior and concluded that the use of swift, brief time-out can be an effective procedure for the control of classroom misbehavior. They hypothesized that the procedure was effective because it was neither so severe that it encouraged peer group support nor so demeaning that it produced resistance from the inmate.

Burchard (1967) provided an example of how response cost may contribute to the control of antisocial behavior, such as stealing, lying, cheating, and fighting, in another study with mentally retarded adolescents and young adults in a residential program. In a reversal design, the loss of tokens in a classroom token economy was first contingent, then non-contingent, and then again contingent upon antisocial behavior. Results indicated lower amounts of antisocial behavior during response cost.

Burchard and Barrera (1972) compared the effectiveness of time-out and response cost with four groups of incarcerated mentally retarded delinquent youths in a token economy classroom. Time-out durations of five and 30 minutes and response cost magnitudes of five and 30 tokens were applied to all groups in counterbalanced sequences. The target behaviors were aggressive acts such as swearing, personal assaults, and destruction of property. The 30-minute time-out and 30-token response cost procedures were most and equally effective in reducing the aggressive acts. Next most effective was a combination of five-minute time-out and five-token response cost, followed by five-minute time-out and finally by five-token response cost. Burchard and Barrera concluded that response cost appears preferable to time-out because it does not terminate participation in the classroom program.

These representative studies make it clear that time-out and response cost are viable alternatives to more severe practices in the management of undesirable behavior in institutional settings. However, when the time-out and response cost procedures are terminated, at least after a short period of use, the suppressed behavior typically reappears. These procedures may therefore be advocated only as ingredients in programs that include procedures for the generalization and maintenance of time-out and response cost effects and, perhaps most importantly, teach skills that are both incompatible with undesirable behaviors and likely to be sustained when the procedures used to instill them are discontinued. Representative procedures used in correctional settings to foster skills and desirable behavior that are incompatible with undesirable behavior are described in the following section.

PROCEDURES TO INCREASE DESIRABLE BEHAVIOR

Helping inmates improve their academic and vocational preparation and, whenever possible, earn a high school degree or its equivalent so that they may qualify for meaningful employment and find a satisfying place in the community upon release is undoubtedly one of the most beneficial uses of a period of incarceration. It should not be surprising that behaviorists have addressed these goals in many of their correctional rehabilitation efforts. In one of the earliest investigations of the applicability of behavioral procedures to an educational classroom in a correctional institution, Burchard (1967) examined the effect of token reinforcement on the appropriate classroom behavior of antisocial retarded students. In a reversal design, tokens were awarded either contingent upon, or independent of, in-seat behavior. As would be expected, the students were in their seats considerably more during the contingent condition.

Subsequent studies have examined the effects of contingency management procedures on the acquisition of academic skills in institutional classroom programs, rather than the maintenance of order and discipline alone. Bednar, Zelhart, Greathouse, and Weinberg (1970) compared traditional and token reinforcement procedures in a between-groups study with incarcerated juvenile delinquents studying programmed educational material. One group worked on the material with no tangible reinforcement. A second group earned tokens for on-task behavior and then for the mastery of the material. In addition, bonus tokens were earned whenever individuals' test scores exceeded the average of their previous week's test score performance. The reinforcement group improved significantly more than the non-reinforcement group in reading and word comprehension on a standardized achievement test.

Graubard (1968) used a reversal design to explore the use of a group contract with emotionally disturbed delinquent youths in a classroom of a residential treatment center. Baseline conditions consisted of traditional teaching strategies involving no tangible reinforcers or group contingencies. During intervention conditions the teacher and students negotiated individual goals, reinforcers, and additional reinforcers that the entire group would earn if everyone met their goals. Substantial decreases in antisocial behavior and substantial increases in academic performance occurred during intervention conditions. Although this study indicates that the use of group contingencies can be an effective strategy for developing positive peer group pressure for appropriate behavior, group contingencies may encourage some group members to apply psychological and physical coercion to individuals who will not or cannot attain the requirements of the group contingency. They should therefore not be utilized unless close and continuing supervision that guarantees the protection of participants is possible and in place.

While each of the previous studies provides an example of the potential of the behavior approach in correctional education, the work of McKee and his colleagues (Clements & McKee, 1968; McKee, 1971; McKee & Clements, 1971; McKee, Jenkins, & Milan, 1977) in a maximum security institution provides a model for the extension of the behavioral approach to academic and vocational instruction. McKee's program begins with a specification of each student's strengths and weaknesses. Training objectives are then specified in behavioral terms; material is presented in a logical sequence of small modules; students respond actively at their own rate to the educational material; and immediate feedback is provided for correct and incorrect answers. McKee (1974) reported that 30% more students completed training with these procedures than was predicted on the basis of previous experience with traditional programs.

McKee (1974) summarized several additional studies going beyond the use of feedback alone and reported that:

1. the performance-contingent opportunity to select items from a "reinforcing event" menu resulted in a doubling of the learning rate with no decline in test scores.
2. the self-recording of performance, supplemented with small monetary awards for sustained outstanding performance, resulted in a marked increase in academic progress and output.
3. a change from contingent to non-contingent monetary consequences resulted in a substantial deterioration in academic test performance, thereby confirming the central role of contingency management procedures in his efforts.

Similarly, McKee et al. (1977) found that students earning monetary reinforcement for academic progress had significantly higher learning rates than a comparable group without contingent reinforcement. Clements and McKee (1968) found that contingency contracts were of approximately equal effectiveness whether prescribed unilaterally by the teachers or negotiated with the students. Finally, accelerated rates of learning have been maintained through reinforcement for protracted periods of time (McKee, 1971), with students averaging gains of 1.4 grade levels on standardized achievement tests for 208 hours of study (McKee & Clements, 1971).

The teaching of academic and vocational skills in the correctional setting appears to be an important ingredient of rehabilitation programs, for it most probably increases the likelihood that inmates will find appropriate employment and earn an adequate wage after release from the institution. In general, research such as has been reported in this and the preceding section indicates that behavioral procedures can be effective in decreasing undesirable behavior and fostering participation in rehabilitation activities in institutional classrooms and shops. As Hollin (1989) has noted, however, there is no evidence that institutional social skills training programs by themselves reduce offending following release from custody, and the same can be said of the efforts described in this and the preceding section. Perhaps what is called for are comprehensive programs that combine all those components, and more. The following section provides examples of more comprehensive programs that incorporate both management and rehabilitation components and operate throughout the inmate's day.

TOWARDS COMPREHENSIVE PROGRAMS FOR MANAGEMENT AND REHABILITATION

Behavioral programs that have combined significant management and rehabilitation components have typically utilized a token economy (Ayllon & Azrin, 1968) to do so. Several large-scale token economies for institutionalized offenders have been described in the literature. Levinson and his colleagues (Ingram, Gerard, Quay, & Levinson, 1970; Karacki & Levinson, 1970) described a program for youthful offenders diagnosed as psychopathic and incarcerated at a federal institution for older, "hard-core" delinquent youths. Inmates earned tokens for appropriate behaviors and for winning in games and contests. A response cost procedure was applied to minor forms of inappropriate behavior, and seclusion was used with more serious and aggressive forms of inappropriate behaviors. Seclusion periods were typically in hours rather than in minutes as is the case with time-out procedures. Outcome measures included the time spent in rehabilitation programs, the occurrence of assaults, and whether an inmate's release from the institution was considered to be "positive" (i.e. paroled or remaining in the institution after completion of the program) or "negative" (i.e. disciplinary transfer or escape). Comparisons between the youths in the program and comparable inmates revealed that all differences favored the youths who were enrolled in the behavioral program, with many of the differences achieving statistical significance.

Hobbs and Holt (1976) evaluated a token economy in the cottages of a residential facility for older delinquent males. Outcome measures included following rules in group games, completing assigned chores, avoiding assaultive behavior, and staying with the group while walking between buildings. A multiple baseline design across cottages indicated that the token economy produced significant improvements in the target behaviors. Hobbs and Holt employed a reversal design to also evaluate the effects of their program on academic performance, including completion of assignments and appropriate social interactions. The token economy was found to produce significant improvements in target behaviors.

Several additional studies examining the effectiveness of token reinforcement procedures were conducted by Ayllon and his colleagues and have been reported by Ayllon, Milan, Roberts, and McKee (1979) in their collaborative description of the Motivating Offender Rehabilitation Environment (MORE) project. MORE extended the scope of the token economy in several studies to include vocational training activities. In one study, MORE explored the effects of incentives on the mastery of instructional material dealing with both the theory underlying auto mechanics and the actual operation of various mechanical parts of the automobile. By alternately reinforcing inmates' mastery of theoretical and applied materials, Ayllon and his colleagues demonstrated that the inmates' efforts could be distributed among these two areas and maintained at high levels of performance. In a second study, MORE examined the effects of a "progressive" differential reinforcement of other behavior (DRO) schedule in a barbering class. In the progressive DRO schedule, progressively more error-free performances earned progressively larger amounts of token reinforcement. The number of errors made in the same amount of time during the progressive DRO reinforcement contingency was less than half the number made during the time that it was not in effect. Unfortunately, no outcome data assessing the effect of the program on post-release adjustment were provided for this and the preceding token economies. Such data were reported for the following four token economy programs.

The Contingencies Applicable to Special Education (CASE) projects and the Karl Holton School for Boys token economy were both large-scale token economies for institutionalized older delinquent youths. Although neither program included systematic investigations of specific program components and motivational strategies, some outcome data were provided. In the CASE projects (Cohen, 1973; Cohen & Filipczak, 1971; Cohen, Filipczak, & Bis, 1970), tokens were earned for academic activities, such as completing assignments and passing examinations, and for engaging in personal hygiene and facility maintenance activities. Perhaps most noteworthy was the effect in the academic program: for every 90 hours of educational work, the inmates increased an average of 1.89 academic months on the Sanford Achievement Test, 2.70 academic months on the Gates Reading Survey, and 12.09 IQ points as assessed by the Revised Beta (Cohen, 1973). Filipczak and Cohen (1972) have asserted that their three-year follow-up indicated that CASE releasees had fewer violator warrants than did similar releasees. Filipczak and Cohen note, however, that trends in the violator warrant data indicate that CASE releasees would eventually recidivate near the national norm.

The Karl Holton token economy (Jesness & DeRisi, 1973) served incarcerated young adults similar to those in the CASE projects. The program used two types of tokens: Karl Holton Dollars that were earned for various academic behaviors and routine hygiene and living hall maintenance activities, and Behavior Change Units that were awarded for progress in the remediation of individual problems. Follow-up involved a comparison of parole violation rates before and after implementation of the program as well as comparisons with a transactional analysis program and two traditional programs, all of which served similar inmates (Jesness, 1979). Jesness found no difference in parole violations between the token economy and transactional analysis programs at the end of the 12-month follow-up period. Parole violation dropped to an average of 33% for the token economy and transactional analysis programs in comparison with 43% for the two traditional programs.

Milan and his colleagues (Milan & McKee, 1976; Milan, Throckmorton, McKee, & Wood, 1979; Milan, Wood, & McKee, 1979) systematically explored the effects of the token economy with an array of management and rehabilitation behaviors in a maximum security correctional institution for adult male felons. Milan and McKee (1976) described the Cellblock Token Economy that served as a basis for their rehabilitation and management efforts. Target behaviors included educational activities during evening and weekend times as well as personal hygiene and cellblock maintenance tasks. All target behaviors were operationally defined, and inmates were provided with instruction in the performance of each. The initial criteria for reinforcement allowed successive approximations of the target behaviors to ensure that inmates earned reinforcement as they mastered the skills required. Backup reinforcers included activities available on the token economy cellblock, such as access to a television room, a pool room and a comfortable lounge, the purchase of coffee, soft drinks, sandwiches, cigarettes and the like in the token economy canteen, and additional activities available off the cellblock, such as movies and recreational athletics. Inmates had access to the backup reinforcers throughout the day. The tokens consisted of tokens credited to inmate checking accounts as they were earned, and the inmates purchased the backup reinforcers by writing and exchanging checks. Accounts were balanced at the end of each day.

The first of the two studies described by Milan and McKee (1976) focused on the management of cellblock maintenance activities normally expected of individuals living in group settings. In an extended withdrawal design consisting of 13 experimental conditions spanning 420 days, the best efforts of a correctional officer to encourage inmates to perform these activities were compared with the effect of the non-contingent award of tokens, the contingent earning of tokens, and an increase in the number of tokens earned. Results indicated that the correctional officer's efforts, which typically consisted of threats and intimidation, and the non-contingent award of tokens were no more effective than the routine conditions of baseline periods. Indeed, the data suggest that performance deteriorated and aggressive behavior increased in response to the correctional officer's intensified efforts. The contingent earning of tokens produced a significant and enduring increase in the performance of the targeted behaviors.

Continued monitoring of performance revealed a gradual and continuing improvement in performance and a reduction in variability over a period of a year.

The second of Milan and McKee's (1976) two studies indicated that reinforcement for participation and performance in the educational program produced an increase in the amount of time spent in the classrooms on the cellblock. In addition, the token economy did not impose a discernible hardship upon the inmates as indexed by their ability to come and go from the token economy cellblock in order to participate in activities elsewhere in the prison. Finally, reinforcement for personal hygiene and cellblock maintenance activities did not produce noticeable increases in the amount of time devoted to these activities, although the quality of each improved. However, a small number of inmates consistently abused the rules governing the operation of the token economy cellblock. Strategies to increase the generality of the token economy so that it encompassed such inmates were examined in subsequent studies.

Milan, Throckmorton et al. (1979) used a reversal design to explore a procedure to encourage adherence to the requirements of the Cellblock Token Economy in the first of their two studies. They chose not to discourage rule violations through punishment but instead to achieve the same result through the reinforcement of its incompatible opposite: adherence to the rules of the token economy. The study focused on the inmates' use of a time clock to record the amount of time they spent away from the token economy cellblock, a backup reinforcer for which they had to pay at the end of the day. During baseline, the amount of time between the time at which inmates were last identified as being on the cellblock during a routine attendance check and the time at which they returned was added to their recorded time off the cellblock. During intervention, inmates earned a half hour of free time off the cellblock each day the routine attendance checks indicated that they were recording all their time away from the cellblock. Results indicated that the reinforcement condition produced a significant increase in adherence to the time clock rule.

Milan, Throckmorton et al. (1979) next explored the relationship between the magnitude of token reinforcement and the performance of target behaviors. The study focused on keeping abreast of current events. During the 11 conditions of their parametric reversal study, the magnitude of token reinforcement for attendance at the evening news program was gradually increased and then decreased. The results showed that the average number of inmates attending the program was functionally related to the magnitude of reinforcement, with progressively more inmates in attendance at the progressively higher magnitudes of reinforcement. Some inmates, however, were unaffected by the magnitude of reinforcement. A strategy to motivate inmates who seemed insensitive to reasonable magnitudes of token reinforcement in token economies was explored in the following study.

The use of response chaining to maximize performance in the cellblock education program when tokens alone produced less than optimal participation and progress was tested by Milan, Wood, and McKee (1979) using an extended reversal design. In the baseline conditions the importance of remedial education activities was emphasized, and inmates were encouraged to participate in the program during their leisure-time hours. Virtually no inmates participated. Next, inmates earned tokens for completing and passing module tests. Participation in the education program increased somewhat, but in general the inmates devoted little time to the educational program and mastered little material. Finally, a chaining procedure was established in which achievement in the education program was a prerequisite for access to selected backup reinforcers. Inmates who mastered material representing 10 hours of study time during a week earned access to the reinforcers for the whole of the following week. Inmates who mastered less material earned access to the reinforcers for proportionately less of the week. The procedure resulted in marked increases in both participation in the educational program and the amount of material mastered. The chaining procedure is an alternative to procedures that use increased magnitudes of token reinforcement in an attempt to increase appropriate behavior when those strategies risk the dilution of the token economy itself by the availability of "cheap money".

Jenkins et al. (1974) reported an 18-month post-release follow-up of Cellblock Token Economy inmates and other inmates who either received vocational training or participated in routine prison activities. During the early months of the follow-up period, the percentage of token economy releasees who were returned to prison for either parole violations or the commission of new crimes was markedly lower than for any of the comparison groups. By the end of the follow-up period, however, the rate of return for the token economy group, although still lowest, approximated those of the comparison groups. None the less, the severity of the offenses for which the Cellblock Token Economy inmates were returned to prison was markedly less than those of the comparison groups, with more of the token economy inmates returned for minor parole violations and fewer returned for serious crimes against persons.

The potential contribution of token economy procedures to the rehabilitation of delinquent soldiers with character and behavior disorders in a closed treatment unit was explored by Colman and his colleagues (Boren & Colman, 1970; Ellsworth & Colman, 1970). The target behaviors consisted of the requirements of military life. Educational offerings involved courses in a variety of practical skills, such as overcoming problems with authority and work projects in which the group worked as a team toward common goals. In his description of the immediate effects of the Walter Reed program, Colman (1970) stated that psychotic episodes and suicidal gestures, previously chronic hazards in the group, stopped completely.

An outcome assessment (Colman & Baker, 1969) compared successful outcomes, defined as either completion of a tour of duty and honorable discharge or continuing satisfactory adjustment in a military unit and unsuccessful outcomes, defined as less than honorable discharge, absence without leave, or presence in a military stockade at the time of follow-up, for 46 soldiers participating in the program and another 48 soldiers who received either general psychiatric treatment or routine disciplinary action. The results indicated that 69.5% of the soldiers who participated in the token economy were successful outcomes, while only 28.3% of the comparison group were successful outcomes.

CONCLUSIONS

The research reported herein indicates that behavioral procedures show much promise in the management of correctional institutions and the operation of rehabilitation programs. When combined in comprehensive token economy programs, these procedures also demonstrate potential to improve adjustment following release from confinement. Taken together, the latter four token economy outcome studies reported continuing, albeit not permanent, effects on offenders' behavior following release from custody. As would be expected, the most promising results were generated by a program in a military setting that returned soldiers to similar military service, supporting the well-established finding (e.g. Miltenberger, 1997) that the more similar the rehabilitation setting is to the setting in which the releasees will find themselves, the more pronounced and enduring will be the effects of intervention.

The lack of more permanent effects of the non-military token economies highlights the need for transition and community programs that maintain and build upon the accomplishments of institutional programs. It is, therefore, discouraging that the social and political climate in the United States has brought correctional rehabilitation efforts to an end and dictates that the criminal justice system will not, for the foreseeable future, build upon the foundation of effective rehabilitation and management practices laid by these early programs so many years ago. For the sake of both incarcerated offenders and their potential victims in the community, one can only hope that era will soon come.

REFERENCES

Akers, R. L. (1973). *Deviant behavior: A social learning approach.* Belmont, CA: Wadsworth.

Akers, R. L. (1977). *Deviant behavior: A social learning approach* (2nd ed.). Belmont, CA: Wadsworth.

Akers, R. L. (1985). *Deviant behavior: A social learning approach* (3rd ed.). Belmont, CA: Wadsworth.

Akers, R. L. (1998). *Social learning and social structure: A general theory of crime and deviance.* Boston, MA: Northeastern University.

Ayllon, T., & Azrin, N. (1968). *The token economy: A motivational system for therapy and rehabilitation.* New York: Appleton–Century–Crofts.

Ayllon, T., & Milan, M. A., with the assistance of Roberts, M. D., & McKee, J. M. (1979). *Correctional rehabilitation and management: A psychological approach.* New York: Wiley.

Bednar, R. L., Zelhart, P. F., Greathouse, L., & Weinberg, S. (1970). Operant conditioning principles in the treatment of learning and behavior problems with delinquent boys. *Journal of Counseling Psychology, 17*, 402–407.

Boren, J. J., & Colman, A. D. (1970). Some experiments on reinforcement principles within a psychiatric ward for delinquent soldiers. *Journal of Applied Behavior Analysis, 3*, 29–37.

Burchard, J. D. (1967). Systematic socialization: A programmed environment for the habilitation of antisocial retardates. *Psychological Record, 17*, 461–476.

Burchard, J. D., & Barrera, F. (1972). An analysis of timeout and response cost in a programmed environment. *Journal of Applied Behavior Analysis, 5*, 270–282.

Burchard, J. D., & Tyler, V. O. (1965). The modification of delinquent behavior through operant conditioning. *Behaviour Research and Therapy, 2*, 245–250.

Burgess, R. L., & Akers, R. L. (1966). A differential association-reinforcement theory of criminal behavior. *Social Problems, 14*, 128–147.

Clements, C. B., & McKee, J. M. (1968). Programmed instruction for institutionalized offenders: Contingency management and performance contracts. *Psychological Reports, 22*, 957–964.

Cohen, H. L. (1973). Motivationally-oriented designs for an ecology of learning. In A. R. Roberts (Ed.), *Readings in prison education* (pp. 142–154). Springfield, IL: Charles C. Thomas.

Cohen, H. L., & Filipczak, J. A. (1971). *A new learning environment.* San Francisco, CA: Jossey-Bass.

Cohen, H. L., Filipczak, J. A., & Bis, J. S. (1970). A study of contingencies applicable to special education: CASE I. In R. E. Ulrich, T. Stachnik, & J. Mabry (Eds.), *Control of human behavior* (Vol. 2, pp. 51–69). Glenview, IL: Scott, Foresman.

Colman, A. D. (1970). Behavior therapy in a military setting. *Current Psychiatric Therapies, 10*, 171–178.

Colman, A. D., & Baker, S. L. (1969). Utilization of an operant conditioning model for the treatment of character and behavior disorders in a military setting. *American Journal of Psychiatry, 125*, 101–109.

Ellsworth, P. D., & Colman, A. D. (1970). The application of operant conditioning principles: Reinforcement systems to support work behavior. *American Journal of Occupational Therapy, 24*, 562–568.

Eysenck, H. J. (1967). *The biological basis of personality.* Springfield, IL: Charles C. Thomas.

Eysenck, H. J. (1977). *Crime and personality* (3rd ed.). London: Paladin.

Eysenck, H. J. (1981). *A model for personality.* New York: Springer.

Eysenck, H. J., & Gudjonsson, G. H. (1989). *The causes and cures of criminality.* New York: Plenum.

Filipczak, J., & Cohen, H. L. (1972, September). *The CASE II contingency management system and where it is going.* Paper presented at the meeting of the American Psychological Association, Honolulu, HI.

Graubard, P. S. (1968). Use of indigenous groupings as the reinforcing agent in teaching disturbed delinquents to learn. *Proceedings of the 6th Annual Convention of the American Psychological Association* 613–614.

Haney, C., & Zimbardo, P. (1998). The past and future of U.S. prison policy. *American Psychologist, 7*, 709–727.

Hobbs, T. R., & Holt, M. M. (1976). The effects of token reinforcement on the behavior of delinquents in cottage settings. *Journal of Applied Behavior Analysis, 9*, 189–198.

Hollin, C. R. (1989). *Psychology and crime: An introduction to criminological psychology.* New York: Routledge.

Ingram, G. L., Gerard, R. E., Quay, H. C., & Levinson, R. B. (1970). An experimental program for the psychopathic delinquent: Looking in the "correctional wastebasket". *Journal of Research in Crime and Delinquency, 7*, 24–30.

Jenkins, W. O., Witherspoon, A. D., Devine, M. D., deValera, E. K., Muller, J. B., Barton, M. C., & McKee, J. M. (1974). *The post-prison analysis of criminal behavior and longitudinal follow-up evaluation of institutional treatment.* Elmore, AL: Rehabilitation Research Foundation.

Jesness, C. F. (1979). The youth center project: Transactional analysis and behavior modification programs for delinquents. In J. S. Stumphauzer (Ed.), *Progress in behavior therapy with delinquents* (pp. 56–72). Springfield, IL: Charles C. Thomas.

Jesness, C. F., & DeRisi, W. M. (1973). Some variations in techniques of contingency management in a school for delinquents. In J. S. Stumphauzer (Ed.), *Behavior therapy with delinquents* (pp. 196–235). Springfield, IL: Charles C. Thomas.

Karacki, L., & Levinson, R. B. (1970). A token economy in a correctional institution for youthful offenders. *The Howard Journal of Penology and Crime Prevention, 13*, 20–30.

McCorkle, R. C. (1992). Personal precaution to prison violence. *Criminal Justice and Behavior, 19*, 160–173.

McKee, J. M. (1971). Contingency management in a correctional institution. *Educational Technology, 11*, 51–54.

McKee, J. M. (1974). The use of contingency management to affect learning performance in adult institutionalized offenders. In R. Ulrich, T. Stachnik, & J. Mabry (Eds.), *Control of human behavior* (Vol. 3, pp. 177–186). Glenview, IL: Scott, Foresman.

McKee, J. M., & Clements, C. B. (1971). A behavioral approach to learning: The Draper model. In H. C. Rickard (Ed.), *Behavioral interventions in human problems* (pp. 201–222). New York: Pergamon Press.

McKee, J. M., Jenkins, W. O., & Milan, M. A. (1977). The effects of contingency management procedures on the rate of learning. *Quarterly Journal of Corrections, 1*, 42–44.

Milan, M. A. (1987a). Basic behavioral procedures in closed institutions. In E. K. Morris & C. J. Braukmann (Eds.), *Behavioral approaches to crime and delinquency* (pp. 161–193). New York: Plenum.

Milan, M. A. (1987b). Token programs in closed institutions. In E. K. Morris & C. J. Braukmann (Eds.), *Behavioral approaches to crime and delinquency* (pp. 195–222). New York: Plenum.

Milan, M. A., & Evans, J. H. (1987). Intervention with incarcerated offenders: A correctional community psychology perspective. In I. B. Weiner & A. K. Hess (Eds.), *Handbook of forensic psychology* (pp. 557–583). New York: Wiley.

Milan, M. A., & Long, C. K. (1980). Crime and delinquency: The last frontier? In D. Glenwick & L. Jason (Eds.), *Behavioral community psychology: Progress and prospects* (pp. 194–230). New York: Praeger.

Milan, M. A., & McKee, J. M. (1974). Behavior modification: Principles and applications in corrections. In D. Glaser (Ed.), *Handbook of criminology* (pp. 745–775). Chicago, IL: Rand McNally.

Milan, M. A., & McKee, J. M. (1976). The cellblock token economy: Token reinforcement procedures in a maximum security correctional institution for adult male felons. *Journal of Applied Behavior Analysis, 9*, 253–275.

Milan, M. A., Throckmorton, W. R., McKee, J. M., & Wood, L. F. (1979). Contingency management in a cellblock token economy: Reducing rule violations and maximizing the effects of token reinforcement. *Criminal Justice and Behavior, 6*, 307–325.

Milan, M. A., Wood, L. F., & McKee, J. M. (1979). Motivating academic achievement in a cellblock token economy: An elaboration of the Premack principle. *Offender Rehabilitation, 3*, 349–361.

Miltenberger, R. (1997). *Behavior modification: Principles and procedures.* Pacific Grove, CA: Brooks/Cole.

Paulus, P. B. (1988). *Prison crowding: A psychological perspective.* New York: Springer-Verlag.

Raine, A. (1993). *The psychopathology of crime.* San Diego, CA: Academic Press.

Toch, H. (1992). *Mosaic of human despair: Human breakdown in prison.* Washington, DC: American Psychological Association.

Tyler, V. O., & Brown, G. D. (1967). The use of swift, brief isolation as a group control device for institutionalized delinquents. *Behaviour Research and Therapy, 5,* 1–9.

Chapter 5

Programming in Cognitive Skills: The Reasoning and Rehabilitation Programme

David Robinson
and
Frank J. Porporino
T³ Associates, Ottawa, Canada

INTRODUCTION

The Reasoning and Rehabilitation programme, frequently referred to as *R&R* or *Cognitive Skills*, has become a popular correctional treatment intervention offered in a variety of settings in several countries. Since the mid 1980s the programme has been implemented quite broadly throughout Canada and the United States, and as well in England and Scotland, the Scandinavian countries, Spain, the Canary Islands, Germany, Australia, and New Zealand. In this chapter we outline the essential tenets of the R&R programme, including the theoretical and conceptual model on which it is based and the intervention techniques employed in delivering the programme. We then review existing research on the effectiveness of the programme.

First developed and tested with Canadian offender populations (Ross, Fabiano, & Ewles, 1988), R&R is a structured cognitive behavioural approach to facilitating change in offender behaviour. The approach focuses specifically on the thinking skills which guide (or fail to guide) the behaviour of offenders. It attempts to replace maladaptive and well-established thinking patterns with cognitive skills that promote pro-social behavioral choices. There is emphasis on teaching offenders to become more reflective rather than reactive, more anticipatory and planful in their responses to potential problems, and more generally

The Essential Handbook of Offender Assessment and Treatment. Edited by C. R. Hollin.

flexible, open-minded, reasoned, and deliberate in their thinking. Using step-by-step instruction and purposeful repetition, skills-building is sequenced and refined as the programme unfolds, and skills-use is integrated and made relevant with concrete examples from offenders' lives. Application of skills is encouraged through constant use of modelling and reinforcement techniques. However, the programme's underlying philosophy is that offenders should be given "choice" to apply the skills they learn. They are told to see one of their pockets as filled with their "old" skills. The programme will attempt to fill their other pocket with "new" skills. They will then have the choice of which pocket they wish to draw from in negotiating problems or conflicts in their lives. In this fashion, the programmme attempts to motivate offenders subtly rather than confrontationally.

The programme focuses on the "how" of thinking. A key concept that has become associated with R&R is that offenders are taught "how" to think, not "what" to think. Another way of saying this is that they are taught the "process" of thinking before attempting to redirect the "content' of their thinking. In this context the term "skill" has been applied to the notion of thinking. The process of learning new methods of thinking, which is most frequently manifested in improved problem-solving skills, allows broad generalization of the skills to a variety of typical living situations involving choices that might lead to pro-social or anti-social outcomes (Fabiano, Porporino, & Robinson, 1990).

The supposition that offenders lack some of the thinking skills necessary for pro-social adaptation is based on a body of empirical evidence drawn from both juvenile and adult offender samples (Ross & Fabiano, 1985; Zamble & Porporino, 1988). For example, in their review of literature, Ross and Fabiano (1985) found a number of studies indicating that thinking processes affect social perceptions and that inter-personal relationships are different across offender and non-offender samples. For example, the evidence presented suggested that many offenders have the propensity to act quickly before thinking, failing to consider the circumstances and emotions of other persons in their choices, and showing cognitive rigidity in their approaches to solving problems. A critical deficit area concerns offender attributions regarding the intentions and actions of other persons. A good example of this phenomenon is illustrated in the work of Dodge and Frame (1982). In contrast to non-aggressive boys, they showed that aggressive boys tend to attribute hostile intent to the ambiguous actions of others. In terms of more general problem-solving deficits that may be linked to thinking skills, Zamble and Porporino (1988) described numerous deficits in the way their sample of incarcerated men solved everyday problems. Their problem-solving was characterized by unsystematic methods that often tended to exacerbate problems, more palliative rather than problem-oriented coping, and a general lack of planful or pro-active behaviour.

According to the theory on which the R&R is based, the skill deficits described above are viewed as playing a role in the onset of criminality and are highly instrumental in the maintenance of offending behaviour. In addition, these skill deficits are viewed as amenable targets of change when addressed using social-learning-based interventions. Again drawing from social learning theory, the model proposes that for many offenders the cognitive skills needed for pro-social adjustment are not acquired as part of the usual socialization process in childhood. Temperamental qualities that can lead to generalized conduct disorder and the early emergence of aggressivity place these individuals particularly at risk. Conceivably, a broad range of skill deficits develops because of the absence of appropriate adult models or the presence of poor parenting practices associated with reinforcement of pro-social skills through childhood and adolescence. Early school failure and delinquent peer-group influence further strengthen an anti-social developmental pattern. At the same time, the R&R approach is based on the assumption that essential skills can be newly acquired or relearned through structured interventions at a later time in adolescence or adulthood. Hence, the programme combines direct training and pro-social modelling techniques to address the skill deficits. The programme also helps offenders to learn to generalize the skills to a variety of situations which have the potential for criminal outcomes when the skills are not applied.

CONTENT OF THE PROGRAMME

The principal targets for the programme include self-control (e.g. thinking before acting), inter-personal problem-solving skills (e.g. early recognition of problems, ability to examine alternatives, assess consequences and interpersonal goals and respond appropriately), social perspective-taking (e.g. acknowledging that the behaviour of others has an impact on ourselves and that there are consequences of one's behavioural choices for other persons), critical reasoning (e.g. evaluating ideas objectively and considering a variety of sources of information in the process of decision-making), cognitive style (e.g. becoming less rigid and narrow in one's thinking and less prone to externalize blame) and values (e.g. acknowledge values that govern one's behaviour and learning to identify inconsistencies between what we believe and how we behave). The R&R programme is delivered in a series of 36 two-hour sessions which are designed to build thinking or "cognitive" skills in a progressive manner but are also designed to move offenders through stages of change—from accepting the existence of problems, decision-making about choices, taking action, maintaining new behaviours, and preventing relapse through learning to monitor and self-correct thinking in new situations. Normally, the programme is delivered to appropriately selected groups of 6–12 participants.

Throughout the 36-session curriculum, there is a consistency in focusing on skills acquisition in all programme content. Programme delivery staff are viewed as "trainers" or "coaches" who teach the requisite skills to the offenders. R&R is multi-modal in that it exposes offenders to a variety of techniques in acquiring the skills. These techniques include role-playing, dilemma games, cognitive exercises (e.g. cognitive puzzles), board games aimed at examining values, and other methods aimed at gaining and maintaining the attention of the participants.

Maximum use is made of the groups setting to break participants into dyads and triads to complete various exercises. Coaches also combine a variety of visual techniques to cover the didactic components of the curriculum, including pictures, posters, overhead transparencies, flip charts, and chalk boards.

Practice and repetition are also important components of the skill acquisition process within the programme. Participants learn many of the social skills which are based on the work of Goldstein (1988) through repeated rehearsal using video-taped feedback to perfect their performance of the skill. Content presented in the programme is frequently repeated and participants are often exposed to rapid reviews of previous material before the introduction of new content. In addition, the importance of memory in learning has been used in the R&R programme through the presentation of skills in a series of steps which participants are encouraged to memorize so that they can easily produce the required behaviours when various situations emerge which call for the performance of the skills. Techniques are used to help students develop memory devices and many of the skills have easily memorized acronyms to assist participant recall. For example, DeBono's (1982) creative thinking skills are employed within the programme to assist offenders in problem-solving. Each skill has a clever acronym (e.g. CAF— Consider All Factors) which participants can easily retrieve when the skill is indicated.

A variety of learning techniques have been purposely integrated within the curriculum of the programme. This approach to the design of the programme was intended to keep skill-learners stimulated, but also to ensure that the diversity of learning styles observed within offender populations is represented. The programme was intended to be delivered at a steady and rather rapid pace. Programme coaches should refrain from lecturing or instructing. Rather, they are trained to teach "Socratically"; not to tell but to elicit answers by asking questions. Ultimate mastery in the delivery of R&R implies that coaches must constantly attend to the diversity of learning styles and ensure that each individual participant is motivated by and able to grasp the material.

The programme is not simply didactic in focus but also incorporates a number of principles of guided discovery whereby participants must pose and answer questions as they master the content. The programme devotes considerable time to problem-solving skills. In learning thinking skills for problem-solving, participants must learn to question in a critical fashion. They must also learn tools of analysis which they can use to make judgements about various pieces of information and choose the best course of action when it is time to make decisions. In teaching problem-solving, R&R coaches provide information on the various steps that must be taken before decision-making is possible. However, they must also use the material generated by the offenders (e.g. problem situations) to guide them through the various steps required to solve a problem. During the training, coaches learn that they must resist the temptation to specify the correct solutions to problems. Rather, they assist the participants in arriving at the best solutions by helping them apply the various cognitive skills covered in the curriculum.

PROGRAMME DELIVERERS

While coaches use their own problem-solving examples and encourage the offender participants to offer scenarios for problem-solving practice, the programme is highly structured. The detailed programme manual guides coaches through the various sessions in a carefully ordered sequence. The programme was not designed to be delivered solely by highly trained professional therapists. In fact, programme coaches are frequently drawn from correctional officer, probation officer, and case management officer ranks within correctional jurisdictions. The possession of the cognitive skills covered in the programme is a key criteria used in selecting coaches. In addition, good rapport with offenders, the ability to manage group situations, and a degree of discipline, flexibility, attentiveness, and exuberance are characteristics of individuals who will become successful coaches. The use of line level correctional staff is a conscious programme implementation principle for many jurisdictions. A benefit of this approach is that support for the objectives of the programme can be more easily obtained when staff from all levels of the correctional setting have ownership and understanding of the programme principles. In this way, line staff can begin to encourage other line staff to support and reinforce the progress of offenders in acquiring the programme skills.

Rather than therapy, R&R is a training programme. While para-professionals are most often used to deliver the curriculum, they must complete an intensive training programme before delivering the programme. Coach preparation consists of at least one week of formal training which includes practicing delivery techniques before trainers and other trainees, and feedback on delivery style and mastery of the programme materials. Following training, new coaches are monitored using video-tapes of their programme sessions and follow-up training assists the coaches to refine their delivery in areas of weakness. A programme of coach certification is regarded as the key to maintaining a high-quality programme delivery system for R&R.

R&R places considerable emphasis on coach training, careful implementation of programme principles, and the ongoing integrity of programme delivery. While the manual is helpful, coaches must prepare each two-hour session in advance so that they are familiar with all the exercises in the session and ready to instil confidence among participants in the content of the programme. The preparation includes set-up of materials and generation of examples or scenarios that are appropriate for the particular group being trained. The programme is not easily "done-on-the-fly", without a full understanding of the sequencing of skills learned and the interdependence between the various programme components. During the training, neophyte coaches receive instruction on each session within the 36-session curriculum. They learn to deal with questions from participants in each of the key areas of the programme. Coaches are also exposed to the group management techniques that are necessary to lead groups of 6–12 participants.

RESEARCH

From its first development, adherents of R&R have emphasized the necessity of research-based knowledge for programme development in corrections. As alluded to above, the selection of the major targets of the programme was based on a review of research on cognitive correlates of criminal behaviour (Ross & Fabiano, 1985). Recently, there have been a number of meta-analyses suggesting that programmes based on cognitive behavioural principles are most promising in treating criminal offenders (Andrews et al., 1990; Izzo & Ross, 1990; Lipsey 1995; Lösel, 1995). The conclusions of these studies have found further empirical support from the preliminary results of the most ambitious meta-analytic review undertaken to date by Lipton and his colleagues (Lipton, Pearson, Cleland & Yee, 1998). Based on more than 900 treatment studies with offender populations, their data suggest that programmes borrowing from cognitive behavioural approaches appear to be more effective than programmes based on alternative models.

Cognitive-based approaches are now quickly becoming the fashion in corrections and criminal justice. However, it is the particular design, and the mode of delivery of a cognitive intervention, that will determine its effectiveness. Regardless of how they are labelled, all programmes should therefore pass the litmus test of controlled research.

There has been considerable commitment by proponents of the R&R to subject the programme to empirical investigations. In particular, there has been an interest in assessing the impact of R&R on participants' post-programme recidivism. In this chapter we concentrate on the research which addresses the impact on recidivism. However, we also draw attention to some studies which have examined more intermediate programme outcomes such as changes in attitudes and indicators of client satisfaction. In our review of the research we examine studies conducted on different offender populations, including adults, juveniles, substance abusers, and mentally disordered offenders.

Adult Offenders

The earliest study conducted on the R&R programme was reported by Ross et al. (1988). At the time of their study they commented that the research represented an "experimental project designed to assess the efficacy of an unorthodox treatment" (p. 29) for high-risk adult probationers. Known as the "Pickering Experiment", the study compared post-programme outcomes of probationers who had been exposed to R&R with the outcomes of a group of offenders who had received "life skills", and a third group of regular probation clients. The offenders ($n = 62$) were all randomly assigned to the three comparison groups. The R&R group showed far superior outcomes than the other two groups in terms of recidivism. For example, only 18.1% of the R&R probationers recidivated compared with 47.5% in the life skills and 69.5% in the regular probation group. In addition, none of the R&R offenders was incarcerated in comparison with 11% of the life skills and 30% of the regular probation groups. Therefore, although the sample size was modest, the first experimental assessment of the effectiveness of the R&R was highly positive.

A series of larger studies on the efficacy of R&R for adult offenders was conducted by researchers at Correctional Service Canada (CSC), where the programme was nationally implemented with Canadian federal offenders. In the Canadian federal system the programme has come to be known as Cognitive Skills Training. For the most part these studies were conducted by the current authors and our colleagues (Fabiano, Robinson & Porporino, 1990; Porporino & Robinson, 1995; Robinson, 1995; Robinson, Grossman & Porporino, 1991) and we relied generally on samples of offenders who had received the programme while they were incarcerated. However, a smaller sub-sample of offenders also had received the programme in community settings.

The introduction of the R&R programme with Canadian federal offenders[1] represented a massive implementation strategy and, in many senses, the strategy has been used as a model by other jurisdictions. The implementation included a commitment to providing resources for delivering the programme across the country in both institutional and community sites. In addition, field staff were given awareness training so that they could support the implementation of the programme. Methods for carefully selecting offenders with the cognitive deficits targeted by the programme were also put in place. Importantly, a large-scale research and evaluation component was included that would provide for an assessment of programme efficacy and ongoing monitoring of programme integrity.

The first research to be reported on CSC's implementation of the programme involved pilot data from initial runs of the programme carried out in 1989 in four sites (Fabiano, Robinson, & Porporino, 1990). Based on a sample of 50 treated offenders and 26 waiting-list comparison offenders, the data provided good evidence that the programme was being targeted to high-risk offenders. Moreover, after 18-month post-release follow-up, there was evidence that the treated group was less likely to be reconvicted (20%) than the comparison group (30.4%). The results remained stable after the initial follow-up was extended for a longer period (mean follow-up = 32.1 months) (Porporino & Robinson, 1995). By this time the overall base rate of recidivism had increased (61%), reflecting the high-risk nature of the treated federal offenders. Of the comparison offenders 70% had been reincarcerated over the follow-up period compared with 57% of the treated group. In addition, the treatment effect appeared to be more marked when official reconvictions were used as the criteria of recidivism, a finding that has been confirmed in several samples with this population of treated offenders. In total, 55% of the comparison group had been reconvicted during follow-up

---

[1] In Canada, offenders who have been sentenced to incarceration for two years or more are under federal jurisdiction. All other offenders are under provincial jurisdictions.

compared with 35% among the offenders who had completed R&R. The difference represented a 36.4% reduction in recidivism for the R&R group. Hence, as
the implementation of the programme grew in federal corrections in Canada, the
data provided considerable optimism about the efficacy of the programme with
high-risk offenders.

In addition to the recidivism data reported for the Canadian pilot study, there
was also evidence that the offenders had made positive gains on programme
relevant targets as assessed through a number of pre-test/post-test measures
(Fabiano, Robinson, & Porporino, 1990). These gains included social perspective-
taking, conceptual complexity, generation of solutions to inter-personal conflicts,
attitudes toward the law, courts, and police, less tolerance for law violations, and
less identification with criminal others. Client satisfaction responses provided by
R&R participants also indicated favourable assessment of the programme's
ability to assist them with problem-solving, inter-personal relationships, goal
setting, controlling anger and other emotions, and handling stress.

The most ambitious effort to assess the effectiveness of the R&R programme
was based on a sample of more than 4000 Canadian federal offenders who had
completed the programme between 1989 and 1994 (Robinson, 1995). A sub-
sample of released offenders ($n = 2125$) had been followed up for a minimum of
one year, including 1444 programme completers and 379 offenders who were randomly assigned to a waiting list control group and had never been exposed to
the programme. In addition, the follow-up sample included 302 offenders who
had terminated their participation in the programme before completion.

As the implementation of the programme proceeded, it became increasingly
difficult for the researchers to maintain field commitment to randomly assigning
offenders to the waiting list control group. For this reason, the control group
failed to grow to a size that was comparable to the treatment group. Nevertheless, the control group size ($n = 379$) remained sufficiently large to allow for a
number of tests of moderating variables to identify offender characteristics that
were most predictive of positive treatment outcomes. The control group, although
differing slightly on some characteristics when compared with treated offenders
(e.g. sentence length, frequency of non-violent property offences), was methodologically suitable for conducting controlled comparisons of outcomes. Because
of the sample size, minor differences between the two groups could be statistically controlled in most analyses to ensure that treatment effects were not resulting due to the non-equivalence of groups.

The overall base rate of recidivism for the sample remained high as had been
observed in the earlier pilot results, a finding that confirmed the high-risk nature
of the population under treatment. Among waiting list control group members,
50.1% were readmitted to custody compared with 44.5% among offenders who
had completed R&R—a reduction in recidivism of 11.2%. The readmission rate
was higher for programme dropouts (58.2%). However, trends showing a positive effect of treatment remained even when the dropouts were included in some
of the recidivism analysis. As observed in the pilot study, the impact of the programme appeared to be greatest for official reconvictions (24.8% among controls

versus 19.7% among R&R participants). Hence, there was a 20% reduction in new reconvictions associated with programme participation during the first year after release.

As noted above, the CSC sample was sufficiently large to examine a variety of treatment moderator variables. Of particular interest were tests of differential treatment outcome for groups differing on risk for recidivism. The programme implementation model specified that R&R was intended for offenders who possessed the cognitive deficits targeted by the programme and participants should generally be drawn from offenders who were at higher risk for poor outcomes following release. Implementation of the programme by CSC attempted to follow the "risk principle" (see Andrews, Bonta, & Hoge, 1990) for selecting candidates to participate in the programme. This approach recognized that lower risk offenders were less likely to recidivate and would therefore receive no benefits from participating in an intensive intervention such as the R&R programme.

A simple actuarial measure based on criminal history indicators (e.g. previous federal admission, failure while under community supervision, history of property offences, robbery, and young age at admission) was used to divide the R&R sample into "low-" and "high-" risk groups. However, even the low-risk portion of the sample demonstrated relatively high rates of recidivism (36.2% versus 58.2% among high-risk offenders). Somewhat unexpectedly, the programme showed greater efficacy with the lower risk participants. For example, there was a 34.2% reduction in reconvictions associated with participation in R&R among low-risk offenders compared with no reduction in reconvictions among high-risk offenders.

Initially, the findings appeared to contradict the risk principle hypothesis that the R&R programme would be most effective with higher risk cases. However, the results were viewed as more consistent with the risk principle when it was considered that even the so-called "low-" risk cases from this sample returned to prison at relatively high rates. In addition, all of the programme participants had been screened into the programme using selection criteria that ensured that candidates were high need with respect to interventions to develop cognitive skills. In Canada, federal offenders generally present a profile of higher risk and need than offenders under provincial jurisdiction (Robinson, Porporino, Millson, Trevethan, & MacKillop, 1998). Andrews et al. (1990) argued that medium- to high-risk offenders are likely to benefit most from treatment. In examining the full spectrum of risk of Canadian offenders, it was assumed that the so-called "low-" risk cases in the CSC sample actually fall toward the higher end of the risk continuum. Hence, the lower risk CSC cases which responded to the R&R intervention might be described more accurately as medium- to high-risk offenders. The higher risk offenders, for whom no programme effect was produced, are likely to be at the extreme end of the risk continuum representing correctional clientele who are most resistant to treatment.

Another important finding from the 1995 CSC study was that offenders who were exposed to the R&R programme in community settings appeared to benefit more from the intervention than those who had been treated while incarcerated.

A 66.3% reduction in new convictions was observed for offenders treated in the community compared with a 16.2% reduction among those from institutional programmes. While the effect for those treated in institutional programmes could not be dismissed, the data suggested that continued efforts should be made to expand delivery of R&R in community sites. It was also discovered that the higher risk CSC cases, when exposed to the programme in a community, rather than institutional, setting, also benefited from participation. Hence, the data suggested that more resistant clients may benefit when their exposure to the R&R was combined with community supervision.

There were also differential programme effects observed across offence type in the CSC sample. Specifically, in the controlled comparisons offenders with violent, sexual, and drug offences benefited from programme participation to a greater extent than property offenders (e.g. break and enter, and robbery). This effect was partly due to the finding that the highest risk cases were less responsive to the intervention. The property offender group tended to be particularly high in risk for recidivism when compared with offenders with other types of offences. This phenomenon is typical of federally sentenced property offenders in Canada.

Controlled outcome comparisons have also been reported for adult offenders who received the R&R programme while on probation in Britain. The Mid-Glamorgan Experiment, reported by Raynor and Vanstone (1996), compared follow-up results for probationers who had received the R&R programme (referred to as Straight Thinking on Probation, STOP, $n = 107$) with results for offenders who had received a variety of other correctional dispositions, including regular probation and incarceration ($n = 548$). Using an actuarial prediction device to predict reconvictions, Raynor and Vanstone found lower than predicted reconviction rates after 12 months of follow-up (35% versus 42% predicted) for completers of the STOP programme. Offenders with other dispositions (e.g. incarceration, other probation) tended to have similar or higher rates of reconviction when their actual rates were compared with predicted rates. However, the STOP participants failed to show reductions on recidivism when the follow-up period was extended from 12 months to 24 months.

An interesting finding from the Mid-Glamorgan Experiment concerned more pronounced impacts of participating in STOP when offence type and disposition for reconvictions were examined. Compared with the combined sample of offenders who had received custodial sentences, those who had completed the R&R intervention while on probation were much less likely to have a serious offence (8%) than those who had been incarcerated (21%). The more positive effects favouring STOP participation were limited to the 12-month follow-up period and were not observed at the 24-month follow-up point. Another finding concerned an apparent impact of programme participation on judicial dispositions whereby a negligible number of STOP participants (2%) received custodial sentences upon reconviction in comparison with those who had been initially incarcerated (15%).

Juvenile Offenders

The efficacy of the R&R programme has also been tested using juvenile offender populations. One of the first studies to evaluate the programme with juveniles was conducted in Spain (Garrido & Sanchis, 1991). Although the sample size was small (R&R group, $n = 14$; control group, $n = 17$), the study provided pre-liminary evidence that the programme could produce beneficial results with incarcerated juvenile populations. The authors noted that the control group, which was recruited from alternative custodial centres, presented an overall lower risk profile than the group that had received the programme. However, the R&R subjects improved to a greater extent on a number of measures designed to operationalize the targets used in the programme (e.g. role-taking, problem-solving). The authors also noted that compared with the control group, the experimental group also demonstrated behavioural improvements as measured by staff ratings on a number of dimensions (e.g. social with-drawal, obsessive–compulsive, self-destruction, inattention, aggressive familial relationships).

A second study based on a sample of incarcerated juvenile offenders was reported from the state of Georgia in the United States (Murphy & Bauer, 1996) The recidivism follow-up was based on a sample of 33 offenders who had received the R&R programme and 16 "control" offenders who were "randomly selected" but did not participate in the programme. While the method of random selection was not described, the authors noted that the treatment group tended to have somewhat higher risk characteristics than the controls. After a mean follow-up period of 16 months, 39% of the R&R offenders had been rearrested compared with 75% of the comparison group. Of those who were rearrested, only 67% of the treated juveniles were convicted compared with 83% of the comparison group. The study also included a number of pre-test/post-test measures of programme-relevant targets. Generally, the psychometric data, which included behavioural ratings completed by staff, indicated more positive scores following participation for the R&R group and superior performance relative to the comparison group.

A final study on juvenile offenders was reported by Pullen (1996) and described an intervention used in the context of juvenile intensive probation supervision in the state of Colorado. Unfortunately, the process evaluation of the R&R programme indicated that implementation procedures were lacking in many respects and the author noted that many of the programme delivery staff failed adequately to prepare to deliver the training. The researcher compared pre-test/post-test results for a group of 20 juvenile probationers who were ran-domly assigned to R&R with 20 probationers who were randomly assigned to a control group. Perhaps as a function of the poor implementation procedures, the data provided only limited evidence of improvement in pre-test/post-test scores on various cognitive measures. In addition, there was little evidence of an impact of programme participation on recidivism. Overall, 50% of the R&R offenders recidivated during supervision compared with 35% among the controls. On the other hand, the rates for post-supervision recidivism were 20% for the R&R group and 25% for the control group.

Substance Abusing Offenders

R&R outcome data from two samples based on substance abusing offenders have been reported. Generally, the data suggests that the R&R programme, when combined with other substance abuse treatment has beneficial recidivism reduction effects. In addition, in one study, the effect of R&R participation was as promising when delivered on its own as was a competing treatment intervention that focused specifically on substance abuse.

The National Council on Crime and Delinquency (NCCD) (Austin, 1997) evaluated the implementation of the R&R programme ($n = 70$) along with a multi-phase drug treatment approach ($n = 65$) by the Northern District of California Probation Service. The latter programme, referred to as the Drug Aftercare Programme (DAC) included urinalysis, psycho-social assessment, drug counselling, and treatment planning. The efficacy of the two approaches was compared with respect to programme implementation and outcome using a random assignment design. The NCCD was critical of the implementation procedures that were used for the R&R programme, noting that delivery staff did not consistently follow the programme procedures and that there was insufficient implementation support within the programme environment. Despite the lack of integrity in the implementation of R&R in this setting, programme participants were slightly less likely to be arrested (25.3%) during the follow-up than those receiving the DAC (32.3%) intervention. In addition, the report concluded that the R&R programme was most cost-effective in that the per-capita cost of delivering the intervention was less than the cost associated with the alternative drug treatment approach.

A second study focusing on assessing the efficacy of the R&R programme with substance abusing offenders was conducted in Colorado using a randomized experimental method (Johnson & Hunter, 1995). The study compared three groups: regular probation service ($n = 36$); specialized drug offender programme (SDOP) ($n = 51$); and SDOP + R&R ($n = 47$). The SDOP and SDOP + R&R yielded considerable reductions in recidivism when compared against the regular probation condition. In total, 41.7% of regular probationers were revoked compared with 29.4% among SDOP probationers and 25.5% among SDOP + R&R probationers. While the R&R probationers performed only marginally better than the SDOP probationers, offenders who had the most severe drug/alcohol problems appeared to benefit to a much greater extent when exposed to the R&R enhancement of the SDOP. Only 18% of this group were revoked compared with 43% among SDOP probationers and 60% among regular service probationers. There was also evidence that probationers who had received the R&R programme achieved more positive results on a variety of pre-test/post-test measures such as empathy, problem-solving, anti-criminal attitudes, and other targets of cognitive skill training.

Mentally Disordered Offenders

There has been some interest in use of the R&R programme for treating mentally disordered offenders. The programme has been implemented with such populations in the state of New York in the United State and in Germany. A post-programme client satisfaction study was conducted at a forensic psychiatric facility in New York city in order to provide information about how offenders perceived the utility of such programmes (Otis, 1997). Although the sample size was small ($n = 12$), the patients were very positive about their experience in completing the R&R programme. The majority of patients believed that the programme was easy to understand and enjoyable and most indicated that they would recommend the programme to other patients. The efficacy of the programme with this type of offender population awaits empirical investigation.

CONCLUSIONS

The R&R programme is based on a well-defined set of theoretical principles which provide explanations of the link between programme targets and criminal behaviour. The programme is skill-based and stresses the "training" approach that is used to help offenders acquire the thinking skills necessary to obtain pro-social adjustment. The programme is highly structured and programme developers have placed considerable emphasis on effective implementation strategies. Because of the high degree of structure characterizing programme delivery, the programme is highly replicable across sites and para-professional staff can master the techniques for programme delivery given motivation and a base of cognitive skills. The manual and training for the programme provide instructions about the optimal conditions that should be achieved before delivering the programme. This not only includes adequate preparation of materials by programme delivery staff, but also a network of support for the principles of the programme within the correctional setting where R&R is being implemented.

The research reviewed above does not include all of the studies that have been conducted on the programme to date. There are now on-going studies in Sweden, Norway, Finland, and a number of state jurisdictions in the United States. However, the available body of literature on this specific approach to the rehabilitation of criminal offenders suggests that the programme can produce beneficial effects for many groups of offenders. Ideally, the programme is suited to offenders who are at medium to high risk of recidivism and exhibit deficits in the various cognitive skills that are included in the programme. Evidence for effectiveness with high-risk adult offenders, substance abusing offenders, and juveniles is available from the studies conducted to date. As the numbers of offenders who have completed the R&R programme increase, researchers should turn their attention to identifying which offenders appear to benefit most from the programme, and which staff are most effective in delivering this kind of structured cognitive intervention.

The content of the programme covers a broad range of cognitive skills which are not only applicable to offenders, but may be important for a number of categories of individuals who are at high risk for negative social outcomes. In most jurisdictions where R&R has been used, the explicit objective of the intervention is to reduce recidivism among adjudicated offenders. An adaptation of the approach is also now being used as a delinquency prevention programme with adolescent age schoolchildren in Norway. In the most recent adaptation, the R&R principles are being used with an intervention designed to teach chronically "unemployable" individuals the requisite skills for securing and maintaining employment.

REFERENCES

Andrews, D. A., Bonta, J., & Hoge, R. D. (1990). Classification for effective rehabilitation: Rediscovering psychology. *Criminal Justice and Behavior, 17*, 19–52.

Andrews, D. A., Zinger, I., Hoge, R. D., Bonta, J., Gendreau, P., & Cullen, F. T. (1990). Does correctional treatment work? A clinically relevant and psychologically informed meta-analysis. *Criminology, 28*, 369–404.

Austin, J. (1997). *Evaluation of the drug aftercare program and the reasoning and rehabilitation program in California probation*. Unpublished manuscript. Washington DC: National Council on Crime and Delinquency.

DeBono, E. (1982). *DeBono's thinking course*. London: BBC Books.

Dodge, K. A., & Frame, C. L. (1982). Social cognitive biases and deficits in aggressive boys. *Child Development, 53*, 620–635.

Fabiano, E. A., Porporino, F. J., & Robinson, D. (1990). *Rehabilitation through clearer thinking: A cognitive model of correctional intervention, R-04*. Ottawa, Canada: Correctional Service Canada.

Fabiano, E., Robinson, D., & Porporino, F. (1990). *A preliminary assessment of the cognitive skills training programme: A component of living skills programming. Programme description, research findings and implementation strategy*. Ottawa, Canada: Correctional Service Canada.

Garrido, V., & Sanchis, J. R. (1991). The cognitive model in the treatment of Spanish offenders: Theory and practice. *Journal of Correctional Education, 42*, 111–118.

Goldstein, A. (1988). *The prepare curriculum: Teaching prosocial competencies*. Champaign, IL: Research Press.

Izzo, R. L., & Ross, R. R. (1990). Meta-analysis of rehabilitation programmes for juvenile delinquents: A brief report. *Criminal Justice and Behavior, 17*, 134–142.

Johnson, G., & Hunter, R. M. (1995). Evaluation of the specialized drug offender program. In R. R. Ross & R. D. Ross (Eds.), *Thinking straight: The reasoning and rehabilitation programme for delinquency prevention and offender rehabilitation* (pp. 215–234). Ottawa, Canada: AIR.

Lipsey, M. W. (1995). What do we learn from 400 research studies on the effectiveness of treatment with juvenile delinquents? In J. McGuire (Ed.), *What works: Reducing reoffending—Guidelines from research and practice* (pp. 63–78). Chichester, UK: Wiley.

Lipton, D. S., Pearson, F. S., Cleland, C., & Yee, D. (1998). *How do cognitive skills training programmes for offenders compare with other modalities: A meta-Analytic perspective.* Presented at the Stop and Think Conference, Her Majesty's Prison Service, York, UK.

Lösel, F. (1995). The efficacy of correctional treatment: A review and synthesis of meta-evaluations. In J. McGuire (Ed.), *What works: Reducing reoffending—Guidelines from research and practice* (pp. 79–111). Chichester, UK: Wiley.

Murphy, R., & Bauer, R. (1996). *Evaluating the effectiveness of a cognitive skills training programme for juvenile delinquents.* (Unpublished Manuscript) Georgia: Valdosta State University.

Otis, D. (1997). *Kirby Forensic Psychiatric Center Patient Satisfaction of the Cognitive Skills Programme: A Formative Evaluation.* Unpublished Manuscript. New York: Kirby Forensic Psychiatric Center.

Porporino, F. J., & Robinson, D. (1995). An evaluation of the reasoning and rehabilitation programme with Canadian federal offenders. In R. R. Ross & R. D. Ross (Eds.), *Thinking straight: The reasoning and rehabilitation programme for delinquency prevention and offender rehabilitation* (pp. 155–191). Ottawa, Canada: AIR.

Pullen, S. (1996). *Evaluation of the reasoning and rehabilitation cognitive skills development programme as implemented in juvenile ISP in Colorado.* Unpublished Report. Denver, CO: Colorado Division of Criminal Justice.

Raynor, P., & Vanstone, M. (1996). Reasoning and rehabilitation in Britain: The results of the straight thinking on probation (STOP) programme. *International Journal of Offender Therapy and Comparative Criminology, 40,* 272–284.

Robinson, D. (1995). *The impact of cognitive skills training on post-release recidivism among Canadian federal offenders.* No. R-41. Research Branch). Ottawa, Canada: Correctional Service Canada.

Robinson, D., Grossman, M., & Porporino, F. J. (1991). *Effectiveness of the cognitive skills training programme: From pilot to national implementation, B-07.* Ottawa, Canada: Correctional Service Canada.

Robinson, D., Porporino, F. J., Millson, W. A., Trevethan, S., & MacKillop, B. (1998). *A one-day snapshot of inmates in Canada's adult correctional facilities* (Juristat, Vol. 18, no 8). Ottawa, Canada: Canadian Centre for Justice Statistics, Statistics Canada.

Ross, R. R., & Fabiano, E. A. (1985). *Time to think. A cognitive model of delinquency prevention and offender rehabilitation.* Johnson City, TN: Institute of Social Sciences and Arts.

Ross, R. R., Fabiano, E. A., & Ewles, C. D. (1988). Reasoning and Rehabilitation. *International Journal of Offender Therapy and Comparative Criminology, 32,* 29–36.

Zamble, E., & Porporino, F. (1988). *Coping, behaviour, and adaptation in prison inmates.* New York: Springer-Verlag.

Chapter 6

Family-Based Treatments

Cynthia Cupit Swenson
Scott W. Henggeler
and
Sonja K. Schoenwald
Medical University of South Carolina, Charleston, USA

INTRODUCTION

Overwhelming evidence supports the view that antisocial behavior in adolescents is multidetermined (i.e. from the interplay of individual, family, peer, school, and community factors) and that family relations play a key role in the development and maintenance of adolescent criminal activity and drug use (Elliott, 1994; Henggeler, 1997; Thornberry, Huizinga, & Loeber, 1995; Tolan & Guerra, 1994). Moreover, in light of the failure of individually-based treatment approaches to realize positive long-term outcomes in treating serious antisocial behavior, reviewers have argued for greater emphasis on addressing difficulties within the key systems in which youths are embedded (Dodge, 1993; Henggeler, 1996; Tate, Reppucci, & Mulvey, 1995). In the vast majority of instances, the family is the key system in which youths are involved—with parents and guardians being the adults primarily responsible for providing their children with the love, structure, and guidance needed for healthy psychosocial adjustment.

Various models of family-based treatment have been applied to the problems presented by antisocial youth. Indeed, meta-analytic reviews have shown that family therapy is effective for resolving a variety of problem behaviors compared with no treatment (Hazelrigg, Cooper, & Borduin, 1987) and alternative treatments (Shadish et al., 1993). Conclusions regarding the efficacy of family therapy, however, are mitigated by the fact that the majority of family-based treatments have received no empirical support. While some family-based treatment approaches have been rigorously evaluated, many others are based primarily on

The Essential Handbook of Offender Assessment and Treatment. Edited by C. R. Hollin.
© 2004 John Wiley & Sons Ltd.

unsubstantiated theory and clinical anecdote. In general, family treatment approaches that follow unstructured models, such as client-centered, intergenerational, and psychodynamic, have not evinced the positive outcomes of more structured treatments (Henggeler, Borduin, & Mann, 1993; Kazdin, 1994). A central contention of this chapter is that family work concerned principally with behavioral changes and that has at least some empirical support carries the greatest likelihood of producing positive outcomes for youths and their families.

As such, the purpose of this chapter is to describe family-based approaches that: (a) have been applied to youth who exhibit criminal activity or substance abuse; and (b) have been examined empirically. These approaches include: *family preservation models* (Nelson, 1990); *functional family therapy* (Alexander & Parsons, 1982); *structural family therapy* (Kurtines & Szapocznik, 1996; Minuchin, 1974; Minuchin & Fishman, 1981); *multidimensional family therapy* (Liddle, Dakof, & Diamond, 1991; Liddle, 1995); and *multisystemic therapy* (Henggeler & Borduin, 1990; Henggeler, Schoenwald, Borduin, Rowland, & Cunningham, 1998). For each of these approaches, the theoretical basis, central treatment goals, and an overview of outcome studies is provided.

DEFINING FAMILY-BASED TREATMENT

In general, the underlying assumptions of family-based treatments are that factors within the family maintain problem behavior and, consequently, changes in family interactions can lead to improved youth behavior. In some clinical settings, however, the youth's problem behavior may not be conceptualized as related to family factors, and inclusion of the family may play a different role. Liddle and Dakof (1995), for example, have distinguished between family therapy (family-based treatment) and family-involved interventions. The former addresses the connection between family relationships and the youth's problem of concern, while the latter involves the family in more adjunctive ways, such as providing information. For the purpose of this chapter, the terms family therapy, family-based treatment, and family work are used interchangeably.

Family therapy models that view family relations as an etiological or maintaining factor in youth behavior problems and seek to change interactions within the family as a means for changing youth behavior are presented. A caveat, however, pertains to the first presentation concerning family preservation programs. Like family therapy in the generic, family preservation programs follow a wide variety of treatment models, some of which may or may not address the role of family interactions in youth behavior problems. However, given that services based on this model have expanded at a rapid rate in the United States and many antisocial youth are being served through these programs, the reader should be aware of the effectiveness of family preservation models with antisocial youth.

FAMILY PRESERVATION PROGRAMS

During the past decade, family preservation programs have proliferated in the United States, primarily within child welfare systems. More recently, family preservation models have been applied to youths in the juvenile justice system (Nelson, 1990). Although family preservation may be viewed as an intervention, it is most accurately described as a model of service delivery encompassing a variety of therapeutic interventions and concrete services in the youth's home and community (Schoenwald & Henggeler, 1997). The characteristics of the family preservation model of service delivery differ from traditional office-based counterparts in several important ways: treatment is time limited (1–5 months), sessions are scheduled at times convenient for family members (including weekends and evenings), services are generally provided in the home and other community settings, therapists have low caseloads (2–6 families) and make multiple contacts weekly, and most programs include 24 hour/7 day availability of service providers (Farrow, 1991; Fraser, Nelson, & Rivard, 1997). The intensity of family preservation is designed to help attain the primary goal of preventing an out-of-home placement for the youth. Thus, such an intense (and costly relative to outpatient treatment) treatment can be cost effective if relatively expensive out-of-home placements are avoided.

The nature of the family-based treatment provided in family preservation varies across programs, but three distinct practice models have been identified (Nelson, 1990, 1994):

1. crisis intervention,
2. home-based model, and
3. family treatment model.

Homebuilders is the national prototype of the crisis intervention model. Interventions are very brief (4–6 weeks) and include concrete services (e.g. food, clothing) and counseling that primarily targets family communication, behavior management, and problem-solving skills from a social learning orientation (Kinney, Haapala, Booth, & Leavitt, 1990). Home-based models tend to be more clinically oriented than crisis models, with interventions targeting problematic interactions between family members and between the family and community (Lloyd & Bryce, 1984). Family treatment models share a similar orientation with the home-based models in that interventions are based on family systems theory. The primary difference between the two models is that concrete services are generally provided by case managers rather than therapists and service delivery is in the outpatient office, as well as the home.

Outcome Studies

Family preservation outcome studies consist mainly of program evaluations and studies with quasi-experimental designs. Within these studies, methodological problems (e.g. selection bias, non-equivalent control groups) render the results equivocal. Studies that included appropriate comparison groups (e.g. Mitchell, Tovar, & Knitzer, 1989; Wood, Barton, & Schroeder, 1988) failed to support the effectiveness of family preservation in preventing placement in child welfare, or combinations of child welfare, juvenile justice, and mental health populations. A recent meta-analytic review (Fraser et al., 1997) suggests that family preservation programs may be more successful with older children referred for aggressive or oppositional behavior than with child maltreatment referrals. However, the majority of the family preservation studies conducted with older youths referred for aggressive behavior used multisystemic therapy (MST) as the model of treatment (randomized trials of MST with violent and serious juvenile offenders are presented later in this chapter). Therefore, with the exception of MST, little evidence supports the effectiveness of family preservation programs with youths engaging in antisocial behavior.

Aside from the MST studies, one randomized trial including antisocial youths has been reported in the family preservation literature (Feldman, 1991). In this study, youths and families were referred by multiple agencies (i.e. juvenile justice, child welfare, and community mental health crisis centers) and randomly assigned to the New Jersey Family Preservation Services program, modeled after Homebuilders, or traditional preventive services (e.g. referral to mental health services, agency monitoring of youths). Family preservation services achieved better placement results up to 9 months after service completion, at which time the effects diminished. Families who received the family preservation services also appeared to function at higher levels on measures of family functioning and stress upon case closure, but the improvements were not greater than those of families who received traditional services. Thus, little evidence supports the effectiveness of family preservation, *per se*, in treating youths with serious antisocial behavior.

FUNCTIONAL FAMILY THERAPY

Functional family therapy (FFT; Alexander & Parsons, 1982) was one of the first family-based treatments applied to antisocial youth. Within an FFT framework, the family is viewed as a constellation of interacting groups that behave according to certain principles and these principles can be used to effect change. A central focus of the treatment is on the functions that problem behaviors play and how the family functions interrelate. Treatment targets behaviors that maintain the functions and strives to help families determine how to achieve the same functions through new behavior patterns. For example, if a youth's tantruming behavior serves the function of gaining parental attention, intervention focuses on obtaining attention with more pleasant behaviors. Responsibility for motivation for treatment is with the therapist who must be proficient in three skill categories:

1. conceptual (i.e. understanding the functions of behaviors and the dynamics of interactions);
2. technical (i.e. knowledge of procedures that produce change in perceptions, feelings and behaviors); and
3. interpersonal skills (i.e. how to apply techniques).

FFT combines interventions from behavior therapy, cognitive behavioral therapy, and family systems models to change family interactions, communication, and problem solving in ways that no longer support the maladaptive behavior (Kazdin, 1994).

Outcome Studies

Several outcome studies show that FFT holds promise as a treatment for mild antisocial behavior in adolescents. An initial evaluation of FFT was conducted with first-time male and female status offenders, mainly from middle class Mormon families (Alexander & Parsons, 1973). FFT was effective at reducing further status offenses, but not criminal offenses. Three subsequent quasi-experimental evaluations were conducted with families of status offenders or youths engaged in delinquency (Barton, Alexander, Waldron, Turner, & Warburton, 1985). Interestingly, the treatment was provided by individuals with varied levels of training: (a) undergraduate students (single-group design), (b) probation workers (*post hoc* comparison of FFT and standard probation services), and (c) doctoral students (planned comparison of FFT and behavioral group home treatment). Across these studies, data regarding recidivism favored FFT. Though outcomes appeared positive, the conclusiveness of these studies is limited by the exclusive reliance on archival data and use of non-experimental designs (i.e. absence of random assignment).

The most recent evaluation of FFT with adolescent offenders was conducted using a quasi-experimental design by Gordon and colleagues (Gordon, Arbuthnot, Gustafson, & McGreen, 1988). Fifty-four White juveniles were assigned to either FFT or a no-treatment control condition. Participants had committed status offenses, misdemeanors, or felonies. The FFT group was composed of 15 male and 12 female youths, and the comparison group contained 23 male and 4 female youths. A significant aspect of this study was the delivery of FFT in the families' homes. FFT was provided by graduate students over an average of 5.5 months, and included an average of 16 sessions (ranging from 7 to 38 sessions), each lasting approximately 1.5 hours. Archival data, reviewed after a follow-up period of 27.8 months for the treatment group and 31.5 months for the comparison group, favored FFT for recidivism rates of all types of offenses combined. An examination of adult court records of the original sample was conducted 3 years after the initial follow-up, when most of the youths were in young adulthood. Data favored FFT for misdemeanor but not felony recidivism rates (Gordon, Graves, & Arbuthnot, 1995).

In addressing the problem of youth substance abuse, Friedman (1989) randomly assigned the families of 135 substance-abusing adolescents to either FFT or a parent group. Noteworthy is that in 93% of families in the FFT condition, one or both parents participated, and in 67% of families in the parent group condition, one or both parents participated. Thus, FFT was more effective at engaging parents in treatment. Families received a 6-month course of treatment. Follow-up was conducted at 9 months. Although time effects emerged during the course of the 9-month follow-up (i.e. decreased substance use and psychiatric symptoms, improved family relations), no FFT treatment effects were observed. In a later report, Friedman, Tomko, and Utada (1991) found that positive family relations at the time of intake was a predictor of positive outcomes for families in the FFT condition.

As a whole, the FFT outcome studies suggest promise for this treatment with youths who do not present serious criminal activity and who have relatively positive family relations. The lack of favorable outcomes or rigorous evaluations of FFT with youths presenting serious antisocial behavior, however, limits the external validity of this treatment model.

STRUCTURAL FAMILY THERAPY

Structural family therapy (SFT; Minuchin, 1974; Minuchin & Fishman, 1981) views the family as a system that operates through patterns of interactions. These interactional patterns regulate the behavior of family members and maladaptive patterns prevent achievement of the family's goals. Problem behaviors may result from the family system's way of organizing itself as it attempts to cope with changes and stresses. Thus, problems are viewed as an expression of the family dysfunction (Szapocznik et al., 1988). SFT is an action-oriented, present-focused therapy directed toward changing the organization or structure of the family (e.g. how they interact, alliances, subsystems). Change in the family structure contributes to changes in the behavior of family members.

SFT therapists form a new therapeutic system with the family and use themselves to change the family system in a way that repairs the family's functioning and enables them to better perform the tasks of support, regulation, nurturance, and socialization of members (Minuchin, 1974). Change mechanisms associated with SFT include (a) joining (techniques the therapist uses to enter the family system); (b) diagnosing or identifying maladaptive interactional patterns; and (c) restructuring or changing maladaptive interactions that are related to problem interactions within the family (Kurtines & Szapocznik, 1996).

Outcome Studies

The most conceptually and methodologically rigorous research on SFT has been conducted by Szapocznik and his colleagues, focusing on specialized applications of SFT for Hispanic families (Kurtines & Szapocznik, 1996). Early studies established the efficacy of SFT in reducing drug use among adolescents upon treatment termination (Szapocznik, Santisteban et al., 1986; Szapocznik, Santisteban, Rio, Perez-Vidal, & Kurtines, 1989). Other studies comparing conjoint family therapy and one-person family therapy (both forms of SFT) documented improvements in youth behavior problems and family relations for both groups at termination of treatment and follow-up (Szapocznik, Kurtines, Foote, Perez-Vidal, & Hervis, 1983, 1986).

A subsequent series of studies focused on the engagement of adolescents and their families in treatment. Strategic Structural Systems Engagement (SSSE; Szapocznik & Kurtines, 1989; Szapocznik et al., 1988), designed to begin the work of joining, diagnosing, and restructuring the family on the first contact, was compared with usual engagement techniques (i.e. minimal joining techniques such as expressing polite concern, asking about problems and well-being of the family). SSSE was more effective in engaging and retaining adolescent substance abusers and their families in treatment. Ninety-three percent of the SSSE families engaged in treatment and 75% of those completed treatment, which compares favorably with the engagement (42%) and completion (25%) rates of families in the control condition (Szapocznik et al., 1988). In a later study comparing SSSE with family therapy without SSSE and group therapy without SSSE, Santisteban et al. (1996) replicated the 1988 findings, but also found that SSSE more successfully engaged non-Cuban Hispanic than Cuban Hispanic families. They hypothesized that Cuban Hispanic families were more incorporated into the mainstream US culture, as evidenced by requesting hospitalization and individual therapy for their child.

The work of Szapocznik and colleagues has made a significant contribution to the adolescent substance abuse treatment field, especially with regard to the engagement process and cultural competence. Additional research is needed to assess further the effectiveness and generalizability of the SFT treatment model. That is, scant results have supported the clinical effectiveness of SFT and applicability of extant findings should be extended to other cultural groups.

MULTIDIMENSIONAL FAMILY THERAPY

Multidimensional family therapy (MDFT; Liddle et al., 1991; Liddle, 1995) is an empirically-derived, multicomponent intervention that was developed for treating adolescent substance abuse. The underlying principle of MDFT is that individual behavior change results from change in the family system. Youth behavior problems are defined as developmental detours or behaviors that prevent adolescents from achieving developmentally appropriate milestones. Conceptualization of the problem emphasizes the multiple, interacting social contexts in which the problem forms and solvability of the problem.

MDFT is theme-driven, as it relies on mutually-agreed-upon themes or areas of work that have personal meaning to the youth and parent. Engagement of the youth, parent, and all subsystems is viewed as basic to treatment success and is ongoing and aggressive. The therapeutic alliance and developing mutually-agreed-upon goals are central to engagement. Parental involvement is viewed as critical to change, but MDFT therapists may treat the adolescent alone in an effort to increase engagement. For the youth, drug screens are required and results are revealed to the parent and involved professionals (e.g. probation officer). Service delivery is designed to engage families, and thus treatment is conducted in the office, by telephone, or in the home (Liddle, 1995). Interventions target four domains: (a) the youth's intrapersonal and interpersonal functioning (e.g. peers); (b) the parent's intrapersonal and interpersonal functioning (adult peers); (c) parent–youth interactions observed in sessions and reported by the parent and adolescent; and (d) family interactions with extrafamilial sources of influence (e.g. school) (Schmidt, Liddle, & Dakof, 1996).

Outcome Studies

Liddle and colleagues have demonstrated the potential merits of MDFT with substance-abusing adolescents. A controlled clinical trial (Liddle & Dakof, 1995) comparing MDFT with peer group therapy and family education indicated that MDFT was more effective in reducing drug use post treatment and at maintaining reductions in use at 1-year follow-up. Youth receiving MDFT also evinced more improvement in school performance relative to youth in the other two treatment conditions. Schmidt et al. (1996) examined the parenting practices of 29 families who completed 16 sessions of MDFT and found significant improvement in parenting (i.e. decreased negative practices and affect and increased positive practices and affect) in 69% of parents. Although most parents and adolescents improved simultaneously, change patterns varied, with 21% of families experiencing adolescent change without parent change and 10% experiencing parent change without adolescent change. In explaining these patterns, Schmidt and colleagues suggest that if MDFT interventions with the primary target (e.g. the parent) fail, treatment should focus on alternative domains (e.g. the youth). MDFT is noteworthy as it represents a relatively new family-based treatment model that is supported by cogent theory and is being validated by a skilled team of investigators. Thus, the field should be informed by future evaluations of MDFT.

MULTISYSTEMIC THERAPY

Multisystemic therapy (MST; Henggeler & Borduin, 1990; Henggeler et al., 1998) was developed as a treatment for adolescent offenders (Henggeler et al., 1986) and is the only treatment approach to demonstrate long-term reductions in rearrest and incarceration in randomized clinical trials. The theoretical foundation of MST lies in Bronfenbrenner's (1979) theory of social ecology and pragmatic family systems models of behavior (Haley, 1976; Minuchin, 1974). Individuals are viewed as nested within interconnected systems (i.e. individual, family, extrafamilial, peers) that influence behavior in a reciprocal fashion, and youth behavior problems are viewed as maintained by problematic transactions within and/or between any one or combination of these systems. Thus, interventions target interactions within the family, and between the family and other systems in the youth's and family's natural (e.g. peers, work) and service (e.g. mental health, child welfare) ecologies (Schoenwald, Borduin, & Henggeler, 1998). Nine treatment principles guide the conceptualization of the problem behavior (i.e. how the behavior makes sense in the context of the youth's social ecology) and the development and implementation of interventions individually tailored to meet the specific needs of the youth and family. Specific intervention techniques are integrated from the best of the existing pragmatic and problem-focused child psychotherapy approaches that have at least some empirical support.

In MST clinical trials, considerable attention has been devoted to the applicability of MST to real-world populations seen in community mental health and juvenile justice settings. As such, clinical trials have been conducted in community-based settings, with a home-and-community-based model of service delivery and 3–5 month length of treatment. Providing treatment in places convenient to families (home, school, church, community) has been important in removing barriers to services access and thus, in the low dropout rates in MST studies (see Henggeler, Pickrel, Brondino, & Crouch, 1996). In accordance with a family preservation service delivery model, MST treatment of the youth and family involves frequent, intensive contacts (sometimes daily) and round-the-clock therapist availability. Therapists carry small caseloads of 4–6 families and receive regular (sometimes daily) clinical and supervisory support. Because empirical demonstrations indicate that MST treatment fidelity is essential to obtaining positive outcomes (Henggeler, Melton, Brondino, Scherer, & Hanley, 1997), therapists are provided with extensive training, supervision, and ongoing mechanisms to promote quality assurance.

Outcome Studies

Following several early clinical trials supporting the short-term efficacy of MST with inner-city adolescents (Henggeler et al., 1986), maltreating families (Brunk, Henggeler, & Whelan, 1987), and a small sample of adolescent sex offenders (Borduin, Henggeler, Blaske, & Stein, 1990), several randomized trials have been conducted with youths presenting serious antisocial behavior. In a study conducted through a community mental health center (Henggeler, Melton, & Smith, 1992; Henggeler, Melton, Smith, Schoenwald, & Hanley, 1993), 84 violent and chronic juvenile offenders at imminent risk of out-of-home placement were randomly assigned to MST or usual juvenile justice services. The latter condition included services such as court ordered curfew and referral to community agencies. MST was more effective than usual community services at reducing criminal behavior and out-of-home placement. At a 59-week follow-up, youths who participated in MST had significantly fewer arrests ($M = 0.87$ vs. 1.52) and fewer weeks of incarceration (5.8 vs. 16.2) than youths receiving usual community services. Moreover, in comparison with families receiving usual services, families who received MST reported increased cohesion and decreased peer aggression among their youths. MST treatment effects were maintained at a 2.4-year follow-up, with MST almost doubling the survival rate (percentage of participants not rearrested) of the serious offenders (Henggeler, Melton et al., 1993). Finally, a comparison of cost indicated that the cost per client for MST treatment was approximately $3500, which compares favorably with the cost of institutional placement received by over 70% of the youths in the comparison condition.

More recently, Borduin et al. (1995) randomly assigned families of 176 chronic adolescent offenders to MST or individual therapy. Following treatment, adolescents whose families received MST had significantly fewer behavior problems and parents reported greater cohesion and adaptability in family relations— reports that were supported by observational data. Importantly, at a 4-year follow-up evaluating rearrest of participants, MST substantially reduced violent criminal activity, other criminal activity, and drug-related arrests (Borduin et al., 1995).

In a third randomized trial of MST with violent and chronic juvenile offenders (Henggeler, Melton et al., 1997), services were provided across two community-based treatment sites to 155 youths and families. A key aspect of this study was ongoing treatment fidelity checks aimed at promoting adherence to the MST treatment protocol. Although MST improved adolescent symptomology at post-treatment and decreased incarceration by 47% at a 1.7-year follow-up, findings for decreased criminal activity were not as favorable as observed in other recent trials of MST. Analyses of parent, adolescent, and therapist reports of MST treatment adherence, however, indicated that outcomes were substantially better in cases where treatment adherence ratings were high. These results highlight the importance of maintaining treatment fidelity when treating youths with serious antisocial behavior and their families.

In addition to the recent MST trials with violent and chronic juvenile offenders and their families, a randomized trial of MST vs. usual community services has been completed with 118 substance abusing or dependent adolescent offenders. At post-treatment, MST participants showed greater reductions in soft- and hard-drug use; and at 12 months post-referral, youths in the MST condition had fewer days incarcerated and in other out-of-home placements (Henggeler, Pickrel, & Brondino, in press). Moreover, 98% of the families referred to the MST condition completed a full course of treatment—demonstrating the effectiveness of MST engagement and retention strategies (Henggeler et al., 1996). Finally, 1 year following referral, cost analyses indicate that the incremental costs of MST were nearly offset by savings accrued as a result of reductions in days of out-of-home placement (e.g. hospital, residential) in the MST condition relative to usual community services (Schoenwald, Ward, Henggeler, Pickrel, & Patel, 1996).

In summary, several randomized trials with youths presenting serious antiso-cial behavior have demonstrated the short-term capacity of MST to improve family relations and the long-term ability of MST to reduce rates of rearrest and out-of-home placement. Importantly, some of these studies have been conducted in real-world community contexts. Moreover, findings support the importance of treatment fidelity in dissemination to such contexts as well as the potential cost saving produced by effective family-based treatment models. Current studies are examining the effectiveness of MST with other populations of youths presenting serious problems (e.g. MST as an alternative to the emergency psychiatric hos-pitalization of youths) and MST provided via other models of service delivery (e.g. outpatient, school-based, within a system of care).

FUTURE DIRECTIONS OF FAMILY-BASED TREATMENT

The family therapy models described in this chapter represent important advances in treating adolescent offenders, substance abusing youths, and their families. The promising short- and long-term outcomes from these studies are especially encouraging after a long history of research demonstrating ineffective results from individually-focused treatment models. Taken together, the family therapy outcome studies provide a number of lessons regarding characteristics of effective interventions for antisocial youth.

1. *Treatment should be provided in the youth's and family's natural environment.* In outpatient settings, services are often underused by child clinical popula-tions, as reflected by retention rates of 50%–70% (Tuma, 1989). In MST studies, where services for antisocial youths and their families were provided in the home and community, treatment completion rates have been as high as 98% (Henggeler et al., 1996). Treatment in the home reduces barriers to service access often faced by multineed families (e.g. lack of transportation or child care) and provides opportunities for the therapist directly to observe family and community interactions. Moreover, families are afforded the chance to practice new behaviors in the settings where they must adapt, which may increase the probability that acquired skills will be maintained.

2. *Treatment should include the primary care giver and principal participants in the various systems in which the youth is embedded.* Interactions within and between systems important to the youth and family may maintain or reduce problem behavior. For example, due to school failure, the youth may leave the school building and once unsupervised, engage in criminal activities. In this case, interventions aimed solely at the family will exclude the very systems that, when targeted, may carry the greatest likelihood of reducing the youth's antisocial opportunities. Traditional family therapy models include the family system but often fail directly to address factors in extrafa-milial systems that are crucial to resolving identified problems. Comprehen-sive interventions that pay careful attention to ecological validity have

empirically demonstrated the importance of addressing needs and building competencies across multiple systems.

3. *Treatment should address the known correlates of antisocial behavior.* Addressing the correlates of a problem behavior requires that services be based on the needs of the youth and family within their ecological context, rather than based on the programmatic or policy needs of the agency or philosophical preference of the provider (Tolan, 1996). As noted earlier, causal models have shown that youth antisocial behavior relates to multiple factors across multiple systems (Henggeler, 1991, 1997). In part, the poor outcomes of individually-focused treatments may be due to their failure to target factors that are maintaining the youth's behavior. For example, if parental substance abuse is a barrier to parental monitoring of youth's behavior, then treatment of the youth alone will have little effect on a major factor that may be maintaining the youth's behavior problems. MST clinical trials have demonstrated that with multineed families presenting complex clinical problems, targeting the multiple correlates of antisocial behavior is possible and essential to obtaining positive outcomes.

4. *Interventions should include techniques whose effectiveness is empirically supported.* According to a national survey, psychological practitioners value research and read research journals (Beutler, Williams, Wakefield, & Entwistle, 1995). However, practicing clinicians report that psychotherapy research holds little value to them (Weisz, Donenberg, Han, & Weiss, 1995) and, as noted by Kazdin, Mazurick, and Bass (1993), few child clinicians rely on research in practice. When therapeutic techniques with no established efficacy are used with families, the probability is increased that services will be of little benefit and may actually exacerbate the problem. To assist practitioners in using empirically validated family-based treatments, researchers may need to collaborate more carefully with service providers to ensure that treatments meet the test of implementation in clinical settings.

5. *Interventions should be sensitive to and informed by an understanding of the youth's and family's cultural beliefs and background* (Tolan, 1996). To facilitate engagement of the family in the treatment process, therapists must develop a critical level of cultural competence (i.e. the ability to share the world view of the family and adapt clinical practice to respect that view) (Abney & Gunn, 1993). By increasing awareness of the family's culturally-influenced beliefs, the therapist may come to understand the important distinction between characteristics of the family that are culturally congruent and those that are dysfunctional (Heras, 1992). The work of Szapocznik and colleagues, demonstrating success in engaging and maintaining adolescents and their families in treatment, is an exemplary model of integrating cultural context into a treatment approach.

In conclusion, future directions for family-based treatment should incorporate lessons learned from current research into clinical practice. Continued progress in research will require procedures to ensure that treatment methods: are transportable to real-world settings; consider the practical needs of families (i.e. service delivery that meets the family's needs); are ecologically valid; and are sensitive to the family's cultural context. Only by integrating the lessons from clinical practice into research and those from research into clinical practice, can effective family therapy models continue to be developed and disseminated.

ACKNOWLEDGMENTS

Preparation of this chapter was supported by the National Institute of Mental Health Grant R01-MH-51852; National Institute on Drug Abuse Grant R01-DA10079; the Center for Mental Health Services, Substance Abuse and Mental Health Services Administration 90FYF0012; and the Annie E. Casey Foundation.

Correspondence concerning this chapter should be addressed to Cynthia Cupit Swenson, Family Services Research Center, Department of Psychiatry and Behavioral Sciences, Medical University of South Carolina, 67 President Street—Suite CPP, P.O. Box 250861, Charleston, SC 29425, USA.

REFERENCES

Abney, V. D., & Gunn, K. (1993). A rationale for cultural competency. *APSAC Advisor*, *6*(3), 19–22.

Alexander, J. F., & Parsons, B. V. (1973). Short-term behavioral intervention with delinquent families: Impact on family process and recidivism. *Journal of Abnormal Psychology*, *81*, 219–225.

Alexander, J. F., & Parsons, B. V. (1982). *Functional family therapy*. Monterey, CA: Brooks/Cole.

Barton, C., Alexander, J. F., Waldron, H., Turner, C. W., & Warburton, J. (1985). Generalizing treatment effects of functional family therapy: Three replications. *American Journal of Family Therapy*, *13*, 16–26.

Beutler, L. E., Williams, R. E., Wakefield, P. J., & Entwistle, S. R. (1995). Bridging scientist and practitioner perspectives in clinical psychology. *American Psychologist*, *50*, 984–994.

Borduin, C. M., Henggeler, S. W., Blaske, D. M., & Stein, R. (1990). Multisystemic treatment of adolescent sexual offenders. *International Journal of Offender Therapy and Comparative Criminology*, *34*, 105–113.

Borduin, C. M., Mann, B. J., Cone, L. T., Henggeler, S. W., Fucci, B. R., Blaske, D. M., & Williams, R. A. (1995). Multisystemic treatment of serious juvenile offenders: Long-term prevention of criminality and violence. *Journal of Consulting & Clinical Psychology*, *63*, 569–578.

Bronfenbrenner, U. (1979). *The ecology of human development: Experiments by nature and design*. Cambridge, MA: Harvard University Press.

Brunk, M., Henggeler, S. W., & Whelan, J. P. (1987). A comparison of multisystemic therapy and parent training in the brief treatment of child abuse and neglect. *Journal of Consulting and Clinical Psychology*, *55*, 311–318.

Dodge, K. A. (1993). The future of research on the treatment of conduct disorder. *Development and Psychopathology*, *5*, 311–319.

Elliott, D. S. (1994). *Youth violence: An overview*. Boulder, CO: University of

Colorado, Institute for Behavioral Sciences, Center for the Study and Prevention of Violence.

Farrow, F. (1991, May). Services to families: The view from the states. *Families in Society: the Journal of Contemporary Human Services*, 268–275.

Feldman, L. H. (1991). Evaluating the impact of intensive family preservation services in New Jersey. In K. Wells & D. E. Biegel (Eds.), *Family preservation services: Research and evaluation* (pp. 33–47). Newbury Park, CA: Sage.

Fraser, M. W., Nelson, K. E., & Rivard, J. C. (1997). The effectiveness of family preservation services. *Social Work Research*, *21*, 138–153.

Friedman, A. S. (1989). Family therapy vs. parent groups: Effects on adolescent drug abusers. *American Journal of Family Therapy*, *17*, 335–347.

Friedman, A. S., Tomko, L. A., & Utada, A. (1991). Client and family characteristics that predict better family therapy outcome for adolescent drug users. *Family Dynamics Addiction Quarterly*, *1*, 77–93.

Gordon, D. A., Arbuthnot, J., Gustafson, K., & McGreen, P. (1988). Home-based behavioral-systems family therapy with disadvantaged juvenile delinquents. *American Journal of Family Therapy*, *16*, 243–255.

Gordon, D. A., Graves, K., & Arbuthnot, J. (1995). The effect of functional family therapy for delinquents on adult criminal behavior. *Criminal Justice and Behavior*, *22*, 60–73.

Haley, J. (1976). *Problem solving therapy*. San Francisco, CA: Jossey-Bass.

Hazelrigg, M. D., Cooper, H. M., & Borduin, C. M. (1987). Evaluating the effectiveness of family therapies: An integrative review and analysis. *Psychological Bulletin*, *101*, 428–442.

Henggeler, S. W. (1991). Multidimensional causal models of delinquent behavior and their implications for treatment. In R. Cohen & A. W. Siegel (Eds.), *Context and development* (pp. 161–181). Hillsdale, NJ: Lawrence Erlbaum.

Henggeler, S. W. (1996). Treatment of violent juvenile offenders—We have the knowledge: Comment on Gorman-Smith et al. (1996). *Journal of Family Psychology*, *10*, 137–141.

Henggeler, S. W. (1997). The development of effective drug abuse services for youth. In J. A. Egertson, D. M. Fox, & A. I. Leshner (Eds.), *Treating drug abusers effectively* (pp. 253–279). New York: Blackwell.

Henggeler, S. W., & Borduin, C. M. (1990). *Family therapy and beyond: A multisystemic approach to treating the behavior problems of children and adolescents*. Pacific Grove, CA: Brooks/Cole.

Henggeler, S. W., Borduin, C. M., & Mann, B. J. (1993). Advances in family therapy: Empirical foundations. In T. H. Ollendick & R. J. Prinz (Eds.), *Advances in Clinical Child Psychology*, (Vol. 15, pp. 207–241). New York: Plenum.

Henggeler, S. W., Melton, G. B., Brondino, M. J., Scherer, D. G., & Hanley, J. H. (1997). Multisystemic therapy with violent and chronic juvenile offenders and their families: The role of treatment fidelity in successful dissemination. *Journal of Consulting and Clinical Psychology*, *65*, 821–833.

Henggeler, S. W., Melton, G. B., & Smith, L. A. (1992). Family preservation using multisystemic therapy: An effective alternative to incarcerating serious juvenile offenders. *Journal of Consulting and Clinical Psychology*, *60*, 953–961.

Henggeler, S. W., Melton, G. B., Smith, L. A., Schoenwald, S. K., & Hanley, J. (1993). Family preservation using multisystemic therapy: Long-term follow-up to a clinical trial with serious juvenile offenders. *Journal of Child and Family Studies*, *2*, 283–293.

Henggeler, S. W., Pickrel, S. G., & Brondino, M. J. (1997). *Multisystemic treatment of substance abusing and dependent delinquents: Outcomes, treatment fidelity, and transportability*. Mental Health Services Research.

Henggeler, S. W., Pickrel, S. G., Brondino, M. J., & Crouch, J. L. (1996). Eliminating (almost) treatment dropout of substance abusing or dependent delinquents through home-based multisystemic therapy. *American Journal of Psychiatry*, *153*, 427–428.

Henggeler, S. W., Rodick, J. D., Borduin, C. M., Hanson, C. L., Watson, S. M., & Urey, J. R.

(1986). Multisystemic treatment of juvenile offenders: Effects on adolescent behavior and family interaction. *Developmental Psychology, 22*, 132–141.

Henggeler, S. W., Schoenwald, S. K., Borduin, C. M., Rowland, M. D., & Cunningham, P. B. (1998). *Multisystemic treatment for antisocial behavior in youth.* New York: Guilford.

Heras, P. (1992). Cultural considerations in the assessment and treatment of child abuse. *Journal of Child Sexual Abuse, 1*, 119–124.

Kazdin, A. E. (1994). Psychotherapy for children and adolescents. In A. E. Bergin & S. L. Garfield (Eds.), *Handbook of psychotherapy and behavior change* (pp. 543–594). New York: Wiley.

Kazdin, A. E., Mazurick, J. L., & Bass, D. (1993). Risk for attrition in treatment of antisocial children and families. *Journal of Clinical Child Psychology, 22*, 2–16.

Kinney, J., Haapala, D., Booth, C., & Leavitt, S. (1990). The Homebuilders model. In J. K. Whittaker, J. Kinney, E. M. Tracey, & C. Booth (Eds.), *Reaching high risk families: Intensive family preservation in human services* (pp. 31–64). New York: Aldine.

Kurtines, W. M., & Szapocznik, J. (1996). Family interaction patterns: Structural family therapy within contexts of cultural diversity. In E. D. Hibbs & P. S. Jensen (Eds.), *Psychosocial treatments for child and adolescent disorders: Empirically based strategies for clinical practice* (pp. 671–697). Washington, DC: American Psychological Association.

Liddle, H. A. (1995). Conceptual and clinical dimensions of a multidimensional, multisystemic engagement strategy in family-based adolescent treatment. *Psychotherapy, 32*, 39–58.

Liddle, H. A., & Dakof, G. A. (1995). Efficacy of family therapy for drug abuse: Promising but not definitive. *Journal of Marital and Family Therapy, 21*, 511–543.

Liddle, H. A., Dakof, G. A., & Diamond, G. (1991). Adolescent substance abuse: Multi dimensional family therapy in action. In E. Kaufman & P. Kaufman (Eds.), *Family therapy with drug and alcohol abuse* (pp. 120–171). Boston, MA: Allyn & Bacon.

Lloyd, J. C., & Bryce, M. E. (1984). *Placement prevention and family reunification: A handbook for the family-centered service practitioner.* Iowa City, IA: University of Iowa, National Resource Center for Family Based Services.

Minuchin, S. (1974). *Families and family therapy.* Cambridge, MA: Harvard University Press.

Minuchin, S., & Fishman, H. C. (1981). *Family therapy techniques.* Cambridge, MA: Harvard University Press.

Mitchell, C., Tovar, P., & Knitzer, J. (1989). *The Bronx Homebuilders Program: An evaluation of the first 45 families.* New York: Bank Street College of Education.

Nelson, K. E. (1990). Family based services for juvenile offenders. *Children and Youth Services Review, XII*, 193–212.

Nelson, K. E. (1994). Family-based services for families and children at risk of out-of-home placement. In R. Barth, J. D. Berrick, & N. Gilbert (Eds.), *Child welfare research review*, (Vol. 1, pp. 83–108). New York: Columbia University Press.

Santisteban, D. A., Szapocznik, J., Perez-Vidal, A., Kurtines, W. M., Murray, W. J., & LaPerriere, A. (1996). Engaging behavior problem drug abusing youth and their families into treatment: An investigation of the efficacy of specialized engagement interventions and factors that contribute to differential effectiveness. *Journal of Family Psychology, 10*, 35–44.

Schmidt, S. E., Liddle, H. A., & Dakof, G. A. (1996). Changes in parenting practices and adolescent drug abuse during multidimensional family therapy. *Journal of Family Psychology, 10*, 12–27.

Schoenwald, S. K., Borduin, C. M., & Henggeler, S. W. (1998). Multisystemic therapy: Changing the natural and service ecologies of adolescents and their families. In M. H. Epstein, K. Kutash, & A. Duchnowski (Eds.), *Outcomes for children and youth with behavioral and emotional disorders and their families: Programs and evaluation best practices* (pp. 485–511). Austin, TX: PRO-Ed.

Schoenwald, S. K., & Henggeler, S. W. (1997). Combining effective treatment strategies with family preservation models of service delivery: A challenge for mental health. In R. J. Illback, H. Joseph, Jr., & C. Cobb (Eds.), *Integrated services for children and families: Opportunities for psychological practice* (pp. 121–136). Washington, DC: American Psychological Association.

Schoenwald, S. K., Ward, D. M., Henggeler, S. W., Pickrel, S. G., & Patel, H. (1996). MST treatment of substance abusing or dependent adolescent offenders: Costs of reducing incarceration, inpatient, and residential placement. *Journal of Child and Family Studies*, *5*, 431–444.

Shadish, W. R., Montgomery, L. M., Wilson, P., Wilson, M. R., Bright, I., & Okwumabua, T. (1993). Effects of family and marital psychotherapies: A meta-analysis. *Journal of Consulting and Clinical Psychology*, *61*, 992–1002.

Szapocznik, J., & Kurtines, W. M. (1989). *Breakthroughs in family therapy with drug-abusing and problem youth*. New York: Springer-Verlay.

Szapocznik, J., Kurtines, W. M., Foote, E., Perez-Vidal, A., & Hervis, O. E. (1983). Conjoint versus one-person family therapy: Some evidence for the effectiveness of conducting family therapy through one person. *Journal of Consulting and Clinical Psychology*, *51*, 889–899.

Szapocznik, J., Kurtines, W. M., Foote, E., Perez-Vidal, A., & Hervis, O. E. (1986). Conjoint versus one-person family therapy: Further evidence for the effectiveness of conducting family therapy through one person. *Journal of Consulting and Clinical Psychology*, *54*, 395–397.

Szapocznik, J., Perez-Vidal, A., Brickman, A. L., Foote, F. H., Santisteban, D., Hervis, O., & Kurtines, W. (1988). Engaging adolescent drug abusers and their families in treatment: A strategic structural systems approach. *Journal of Consulting and Clinical Psychology*, *56*, 552–557.

Szapocznik, J., Santisteban, D., Rio, A. T., Perez-Vidal, A., & Kurtines, W. M. (1989). Family effectiveness training: An intervention to prevent problem behaviors in Hispanic adolescents. *Hispanic Journal of Behavioral Sciences*, *11*, 4–27.

Szapocznik, J., Santisteban, D., Rio, A. T., Perez-Vidal, A., Kurtines, W. M., & Hervis, O. E. (1986). Bicultural effectiveness training: An experimental test of an intervention modality for families experiencing intergenerational/intercultural conflict. *Hispanic Journal of Behavioral Sciences*, *8*, 303–330.

Tate, D. C., Reppucci, N. D., & Mulvey, E. P. (1995). Violent juvenile delinquents: Treatment effectiveness and implications for future action. *American Psychologist*, *50*, 777–781.

Thornberry, T. P., Huizinga, D., & Loeber, R. (1995). The prevention of serious delinquency and violence: Implications from the program of research on the causes and correlates of delinquency. In J. C. Howell, B. Krisberg, J. D. Hawkins, & J. J. Wilson (Eds.), *A sourcebook: Serious, violent, and chronic juvenile offenders* (pp. 213–237). Newbury Park, CA: Sage.

Tolan, P. H. (1996). Characteristics shared by exemplary child clinical interventions for indicated populations. In M. C. Roberts (Ed.), *Model programs in child and family mental health* (pp. 91–107). Mahwah, NJ: Lawrence Erlbaum.

Tolan, P. H., & Guerra, N. C. (1994). *What works in reducing adolescent violence: An empirical review of the field*. Boulder, CO: University of Colorado, Institute for Behavioral Sciences, Center for the Study and Prevention of Violence.

Tuma, J. M. (1989). Mental health services for children. *American Psychologist*, *46*, 188–189.

Weisz, J. R., Donenberg, G. R., Han, S. S., & Weiss, B. (1995). Bridging the gap between laboratory and clinic in child and adolescent psychotherapy. *Journal of Consulting and Clinical Psychology*, *63*, 688–701.

Wood, K. M., Barton, K., & Schroeder, C. (1988). In-home treatment of abusive families: Cost and placement at one year. *Psychotherapy*, *25*, 409–414.

Chapter 7

Delinquency Prevention Programs in Schools

David LeMarquand
and
Richard E. Tremblay
Université de Montréal, Montréal, Canada

INTRODUCTION

Chronic adult offenders commonly begin their criminal careers as chronic juvenile offenders (Lynam, 1996; see also Loeber & Stouthamer-Loeber, 1998). Ideally, intervention strategies for criminal behavior should be initiated early, before violent and criminal behavior becomes a stable part of an individual's repertoire. One method of intervening in treating or preventing chronic juvenile delinquency is through the school (Durlak, 1995; Lane & Murakami, 1987). This strategy may be effective for a number of reasons.

First, longitudinal studies have demonstrated that low intelligence, poor academic achievement, small vocabulary, and poor verbal reasoning are predictors of chronic delinquency (Farrington, 1985, 1987; Hawkins et al., 1998; Loeber & Dishion, 1983). Poor "executive functions", including the ability to plan and sequence behavior, have also been associated with stable aggressive behavior in early-adolescent boys (Séguin, Pihl, Harden, Tremblay, & Boulerice, 1995). Low cognitive ability is commonly thought to precede the development of delinquent behavior; however, it is possible that early aggressive behavior may lead to lower IQ, or that third variables (e.g. parental psychopathology) may account for the cognitive deficit/delinquency association. At present there is not enough evidence to clearly specify a direction of causality (Yoshikawa, 1994). A causal link between low cognitive ability and delinquency might be mediated by academic success and bonding to the school environment. Low bonding to school, truancy

The Essential *Handbook of Offender Assessment and Treatment.* Edited by C. R. Hollin.
© 2004 John Wiley & Sons Ltd.

and school dropout have been related to later delinquency (Hawkins et al., 1998). Low cognitive ability leading to academic failure and reduced bonding to the school may lead to skipping school and dropping out, increasing the time available for becoming involved in delinquent behavior. School interventions designed to improve cognitive functioning could contribute to a reduction in delinquency and provide confirmation of a causal link between reduced cognitive ability and later delinquency.

Second, behavior problems exhibited in school are important targets for intervention in and of themselves. Disruptive behavior in the classroom consumes a teacher's time and energy, and interferes with the learning processes of disruptive and non-disruptive students, which may lead to a classwide reduction in academic achievement. Moreover, classroom behavior problems may represent early expressions of disruptiveness that later develop into delinquent behavior. Childhood aggressive behavior, as well as hyperactivity, attentional difficulties, impulsivity, and oppositional behavior, are related to delinquent behavior in adolescence (Farrington, 1991; Huesmann, Eron, Lefkowitz, & Walder, 1984; White, Moffitt, Earls, Robins, & Silva, 1990). More specifically, teacher-rated aggressive behavior in school is related to later delinquency, particularly in males (Stattin & Magnusson, 1989; Tremblay et al., 1992).

Third, school processes and climate are related to levels of achievement and delinquency (Fiquera-McDonough, 1986; Rutter, 1983). A number of early studies (summarized in Rutter, 1983) have demonstrated a wide variability in delinquency rates across schools, although some of this variability may be a function of school intake characteristics. A school environment characterized by competitive academic achievement, routine handling of discipline and unpredictable supervision (versus a broader definition of success, more specialized discipline, and predictable supervision) is associated with higher rates of minor delinquency (Fiquera-McDonough, 1986).

Another advantage of intervening in schools to impact on delinquency, particularly from a prevention point of view, is that the great majority of children attend school. This facilitates the early identification of children who exhibit aggressive behavior and/or academic difficulties, which are known predictors of later delinquent behavior (Farrington, 1994; Loeber & Dishion, 1983; Stattin & Magnusson, 1989). Following identification, a school intervention can be implemented for indicated individuals with greater ease than if implemented in the home or clinic.

In this chapter, school interventions designed to prevent and treat juvenile delinquency are reviewed. Only those studies implementing a school intervention and assessing juvenile delinquency outcomes using controlled experimental or quasi-experimental designs are included for review. The majority of studies in this review include school interventions implemented before the onset of delinquent behavior, designed to prevent the subsequent development of serious delinquency. Thus, these are prevention studies, as opposed to treatment studies, seeking to reduce criminal behavior in youth already identified as juvenile delinquents. Interest in the prevention of delinquency is growing. Early intervention, before the development of serious delinquent behavior, may avert significantly greater societal and individual suffering than by treating the individual after the development of delinquent behavior.

PRIMARY FINDINGS

Table 7.1 summarizes the studies of school interventions to reduce delinquent behavior. The studies are grouped by type of intervention. Preventive interventions can be classified according to the characteristics of the sample chosen for the intervention (Gordon, 1987). A universal preventive intervention is applied to an entire population, a selective intervention to individuals at above average risk for a disorder, and an indicated intervention to asymptomatic individuals who manifest a risk factor which places them at high risk for the development of a disorder. In the present review, interventions were classified as selective if participants manifested one or more environmental risk factors (i.e. poverty), whereas indicated interventions involved participants manifesting personal risk factors (e.g. disruptive behavior, low IQ) placing them at higher risk for the development of delinquency. Within each intervention type, studies are ordered by decreasing age of the participants.

Also included in Table 7.1 are effect sizes (ESs), calculated for delinquency outcomes. ESs represent the mean of the control group subtracted from the mean of the intervention group, and divided by the pooled within-group standard deviation, and are unweighted (Hedges & Olkin, 1985). They are calculated so that positive scores reflected improvement in the intervention group relative to the controls. ESs of 0.2 are generally considered small, 0.5 medium, and 0.8 large (Cohen, 1977).

Three universal interventions have incorporated school intervention components to prevent juvenile delinquency (among other negative outcomes), including two carried out by Hawkins and his associates involving altering teaching methods to reduce delinquent behavior. A third reported by Farrell and Meyer (1997) involved the implementation of a classroom information curriculum to prevent violent behavior. An additional universal intervention (Kellam, Rebok, Ialongo, & Mayer, 1994) reported on the effects of a classroom-based behavior management strategy on aggressive behavior; however, delinquency outcome data have yet to be reported on this sample. Another large-scale universal intervention designed to prevent bullying in schools found reductions in antisocial behavior after 20 months of intervention; however, this study did not employ a no-treatment control group, using instead a "time-lagged contrasts between age-equivalent cohorts" design (Olweus, 1991).

Hawkins and his associates (Hawkins, Doueck, & Lishner, 1988; Hawkins & Lam, 1987) implemented an intervention experiment in grade seven classrooms of five Seattle middle schools. Three of these schools were randomly assigned to either the intervention or control condition, while the classes of a fourth school were assigned to the intervention and the classes of a fifth school to the control

Table 7.1 School interventions and their effects on delinquent behavior

Author(s)	Number of participants at pretest (I = intervention, C = control)	Age at intervention (years)	Design	Type of intervention	Description of intervention	Context of intervention	Length of intervention	Follow-up: length (years); sample size at follow-up	Results for delinquency for intervention group, compared to controls, at latest assessment (effect size)
Farrell & Meyer (1997)	978	11	random assignment	universal	violence information curriculum	school	18 weeks	0; 698 (385 girls); 348 I, 350 C	• significant decreases in boys' self-reported problem behavior (0.24) and drug use (0.20) • trend for decreased boys' self-reported violent behavior (0.18) • no effect on girls self-reported violent behavior (−0.12), problem behavior (−0.14), and drug use (−0.02)
Hawkins & Lam (1987)	1166 boys and girls; 513 I, 653 C	mean = 13.3	quasi-experimental (partial randomization)	universal	teacher training	school	1 year	0; 766	• negative relationship between teacher practices and school disciplinary reports (0.90), days suspended (0.98), and self-report times suspended or expelled
Hawkins et al. (1999); SSDP	643 (316 girls); 156 full I, 267 late I, 220 C	6	quasi-experimental (partial randomization)	universal	teacher training, child training, parent training	school, family	6 years	6 years; 598 (299 girls); 149 full I, 243 late I, 206 C	• full I significantly reduced self-report violent delinquency (0.23), officially-recorded school misbehavior (0.25) • full I tended to reduce self-report non-violent delinquency (0.11), police arrests (0.14), and official court-recorded delinquency (0.17)

Study	Sample	Age	Design	Type	Intervention	Setting	Duration	Follow-up	Outcomes
Clarke & Campbell (1997); The Abecedarian Project	111 (59 girls); 57 I, 54 C	mean = 4.4 m	random assignment	selective	preschool	daycare	5 years	13 years; 105, 54 I, 51 C	• no differences in officially-recorded adult criminal charges and arrests (including percentage receiving any charge (0.03), mean number of charges, mean number of arrests)
Gottfredson (1987); PCD	360 boys and girls; 184 I, 176 C	14–17; mean = 15.4	random assignment	indicated	group counselling with peers/leaders	school	15 weeks	0	• marginally greater self-report serious delinquency (−0.20) • no difference in police contacts (−0.05) • greater drug use (−0.25)
Gottfredson & Gottfredson (1992); STATUS	247 boys and girls; 120 I, 127 C	12 to 17	quasi-experimental (failed random assignment)	indicated	social studies curriculum	school	1 year	0	• less self-report serious delinquency in junior (0.33) and senior (0.42) schools • marginally lower rates of court contact in junior (0.07) and senior (0.18) schools less drug involvement in junior (0.42) and senior (0.35) schools
Arbuthnot & Gordon (1986)	48 (13 girls); 24 I, 24 C	mean = 14.5	pairing, random assignment	indicated	group discussions around moral reasoning	school	16–20 weeks	1 year; 22, 13 I, 9 C	• no differences in police/court contacts • decreased school absenteeism
Gottfredson (1986); PATHE	869 boys and girls; 468 I, 401 C	11–17	random assignment	indicated	individualized intervention programs, alterations in school management and organization	school	2 years	0	• no change in self-report serious delinquency (0.00), number of court contacts (0.00), school-recorded suspensions (−0.02), expulsions (0.10), disciplinary infractions (0.16) • greater self-report drug involvement (−0.21)

continued overleaf

Table 7.1 *(continued)*

Author(s)	Number of participants at pretest (I = intervention, C = control)	Age at intervention (years)	Design	Type of intervention	Description of intervention	Context of intervention	Length of intervention	Follow-up: length (years); sample size at follow-up	Results for delinquency for intervention group, compared to controls, at latest assessment (effect size)
Ahlstrom & Havighurst (1982)	Group 2: 167 boys; 95 I, 72 C	13–14	random assignment	indicated	individualized classroom education program; work program	school	approx. 5.5 years	0	• higher police-reported arrests in early adolescence (–0.29); slightly lower percentage of arrests in late adolescence (0.04)
Wodarski & Filipczak (1982); PREP	60 (18 girls); 30 (9 girls) I; 30 (9 girls) C	13.2 (grades 7–9)	matching, random assignment	indicated	individualized and small group instruction, social skills training, behavioral contracts with incentives	school	1 year	4 years; 21 I, 19 C	• no differences on 31 I-C comparisons on self- and parent-reported juvenile problem behavior variables • less self-reported participation in gang fights (0.51) greater attempts to avoid trouble (0.52)
Reckless & Dinitz (1972); YDP	1094 boys; 632 I, 462 C	13 (7th grade)	random assignment	indicated	remedial reading, teacher group lesson planning, teacher group discussion, social role-modelling	school	1 year	3 years; 536 I, 379 C	• no differences on police contacts (–0.03) • no differences on self-report delinquency • teacher-rated delinquency lower in one cohort
Stuart et al. (1976)	60; 30 I, 30 C	11–15 (grades 6–10)	random assignment	indicated	behavioral contacts with incentives, costs	school	4 months	0	• no differences in court contacts (0.37)
Bry (1982)	66 (22 girls); 33 I, 33 C	mean = 12.5 (grader 7)	pairing, andom assignment	indicated	behavior contingencies, school monitoring	school	2 years	5 years; 60 (20 girls), 30 I, 30 C	• fewer serious or chronic delinquency probation dept. files (0.51)

Study	Age	Design	Level	Intervention	Setting	Duration	Follow-up	Results
Lochman (1992)	145 boys; 31 anger-coping (AC), 52 untreated aggressives (UA), 62 nonaggres-sives (NON)	9–12	random assignment of some cohorts to treatment and control groups	indicated	cognitive–behavioral, anger control	school	4–5 months	2.5–3.5 years	• no differences in self-report general behavioral deviance (0.11, including crimes against persons (–0.12) or general theft (0.19)) between AC and UA boys
Tremblay et al. (1995); MLES	166 boys; 43 I, 82 attention/observation C, 41 C	7	random assignment	indicated	parent training in effective child rearing; social skills training for children	home, school	2 years	6 years	• less self-reported delinquent behaviors 1 to 6 years after end of intervention (0.24) • no difference in court registered delinquent offenses (–0.07)
Schweinhart et al. (1993); Perry Preschool Study	123 (51 girls); 58 (25 girls) I, 65 (26 girls) C	3–4	random assignment	indicated	preschool; teacher home visits	school, home	1–2 years	22 years	• fewer mean officially-recorded lifetime arrests (0.54) • no differences on self-report misconduct variables (0.29)
Schweinhart & Weikhart (1997); Preschool Curriculum Study	68 (37 girls); 23 Direct Instruction (DI), 22 High/Scope (HS), 23 Nursery School (NS)	3–4	random assignment	indicated	preschool (either DI—teacher-initiated activities, HS—teacher and child planned & initiated activities, or NS—child-initiated activities); teacher home visits	school, home	1–2 years	18 years, 52; 19 DI, 14 HS, 19 NS	• DI had higher self-report mean frequency of work suspensions (0.22 for all self-report delinquency variables, HS vs. other two groups) • DI had higher lifetime arrests, adult arrests, felony arrests (specifically property felonies) and property misdemeanour arrests according to official records (0.21 for lifetime arrests, juvenile and adult, HS vs. other two groups)

condition. The intervention focused on maintaining low achievers in regular class-rooms and modifying teaching practices to provide them with opportunities for active involvement, skills for successful participation, and constant reinforcement for work involvement. Hypothetically, these opportunities would increase school success, increase bonding to school, and decrease disruptive behavior. To this end, teachers were provided with training programs emphasizing proactive classroom management (how to create a learning environment in the classroom), interactive teaching (including mastering objectives before moving to higher learning levels), and cooperative learning (grouping students of different abilities to work together). Teachers were also supervised in these instructional methods in the classroom.

Data for the entire sample were analyzed by looking for correlations between the use of the prescribed teacher practices and delinquent behaviors, rather than comparing the intervention and control groups on delinquency outcomes. At the end of the school year, inverse relationships were found between the extent to which teachers employed project teaching practices and the number of school disciplinary reports and days suspended, as well as students' self-report number of times suspended/expelled and high on drugs at school. There were no relationships between use of teacher practices and student self-reports of truancy, school theft, or trouble due to drug/alcohol use (Hawkins & Lam, 1987). In a subset of the entire sample chosen on the basis of low math achievement test scores, the intervention group was suspended or expelled less often than the control group according to school records and self-report (ES = 0.36); however, again there were no group differences in self-report property crimes (ES = 0.06), interpersonal violence (ES = 0.04), serious crime (ES = 0.13), or drug use (ES = 0.11). This despite the fact that intervention students reported more positive attitudes toward school and higher expectations for future education (Hawkins et al., 1988). It may be that not enough time had elapsed for the change in attitudes and school behaviors to have "trickled down" to impact on delinquency. An additional follow-up might demonstrate the desired effects.

A second, more extensive universal intervention experiment designed to prevent delinquency and other undesirable behavioral outcomes is the Seattle Social Development Project (SSDP) (Hawkins, Catalano, Kosterman, Abbott, & Hill, 1999). First grade classrooms in one Seattle public school were assigned to the intervention condition, classrooms in a second school to the control condition, and classrooms in the remaining six schools were randomly assigned to intervention or control conditions. At the beginning of grade five, the sample was non-randomly expanded with the addition of 18 schools to the late treatment and control conditions, resulting in a quasi-experimental design. The intervention was 6 years in length. In this study, the classroom intervention was one component of a multimodal intervention. For this component, teachers received 5 days of in-service training per year in proactive classroom management, interactive teaching, and cooperative learning. As a manipulation check, teachers in the intervention and control conditions were observed in the fall and spring of each year to document the use of the targeted teaching strategies.

Greater use of the targeted teaching strategies in the intervention classrooms compared with the control classrooms was confirmed. In addition to the teacher-training component, the intervention included cognitive and social skills training administered to the children by the teachers, as well as parent training in behavior management skills. A recent 6-year follow-up of this study has demonstrated that the full intervention significantly reduced officially-recorded school misbehavior (ES = 0.25) and self-report violent delinquency (ES = 0.23), and tended to reduce self-report non-violent delinquency (ES = 0.11), police arrests (ES = 0.14), and official court records (ES = 0.17) (Hawkins et al., 1999). Since the teacher-training intervention was but one component of a multimodal intervention package, it is not possible to know the proportion of the reduction in disruptive behavior that was due to the school intervention component alone.

Farrell and Meyer (1997) reported on a classroom-based curriculum designed to teach high-school-aged youth about the nature of violence. This program was implemented and evaluated in six of eight middle schools with predominantly low-income African-American students. Classrooms were randomly assigned to the immediate intervention or waiting-list control conditions. The 18-week intervention focused on building trust, teaching respect for individual differences, imparting information on the nature of violence and risk factors, teaching anger management, discussing personal values, discussing the precipitants and consequences of fighting, and generating non-violent alternative responses to fighting. It was implemented in the classroom by four college-educated, African-American male prevention specialists, working in pairs. Post-intervention assessment was completed after those in the immediate intervention condition had finished the intervention, but before the waiting-list control condition received the curriculum. Data were available for 348 students in the intervention condition, and 350 students in the waiting-list control condition.

Three subscales of the Behavioral Frequency Scales were the primary dependent measures: the Violent Behavior Scale, with items such as "been in a fight in which someone was hit", "threatened to hurt a teacher", "threatened someone with a weapon (gun, knife, or club)", "brought a weapon to school", and "been in a fight in which you were injured and had to be treated by a doctor or nurse"; the Problem Behavior Scale, tapping the frequency of vandalism and shoplifting, in addition to violent behaviors; and the Drug Use Scale, assessing the frequency of alcohol, cigarette, and marijuana use. Results showed definite sex effects. Scores on the Problem Behavior and Drug Use scales were significantly decreased for boys (ESs = 0.24 and 0.20, respectively), but not for girls (ESs = −0.14 and −0.02), in the intervention condition compared with the waiting-list control condition. Scores on the Violent Behavior Scale also tended to be lower for boys in the intervention condition relative to controls (ES = 0.18), with no differences for girls (ES = −0.12). The authors speculate that the intervention may have been more effective for boys because they more readily identified with the African-American men who implemented the program.

The only selective intervention located that involved a school component was the Abecedarian project (Clarke & Campbell, 1997). This study is notable, however, in that the intervention was initiated when the participants were born, presumably when the potential for influence on future behavior is greatest. It is distinguishable from other preventive interventions beginning at or near birth (Olds et al., 1997; Seitz, Rosenbaum, & Apfel, 1985) in that it focused specifically on cognitive development through a preschool intervention, whereas the latter interventions were daycare-oriented. One hundred and eleven infants were randomly assigned at birth to receive either 5 years of preschool education in a child-care setting, or no treatment. The infants were considered to be at risk for suboptimal cognitive development due to conditions of poverty, low parental education levels, low parental IQ, and poor maternal social/family support, among others (Campbell & Ramey, 1995). The intervention covered four primary domains: cognitive and fine motor development; social and self-help skills; language; and gross motor skills. Areas within the child care center were set up for art, housekeeping, blocks, fine motor manipulation, language, and literacy. Language instruction was less focused on syntax and more on practical usage. Prephonics training to prepare children for reading was also provided. Follow-up 13 years later (at age 18) failed to reveal significant differences between the intervention and control groups in the (officially-recorded) percentage of participants receiving any criminal charge (ES = 0.03), the percentage receiving violent (ES = 0.08), property (ES = –0.12), drug (ES = 0.01), or other (ES = 0.09) charges, the mean number of total charges, the mean number of specific charges, the mean number of all arrests, or the mean number of specific arrests. This despite the fact that the intervention group had higher IQs, higher reading test scores, fewer students retained in a grade at least once, and fewer students assigned to special education classes relative to the control group at age 15 follow-up (Campbell & Ramey, 1995). These authors have hypothesized that the lack of positive results may have been due to the exclusion of a home visit/parent training component in the intervention.

The remaining 13 studies in this review are indicated or treatment interventions (some study samples contain both individuals at high risk for delinquency, as well as those who have engaged in delinquent behavior already, making classification of the study as an indicated preventive or treatment intervention difficult). Of note, some studies incorporated interventions implemented in schools (e.g. Kolvin et al., 1986) but did not report specifically on delinquent behavior outcomes, and thus were not reviewed below. Studies in the following section are ordered by decreasing age of the sample at the start of intervention.

Gottfredson and Gottfredson (1992) reported on three indicated interventions for adolescents involving school intervention components. The first of these, the Peer Culture Development (PCD) program (Gottfredson, 1987), was a 15-week peer counselling program implemented in three public secondary schools for students ages 14–17 years. The program involved daily group counselling sessions with peers and a leader, and was offered as a social studies course for credit. The principle behind the intervention was that delinquents would learn to conform to societal rules by receiving more social rewards for conformity than non-conformity. The emphasis in the sessions was on problem-solving and conformity to social rules. Equal numbers of students in trouble at school and positive role models were included in the peer groups. Participants (volunteers, or referrals from teachers, peers) were randomly allocated to intervention or control groups separately by gender and within pools of:

1. negative leaders (youths demonstrating leadership and delinquent socialization);
2. positive leaders (youths demonstrating leadership and conventional socialization);
3. students in trouble; and
4. students with no difficulties.

There were 184 intervention and 176 control participants. Post-intervention outcome assessment revealed that the intervention group tended to show higher rates of self-report serious delinquency (ES = –0.20) and significantly greater drug use (ES = –0.25), relative to the control group. There was no effect of the intervention on number of police contacts (ES = –0.05), as derived from archival records.

Another strategy tested to prevent school delinquency involved exposure to an English and law/social studies school curriculum emphasizing instruction in various facets of society, such as the school, human nature and interpersonal relations, the family, social contracts, and the justice system. This intervention was called the Student Training Through Urban Strategies (STATUS) project (Gottfredson & Gottfredson, 1992). Personal responsibility and the importance of order and rules were emphasized. This curriculum involved active participation, including visits to community organizations/agencies, independent and small group research, role-playing and simulation, and guest speakers. Teachers used student teams for tutoring and support, rewarded progress, and created individualized learning plans. The overarching principle behind the intervention was to allow students the opportunity to gain a first-hand appreciation for the functioning of society and their place as citizens within it. This, in turn, would reduce their alienation from learning, increase academic success, and decrease disruptive behavior. This program was implemented in one junior (ages 12–13 years) and one senior (ages 15–17 years) secondary school in California. Participants were recruited through school–staff referrals or self-nominations. Random allocation of students to intervention or control conditions was attempted but not fully achieved due to scheduling difficulties. As such, in the senior cohort, there were more females and African-American students in the intervention group compared with the control group. There were 120 intervention and 127 control students. Results at the end of the school year, controlling for pretreatment differences between the intervention and control groups (where necessary) revealed that, in the junior school, the program reduced self-report serious delinquency (ES = 0.33; non-significant) and drug use (ES = 0.42; significant), and lowered the rate of court contact (ES = 0.07; non-significant). In the senior school, the program significantly reduced self-report serious delinquency (ES = 0.42) and drug use (ES = 0.35), and non-significantly reduced court contacts (ES = 0.18).

A similar intervention by way of its focus on learning personal responsibility was that of Arbuthnot and Gordon (1986). They reported on an indicated preventive intervention to enhance the moral reasoning of adolescents teacher-rated as seriously behavior-disordered. Forty-eight young adolescents were randomly assigned into intervention or no-treatment control groups. The intervention consisted of 16–20 weekly sessions, each one class period (45 minutes) long, in which the intervention participants discussed moral dilemmas in groups of five to eight students. The leader used questioning, role-playing, and perspective-taking techniques to facilitate discussion of moral dilemmas. Active listening, communication, problem-solving, and decision-making skills were taught. At post-intervention, the intervention group demonstrated increases in moral reasoning abilities and grades, as well as decreases in school-recorded disciplinary referrals and tardiness. There was also a significant difference between groups in officially-recorded police/court contacts (ES = 0.66) favoring the intervention group. At one-year follow-up, however, there was no group difference in police/court contacts, as neither group had any recorded contacts (note that the numbers of participants followed-up was low, particularly in the control group). Differences in moral reasoning, academic performance, school behavior referrals, absenteeism, and teacher-ratings of school adjustment were found, again favoring the intervention group.

A third school-based intervention for delinquency presented by Gottfredson and Gottfredson (1992) endeavored to alter school organization and management and intervene directly with high-risk youths (the Positive Action Through Holistic Education, or PATHE, program; Gottfredson, 1986). Youths were identified through teacher referrals and screenings of academic and behavioral records. Once identified, academic and behavioral objectives were defined, and the intervention specialists created individualized treatment programs to work toward the objectives. These treatment plans could include counselling, tutoring services, extracurricular activities (field trips, clubs), peer counselling and rap sessions, and community services for families. Specialists worked with teachers to recommend instructional strategies as well. School organization and management were also altered to increase school bonding and reduce disorder. It was hypothesized that by intervening in such a fashion, commitment to school would increase, and delinquency would decrease.

The program was implemented in seven secondary schools for students from ages 11–17. Four hundred and sixty-eight students were randomized to the treatment group, 401 to the control group. Following two years of intervention (at post-test), there were no changes in self-report serious delinquency (ES = 0.00) or officially-recorded court contacts (ES = 0.00). There were also no changes in school-recorded suspensions (ES = –0.02), expulsions (ES = 0.10), or disciplinary infractions (ES = 0.16). There was, however, greater self-reported drug involvement in the intervention group (ES = –0.21). Thus, the intervention failed to have a positive effect on delinquency, despite improvements in academics (e.g. better grades, better promotion, and graduation rates).

Two interventions implemented in the 1960s to prevent delinquency had school components. Ahlstrom and Havighurst (1982) reported on a combined school/work intervention with 13–14 year-old socially, behaviorally, and educationally maladjusted boys begun in 1962. The intervention began when the boys entered grade eight, and was divided into stages. In stage one, half of each day was spent in the classroom in an educational program geared toward each boy's needs, interests, and personal orientations. The boys had their own teachers. The other half of each day was spent in supervised work programs for token pay (e.g. landscaping, woodworking, and warehouse work). In stage two, at approximately 15 years of age, part-time paid employment in the community was sought for each participant, while the half day of classroom study continued. In stage three, the boys were no longer in the school program, and moved into full-time employment. Control group boys were enrolled in regular classrooms. Post-treatment assessment was done when the boys were 19 years old.

Prior to the eighth grade (i.e. pretreatment), the intervention group had a higher percentage of police reports of arrests relative to the control group (ES = −0.12). From ages 13 to 16, the intervention group continued to show a higher percentage of arrests relative to the control group (ES = −0.29), including a higher percentage of arrests for more than one offense (ES = −0.18) and for serious offenses (ES = −0.24). Between ages 17 and 19, the intervention had a slightly lower percentage of arrests compared with the control group (ES = 0.04), including a lower percentage of arrests for more than one offense (ES = 0.10), and for serious offenses (ES = 0.23). The authors suggest that the absence of an intervention effect on arrest rates in early adolescence may have been due to grouping delinquent boys together in work and classroom settings, an effect that has been found more recently (Dishion & Andrews, 1995; McCord, 1997). They also suggest that the suppressive effect regular school had on arrest rates in the control group in early adolescence was not present in later adolescence.

The Youth Development Project (YDP; Reckless & Dinitz, 1972) investigated whether a one school year intervention with potentially delinquent boys would lower delinquency and dropout rates over a 3-year follow-up period compared with untreated controls. Boys identified by their sixth-grade teachers as likely candidates for future delinquency were randomly assigned to all-boy intervention or control regular classrooms in grade seven. The intervention consisted of remedial reading exercises, teacher group lesson planning in consultation with project staff, teacher group discussion of student behavior problems with a psychiatrist, and role-modelling of social relationships. The intervention failed to have an effect on police contacts in the 3 years following the end of the intervention, relative to controls (ES = −0.03). Project teachers rated the intervention boys as lower in delinquency potential relative to control boys in one cohort of participants 2 years after the seventh grade. Self-report delinquency was not significantly lower in the intervention boys compared with controls at this assessment point either. The authors hypothesized that the intervention may not have been strong enough to effect behavioral change.

At least three school interventions implemented at the middle or early high school level to prevent delinquent behavior have applied behavioral techniques to alter the classroom environment. In one of a number of cohorts of the Preparation through Responsive Educational Program (PREP; Wodarski & Filipczak, 1982; Wodarski, Filipczak, McCombs, Koustenis & Rusilko, 1979), 60 students, mean age 13 years, who exhibited evidence of academic or social problems in the prior year were matched and randomly assigned to either the intervention or a no-treatment control group. The intervention involved individualized and small-group instruction in core courses (reading, English, mathematics), daily social skills training, and family skills training to promote increased parental involvement in school and management programs at home. Behavioral contracts were negotiated for classes taken in the regular school program, with positive reinforcers delivered for academic performance and appropriate social behavior. The intervention lasted for one year. At 4-year follow-up, 40 students were assessed. Of 33 intervention–control comparisons on self- and parent-reported juvenile problem behaviors, only two comparisons were statistically significant. Thus, the intervention was not successful in reducing delinquency in the long term.

A second school intervention based on behavioral principles was the Family and School Consultation Project (Stuart, Jayaratne, & Tripodi, 1976; Stuart & Tripodi, 1973). In this study, 60 students, primarily ages 13–15 years, and referred by assistant principals for prior problem behavior, were randomly assigned to an intervention or placebo control group. The intervention centered around the negotiation of behavioral contracts at school. Special privileges were given for meeting specific responsibilities; sanctions were imposed for lapses in contract compliance. Home-based consequences were made contingent on academic and behavioral outcomes in school and, later, behavioral goals at home. The intervention continued for 4 months. Only one measure of delinquency was reported: court contacts. At baseline, before the intervention, one of 30 participants in the intervention group and none of the 30 control group participants had had contact with the court system. At post-treatment, none of the intervention group and two of the 30 control group participants had court contacts. This difference was not statistically significant (ES = 0.37).

A final intervention using behavioral techniques to alter the classroom environment was reported by Bry and George (1980). They developed an intervention based on the notion that adolescent problem behaviors are preceded by feelings of cynicism concerning the predictability of the world and feelings of decreased coping self-efficacy. They endeavored to create environments in which desired consequences were obtainable through one's actions. Their two-year program was administered to seventh-grade urban adolescents with some combination of: (a) low academic achievement motivation, (b) family problems, or (c) frequent or serious discipline referrals. Participants within the same classroom with similar sixth-grade records were paired and randomly assigned to an intervention or control group. Working closely with teachers, the participants' school behaviors (e.g. attendance, tardiness, disciplinary actions) were closely monitored. Positive reinforcement (e.g. praise, a positive letter sent home, points that allowed the student to participate in a school trip) for decreases in undesirable school behaviors (e.g. tardiness) and increases in desirable behavior (e.g. following rules) was given. Failing these methods, individual schoolwork monitoring sessions were scheduled with a paraprofessional.

At age $15^{1}/_{2}$, one year after the end of the intervention, self-reported criminal behavior was significantly lower in the intervention group ($n = 29$) compared with the controls ($n = 29$). At age $19^{1}/_{2}$, five years after the intervention, significantly fewer of the intervention participants (three of 30) had county court files, compared with the control group (nine of 30; ES = 0.51) (Bry, 1982).

Two studies have reported on interventions carried out in a school setting, but did not directly involve the alteration of the classroom/school environment or teaching styles of instructors. Lochman (1992) reported on a 3-year follow-up of a cognitive–behavioral anger control intervention in a large number of teacher-nominated aggressive pre-adolescent boys. The intervention involved weekly, hour-long group sessions in school, for four to five months, in which participants learned about using self-statements to inhibit impulsive behavior, identified problems and generated response alternatives to them, watched videotapes of children modelling adaptive problem-solving, planned and made their own videos portraying adaptive problem-solving, and used discussions, role-playing and dialoguing to develop problem-solving skills. Three years post-treatment, relative to untreated aggressive boys, the anger control group did not show differences in their self-reported levels of general behavioral deviance (ES = 0.11), including crimes against persons (ES = –0.12), or general theft (ES = 0.19). There were differences between the anger control and untreated aggressive boys on substance abuse, self-esteem, and problem-solving skills, with the anger control boys fairing better on these dimensions.

An intervention component of the Montréal Longitudinal-Experimental Study (MLES; Tremblay, Kurtz, Mâsse, Vitaro, & Pihl, 1995) was also administered in a school setting. In this indicated intervention to prevent conduct problem behavior, low SES boys who scored high on disruptiveness were randomly assigned to either an intervention, attention/observation control, or no-treatment control groups. The intervention had two components: parent training in effective child-rearing and social skills training in children. The social skills training sessions were administered by professional child-care workers in the schools over lunch period, and involved training in prosocial skills, problem-solving, and self-control in conflict situations. This component was administered in a group format, composed of four to seven school peers, with a ratio of teacher-nominated prosocial to disruptive youth of three to one. The parent training component was administered in the boys' homes. The intervention was 2 years long; after this the groups were assessed yearly for 6 years on self-report delinquency. Court records were also searched for evidence of extreme delinquent behavior. The results indicated a reduction of self-reported delinquency in the intervention group compared with the combined (attention/observation and no-treatment) control group (ES across all six years = 0.24). There were no differences between the intervention and combined control groups on court-registered delinquent offenses, however (ES = –0.07).

The final two indicated school interventions are unique in that they were applied at an early age, similar to the Abecedarian Project (Clarke & Campbell, 1997) reviewed above. These two well-known preschool prevention studies utilized the High/Scope classroom curriculum (Schweinhart, Barnes, & Weikart, 1993; Schweinhart & Weikart, 1997). This curriculum encourages an open-framework approach to education where both the teacher and the child initiate learning activities. Children are encouraged daily to plan, do, and review. One might hypothesize that it may be this continual focus on planning and reviewing that impacts positively on delinquency, particularly given that early-adolescent aggressive boys have been shown to have poorer executive functions, including the ability to plan and sequence behavior (Séguin et al., 1995). Both studies were indicated preventive interventions; the children selected had lower IQs and were from low SES families. In one study, children were paired on IQ and randomly assigned to either the High/Scope curriculum or a no-treatment control group (Schweinhart et al., 1993). In the second study, children were randomly assigned to either the High/Scope curriculum, a Direct Instruction curriculum (character-ized as a programmed-learning approach, in which the teacher initiates/instructs and the children respond), or a Nursery School curriculum model (characterized as a child-centered approach, in which the child initiates and the teacher responds) (Schweinhart & Weikart, 1997). Intervention began when the children were 3 to 4 years old, and lasted for one to two years. Children in the first study have been followed for 22 years, to age 27 (Schweinhart et al., 1993), and in the second study for 18 years, to age 22 (Schweinhart & Weikart, 1997). Both studies have demonstrated significant reductions in self-report and officially-recorded delinquency at follow-up (ESs between 0.20 and 0.50; see Table 7.1).

ON-GOING SCHOOL INTERVENTION TRIALS

Two on-going large-scale preventive interventions for conduct disorder contain prominent school components. The Fast Track Project (Conduct Problems Prevention Research Group, 1992) combines a universal program (a five-year, teacher-led classroom curriculum focusing on the development of emotional con-cepts, social understanding, and self-control) with an indicated intervention for high-risk children (child social skills training, tutoring in reading, and classroom friendship enhancement, as well as parent-training). This package has been imple-mented in elementary school children beginning in grade one. Preliminary results indicate that both the universal and indicated components demonstrate positive effects on disruptive behavior after one to two years of intervention (Coie & Conduct Problems Prevention Research Group, 1997; Conduct Problems Prevention Research Group, 1997). It is expected that this sample will be fol-lowed into early adulthood, allowing for the assessment of delinquent behavior.

In the Metropolitan Area Child Study (Metropolitan Area Child Study Research Group, 1997), 16 schools have been randomly assigned to one of three increasingly intensive intervention conditions or a no-treatment control condi-tion to test their effects on aggressive behavior in elementary school children.

The first intervention group has received a classroom enhancement program (involving a teacher education program, collaborative support for project staff, and a 40-session social cognitive curriculum for the children); the second has received the classroom enhancement program plus small group social skills training for high-risk children; and the third has received both the classroom enhancement program and small group training plus a family intervention for high-risk children and their families. Preliminary results after two years of intervention reveal reduced aggression in the most extremely aggressive children, with the greatest impact from the full intervention condition. Follow-up into late adolescence will similarly allow for the measurement of delinquent behavior.

WHAT WORKS?

There are a number of advantages to intervening in the schools to prevent delinquency. The majority of children attend school. This facilitates the identification of children exhibiting aggressive behavior at an early age. These children may be targeted for intervention to improve academic achievement and promote prosocial behavior. Children in school are also more accessible for the application of an intervention. Also, variability in delinquency rates across schools (Rutter, 1983) indicates that the potential for effective intervention at the classroom or school level to reduce delinquency exists.

From this review, it is evident that wide variability exists between studies in the types of interventions implemented, the characteristics of the study participants (age, risk factors), the length of the interventions, the length of follow-up periods, and the types of outcome measures. This makes the task of drawing conclusions concerning which school interventions, or components thereof, are effective in reducing delinquency, difficult. A few general conclusions can be advanced, however. The application of behavioral techniques in the classroom may hold promise for the prevention of delinquency. The studies by Hawkins and his associates demonstrate that teacher training in classroom management, interactive teaching, and cooperative learning, particularly in the context of a multimodal intervention package, can lead to reductions in delinquent behavior and other negative outcomes (Hawkins et al., 1988; 1999). Two studies utilizing behavioral contracts for the completion of academic and behavioral goals, with clear rewards for successful completion and costs for breaches, demonstrated both short-term (Stuart et al., 1976) and long-term (Bry, 1982) reductions in delinquency. Notably, and regrettably, one study utilizing behavioral techniques along with other components such as social skills training for a substantial period of time, and with a substantial follow-up, failed to demonstrate effects on delinquency outcomes (Wodarski & Filipczak, 1982). The reasons for this lack of effect are not readily apparent.

School interventions emphasizing moral reasoning or social studies have also demonstrated some efficacy in reducing delinquent behavior. Although Arbuthnot and Gordon (1986) found no effect of their moral reasoning intervention on delinquency after one year, at post-treatment there was a significant reduction in delinquency in the intervention group, similar to that demonstrated in the STATUS project, an intervention emphasizing personal responsibility and the importance of order and rules (Gottfredson & Gottfredson, 1992). It may be that longer, more intensive moral reasoning interventions might reduce delinquency over the long term.

More generally, interventions that incorporate school components along with other components, such as home visits (Schweinhart et al., 1993; Schweinhart & Weikart, 1997), parent training (Hawkins et al., 1999; Tremblay et al., 1995), and child social skills training (Hawkins et al., 1999) appear to be more effective than those with only one component. Intuitively, it makes sense that changing relationships and environments in multiple areas (e.g. school, family, peers) would lead to greater behavioral change than altering one area only. For example, the absence of a home visit component in the Abecedarian Project (Clarke & Campbell, 1997), similar to that implemented in the Perry Preschool and Preschool Curriculum Studies, may have led to the negative findings on crime, despite improvements in IQ, reading ability and grade retention rate. A home visit component may have allowed for the generalization of classroom learning to the home environment, perhaps facilitating continued learning after the completion of the intervention.

Intervening at younger ages, before the development of delinquent behavior, may be the most profitable course of action. Of the studies reviewed, the two multimodal interventions beginning in preschool appear to be among the most effective in preventing delinquency (Schweinhart et al., 1993; Schweinhart & Weikart, 1997). Also, interventions should be relatively lengthy. Studies with larger effects on delinquency in the present review tended to be those with intervention periods greater than one year (e.g. Bry, 1982; Gottfredson & Gottfredson, 1992; Hawkins et al., 1999; Schweinhart et al., 1993; Schweinhart & Weikart, 1997; Tremblay et al., 1995) with some notable exceptions (Ahlstrom & Havighurst, 1982; Clarke & Campbell, 1997; Gottfredson, 1986).

GUIDELINES FOR FUTURE INTERVENTIONS

Ramey and Ramey (1998) recently outlined six principles to inform the design of early interventions to improve cognitive, academic, and social outcomes. From their viewpoint, early interventions should:

1. begin at an early age and continue for a substantial time period;
2. be time intensive (i.e. provide much contact within the intervention period);
3. provide direct intervention (i.e. direct contact with the children, as opposed to, for example, parent training only);
4. be multimodal, providing comprehensive services;
5. be cognizant of individual differences in program benefits (i.e. some children benefit more than others); and

6. provide adequate environmental supports after the end of the intervention to maintain attitude and behavior change.

These principles are directly applicable to the design of preventive interventions for delinquency that incorporate a school component. More research into multimodal interventions implemented in preschool or the primary grades is warranted. School components within these interventions might incorporate cognitive training (of the type implemented by Schweinhart et al., 1993), social skills training, and teacher training in behavioral principles. Such multicomponent interventions implemented early in development appear most likely to have salutary effects on delinquency outcomes later in life.

REFERENCES

Ahlstrom, W., & Havighurst, R. J. (1982). The Kansas City work/study experiment. In D. J. Safer (Ed.), *School programs for disruptive adolescents* (pp. 259–275). Baltimore, MD: University Park Press.

Arbuthnot, J., & Gordon, D. A. (1986). Behavioral and cognitive effects of a moral reasoning development intervention for high-risk behavior-disordered adolescents. *Journal of Consulting and Clinical Psychology, 54*, 208–216.

Bry, B. H. (1982). Reducing the incidence of adolescent problems through preventive intervention: One- and five-year follow-up. *American Journal of Community Psychology, 10*, 265–276.

Bry, B. H., & George, F. E. (1980). The preventive effects of early intervention on the attendance and grades of urban adolescents. *Professional Psychology, 11*, 252–260.

Campbell, F. A., & Ramey, C. T. (1995). Cognitive and school outcomes for high-risk African–American students at middle adolescence: Positive effects of early intervention. *American Educational Research Journal, 32*, 743–772.

Clarke, S. H., & Campbell, F. A. (1997). *The Abecedarian Project and youth crime.* Paper presented at the biennial meeting of the Society for Research in Child Development, Washington, DC.

Cohen, J. (1977). *Statistical power analysis for the behavior sciences* (Rev. ed.). New York: Academic Press.

Coie, J. D., & Conduct Problems Prevention Research Group (1997). *Testing developmental theory of antisocial behavior with outcomes from the Fast Track Prevention Project.* Paper presented at the annual meeting of the American Psychological Association, Chicago.

Conduct Problems Prevention Research Group (1992). A developmental and clinical model for the prevention of conduct disorder: The FAST Track Program. *Development and Psychopathology, 4*, 509–527.

Conduct Problems Prevention Research Group (1997). *Prevention of antisocial behavior: Initial findings from the Fast Track Project.* Symposium (R. J. McMahon, chair) presented at the biennial meeting of the Society for Research in Child Development, Washington, DC.

Dishion, T. J., & Andrews, D. W. (1995). Preventing escalation in problem behaviors with high-risk young adolescents: Immediate and 1-year outcomes. *Journal of Consulting and Clinical Psychology, 63*, 538–548.

Durlak, J. A. (1995). *School-based prevention programs for children and adolescents.* Thousand Oaks, CA: Sage.

Farrell, A. D., & Meyer, A. L. (1997). The effectiveness of a school-based curriculum for reducing violence among urban sixth-grade students. *American Journal of Public Health, 87*, 979–984.

Farrington, D. P. (1985). Predicting self-reported and official delinquency. In D. P. Farrington & R. Tarling (Eds.), *Prediction in criminology* (Vol. 8, pp. 150–173). New York: State University of New York Press.

Farrington, D. P. (1987). Early precursors of frequent offending. In J. Q. Wilson & G. C. Loury (Eds.), *From children to citizens (Vol. III). Families, schools and delinquency prevention* (pp. 27–50). New York: Springer-Verlag.

Farrington, D. P. (1991). Childhood aggression and adult violence: Early precursors and life outcomes. In D. J. Pepler & K. H. Rubin (Eds.), *Development and treatment of childhood aggression* (pp. 5–29). Hillsdale, NJ: Erlbaum.

Farrington, D. P. (1994). Childhood, adolescent, and adult features of violent males. In L. R. Huesmann (Ed.), *Aggressive behavior: Current perspectives* (pp. 215–240). New York: Plenum.

Fiquera-McDonough, J. (1986). School context, gender, and delinquency. *Journal of Youth and Adolescence, 15*, 79–98.

Gordon, R. (1987). An operational classification of disease prevention. In J. A. Steinberg & M. M. Silverman (Eds.), *Preventing mental disorders: A research perspective* (pp. 20–26). Rockville, MD: Department of Health and Human Services.

Gottfredson, D. C. (1986). An empirical test of school-based environmental and individual inter entions to reduce the risk of delinquent behavior. *Criminology, 24*, 705–731.

Gottfredson, D. C., & Gottfredson, G. D. (1992). Theory-guided investigation: Three field experiments. In J. McCord & R. E. Tremblay (Eds.), *Preventing antisocial behavior: Interventions from birth through adolescence* (pp. 311–329). New York: Guilford.

Gottfredson, G. D. (1987). Peer group interventions to reduce the risk of delinquent behavior: A selection review and new evaluation. *Criminology, 25*, 671–714.

Hawkins, J. D., Catalano, R. F., Kosterman, R., Abbott, R., & Hill, K. G. (1999). Preventing adolescent health-risk behaviors by strengthening protection during childhood. *Archives of Pediatrics and Adolescent Medicine, 153*(3), 226–234.

Hawkins, J. D., Doueck, H. J., & Lishner, D. M. (1988). Changing teaching practices in mainstream classrooms to improve bonding and behavior of low achievers. *American Educationnal Research Journal, 25*, 31–50.

Hawkins, J. D., Herrenkohl, T., Farrington, D. P., Brewer, D., Catalano, R. F., & Harachi, T. W. (1998). A review of predictors of youth violence. In R. Loeber & D. P. Farrington (Eds.), *Serious and violent juvenile offenders: Risk factors and successful interventions* (pp. 106–146). Thousand Oaks, CA: Sage.

Hawkins, J. D., & Lam, T. (1987). Teacher practices, social development and delinquency. In J. D. Burchard & S. N. Burchard et al. (Eds.), *Prevention of delinquent behavior: Primary prevention of psychopathologyp* (Vol. X, pp. 241–274). Beverly Hills, CA: Sage.

Hedges, L. V., & Olkin, I. (1985). *Statistical methods for meta-analysis*. New York: Academic Press.

Huesmann, L. R., Eron, L. D., Lefkowitz, M. M., & Walder, L. O. (1984). Stability of aggression over time and generations. *Developmental Psychology, 20*, 1120–1134.

Kellam, S. G., Rebok, G. W., Ialongo, N., & Mayer, L. S. (1994). The course and malleability of aggressive behavior from early first grade into middle school: Results of a developmental epidemiologically-based preventive trial. *Journal of Child Psychology Psychiatry, 35*, 259–281.

Kolvin, I., Garside, R. F., Nicol, A. R., MacMillan, A., Wolstenholme, F., & Leitch, I. M. (1986). *Help starts here*. New York: Tavistock.

Lane, T. W., & Murakami, J. (1987). School programs for delinquency prevention and intervention. In E. K. Morris & C. J. Braukmann (Eds.), *Behavioral approaches to crime and delinquency: A handbook of application, research and concepts* (pp. 305–327). New York: Plenum.

Lochman, J. E. (1992). Cognitive–behavioral intervention with aggressive boys: Three-year follow-up and preventive effects. *Journal of Consulting and Clinical Psychology, 60,* 426–432.

Loeber, R., & Dishion, T. J. (1983). Early predictors of male delinquency: A review. *Psychological Bulletin, 94,* 68–99.

Loeber, R., & Stouthamer-Loeber, M. (1998). Development of juvenile aggression and violence: Some common misconceptions and controversies. *American Psychologist, 53,* 242–259.

Lynam, D. R. (1996). Early identification of chronic offenders: Who is the fledgling psychopath? *Psychological Bulletin, 120,* 209–234.

McCord, J. (1997). *Some unanticipated consequences of summer camps.* Paper presented at the biennial meeting of the Society for Research in Child Development, Washington, DC.

Metropolitan Area Child Study Research Group (1997). *A cognitive–ecological approach to preventing aggression in urban and inner-city settings: Preliminary outcomes.* Manuscript submitted for publication.

Olds, D. L., Eckenrode, J., Henderson, C. R. Jr., Kitzman, H., Powers, J., Cole, R., Sidora, K., Morris, P., Pettitt, L. M., & Luckey, D. (1997). Long-term effects of home visitation on maternal life course and child abuse and neglect: Fifteen-year follow-up of a randomized trial. *Journal of the American Medical Association, 278,* 637–643.

Olweus, D. (1991). Bully/victim problems among schoolchildren: Basic facts and effects of a school based intervention program. In D. J. Pepler & K. H. Rubin (Eds.), *The development and treatment of childhood aggression* (pp. 411–448). Hillsdale, NJ: Lawrence Erlbaum.

Ramey, C. T., & Ramey, S. L. (1998). Early intervention and early experience. *American Psychologist, 53,* 109–120.

Reckless, W. C., & Dinitz, S. (1972). *The prevention of juvenile delinquency: An experiment.* Columbus, OH: Ohio State University Press.

Rutter, M. (1983). School effects on pupil progress: Research findings and policy implications. *Child Development, 54,* 1–19.

Schweinhart, L. L., Barnes, H. V., & Weikart, D. P. (1993). *Significant benefits. The High/Scope Perry School Study through age 27.* Ypsilanti, MI: High/Scope Press.

Schweinhart, L. L., & Weikart, D. P. (1997). *Lasting differences: The High/Scope Preschool Curriculum Comparison Study through age 23.* (Monographs of the High/Scope Educational Research Foundation, 12). Ypsilanti, MI: High/Scope Press.

Séguin, J. R., Pihl, R. O., Harden, P. W., Tremblay, R. E., & Boulerice, B. (1995). Cognitive and neuropsychological characteristics of physically aggressive boys. *Journal of Abnormal Psychology, 104,* 614–624.

Seitz, V., Rosenbaum, L. K., & Apfel, H. (1985). Effects of family support intervention: A ten-year follow-up. *Child Development, 56,* 376–391.

Stattin, H., & Magnusson, D. (1989). The role of early aggressive behavior in the frequency, seriousness and types of later crime. *Journal of Consulting and Clinical Psychology, 57,* 710–718.

Stuart, R. B., Jayaratne, S., & Tripodi, T. (1976). Changing adolescent deviant behavior through reprogramming the behavior of parents and teachers: An experimental evaluation. *Canadian Journal of Behavioral Science, 8,* 132–144.

Stuart, R. B., & Tripodi, T. (1973). Experimental evaluation of three time-constrained behavioral treatments for predelinquents and delinquents. In R. D. Rubin, J. P. Brady, & J. D. Henderson (Eds.), *Advances in behavioral therapy* (Vol. 4, pp. 1–12). New York: Academic Press.

Tremblay, R. E., Kurtz, L., Mâsse, L. C., Vitaro, F., & Pihl, R. O. (1995). A bimodal preventive intervention for disruptive kindergarten boys: Its impact through mid-adolescence. *Journal of Consulting and Clinical Psychology, 63,* 560–568.

Tremblay, R. E., Mâsse, B., Perron, D., LeBlanc, M., Schwartzman, A. E., & Ledingham, J. E. (1992). Early disruptive behavior, poor school achievement, delinquent behavior and delinquent personality: Longitudinal analyses. *Journal of Consulting and Clinical Psychology, 60,* 64–72.

White, J. L., Moffitt, T. E., Earls, F., Robins, L., & Silva, P. A. (1990). How early can we tell? Predictors of childhood conduct disorder and adolescent delinquency. *Criminology, 28,* 507–533.

Wodarski, J. S., & Filipczak, J. (1982). Behavioral intervention in public schools: II. Long-term follow-up. In D. J. Safer (Ed.), *School programs for disruptive adolescents* (pp. 201–214). Baltimore, MD: University Park Press.

Wodarski, J. S., Filipczak, J., McCombs, D., Koustenis, G., & Rusilko, S. (1979). Follow-up on behavioral intervention with troublesome adolescents. *Journal of Behavior Therapy and Experimental Psychiatry, 10,* 181–188.

Yoshikawa, H. (1994). Prevention as cumulative protection: Effects of early family support and education on chronic delinquency and its risks. *Psychological Bulletin, 115,* 28–54.

Chapter 8

Skills Training

Clive R. Hollin
and
Emma J. Palmer
University of Leicester, Leicester, UK

INTRODUCTION

There can be little doubt that social skills training (SST) has proved immensely popular with practitioners working with a vast range of client groups (Hollin & Trower, 1986a, 1986b, 1988). In terms of criminal populations, both young and adult offenders have proved to be popular targets for SST: there are several reviews available (Cunliffe, 1992; Henderson & Hollin, 1983, 1986; Hollin, 1990a; Howells, 1986; Huff, 1987; Spence, 1979; Templeton, 1990), as well as texts to inform the practice of SST with offenders (Priestley et al., 1984; Priestley & McGuire, 1985).

The original social skills model (Argyle & Kendon, 1967) held that socially skilled behaviour, perhaps better termed socially competent behaviour, consists of three related components, namely social perception, social cognition, and social performance (Hollin & Trower, 1986c). Social perception refers to the ability to perceive and understand social cues and signals; social cognition, in this sense, is analogous to social information processing; and social performance is, of course, observable social action. Thus, SST seeks to help the individual develop their social skills in order to function more effectively in their social world.

The application of this way of thinking about social behaviour with respect to offender populations raises two issues. First, is there any evidence to indicate that offenders have particular difficulties in any specific areas of social ability? Second, is an offender's level of social skills related to their offending?

The Essential *Handbook of Offender Assessment and Treatment.* Edited by C. R. Hollin.
© 2004 John Wiley & Sons Ltd.

SOCIAL PERCEPTION

The ability to recognize, understand, and interpret interpersonal cues is central to all social behaviour (Argyle, 1983). In a study of social perception in delinquents, McCown, Johnson, and Austin (1986) investigated the ability of young offenders to recognize emotion from facial expression cues. They found that, compared with non-delinquents, the young offenders could reliably recognize happiness, anger, and fear; but were less able to identify the facial expressions of sadness, surprise, and disgust. In a similar fashion, a body of evidence has accumulated to suggest that children and adolescents who struggle socially, particularly with respect to aggressive behaviour, have difficulties in both the selection and interpretation of social cues (e.g. Akhtar & Bradley, 1991; Dodge, Murphy, & Buchsbaum, 1984; Dodge & Tomlin, 1987). Similarly, a study by Lipton, McDonel, and McFall (1987) suggested that sexually aggressive men may misperceive social cues in male–female social interactions.

The misperception of social cues may in turn lead to misattribution of intent, so that the actions of other people are mistakenly seen as hostile or threatening (Crick & Dodge, 1996; Lochman & Dodge, 1994; Slaby & Guerra, 1988). The way a social encounter is perceived will, in turn, influence the way in which the person deals with a given social encounter.

SOCIAL COGNITION

Following social perception, the individual must decide on a suitable response. This decision-making requires the ability to generate feasible courses of action, consider alternatives, and make plans towards achieving the desired outcome (Spivack, Platt, & Shure, 1976). Several studies have suggested that some offenders, particularly young offenders, may experience difficulties in solving social interaction problems. For example, using the Adolescent Problem Inventory (API; see Palmer & Hollin, 1996), Freedman, Rosenthal, Donahoe, Schlundt and McFall (1978) found that young offenders gave less socially competent responses than non-offenders to a series of social problems. The delinquents used a more limited range of alternatives to solve interpersonal problems, and relied more on verbal and physical aggression. Veneziano and Veneziano (1988) used the API to classify delinquents as "incompetent", "moderately competent", and "competent" in their knowledge of social skills. These three groups differed significantly in the number of behavioural difficulties they experienced, on scores on various measures of personality, and on measures of social values and morality. In general, young people with less knowledge were socially and personally disadvantaged compared with their peers; the delinquents showed a lower knowledge of social skills than a sample of "good citizens". Similarly, Simonian, Tarnowski, and Gibbs (1991), using a revised version of the API, found that API scores were related to delinquent activity (official and self-report). Interestingly, Cole, Chan, and Lytton (1989) found that delinquents accurately perceived themselves as less skilled than their peers.

Gaffney and McFall (1981) developed the Problem Inventory for Adolescent Girls (PIAG), a self-report measure of social competence in dealing with awkward social situations. They reported that delinquent girls gave less socially competent responses with respect to their probable actions in the various social situations. Furthermore, it was found that delinquency was more closely related to skill deficits in interacting with adults in positions of authority rather than in interacting with peers. Ward and McFall (1986), also using the PIAG, found that female young offenders gave less competent responses to the problem situations.

It is clear that, perhaps particularly for children and adolescents, social cognition, including social problem solving, is related to delinquent and antisocial behaviour. There is a weight of research in the tradition illustrated above, that strongly suggests that difficulties in setting social goals, solving social problems, and accurately perceiving social feedback on performance are critical factors in understanding antisocial behaviour (e.g. Akhtar & Bradley, 1991; Crick & Dodge, 1994; Demorest, 1992; Hollin, 1990b; Ross & Fabiano, 1985).

SOCIAL PERFORMANCE

In a typical study, Spence (1981a) compared the social performance skills of young male offenders with non-delinquent controls matched for age, academic performance, and social background. The delinquents showed significantly less eye contact and speech, but more "fiddling" and gross body movements, behaviours shown to relate to poor observer ratings of social skill (Spence, 1981b). On global ratings of social skill, social anxiety, and employability the delinquent group was rated less favourably than the non-delinquents.

In summary, the research suggests that some offenders do experience difficulties with social skills. However, it would be wrong to assume that this is a characteristic of all offenders: clearly offenders are a heterogeneous population with a wide distribution of social ability. Nonetheless, there are offenders with social difficulties and the hypothesis has been formed that there is a link between social ability and offending. If this hypothesis is true, in some cases at least, then remediation of these social difficulties through SST may lead to a reduction in offending. However, as noted in the extant reviews, there is little in the way of convincing evidence that SST has any systematic effect on recidivism. A number of studies have, however, been published since the last reviews and the remainder of this chapter focuses on their contribution to this field.

RECENT EVIDENCE: AN OVERVIEW

The extant reviews give a picture of the field of skills training with offenders up to the 1990s. Since that time it is clear that skills training has increasingly been used as a component of multimodal programmes (e.g. Goldstein, Glick, & Gibbs, 1998) rather than as a "stand alone" intervention. However, several studies with an explicit focus on skills training, published after 1989, were identified and these are discussed below. There are two main groups of studies: the first concerns skills training with general offender groups, the second involves skills training with sex offenders.

Several studies with juvenile offenders have been reported in the post-1989 literature. Lennings (1990) evaluated a social skills programme for three juvenile offenders in a detention centre. The programme focused on enhancing self-esteem, increasing assertion and communication skills, and challenging sex-role behaviours. The evaluation showed that the programme was successful in achieving positive gains in the target areas. Elrod and Minor (1992) also evaluated a programme with juvenile offenders, in which traditional skills training was bundled with outdoor adventure and parent skills training to form "Project Explore". The offending rates of juveniles participating in Project Explore were compared with those of juveniles who received standard probation. At two-year follow-up, both groups showed a reduction in offending, but there was no difference in the offending rates of the two groups. The design of the evaluation makes it impossible to disaggregate the relative effect of the skills training component.

Mathur and Rutherford (1994) took a much narrower focus in an evaluation of a social skills programme designed specifically to improve the conversational skills of female juvenile delinquents. The programme was a clear success in improving a range of conversational skills, such as using names and making positive statements, but did not report offending rates. Leiber and Mawhorr (1995) reported an evaluation of the impact of the "Second Chance" programme with juvenile delinquents. The programme consisted of social skills training, pre-employment training, and exploiting job placement opportunities. The design of the evaluation allowed a comparison of the offending, at one-year follow-up, of juveniles participating in the programme with juveniles who received traditional court juvenile services. The rates of recidivism of the juveniles participating in the Second Chance programme, as measured by official referral to a juvenile or adult court, did not differ significantly from the controls. However, the young people completing the programme, as compared with the controls, were more likely to be charged with *less* severe offences. As Leiber and Mawhorr note, it is not possible to assess the specific effect of the skills training in the general pattern of results. Finally, Wright (1995) reported a study looking at the effectiveness of social skills training (with an explicit cognitive bias) with conduct-disordered boys in residential treatment. The intervention was successful in increasing self-esteem, self-control, and social skills: the lack of a control group makes outcome effectiveness difficult to judge, but there were indications of beneficial effects with respect to later community adjustment and low rates of offending.

Marshall, Turner, and Barbaree (1989) reported an evaluation of a life skills training programme for penitentiary inmates. The focus of the programme was on a range of skills including problem-solving, attitudes towards authority, and

Table 8.1 Summary of recent studies

Study	Offender group	Training methods	Target and generalization measures	Evaluation method and measures	Results
Elrod & Minor (1992)	43 juvenile delinquents: 22 treatment group 21 controls. Males and females. Aged 12–17 years.	Group: instruction, role-play with peers and parents, discussion, homework. 8 weeks plus 3 months a year later. Weekly.	Prevalence of official offending.	Official records. Pre-post training.	Both groups showed a reduction in status and criminal offences over two-year follow-up. No significant differences between the two groups.
Graves, Openshaw & Adams (1992)	18 young sex offenders 12 controls. Aged 12–19 years.	Group: Modelling rehearsal, encouragement, homework. 9 weeks.	Giving and getting feedback, resisting peer pressure, problem-solving, negotiation, following instructions, conversation skills.	Parental self-report scales for parent–child relationship. Adolescent self-report for self-concept. Behaviour checklist completed by parents of adolescents. Pre-post training.	Significantly more social skills shown by treatment group than controls after training. Improvement in parent-child communication after training. Some evidence of improvement in social competence by training group, from adolescents' perceptions. Suggestion that self-concept improved for training group.
Hopkins (1993)	8 sex offenders 7 controls.	Group: discussion, observation, role-play, feedback.	Social anxiety, self-esteem, fear of negative evaluation, appropriate social behaviour.	Staff ratings of behaviour. Ratings of videoed interactions with unknown female.	Increased use of appropriate behaviour among treatment group. Increased self-esteem among treatment group.

continued overleaf

Table 8.1 (continued)

Study	Offender group	Training methods	Target and generalization measures	Evaluation method and measures	Results
		6 weeks, 1 hour/week.		Self-report scales. Pre-post training and 6 month follow-up for treatment group only.	Decrease among controls. Decreased social anxiety among treatment group. No change among controls. Decreased fear of negative evaluation among treatment group. Small increase among controls.
Jones & McColl (1991)	12 male offenders. 12 controls taking part in conventional psychotherapy group.	Group: role-play, feedback, self-evaluation. 3 weeks, 2 sessions/week.	Desire for participation in groups. Need for social inclusion, ability to take on group membership roles, ability to take on prosocial group roles, positive feelings about group membership.	Self-report scales. Pre-post training.	Desire to participate in groups increased for both groups. Treatment group took on more roles post-training than controls, especially as pleaser, risk-taker, and director. Roles occupied valued more positively by treatment group.
Leiber & Mawhorr (1995)	Juvenile delinquents: 57 treatment group, 56 matched controls, 85 non-matched controls. Males and	Group: instruction, discussion, homework. 16 weeks.	Official recidivism.	Official referral to court. Pre-post treatment.	No reduction in recidivism at one-year follow-up for any group. However, treatment group referred for less serious offences.

Study	Sample	Intervention	Target behaviours	Assessment	Results
(continued)	females. Aged 9–18 years.				
Lennings (1991)	3 male juvenile delinquents. Aged 16–19 years.	Group: role-play. 6 sessions over a 3-month period.	Assertion, self-control, self-esteem, and institutional behaviour.	Self-report scales and staff assessment for behaviour. Pre-post training.	No statistical analysis due to small sample. However, results show change in positive direction on assertion, self-control, and self-esteem. Behaviour showed signs of improvement too.
Marshall, Turner, & Barbaree (1989)	68 male offenders. 22 offender controls.	Group: discussion.	Social interaction, social behaviour, attitudes, and criminal disposition.	Videoed role-play with female confederate. Self-report scales. Pre-post training.	Treatment group showed greater change over time. Controls showed little at all. After training, treatment group was less tolerant of crime, less under-assertive, more positive towards the police and courts, less concerned about being negatively evaluated, more empathic, less psychopathic, more socially skilled, and less socially anxious.
Mathur & Rutherford (1994)	9 female juvenile delinquents. Aged 13–17 years	Group: explanation, practise, modelling, role-play, feedback, transfer of skills. 5 phases: baseline, SST & prompting, prompting only,	Using others' names, using manners, making positive statements about self, others, and the present and future.	Direct observation. Throughout all 5 phases.	All targeted behaviours increased during social skills training, although the level decreased after. At follow-up, all target behaviours were at a slightly higher level than the baseline level.

continued overleaf

Table 8.1 (continued)

Study	Offender group	Training methods	Target and generalization measures	Evaluation method and measures	Results
		maintenance, follow-up. SST phase lasted 5 days.			
Valliant & Antonowicz (1991)	19 male sex offenders. 34 male adult non-sex offenders.	Group: instruction, Role-play, discussion. 5 weeks, 2 hours/week.	Anxiety, self-esteem, hostility.	Self-report scales. Pre-post training.	Self-esteem increased, and anxiety and hostility decreased after training. Sex offenders showed higher levels of self-esteem, and lower aggression and anxiety than the general offenders.
Valliant & Antonowicz (1992)	45 sex offenders including controls.	Group: instruction, role-play, discussion. 5 weeks, 2 hours/week.	Restructuring of faulty thinking, self-esteem, anxiety, and hostility.	Self-report scales. Pre-post training.	Increased self-esteem among rapists. Decrease in anxiety among rapists and molesters.
Wright (1995)	30 conduct-disordered boys in a residential setting. Aged 8–11 years.	Group: modelling, role-play, scripting, coaching, video feedback, homework. One hour/week.	Social skill competency, self-esteem, locus of control.	Self-report scales. Pre-post training.	Social skill competency appeared to increase. There were significant increases in levels of self-esteem, and the boys' locus of control became more internal. Longer-term follow-ups suggest that benefits are maintained.

practical living skills. The skills of inmates participating in the programme improved significantly as compared with controls who did not participate in the programme. Jones and McColl (1991) also evaluated a life skills programme for offenders admitted to a Forensic Inpatient Service. The programme aimed to develop skills in interacting with social groups and adopting prosocial roles, and the evaluation suggested that these aims were, in the main, achieved through the training.

Valliant and Antonowicz (1991) report the findings from an evaluation of an intervention, heavily reliant on SST, with imprisoned offenders, including sex offenders. They found that the treatment programme had positive effects on the offenders' levels of self-esteem and reduced their levels of anxiety. Similarly, Valliant and Antonowicz (1992) reported that cognitive and SST with incarcerated sex offenders increased levels of self-esteem. Graves, Openshaw, and Adams (1992) developed a SST programme for use with adolescent sex offenders. They report that the SST had a number of significant benefits, including improved communication with parents, higher levels of social competence, and positive changes in self-concept. Finally, Hopkins (1993) evaluated the effects of SST with groups of sex offenders in prison, finding a range of positive behavioural and psychological changes following training.

CONCLUDING COMMENTS

Set against the earlier reviews, it appears that SST is still a part of practice in working with offenders, but that its use as the primary means of intervention has decreased markedly. The development of the field over the past decade, and particularly the last five years, has seen the growth of multimodal programmes as the optimum means of working with offenders. While the "single modality" studies of the type discussed here are important, this importance is not based on their effects on recidivism (not measured in most of the studies) but in increasing understanding of the strengths and limitations of SST, thereby moderating unrealistic expectations of what SST can achieve (Hollin & Henderson, 1984). This growth in understanding will, in turn, feed the development of the skills training component of the more complex multimodal programmes.

REFERENCES

Akhtar, N., & Bradley, E. J. (1991). Social information processing deficits of aggressive children: Present findings and implication for social skills training. *Clinical Psychology Review, 11*, 621–644.

Argyle, M. (1983). *The psychology of interpersonal behaviour* (4th ed.). Harmondsworth, UK: Penguin Books.

Argyle, M., & Kendon, A. (1967). The experimental analysis of social performance. In L. Berkowitz (Ed.), *Advances in experimental social psychology* (Vol. 3). New York: Academic Press.

Cole, P. G., Chan, L. K. S., & Lytton, L. (1989). Perceived competence of juvenile delinquents and nondelinquents. *Journal of Special Education*, *23*, 294–302.

Crick, N. R., & Dodge, K. A. (1994). A review and reformulation of social information-processing mechanisms in children's social adjustment. *Psychological Bulletin*, *115*, 74–101.

Crick, N. R., & Dodge, K. A. (1996). Social information-processing mechanisms in reactive and proactive aggression. *Child Development*, *67*, 993–1002.

Cunliffe, T. (1992). Arresting youth crime: A review of social skills training with young offenders. *Adolescence*, *27*, 891–900.

Demorest, A. P. (1992). The role of social cognition in children's social maladjustment. *Social Cognition*, *10*, 211–233.

Dodge, K. A., Murphy, R. R., & Buchsbaum, K. (1984). The assessment of intention-cue detection skills in children: Implications for developmental psychopathology. *Child Development*, *55*, 163–173.

Dodge, K. A., & Tomlin, A. M. (1987). Utilization of self-schemas as a mechanism of interpretational bias in aggressive children. *Social Cognition*, *5*, 280–300.

Elrod, H. P., & Minor, K. I. (1992). Second wave evaluation of a multi-faceted intervention for juvenile court probationers. *International Journal of Offender Therapy and Comparative Criminology*, *36*, 247–262.

Freedman, B. J., Rosenthal, L., Donahoe, C. P., Schlundt, D. G., & McFall, R. M. (1978). A social–behavioral analysis of skills deficits in delinquent and non-delinquent adolescent boys. *Journal of Consulting and Clinical Psychology*, *46*, 1448–1462.

Gaffney, L. R., & McFall, R. M. (1981). A comparison of social skills in delinquent and nondelinquent adolescent girls using a behavioral role-playing inventory. *Journal of Consulting and Clinical Psychology*, *49*, 959–967.

Goldstein, A. P., Glick, B., & Gibbs, J. C. (1998). *Aggression Replacement Training* (Rev. ed.). Champaign, IL: Research Press.

Graves, R., Openshaw, D. K., & Adams, G. R. (1992). Adolescent sex offenders and social skills training. *International Journal of Offender Therapy and Comparative Criminology*, *36*, 139–153.

Henderson, M., & Hollin, C. R. (1983). A critical review of social skills training with young offenders. *Criminal Justice and Behavior*, *10*, 316–341.

Henderson, M., & Hollin, C. R. (1986). Social skills training and delinquency. In C. R. Hollin & P. Trower (Eds.), *Handbook of social skills training, Volume 1: Applications across the life span*. Oxford: Pergamon Press.

Hollin, C. R. (1990a). Social skills training with delinquents: A look at the evidence and some recommendations for practice. *British Journal of Social Work*, *20*, 483–493.

Hollin, C. R. (1990b). *Cognitive–behavioral interventions with young offenders*. Elmsford, NY: Pergamon Press.

Hollin, C. R., & Henderson, M. (1984). Social skills training with young offenders: False expectations and the "failure" of training. *Behavioural Psychotherapy*, *12*, 331–341.

Hollin, C. R., & Trower, P. (Eds.) (1986a). *Handbook of social skills training, Volume 1: Applications across the life span*. Oxford: Pergamon Press.

Hollin, C. R., & Trower, P. (Eds.) (1986b). *Handbook of social skills training, Volume 2: Clinical applications and new directions*. Oxford: Pergamon Press.

Hollin, C. R., & Trower, P. (1986c). Social skills training: Critique and future development. In C. R. Hollin & P. Trower (Eds.), *Handbook of social skills training, Volume 2: Clinical applications and new directions*. Oxford: Pergamon Press.

Hollin, C. R., & Trower, P. (1988). Development and applications of social skills training: A review and critique. In M. Hersen, R. M. Eisler, & P. M. Miller (Eds.), *Progress in behavior modification* (Vol. 22). Beverly Hills, CA: Sage.

Hopkins, R. E. (1993). An evaluation of social skills groups for sex offenders. *Issues in Criminological and Legal Psychology*, *19*, 52–59.

Howells, K. (1986). Social skills training and criminal and antisocial behaviour in adults. In C. R. Hollin & P. Trower (Eds.), *Handbook of social skills training, Volume 1: Applications across the life span*. Oxford: Pergamon Press.

Huff, G. (1987). Social skills training. In B. J. McGurk, D. M. Thornton, & M. Williams (Eds.), *Applying psychology to imprisonment: Theory & practice*. London: HMSO.

Jones, E. J., & McColl, M. A. (1991). Development and evaluation of an interactional life skills group for offenders. *The Occupational Therapy Journal of Research, 11*, 80–92.

Leiber, M. J., & Mawhorr, T. L. (1995). Evaluating the use of social skills training and employment with delinquent youth. *Journal of Criminal Justice, 23*, 127–141.

Lennings, C. J. (1990). Skills training in a juvenile detention centre. *Residential Treatment for Children and Youth, 8*, 39–54.

Lipton, D. N., McDonel, E. C., & McFall, R. M. (1987). Heterosocial perception in rapists. *Journal of Consulting and Clinical Psychology, 55*, 17–21.

Lochman, J. E., & Dodge, K. A. (1994). Social–cognitive processes of severely violent, moderately aggressive and nonaggressive boys. *Journal of Consulting and Clinical Psychology, 62*, 366–374.

Marshall, W. L., Turner, B. A., & Barbaree, H. E. (1989). An evaluation of life skills training for penitentiary inmates. *Journal of Offender Counseling, Services and Rehabilitation, 14*, 41–59.

Mathur, S. R., & Rutherford, R. B. (1994). Teaching conversational social skills to delinquent youth. *Behavioral Disorders, 19*, 294–305.

McCown, W., Johnson, J., & Austin, S. (1986). Inability of delinquents to recognize facial affects. *Journal of Social Behavior and Personality, 1*, 489–496.

Palmer, E. J., & Hollin, C. R. (1996). Assessing adolescent problems: An overview of the adolescent problem inventory. *Journal of Adolescence, 19*, 347–354.

Priestley, P., & McGuire, J. (1985). *Offending behaviour: Skills and stratagems for going straight*. London: Batsford.

Priestley, P., McGuire, J., Flegg, D., Hemsley, V., Welham, D., & Barnitt, R. (1984). *Social skills in prison and the community*. London: Routledge & Kegan Paul.

Ross, R. R., & Fabiano, E. A. (1985). *Time to think: A cognitive model of delinquency prevention and offender rehabilitation*. Johnson City, TN: Institute of Social Sciences and Arts.

Simonian, S., Tarnowski, K. J., & Gibbs, J. C. (1991). Social skills and antisocial conduct of delinquents. *Child Psychiatry and Human Development, 22*, 17–27.

Slaby, R. G., & Guerra, N. G. (1988). Cognitive mediators of aggression in adolescent offenders: I. Assessment. *Developmental Psychology, 24*, 580–588.

Spence, S. H. (1979). Social skills training with adolescent offenders: A review. *Behavioural Psychotherapy, 7*, 49–56.

Spence, S. H. (1981a). Differences in social skills performance between institutionalized juvenile male offenders and a comparable group of boys without offence records. *British Journal of Clinical Psychology, 20*, 163–171.

Spence, S. H. (1981b). Validation of social skills of adolescent males in an interview conversation with a previously unknown adult. *Journal of Applied Behavior Analysis, 14*, 159–168.

Spivack, G., Platt, J. J., & Shure, M. B. (1976). *The problem-solving approach to adjustment: A guide to research and intervention*. San Francisco, CA: Jossey-Bass.

Templeton, J. K. (1990). Social skills training for behavior-problem adolescents: A review. *International Journal of Partial Hospitalization, 6*, 49–60.

Valliant, P. M., & Antonowicz, D. H. (1991). Cognitive behaviour therapy and social skills training improves personality and cognition in incarcerated offenders. *Psychological Reports, 68*, 27–33.

Valliant, P. M., & Antonowicz, D. H. (1992). Rapists, incest offenders, and child molesters in treatment: Cognitive and social skills training. *International Journal of Offender Therapy and Comparative Criminology, 36*, 221–230.

Veneziano, C., & Veneziano, L. (1988). Knowledge of social skills among institutionalized juvenile delinquents: An assessment. *Criminal Justice and Behavior, 15,* 152–171.

Ward, C. I., & McFall, R. M. (1986). Further validation of the problem inventory for adolescent girls: Comparing Caucasian and black delinquents and nondelinquents. *Journal of Consulting and Clinical Psychology, 54,* 732–733.

Wright, N. A. (1995). Social skills training for conduct-disordered boys in residential treatment: A promising approach. *Residential Treatment for Children and Youth, 12,* 15–28.

Chapter 9

Anger Treatment with Offenders

Raymond W. Novaco
University of California, Irvine, USA
Mark Ramm
and
Laura Black
The State Hospital, Carstairs, Scotland, UK

INTRODUCTION

Because anger is an important antecedent of violent behaviour and because it is also a significant aspect of psychological distress associated with many clinical syndromes, advances in anger treatment offer important resources for service providers attending to the needs of various offender groups. Despite the transparent relevance of anger to intervention work with offender populations, clinical research in this field is sparse. In no small measure, this is partly due to the formidable challenges presented by the dispositions of angry and aggressive clients and the contexts in which such clients are typically found.

We present our approach to anger treatment with patients at a maximum security psychiatric hospital, aiming to portray that such work can be done efficaciously, even with severely disturbed clients having long-standing histories of violence and institutionalization for mental disorder. A model differentiating levels of anger treatment is put forth, seeking to clarify how interventions for anger problems are understood and might then be resourced in providing clinical service options.

To frame the presentation, we discuss the prevalence of anger among offender populations, highlighting the role of anger as a violence risk factor. However, in

The Essential Handbook of Offender Assessment and Treatment. Edited by C. R. Hollin,
© 2004 John Wiley & Sons Ltd.

addition to clinical interventions for anger being justified by it being a central mediator of aggressive behaviour, it is also the case that anger dyscontrol is a significant component of psychological distress in the clinical profiles of many different types of offenders.

ANGER, AGGRESSION, AND ANGER TREATMENT APPROPRIATENESS

The anger–aggression relationship is a dynamic one. While being neither necessary nor sufficient for aggression, anger is a significant activator of aggression and is reciprocally connected to it. This is generally agreed among a number of theorists (Bandura, 1983; Konecni, 1975; Novaco, 1994; Zillmann, 1983). As a normal emotion, anger does not always result in aggression, because aggressive behaviour is regulated by inhibitory mechanisms engaged by internal and external controls. Regulatory controls on aggression, such as external restraints, expectations of punishment, empathy, or considerations of consequences, can be overridden by disinhibitory influences, such as heightened arousal, aggressive modelling, lowered probability of punishment, biochemical agents, and environmental cues (Bandura, 1983). Aggression can occur independently of anger for instrumental, automatized, or cue-activated reasons.

It is thus readily understood that not all violent offenders are candidates for anger therapy. Howells (1989) cogently discussed the suitability of clients for anger therapy and provided case illustrations of congruities and incongruities. He stated that anger treatment is not indicated for those whose violent behaviour is not emotionally mediated, whose violent behaviour fits their short-term or long-term goals, or whose violence is anger mediated but not acknowledged. We essentially concur with Howells, except to note that persons in the latter category are often found among the type of treatment-resistant clients served by our State Hospital Anger Project.

Across categories of clients, the key issues regarding appropriateness for anger treatment are:

1. the extent to which the person's offending behaviour is an anger regulatory problem, implying that the acquisition or augmentation of anger control capacity would thereby reduce the probability of offending; and
2. whether the person recognizes, or can be induced to see, the costs of his or her anger/aggression routines—i.e. can genuine engagement in treatment be obtained?

Because resolution on the latter issue is so often elusive, an anger treatment "preparatory phase" has been developed and implemented in our work with forensic patients.

ANGER AND INSTITUTIONALIZED OFFENDERS

The presence of anger dyscontrol as a salient characteristic of violent offenders is commonly recognized. Blackburn (1993) gives extensive attention to the involvement of anger in violent crime and as a personal attribute of offenders. Even psychopaths, whose violent offending behaviour might appear to fit with the exclusionary criteria given above, may stand to gain from anger treatment. Blackburn and Lee-Evans (1985) asserted that ". . . psychopaths as a group may be more distinguished by angry reactions to threats or provocation of an interpersonal kind, rather than by reactions to thwarting or frustration" (p. 99). They suggested that anger management interventions might hold promise for their socialization.

Violent criminals are often impulsively aggressive, and anger prompts their harm-doing behaviour by locking-in schemas and scripts associated with threat and retaliation. In Berkowitz's (1986) study of impulsively violent men in Scottish prisons, he found that uncontrolled anger was experienced by 82% of the men before their violent offence. Anger remains salient among prison inmates during long-term incarceration (Zamble, 1992).

The dynamics of anger and violence in prison settings has been aptly characterized by Toch (1989), and a number of prison-based studies have assessed anger psychometrically. Selby (1984) examined five measures of anger or hostility for their ability to discriminate violent from non-violent criminals in a study with 204 adult male felons. He found that most of the measures, including the Buss–Durkee Hostility Inventory (Buss & Durkee, 1957), various MMPI hostility scales, and the Novaco Anger Inventory (NAI; Novaco, 1975), discriminated the violent group from the non-violent group and that the NAI did so with 90% accuracy. Kroner and Reddon (1995) assessed anger using the State Trait Anger Expression Inventory (STAXI; Spielberger, 1991) and examined the relationship of that measure's scales to Basic Personality Inventory (BPI; Jackson, 1989) indices. They found that the STAXI Anger-Out scale was significantly correlated with BPI scales of interpersonal difficulties and alienation, while the Anger-In scale was related to nearly all BPI scales, including depression, anxiety, and self-devaluation. These correlations are not surprising. What is noteworthy about the results is that incarcerated felons will self-report anger and these interpersonal and intra-psychic difficulties. Similarly, Welsh and Gordon (1991) found that STAXI Trait Anger was predictive of aggressive behaviour coded from role-plays in a study with a forensic hospital sample (whose psychiatric status was undefined). These studies suggest that anger self-report is an avenue of opportunity for treatment engagement.

In addition to these studies with incarcerated offenders, there is anger research on offenders in community settings, such as male batterers court-referred to anger management programmes for domestic violence. For example, Maiuro, Cahn, Vitaliano, Wagner, and Zegree (1988) compared domestically violent males with generally assaultive men and with non-violent controls and found that while the domestically violent men were more likely to be depressed, their anger and hostility scores were very similar to those who were generally assaultive. Indeed, there is a growing body of work pertinent to anger management with male batterers, activated by Gondolf (1985). In contrast, there is very little research on the anger dispositions of young offenders in community custodial settings. Gentry and Ostapiuk (1989) discuss violence in such residential treatment environments and present a case illustration that points to considerable anger involvement, but there is little psychometric research in this area. However, there is noteworthy anger treatment research with adolescents in such settings done by Feindler and her colleagues, discussed later. The broad range of cognitive–behavioural interventions with young offenders can be found in Hollin (1990).

One of the most prolifically studied topics in the psychiatric literature is the violence proneness of in-patients, regarding their functioning in the community and within institutions (cf. Monahan & Steadman, 1994; Mullen, Taylor, & Wessely, 1993). Recent community studies have focused on specific psychotic symptoms, rather than mental disorder in general, as violence risk factors. Swanson, Borum, Swartz, and Monahan (1996), following the work of Link and Stueve (1994), found that the presence of delusions, and, most specifically, threat/control-override symptoms doubled the risk of violence, controlling for other effects. Conceptualization of occurrences of violent behaviour as sequelae of illness pathology gives priority to illness symptomology, such as delusions and hallucinations, as crucial activators of assault. Alternatively, anger may be identified as an important mediator of the psychotic stimulus–violent behaviour relationship.

There is now considerable evidence about the violent conduct of psychiatric in-patients in European and North American institutions (cf. Hersen, Ammerman, & Sisson, 1994; Monahan & Steadman, 1994; Rice, Harris, Varney, & Quinsey, 1989). Haller and Deluty (1988), in a review of assaults on psychiatric staff, asserted that the frequency of such behaviour substantially increased during the course of the previous 10 years. However, such trends may have changed since that review, and there may be substantial variation across institutions. Noble's (1997) data from the records at Maudsley and Bethlem Royal Hospitals for the period of 1970–1995 show that since 1986 the incident rate has levelled after having sharply escalated in the previous years.

Among the variables identified by Haller and Deluty (1988) as potentially predictive of patient assault on staff was "level of anger" (p. 177). In an analysis of physical assault data pertaining to over 4000 civil and forensic psychiatric patients in California State Hospitals, Novaco (1994) found level of anger, indexed by clinician ratings, to be significantly related, concurrently and prospectively, to patient assaultiveness, and the prospective analysis controlled for prior assaultive behaviour. Convergently, Novaco and Renwick (1998) found in a prospective analysis of patient assaultiveness of 125 male forensic patients, studied longitudinally for 30 months, that anger was very significantly predictive of the patient being involved in physical assault incidents and in being the precipitator of physical assault. High anger patients were also less likely to be discharged in that prospective analysis.

EXISTING ANGER TREATMENT STUDIES WITH OFFENDERS

In view of the above research, the provision of anger treatment ought to have a high priority for a clinical service with offenders. Indeed, Rice, Harris, Quinsey, and Cyr (1990) found institutional staff to rate anger as the biggest problem in secure psychiatric facilities. Despite such evidence, the treatment of anger continues to be seriously neglected. Historically-driven conceptualizations of emotional disregulation in the illness process may have obscured seeing the mediating influence of anger on violent behaviour. That is to say, clinical staff in mental health facilities may tend to see assaultive patients as ill rather than lacking the capacity for anger control and thus fail to consider self-control treatments as a means of overcoming such difficulties. In correctional settings, because of the connection between anger and aggression, both prison and mental health staff may be inclined to view anger reactions as associated with bad behaviour and not be oriented psychotherapeutically when presented with anger reactions.

As practitioners working with offenders have been mindful of anger and aggression as significant problems, there has been a modicum of research in the treatment realm, although there has been considerable variability in the content and process of the treatment. Most applications have been based broadly on a cognitive–behavioural approach, initially developed by Novaco (1975, 1977), which utilized the stress inoculation approach (Meichenbaum, 1985). Studies with offender populations that are most closely connected to this approach are those of Stermac (1986), Bornstein, Weisser, and Balleweg (1985), Howells (1989), and Renwick, Black, Ramm, and Novaco (1997), all of which concerned forensic hospital patients, as well as the studies by Schlichter and Horan (1981) with institutionalized juvenile delinquents and by Feindler, Marriott, and Iwata (1984) with non-institutionalized juvenile delinquents.

The study by Stermac (1986) utilized a control group design and involved a group treatment of six sessions for male offenders with personality disorders, remanded to a Canadian psychiatric facility. She found significant changes in anger, impulsivity, and coping strategies in her anger treatment condition, compared with a psycho-educational control group. Bornstein et al. (1985) more fully implemented the stress inoculation approach in a multiple baseline design and obtained significant anger treatment gains with three institutionalized forensic patients, as reflected by ratings of behaviour in videotaped role-play, ward behaviour ratings, and self-reported anger. Howells (1989) reported successful anger treatment using the stress inoculation approach in a case study with a patient who had recurrent admissions to penal and psychiatric facilities due to violent offences and anger.

Most recently, Renwick et al. (1997) extended cognitive–behavioural anger treatment to institutionalized mentally disordered patients at a maximum security forensic hospital. The intervention involved an extension of the Novaco (1993) anger treatment protocol, developed in conjunction with a controlled clinical trial with Vietnam veterans with severe PTSD (Chemtob, Novaco, Hamada, & Gross, 1997). The Renwick et al. project modified and substantially developed the Novaco anger treatment protocol to meet the needs of secure hospital patients and was evaluated with four very angry and assaultive men with long histories of institutionalization, who were then found to make significant treatment gains.

Treatment studies with adolescent offenders have also incorporated the stress inoculation approach to anger problems. Schlichter and Horan (1981) implemented this anger treatment in 10 sessions in an experimental study with institutionalized aggressive delinquents. They obtained significant anger treatment effects, compared with a no-treatment group, on various anger self-report measures and on role-play behaviour ratings. Feindler et al. (1984) conducted a 10-session group anger control intervention with many stress inoculation approach elements with junior high school delinquents, as part of an in-school token economy programme. Feindler, Ecton, Kingsley, and Dubey (1986) further modified the intervention and applied it to aggressive adolescents on a psychiatric ward. Compared with a control group, their anger treatment group was found to have reduced aggressive behaviour on the ward, decreased hostile verbalizations in role-play, improved cognitive performance, and increased staff-rated self-control. The book by Feindler and Ecton (1986) gives a full account of this work, which, while not applied to violent offenders, is oriented behaviourally and offers many useful ideas for clinicians dealing with adolescent anger in out-patient, in-patient, and residential settings. Another valuable approach to cognitive–behavioural treatment of adolescent aggression is that of Goldstein and Keller (1987), who incorporate some stress inoculation anger management procedures in their training of prosocial skills.

At the heart of the stress inoculation approach to anger treatment is a focus on emotional dysregulation and a progressive acquisition of self-control coping skills. Other less complex approaches have been adopted with offenders, notably, a psycho-educational programme for anger management, used by McDougall and her colleagues. McDougall, Boddis, Dawson, and Hayes (1990) obtained improvement in self-report and institutional behaviour in 18 young offenders following the completion of a brief anger control course. Curiously, the authors expressed concern about whether anger, as opposed to aggression, epitomized the nature of participants' difficulties. This may have been due to participant selection being determined by the recommendations of prison officers (i.e. the absence of clinical assessment) or to the intervention failing to address the emotional component of the offenders' violent conduct.

Brief cognitive–behavioural anger management interventions have been implemented with adolescents by Valliant, Jensen, and Raven-Brook (1995) with offenders in open custody and by Dangel, Deschner, and Rasp (1989) in a residential treatment facility. Both of these studies used control group designs. However, highly aggressive persons were dismissed from the latter study (cf. Dangel et al., p. 457), and Valliant et al. did not get treatment effects for their brief anger therapy, which they thought may have been due to lack of participant motivation.

A number of other psycho-educational approaches to anger management for violent offenders have been reported. Serin and Kuriychuk (1994) applied a cognitive–behavioural anger control programme to violent offenders in a Canadian prison. They implemented a 12–16 session programme, but their report of its content, sequence, and results are very cursory. Smith, Smith, and Beckner (1994) conducted a three-session series of 2-hour workshops with women in a medium security prison and found significant reductions in anger inventory scores and mood diary ratings. Their intervention involved education about anger, self-monitoring, relaxation techniques, cognitive review of anger events, and strategies to escape from conflict; however, only one of their participants was in prison for a violent crime. Implementation of these basic elements of the cognitive–behavioural approach was done by Daly (1994) with a patient at a maximum security hospital. That patient had a history of substance abuse, paranoid schizophrenia, and serious violence. His anger and confrontational behaviour diminished with treatment, and he was transferred to a lower security unit.

Other anger management intervention work, linked to the Novaco cognitive–behavioural approach, has been conducted in the British Prison Service. Towl (1995) described the nationally implemented courses designed for groups of six to eight prisoners and run for eight 2-hour sessions. In an evaluative study, Hughes (1995) reported results for a 12-session programme involving 52 offenders in a Canadian federal penitentiary, finding significant pre-post changes in anger, physical symptoms, and irrational beliefs, although there was considerable incompleteness in the psychometric data. However, measures of recidivism were obtained for all those released from prison, and those who completed the anger management programme had a significantly longer latency to rearrest and a lower likelihood for conviction for a violent crime. Fitzharding (1997) reported gains for the participants of a group anger management in work with women prisoners, based on pre-post interviews compared with a group of non-participants.

Clearly, there has been considerable variation in the form of anger therapies; it would seem useful to distinguish various types of intervention, particularly as there is corresponding variation in the requirements and objectives for each type.

THERAPEUTIC INTERVENTIONS FOR ANGER: DIFFERENTIATING LEVELS

Psychotherapeutic interventions for anger occur at several levels, which have different aims and degrees of sophistication. Intervention levels reflect the degree of systematization, complexity, and depth of therapeutic approach. Increased depth is associated with greater individual tailoring to client needs. Correspondingly, greater specialization in techniques and in clinical supervision is required with more complex levels of intervention.

Level 1: General Clinical Care for Anger. A client's problems with anger and aggression may be treated in routine clinical care. Here, the clinician identifies anger as a relevant treatment issue and addresses the anger-related difficulties as part of a wider mental health care programme. This level pertains to general treatment strategies of counselling, psychodynamic therapies, cognitive and behavioural therapies, and/or psychopharmacology applied in an individual, couple, family, or group format. In seeking explicitly to address anger, such intervention work will actively incorporate new knowledge about anger and aggressive behaviour. General clinical care for anger, when its operational characteristics are explicitly designated, may indeed serve as a comparison condition for experimental anger treatment, as was done in the Chemtob et al. (1997) study with Vietnam veterans.

Level 2: Anger Management Provision. It is particularly useful to distinguish this level of intervention from more specialized anger treatment. The term "anger management", which was first used in Novaco (1975) to describe an experimental cognitive–behavioural treatment, can now better be used to designate a *psycho-educational* approach that is less treatment intensive. The content and format of this intervention type may vary considerably, although most existing forms of this approach are guided by cognitive–behavioural principles.

This intervention type is structured by a syllabus of some sort. It imparts information about anger, including its determinants, signs, manifestations, and consequences. It also educates about ways of controlling anger, such as changing perceptions or beliefs, using relaxation, and adopting alternative behaviours for dealing with provocation. It aims to increase the person's self-monitoring capacity by calling attention to "anger triggers" and habitual ways of responding. It seeks to promote new coping skills. This type of intervention is often implemented in a group format, providing a forum for the sharing of anger experiences, peer support, and peer modelling, as well as serving the throughput objectives of a clinical service system.

Compared with "anger treatment", the provision of anger management is more time-limited and is more structured. It is generally homogeneous in procedure, not being individually tailored. While there are occasions for participant discussion, it is less interactive than treatment and more unidirectional in information flow. It involves less client disclosure and is thus less threatening. Correspondingly, and because of its structure, the personal investment for the client is lower. However, it thereby does not address the treatment engagement issues intrinsic to the profiles of treatment-resistant patients. Lastly, while evaluative measures are often employed in conjunction with the intervention, there tends not to be explicit use of individual client assessment data.

Level 3: Anger Treatment Provision. At this level of intervention, anger dyscontrol is approached in terms of the client's core needs. However, anger treatment is not a substitute for psychotherapy and should be understood as an adjunctive treatment. It focuses on psychological deficits in self-regulation and explicitly integrates assessment with treatment. Precisely because it must often overcome client resistance to change and centrally involves clients who are characteristically high in threat-sensing, suspicion, and avoidance, it hinges on the provision of a therapeutic relationship.

Anger treatment targets enduring change in cognitive, arousal, and behavioural systems. It centrally involves substantial cognitive restructuring and the acquisition of arousal reduction and behavioural coping skills. It achieves cognitive and behaviour change in large measure through changing valuations of personal priorities and augmenting self-monitoring capacity. Because it addresses anger as grounded and embedded in aversive and often traumatic life experiences, it entails the evocation of distressed emotions—i.e. fear and sadness, as well as anger. Therapeutic work centrally involves the processes of "transference" (the learning of new modes of responding to cues previously evocative of anger in the context of relating to the therapist) and of "counter-transference" (negative sentiment on the part of the therapist to the frustrating, resistive, and unappreciative behaviour of the client). Regarding the latter, it is characteristic of high anger patients to push people away as part of their external blaming and avoidant styles. Thus, advanced therapeutic skill and supervision is essential in delivering anger intervention at this level.

Level 3R: Anger Treatment Protocol Research. This incorporates all of the attributes of Level 3 intervention, but follows a designated protocol in delivering the treatment. To meet research design requirements, inclusion and exclusion criteria are specified for client participation. This level of intervention is explicitly evaluative and stipulates time points and procedures for assessment. As part of the research design procedure, it incorporates checks on treatment protocol fidelity. In the enterprise of scientific discovery, it seeks knowledge about anger assessment and treatment.

Having made this differentiation in anger interventions, we now turn to the context of our Level 3 and 3R work at a maximum security forensic hospital. Prior to our research there (Renwick et al., 1997), existing anger intervention studies had yet to address the treatment of severely mentally disordered violent offenders. Our project participants have been severely disordered, dangerously violent, and have long histories of institutionalization.

THE STATE HOSPITAL ANGER TREATMENT PROJECT

The State Hospital, Carstairs, is the sole national forensic psychiatric facility serving the populations of Scotland and Northern Ireland. It has up to 240 patients at any one time. In addition to having a determined mental illness, patients must demonstrate dangerous, violent, or criminal propensities to warrant detention there, and most patients usually have an extensive history of criminal activity. Admission to the hospital is from courts, prisons, or other National Health Service facilities and requires legal orders of restriction.

The anger project was established under the direction of Dr Stanley Renwick to develop a protocol to assess and treat anger with this client population. For the target group, emphasis was placed on long-standing aggression associated with an inability to control anger. When referral of such patients was invited, almost one-fifth of the hospital's census was referred.

The State Hospital anger treatment protocol substantially modifies the 12-session anger control, stress inoculation approach progressively developed by Novaco (1975, 1993), which involved the following key components:

1. education regarding anger and aggression;
2. self-monitoring of anger frequency, intensity, and situational triggers;
3. construction of a personal anger provocation hierarchy created from the self-monitoring data;
4. cognitive restructuring by altering attentional focus, modifying appraisals, and using self-instruction;
5. arousal reduction through progressive muscle relaxation, breathing-focused relaxation, and guided imagery;
6. training behavioural coping, communication, and assertiveness through modelling and role-play;
7. practising anger control coping skills through visualizing and role-playing progressively intense anger-arousing scenes from personal provocation hierarchies;
8. practising the new anger coping skills in real everyday situations.

Owing to the severity of the patients' disorders and the institutional context, a number of additions to the basic protocol were required for it to be efficacious. First, a comprehensive assessment was needed of the patient, his anger problems, and treatment goals; second, a treatment "preparatory phase" was developed to engender treatment engagement and basic skill prerequisites, such as emotion awareness, emotion intensity level differentiation, and elementary self-monitoring; and third, the outpatient protocol was extended to a 20-session procedure to address the multi-layered needs of the patients.

COMPREHENSIVE ASSESSMENT

Our assessment involves psychometric scales, such as the STAXI and the NAS, but suitability for treatment and identification of anger regulatory deficits can hardly be ascertained from questionnaire procedures—unlike the all too common anger treatment studies done with college students, who are selected as participants by having upper-quartile scale scores and then volunteer by telephone. Assessment with seriously disordered patients must involve: interviews with the patient, doctor, and nursing staff; psychometric testing; observational recordings; examination of case notes; and background reports. Indeed, various members of the clinical team are continually involved in the anger assessment and treatment. A proper assessment of anger problems cannot be gained from psychometric measures alone, particularly when self-reports of anger are given with considerable guardedness.

Assessing therapeutic progress requires evaluation with multiple measures of anger and anger control. This includes self-report psychometric scales, behavioural observation, and scaled ratings by clinical staff. The self-monitoring records of anger experiences maintained by the patients throughout treatment can also provide one form of process measure. Very importantly, we carefully track critical incidents in ward behaviour.

As noted earlier, not all patients are suitable for anger treatment and this treatment approach. Clients who have significant learning difficulties or are acutely psychotic may not benefit. However, they may be suited to adapted protocols or other interventions—for example, Black and Novaco (1993) reported on successful anger treatment of a then hospitalized man with a mild learning disability. Many patients for whom treatment is indicated often refuse to participate in assessment or for various reasons give misleading information. With patience and supportive encouragement this resistance may be overcome. The "preparatory phase" is devised to address engagement issues and to shape the capacity for veridical assessment.

TREATMENT PREPARATORY PHASE

Originally implemented as a five-session procedure (Renwick et al., 1997), this is now a protocol-guided block of seven sessions. The rationale for this "preparatory phase" is to foster therapeutic engagement while conducting further assessment and developing client competencies needed for treatment. Particularly in a forensic setting, patients are likely to be very guarded about self-disclosure and to be motivationally ambivalent. They are not likely to recognize the personal costs that their anger routines incur. Also, they often lack a number of prerequisites for optimal involvement in a self-regulatory, coping skills intervention programme. They may very well have had some training in arousal control, and they may not have much difficulty in identifying emotions or differentiating degrees of intensity. But they are likely to be unaccustomed to making self-observations about their thoughts, feelings, and behaviours, or conduct rudimentary self-monitoring. Many may not recognize the degree to which thoughts, emotions, and behaviours are interconnected. For some patients, the educational aspects of the preparatory phase proceed quite smoothly and are much less crucial than the engagement issues.

The preparatory phase is thus constructed to "prime" the patient motivationally and to establish basic skills of emotion identification, self-monitoring, communication about anger experiences, and arousal reduction. It serves to build trust in the therapist and the treatment programme, providing an atmosphere conducive to personal disclosure and to the collaboration required by this therapeutic approach. While designed to be relatively non-probing and non-challenging, for many patients it elicits considerable distress. Consequently, some follow-up meetings often are needed to support patients in coping with the impact of the sessions. Very importantly, it must be recognized that treatment engagement frequently remains an ongoing issue. The start of the central treatment becomes a second decision to engage, but this issue is likely to be revisited several times throughout the course of therapy.

CENTRAL TREATMENT: MAJOR ISSUES

The completion of the treatment procedure (defined by the completion of the provocation hierarchy) in many cases might be expected to take longer than the 20 meetings specified in the protocol. This can be a function of both institutional circumstances and individual patient conditions that impede scheduled implementation. Clients may override the planned session procedure with their own agenda or resist the therapist's inducements. Importantly, the institutional context must be grasped. In a maximum-security setting, life moves at a slow pace. Forensic hospital patients, in common with prisoners in the penal system, develop strategies to cope with extended periods of incarceration. There is a subtle, but very real, "slowing down". Patients can take a disproportionately long time to complete routine tasks, avoid long-term planning, and live from day to day. Failure to take such needs into account evokes patient resistance. Thus, adjustments have to be made in therapist expectations regarding such things as homework assignments and the number of sessions required to reach therapeutic milestones.

Although essentially cognitive–behavioural, this anger treatment approach views anger dyscontrol as relating to the historically constituted core needs of the person, to ingrained psychological deficits in self-regulation, and to biomedical factors. This Level 3 treatment therefore requires training in a broadbased clinical approach suitable for the evocation of distressed emotions in the therapeutic arena. While this intervention is protocol-driven, we must say, quite emphatically, that its implementation requires clinical sophistication to modulate it.

Being prone to frustration and inclined toward avoidant behaviour, clients may frequently pull back or disengage. It is characteristic of high anger patients that they push people away as part of their avoidant style. As treatment engagement can often be tentative, the therapist must steer a steady course, maintaining focus and patience. As in Motivational Interviewing (Miller & Rollnick, 1993) this is achieved through a gentle therapeutic style and listening to the client's perspective.

For many patients, anger is deeply entrenched in identity, and the costs of chronic anger are discounted. High anger patients are reluctant to surrender this part of their defined sense of self. The anger treatment gives the patients a middle ground. It gives them a way to maintain their self-esteem and also to move on through the system. While fortifying self-worth, it gives the patients a compromise position by allowing them to maintain self-respect and yet enables them to change. The patient thereby finds himself or herself empowered rather than compromised.

Because of the complexity of this work and the potential risk of physical attack when working at an interpersonal level, it is essential that all therapists have adequate clinical supervision and a security plan. Therapists working with such difficult clients need the support and objective eye of another to guard against colluding with the client's view of the world or responding to their hostility with blame or rejection.

FOLLOW-UP

The transition towards coping alone is difficult, particularly as the patient is likely to remain in confinement. As with all established habits, those of angry, aggressive individuals can easily resurface following treatment. Setbacks are to be expected and worked through. Support and refresher sessions in later months are therefore very valuable. This is particularly the case when a person has to deal with a completely new set of circumstances, e.g. when leaving hospital to return to the community or simply being transferred to a less secure facility.

SUMMARY AND FUTURE DIRECTIONS

Given the prevalence of anger and aggression among offender populations, there is a salient need for effective treatment interventions. This is particularly the case for forensic patients who have longstanding difficulties with both mental disorder and violent behaviour. Such severely disordered people do not gravitate to "anger management" interventions and present considerable resistance to engaging and remaining in therapy.

We have here put forward a differentiation of levels of interventions for anger and have described the complexities of providing anger treatment in a high security setting. We also pointed to a newly developed anger treatment protocol, designed for use with Special Hospital patients whose inabilty to control anger presented recurrent, substantial problems for themselves, for care staff, and for society outside the institution. Clinical and empirical data from our preliminary research (Renwick et al., 1997) reflect modest but noteworthy gains in emotional competence, in anger management, and in social–behavioural competencies.

Our most clear indication of treatment success is that our anger project patients are recommended for discharge from the hospital. That this measure of success could be achieved with patients who were so severely disordered is certainly encouraging. These are patients for whom institutions all too easily give up hope, which is quite understandable, given their treatment-resistant characteristics and the institutional incidents that are associated with their behaviour. Having been in and out of many treatment facilities, they are given a poor prognosis by treatment providers, who view them as being "at the end of the line"— so much has been tried, with so little effect. This sense of highly entrenched problems is shared by the patients. We hope that what we have learned in treating such a severely disordered population will be useful for downward extensions anger intervention to less extreme anger clients.

REFERENCES

Bandura, A. (1983). Psychological mechanisms of aggression. In R. G. Geen & E. I. Donnerstein (Eds.), *Aggression: Theoretical and empirical reviews* (Vol. 1, pp. 1–40). New York: Academic Press.

Berkowitz, L. (1986). Some varieties of human aggression: Criminal violence as coercion, rule-following, impression-management, and impulsive behaviour. In A. Campbell & J. J. Gibbs (Eds.), *Violent transactions*. Oxford, UK: Basil Blackwell.

Black, L., & Novaco, R. W. (1993). Treatment of anger with a developmentally handicapped man. In R. A. Wells & V. J. Giannetti (Eds.), *Casebook of the brief psychotherapies*. New York: Plenum.

Blackburn, R. (1993). *The psychology of criminal conduct*. Chichester, UK: Wiley.

Blackburn, R., & Lee-Evans, J. M. (1985). Reactions of primary and secondary psychopaths to anger-evoking situations. *British Journal of Clinical Psychology, 24*, 93–100.

Bornstein, P. H., Weisser, C. E., & Balleweg, B. J. (1985). Anger and violent behavior. In M. Hersen & A. S. Bellack (Eds.), *Handbook of clinical behavior therapy with adults* (pp. 603–629). New York: Plenum.

Buss, A., & Durkee, A. (1957). An inventory for assessing different kinds of hostility. *Journal of Counseling Psychology, 21*, 342–349.

Chemtob, C. M., Novaco, R. W., Hamada, R. S., & Gross, D. M. (1997). Cognitive–behavioral treatment for severe anger in post-traumatic stress disorder. *Journal of Consulting and Clinical Psychology, 65*, 184–189.

Daly, A. (1994). An eclectic approach to nursing an angry young man. *Nursing Times, 90*, 50–51.

Dangel, R. F., Deschner, J. P., & Rasp, R. R. (1989). Anger control training for adolescents in residential treatment. *Behavior Modification, 13*, 447–458.

Feindler, E. L., & Ecton, R. B. (1986). *Adolescent anger control: Cognitive therapy techniques*. New York: Pergamon Press.

Feindler, E. L., Ecton, R. B., Kingsley, R. B., & Dubey, D. R. (1986). Group anger-control training for institutionalized psychiatric male adolescents. *Behavior Therapy, 17*, 109–123.

Feindler, E. L., Marriott, A., & Iwata, M. (1984). Group anger control training for junior high school delinquents. *Cognitive Therapy and Research, 8*, 299–311.

Fitzharding, S. (1997). Anger management groupwork with women prisoners. *Forensic Update, 48*, 3–7.

Gentry, M. R., & Ostapiuk, E. B. (1989). Violence in institutions for young offenders and disturbed adolescents. In K. Howells & C. R. Hollin (Eds.), *Clinical approaches to violence* (pp. 249–266). Chichester, UK: Wiley.

Goldstein, A., & Keller, H. (1987). *Aggressive behavior: Assessment and intervention*. New York: Pergamon Press.

Gondolf, E. W. (1985). *Men who batter*. Holmes Beach, FL: Learning Publications.

Haller, R. M., & Deluty, R. H. (1988). Assaults on staff by psychiatric in-patients: A critical review. *British Journal of Psychiatry, 152*, 174–179

Hersen, M., Ammerman, R. T., & Sisson, L. A. (1994). *Handbook of aggressive and destructive behavior in psychiatric patients*. London: Plenum.

Hollin, C. R. (1990). *Cognitive–behavioral interventions with young offenders*. New York: Pergamon Press.

Howells, K. (1989). Anger-management methods in relation to the prevention of violent behavior. In J. Archer & K. Browne (Eds.), *Human aggression: Naturalistic accounts* (pp. 153–181). London: Routledge.

Hughes, G. V. (1995). Short and long term outcomes for a cognitive–behavioral anger management program. In G. Davies, S. Lloyd-Bostock, M. McMurran, & C. Wilson (Eds.), *Psychology, law, and criminal justice: International developments in research and practice* (pp. 485–494). New York: Walter de Gruyter.

Jackson, D. N. (1989). *The basic personality inventory manual.* Port Huron, MI: Research Psychologist Press.

Konecni, V. J. (1975). The mediation of aggressive behavior: Arousal level versus anger and cognitive labeling. *Journal of Personality and Social Psychology, 32,* 706–712.

Kroner, D. G., & Reddon, J. R. (1995). Anger and psychopathology in prison inmates. *Personality and Individual Differences, 18,* 783–788.

Link, B., & Stueve, C. (1994). Psychotic symptoms and the violent/illegal behavior of mental patients compared to community controls. In J. Monahan & H. Steadman (Eds.), *Violence and mental disorder: Developments in risk assessment* (pp. 21–59). Chicago, IL: University of Chicago Press.

Maiuro, R. D., Cahn, T. S., Vitaliano, P. P., Wagner, B. C., & Zegree, J. B. (1988). Anger, hostility, and depression, in domestically violent versus generally assaultive men and nonviolent control subjects. *Journal of Consulting and Clinical Psychology, 56,* 17–23.

McDougall, C., Boddis, S., Dawson, K., & Hayes, R. (1990). Developments in anger control training. *Issues in Criminological and Legal Psychology, 15,* 39–44.

Meichenbaum, D. (1985). *Stress inoculation training.* Oxford, UK: Pergamon Press.

Miller, W. R., & Rollnick, S. (1993). *Motivational interviewing.* New York: Guilford.

Monahan, J., & Steadman, H. (1994). *Violence and mental disorder.* Chicago, IL: University of Chicago Press.

Mullen, P., Taylor, P. J., & Wessely, S. (1993). Psychosis, violence and crime. In J. Gunn & P. J. Taylor (Eds.), *Forensic psychiatry: Clinical, legal and ethical issues* (pp. 329–372). Oxford, UK: Butterworth–Heinemann.

Noble, P. (1997). Violence in psychiatric in-patients: Review and clinical implications. *International Review of Psychiatry, 9,* 207–216.

Novaco, R. W. (1975). *Anger control: The development and evaluation of an experimental treatment.* Lexington, MA: D. C. Heath.

Novaco, R. W. (1977). Stress inoculation: A cognitive therapy for anger and its application to a case of depression. *Journal of Consulting and Clinical Psychology, 45,* 600–608.

Novaco, R. W. (1993). *Stress inoculation therapy for anger control: A manual for therapists.* Unpublished manuscript, University of California, Irvine.

Novaco, R. W. (1994). Anger as a risk factor for violence among the mentally disordered. In J. Monahan & H. Steadman (Eds.), *Violence and mental disorder: Developments in risk assessment* (pp. 21–59). Chicago, IL: University of Chicago Press.

Novaco, R. W. (1997). Remediating anger and aggression with violent offenders. *Legal and Criminological Psychology, 2,* 77–88.

Novaco, R. W., & Renwick, S. J. (1998). Anger predictors of the assaultiveness of forensic hospital patients. In E. Sanavio (Ed.), *Behavior and cognitive therapy today: Essays in honor of Hans J. Eysenck* (pp. 199–208). Amsterdam: Elsevier Science.

Renwick, S., Black, L., Ramm, M., & Novaco, R. W. (1997). Anger treatment with forensic hospital patients. *Legal and Criminological Psychology, 2,* 103–116.

Rice, M. E., Harris, G. T., Quinsey, V. L., & Cyr, M. (1990). Planning treatment programs in secure psychiatric facilities. In D. N. Weisstub (Ed.), *Law and mental health: International perspective* (Vol. 6, pp. 159–187). Hillsdale, NJ: Erlbaum.

Rice, M. E., Harris, G. T., Varney, G. W., & Quinsey, V. L. (1989). *Violence in institutions: Understanding prevention, and control.* Toronto, Canada: Hogrefe & Huber.

Schlichter, K. J., & Horan, J. J. (1981). Effects of stress inoculation on the anger and aggression management skills of institutionalized juvenile delinquents. *Cognitive Therapy and Research, 5*, 359–365.

Selby, M. J. (1984). Assessment of violence potential using measures of anger, hostility, and social desirability. *Journal of Personality Assessment, 48*, 531–544.

Serin, R. C., & Kuriychuk, M. (1994). Social and cognitive processing deficits: Implications for treatment. *International Journal of Law and Psychiatry, 17*, 431–441.

Smith, L. L., Smith, J. N., & Beckner, B. M. (1994, March). An anger management workshop for women inmates. *Journal of Contemporary Human Services*, 172–175.

Spielberger, C. D. (1991). *State–trait anger expression inventory: Revised research edition.* Odessa, FL: Psychological Assessment Resources.

Stermac, L. E. (1986). Anger control treatment for forensic patients. *Journal of Interpersonal Violence, 1*, 446–457.

Swanson, J. W., Borum, R., Swartz, M. S., & Monahan, J. (1996). Psychotic symptoms and disorders and the risk of violent behaviour in the community. *Criminal Behaviour and Mental Health, 6*, 309–329.

Toch, H. (1989). Violence in prisons. In K. Howells & C. R. Hollin (Eds.), *Clinical approaches to violence* (pp. 267–285). Chichester, UK: Wiley.

Towl, G. (1995). Anger management groupwork. *Issues in Criminological Psychology, 23*, 31–35.

Valliant. P. M., Jensen, B., & Raven-Brook, L. (1995). Brief cognitive behavioural therapy with male adolescent offenders in open custody or on probation: An evaluation of the management of anger. *Psychological Reports, 76*, 1056–1058.

Welsh, W. N., & Gordon, A. (1991). Cognitive mediators of aggression: Test of a causal model. *Criminal Justice and Behavior, 18*, 125–145.

Zamble, E. (1992). Behavior and adaptation in long-term prison inmates: Description of longitudinal results. *Criminal Justice and Behavior, 19*, 409–425.

Zillmann, D. (1983). Arousal and aggression. In R. Geen & E. I. Donnerstein (Eds.), *Aggression: Theoretical and empirical reviews.* New York: Academic Press.

Part III

Assessment and Treatment
of Offenders

Chapter 10

Adult Sexual Offenders Against Women

William L. Marshall
Queen's University, Kingston, Ontario, Canada

INTRODUCTION

It is essential first to clarify what the topic of this chapter involves. There are various legal descriptions of sexual assaults against adult females, and across jurisdictions the same terms can mean quite different offenses. Primarily the offenses discussed in this chapter will match what is usually meant by rape and that term will be used interchangeably with sexual assault, as generic descriptors. However, rape is in practice a problematic term because it has traditionally meant forced, non-consenting vaginal penetration by the male assailant's penis. Such a restricted definition caused so many problems (e.g. having to prove that penile–vaginal penetration took place) that Canada wisely amended its laws in 1983 to eliminate the word rape by replacing all the relevant laws with one that specified the meaning of different levels of sexual assault. Concern about whether or not vaginal penetration occurred was replaced by specifications of the degree of forcefulness, coercion, or the imbalance of power. In this sense, a sexual assault is any unwanted direct sexual contact. This allows us to consider frotteurism within the same category as rape, a position that some researchers (Langevin, 1983) have suggested is more appropriate than viewing them as different behaviours.

The sexual assault of females by males has a very long history. Indeed, socio-biological accounts claim that rape was a common practice in the very earliest part of our history as a species (Quinsey & Lalumière, 1995; Thornhill & Thornhill, 1992). It is also evident that rape occurs in all societies, whether they are industrial, or pre-industrial, or even pre-agricultural societies (Sanday, 1981; Schiff, 1971).

The Essential Handbook of Offender Assessment and Treatment. Edited by C. R. Hollin.
© 2004 John Wiley & Sons Ltd.

Incidence and prevalence studies reveal that the sexual assault of adult females occurs with frightening frequency in Western countries. For example, Koss, Gidycz, and Wisniewski (1987) report that more than half their national sample of women in the United States said they had been sexually victimized sometime after age 14 years. Similarly, 44% of the Californian women Russell (1984) interviewed told her they had been sexually assaulted as adults. Interestingly, only 8% of these women reported the assault to the police. Deriving their data from official police records, and then correcting for the police estimates of unreported rapes, Marshall and Barrett (1990) concluded that every seven minutes an adult Canadian woman is either raped or is the victim of an attempted ~~minutes an adult~~ data from various European countries, including the United ~~ery~~ similar rates of sexual assault (van Dijk & Mayhew, 1992). ~~ims~~ and their families, and the cost to society of these assaults, ~~g~~ and extensive (Koss & Harvey, 1991). This is obviously a very ~~blem~~ that calls for a comprehensive response, one part of which ~~ly~~ with identified offenders.

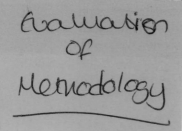

THE NATURE OF THE OFFENDER

Although researchers have made persistent efforts over many years to discern distinctive features of rapists, and while group differences have been found on several variables, it is clear that these offenders are a good deal more like other men than most people would like to think. Research has typically examined one of two populations of men who have engaged in sexually coercive behaviours:

1. men convicted of sexually assaulting adult females (usually incarcerated offenders); or
2. men not identified by the legal system but who either admit to having forced a woman to have sex or who say they would be likely to do so if they knew they could get away with it.

Malamuth and his colleagues (Malamuth, 1986; Malamuth, Heavey, & Linz, 1993) have been the foremost researchers adopting the latter strategy. While Malamuth's research is methodologically exemplary, the underlying assumption that examining males who indicate some likelihood of raping will tell us about the characteristics of men who actually assault women, seems to be problematic. First, these subjects may not all mean the same thing when they rate their likelihood of raping. One man may assume that the context of the possible rape is within his normal living circumstances, whereas another may assume unusual circumstances, such as being stranded on a desert island with a lone woman. Such studies, therefore, have dubious relevance for understanding actual offenders.

However, examining only incarcerated offenders also has its problems. The investigatory and judicial systems are selective, although they presumably do not intend to be so. The rigorous pursuit of an investigation of sexual assault, the decision to prosecute, the likelihood of conviction, and the sentence handed down upon conviction, all appear to be influenced by factors such as race, socioeconomic status, intelligence, style of presentation, admission of guilt, and the expression of remorse, in addition to the facts of the offense.

Unfortunately there is little research available on the characteristics of men who rape outside of those studied in prisons. In addition to the selective processes of the investigative and prosecutorial systems, many women who are raped do not report the offense and this is probably more true when the offender is a boyfriend or a husband. Indeed, in many jurisdictions a husband is still exempt from prosecution for raping his wife. The majority of the data available on rapists, then, represents a distorted picture but it is, unfortunately, the only picture we have. The rest of this chapter will perforce be restricted to a discussion of those rapists who have been identified by the judicial system.

CHARACTERISTICS AND ASSESSMENT OF THE OFFENDER

Few rapists seem to be characterized by the sort of evident psychopathology that the public expects in these offenders. No more than 5%–8% of rapists suffer from either psychosis, serious brain dysfunction, or mental retardation (Abel, Rouleau, & Cunningham-Rathner, 1986; Seghorn, Prentky, & Boucher, 1987).

It is not possible to discuss all of the features of rapists that have been examined in the literature. The following will focus on those features that most clinicians appear to consider relevant to assessment and treatment. Table 10.1 lists some of the more appropriate measures used to assess these various features.

Social Skills

Although it has been expected that rapists would display deficient social skills, in fact the evidence is at best equivocal and some subtypes of rapists appear to be satisfactorily socially competent (Knight, Rosenberg, & Schneider, 1985). While Segal and Marshall (1985) found that all their incarcerated offenders (rapists, child molesters, and non-sexual offenders) were equally skilled and all were less socially skilled than community males, Overholser and Beck (1986) found that rapists tended to be more appropriately assertive than child molesters. Finally, Stermac and Quinsey (1985) found that incarcerated offenders were more deficient than a community group, but the rapists did not display unique social deficits.

Table 10.1 Assessment methods

Problems	Measures
Assertiveness	Rathus Assertiveness Scale (Rathus, 1973).
Intimacy/loneliness	Social Intimacy Scale (Miller & Lefcourt, 1982). Fear of Intimacy Scale (Descutner & Thelen, 1991). UCLA Loneliness Scale (Russell, Peplau, & Cutrona, 1980).
Empathy	Rapist Empathy Measure (Fernandez & Marshall, 1998). Empathy for Women (Hanson & Scott, 1995).
Self-esteem	Social Self-esteem Inventory (Lawson, Marshall, & McGrath, 1979).
Cognitive distortions	Rape Scale (Bumby, 1996). Rape Myth Acceptance Scale (Burt, 1980). Hostility Toward Women Scale (Check, 1984).
Sexual preferences	Phallometric tests (Murphy & Barbaree, 1994). Multiphasic Sex Inventory (Nichols & Molinder, 1984).
Personality	Psychopathy Checklist–Revised (Hare, 1991).
Substance abuse	Michigan Alcoholism Screening Test (Selzer, 1971). Drug Abuse Screening Test (Skinner, 1982).
Anger	State–Trait Anger Expression Inventory (Speilberger, 1988).

Two studies have suggested that rapists may have problems with specific aspects of general social skills. Lipton, McDonel, and McFall (1987) demonstrated that rapists typically either failed to recognize a rebuff by a woman or took the woman's response to reflect a positive interest in them. Marshall, Barbaree, and Fernandez (1995) found that the rapists judged aggressive behaviours to be more socially appropriate than either normal assertiveness or underassertiveness. Perhaps these offenders misread cues from women and consider aggression to be the proper response in dealing with others.

Three other aspects of the social behaviour of rapists have revealed reasonably consistent findings over the past few years.

Intimacy Problems

Marshall (1989) outlined the potential extent of intimacy difficulties and their relationship to the etiology and maintenance of sexual abuse. He suggested that rapists failed to acquire the capacity for intimacy as a result of their poor childhood relationships with their parents and, as a consequence, did not develop the skills and confidence necessary to form satisfactory relationships as adults. Subsequent research has demonstrated that rapists are deficient in intimacy and suffer from emotional loneliness (Garlick, Marshall, & Thornton, 1996; Smallbone & Dadds, in press).

Empathy Deficits

There now exists a reasonably extensive body of literature on empathy deficits in sexual offenders (see the reviews by Hanson, 1997; Marshall, Hudson, Jones, & Fernandez, 1995). Presumably emotional recognition is an essential first step to empathy, and Hudson et al. (1993) showed that rapists had problems recognizing emotions in others. The particular emotions these men confused were anger, disgust, and fear; that is, just the sort of emotions we might expect victims to display. Having subjects respond to vignettes describing adult heterosexual interactions which varied from acceptable behaviours to explicit rape, Hanson and Scott (1995) found that rapists were deficient in perspective taking. Interestingly, those rapists who were intoxicated at the time of their offense, and those who used the least amount of force, were the most accurate in perceiving the distress of the women in the vignettes.

Fernandez and Marshall (1998) developed a measure to assess the capacity of rapists to recognize harm suffered by a woman, and to feel distress over her suffering. Rapists were as empathic as non-offenders toward a woman who had been disfigured in an accident and they were somewhat more compassionate toward the woman who had been raped by someone else. However, they were markedly deficient in empathy toward their own victim. Fernandez and Marshall took their results to indicate that the primary problem for rapists was not so much a generalized deficiency in empathy, but rather an inability to acknowledge the harm they had done. Thus, the apparent empathy deficits among rapists were seen as just another aspect of their ubiquitous, and self-serving, cognitive distortions.

Self-esteem

Marshall, Anderson, and Champagne (1996) suggested that sexual offenders have low self-esteem and that this is both causally related to their offending and problematic for engaging their cooperation in treatment. Self-esteem, and particularly that aspect having to do with confidence in social relationships, has its source in the person's childhood experiences, most notably with their parents. Learning to have confidence in oneself and confidence that others will be trustworthy and positive is largely dependent on the quality of the person's relationship with their parents. Rapists, so Marshall et al. claim, have childhood experiences that make them either cynical of others or self-denigrating.

Recently, Fernandez, Anderson, and Marshall (1997) evaluated the self-esteem of rapists across a number of domains (e.g. in social situations, sexual contexts, occupational functioning, and in personal appearance and athletic performance). They report idiosyncratic patterns of self-confidence across these domains among individual rapists, although all were lacking in self-esteem generally.

Cognitive Distortions

For many years theorists and clinicians have declared that sexual offenders display manifold cognitive distortions. However, a problem with these ideas, and much of the subsequent research, is that it is not always clear what is meant by cognitive distortions. For example, are deliberate misrepresentations (denial and minimization) properly thought of as cognitive distortions, or simply lying? Barbaree (1991), for example, found that 54% of rapists denied having committed an offense and Schlank and Shaw (1997) report that minimization is common. Both denial and minimization must be addressed in treatment whether or not they are construed as distortions.

Abel et al. (1989) developed a scale to measure distortions in child molesters and, although they presented convincing data, other researchers have had trouble replicating these findings (Hanson, Gizzarelli, & Scott, 1994). Hanson et al. suggested that these failures to replicate are due to the transparent nature of the questions which allow the respondents to readily identify the "correct" answer.

Bumby (1996) has devised a scale similar to Abel's to assess distortions in men who sexually assault adult females. His items reflect misinterpretations of the woman's behavior, distorted views of women's sexuality and of the victim's responsibility, as well as denial of harm. Bumby demonstrated that scores on his scale were reliable, were uncontaminated by a socially desirable response set, and distinguished rapists from non-sexual offenders.

Rapists have also been found to harbor attitudes toward women, violence, and rape that are offense-supportive (Burt, 1980). However, other studies have failed to detect differences between the attitudes of rapists and other men (Overholser & Beck, 1986; Segal & Stermac, 1984).

Sexual Preferences

Early studies of the phallometric assessment of rapists found differences between small groups of offenders and non-offenders (Abel, Barlow, Blanchard, & Guild, 1977; Barbaree, Marshall, & Lanthier, 1979; Quinsey, Chaplin, & Varney, 1981). Subsequently, however, large-scale studies have failed to replicate these early findings, with rapists in these recent studies appearing to match non-rapists (Baxter, Barbaree, & Marshall, 1986; Hall, 1989; Wormith, Bradford, Pawlak, Borzecki, & Zohar, 1988). It may be that in the earlier studies there were an unusual number of very vicious or sadistic offenders who we may expect to be highly aroused by the sexual violence depicted in the stimuli (Barbaree, 1990).

Personality Problems

While some authors (e.g. Kalichman, 1991) claim that rapists have distinctive personalities, Marshall and Hall (1995), in their review of MMPI studies, concluded that "there appears to be little support for the claim that any version of MMPI profiles, or any of its derived scales, distinguishes rapists from other subjects" (pp. 211–212). Research on psychopathy, on the other hand, has consistently shown that a proportion of rapists meet the criteria for psychopathy. For example, Quinsey, Rice, and Harris (1990) report that over 30% of sexual offenders scored above the cutoff on Hare's (1991) Psychopathy Checklist—Revised Scale. However, the offenders in these studies were housed in institutions created specifically to accommodate the most dangerous and chronic sexual offenders. When Serin, Malcolm, Khanna, and Barbaree (1994) examined sexual offenders in Ontario prisons, they found only 12.2% of rapists scored above the cutoff on Hare's measure.

Other Problems

Substance use and abuse problems (usually alcohol) appear to be common in rapists (Seto & Barbaree, 1995). We should not infer from these observations, however, that rapists are typically alcoholics or drug addicts. In a re-examination of some early data collected in Canadian prisons, Marshall (1996a) found that 70% of the rapists were intoxicated at the time of their offense, but only 60% of these intoxicated offenders (i.e. 42% of the total) had persistent problems with substance use and even less met the criteria for alcoholism or drug dependence.

Some theories of rape identify anger as a fixed disposition of the offender (e.g. Groth, Burgess, & Holmstrom, 1977), and researchers have found anger to be an immediate precursor to an offense (Pithers, Beal, Armstrong, & Petty, 1989). Marshall and Hambley (1996) found rapists to be hostile toward women, and Hudson and Ward (1997) reported that rapists displayed high levels of trait anger.

Finally, there is evidence that a limited number of rapists have elevated levels of one or another of the sex steroids (Bradford, 1990). Hormonal assays, in those cases where either deviant fantasies are persistent and powerful or behavioral controls are tenuous, appear to be valuable and an appropriate referral should be made.

TREATMENT

Cognitive–behavioural programs appear to be the most popular approach to the treatment of rapists. These programs arose out of strictly behavioral interventions for various other sexual deviations that were developed in the 1960s. When applied to sexual offenders, these programs were progressively modified throughout the 1970s. By the early 1980s they had assumed most of their current form after relapse prevention procedures were co-opted from the field of addictions.

In the first description of a behavioral intervention specifically designed for rapists, Marshall (1973) aimed at modifying deviant sexual preferences. This goal was consistent with the behavioral thesis of the time that acquired sexual preferences drove overt sexual behavior (McGuire, Carlisle, & Young, 1965). While this was a reasonable proposition, it was gradually deemed to be incomplete and theories about sexual offending became progressively more complex, invoking a vast array of factors. As a consequence, assessment and treatment have become far more elaborate. These comprehensive programs are now in widespread use in many countries (Marshall, Fernandez, Hudson, & Ward, 1998).

Marshall and Eccles (1995) have distinguished what they call "offense-specific" treatment targets from "offense-related" targets. The former refer to those features that are thought to be critical to the treatment of all sexual offenders while the latter are seen as relevant to some but not all offenders. This section will describe only the offense-specific components of treatment; other sources describe offense-related components (Schwartz & Cellini, 1997).

Treatment for sexual offenders is typically carried out in groups of 8–10 offenders with one or two therapists. Generally, individual counselling is avoided as it is thought to be uneconomical, unproductive, and lends itself to inadvertent collusion with the offender.

Self-esteem and Treatment Processes

The enhancement of self-esteem is best achieved in three ways:

1. by providing an environment which is conducive to the development of positive self-worth;
2. by adopting a therapist style that encourages trust and respects the client's dignity; and
3. by the use of specific clinical procedures.

While it is certainly difficult to create appropriate circumstances outside the group room, it is part of the treatment providers' responsibility to make every effort to achieve these conditions.

At present there is little information on what constitutes an effective therapist style with sexual offenders. Marshall (1996b), and Kear-Colwell and Pollack (1997) have made a case against using a confrontational approach. Both sets of authors, basing their claims on the work of earlier therapists (e.g. Carl Rogers, Jerome Frank) advocate a more supportive but firmly challenging style that directs attention to the offender's behavior rather than to his character.

In terms of procedures to enhance self-esteem, encouraging clients to increase the frequency and range of their social and pleasurable activities has been shown to increase self-confidence (Khanna & Marshall, 1978) as has having them rehearse positive self-statements (Marshall & Christie, 1982).

Finally, a combination of these treatment approaches significantly improved the self-worth of sexual offenders (Marshall, Champagne, Sturgeon, & Bryce, 1997). While increasing offenders' self-esteem seems valuable in itself, it is essential if we are effectively to engage sexual offenders in treatment. Research with addictions indicates that increasing self-esteem markedly improves compliance with treatment and significantly reduces post-treatment relapse rates (Miller & Rollnick, 1991).

Cognitive Distortions

Many treatment programs do not include deniers or those who markedly minimize what they did or their responsibility for the offense. Unfortunately this seems likely to exclude those offenders most at risk for reoffending or most at risk to reoffend in a particularly damaging way. However difficult these offenders may be to treat, society will be best served by attempting to treat them. Specific programs that deal with denial and minimization have been shown to be effective (Schlank & Shaw, 1997). All other aspects of cognitive distortions (e.g. distorted views of their victim's behavior, seeing others as responsible rather than themselves, various rape-supportive attitudes) are dealt with in treatment by having the offender discuss in detail his offense and challenging any distortions, rationalizations, and justifications as they arise.

Social Skills

Most programs attempt to enhance the offender's general social skills such as assertiveness and conversational skills. Most aspects of general social skills are best shaped throughout the whole program, making a specific component unnecessary. However, empathy and intimacy skills are usually targeted separately.

Empathy

The primary goal here is to sensitize the offender to the harm his sexual assaults cause. However, on this issue therapists must be careful to avoid increasing the satisfaction of the sadistic rapists in the group. For this component, and possibly for the whole program, it may be better to treat the sadists independently.

The focus in this component is on having the offender develop an understanding of the problems victims face as a result of being sexually assaulted, and on generating remorse in the offender. Since rapists appear to be deficient at recognizing emotions, it may be necessary to initially train them in emotional recognition. The full details of empathy training have been described elsewhere (Marshall, O'Sullivan, & Fernandez, 1996) and this report indicates that empathy was effectively enhanced by these procedures.

Intimacy

Marshall, Bryce, Hudson, Ward, and Moth (1996) have described in detail their approach to enhancing intimacy skills and they have demonstrated its effective-

ness. Skills involved in romantic relationships are identified, discussed, and prac-
tised. Issues around jealousy, loneliness, effective communication, sexuality, and
myths about sex are topics for discussion. These various issues are integrated for
each offender and he is encouraged to extend his range of friendships, approach
relationships with caution, and deepen his capacity for intimacy.

Deviant Sexuality

It may not always be necessary directly to target deviant sexual preferences in
rapists. As we have seen, few of them show deviant preferences at phallometric
evaluations, so it would seem inappropriate to have all rapists participate in
arousal modification procedures. However, even with those rapists who reveal
deviant preferences at assessment, Marshall (1997) has shown that deviant preferences can be normalized without specifically targeting these preferences. Of
course, many therapists are unlikely to adopt this approach and will prefer to
employ specific interventions.

Behavioral methods aimed at changing sexual preferences include aversion
therapy, masturbatory reconditioning, and covert sensitization. Aversion therapy,
however, seems to have lost its early popularity (Quinsey & Earls, 1990). Masturbatory reconditioning combines directed masturbation up to orgasm while
fantasizing appropriate sexual acts, with immediate post-orgasm repetition of
deviant fantasies. The evidence in support of these procedures is encouraging but
not strong (Laws & Marshall, 1991). Covert sensitization associates thoughts of
deviant sex with thoughts of unpleasant consequences. Unfortunately, no study
has clearly demonstrated any positive effects for covert sensitization with sexual
offenders.

Pharmacological interventions seem to be at least as effective as behavioral
methods in giving sexual offenders greater control over their urges. Bradford and
Pawlak (1993) demonstrated that cyproterone acetate (an antiandrogen) specifically reduced arousal to deviant fantasies while enhancing arousal to appropriate stimuli. Federoff (1993) has reviewed the evidence on the value of serotonin
reuptake inhibitors, and concluded that they can be effective in bringing deviant
sexual urges under control.

Relapse Prevention

Relapse prevention provides both an integrative framework and specific procedures for developing post-treatment maintenance strategies. Some programs,
most notably those in California (Marques, Day, Nelson, & Miner, 1989) and
Vermont (Pithers, Martin, & Cumming, 1989) have very extensive relapse prevention components, both within treatment and during post-release supervision.
Offenders are rigorously taught the language and meaning of the relapse prevention approach. They are required to provide detailed accounts of their offense

chain, identify all the factors that may put them at risk, and generate an extensive set of plans to avoid or deal with risks. Upon release offenders in these programs are required to enter community treatment and are very thoroughly supervised by trained staff. While this approach has obvious appeal, it does not necessarily follow that it will actually reduce risk. In fact, such comprehensive training and post-release supervision may serve to convince the offender that he cannot function effectively on his own. Once their sentence expires, supervisory control also expires and such a sudden change may precipitate an offense. A less intense approach involving a graduated shift to self-management would seem more sensible.

A review (Marshall & Anderson, 1996) of relapse prevention programs has shown that relapse rates are lower when post-release supervision is less extensive than that employed in the Californian or Vermont programs. In addition, these apparently more effective programs did not employ very extensive within-treatment training in relapse prevention. It may, in fact, be unnecessary to ensure that offenders learn the meaning of relapse prevention terminology. The whole relapse prevention package has largely been adopted without question just because it seems to make such apparent sense, and there have been few attempts to criticize or evaluate the specific procedures of relapse prevention with the exception of the work of Ward and his colleagues (e.g. Ward, Hudson, & Siegert, 1995).

Treatment Benefits

Reviews of treatment outcome with sexual offenders (e.g. Furby, Weinrott, & Blackshaw, 1989; Marshall, Jones, Ward, Johnston, & Barbaree, 1991) have differed in their conclusions about its effectiveness and debate continues. Whatever the eventual outcome of this debate, even the optimists agree that treatment is somewhat less effective with rapists than with child molesters (Marshall & Pithers, 1994). It has been suggested that we need to modify some aspects of treatment with these offenders (Marshall, 1993; Pithers, 1993). However, those who claim treatment does not work (e.g. Quinsey, Harris, Rice, & Lalumière, 1993) reject these suggestions. They advocate withdrawing funding from treatment and diverting it into long-term intensive supervision. Unfortunately, there is no evidence that such supervision reduces recidivism, and the evidence regarding relapse prevention approaches suggests that this might not be a wise decision.

What is important to realize is that continuing to do treatment is the only way we will develop better techniques, and it does not have to be very effective to realize benefits. Employing a cost–benefit analysis, Marshall (1992) demonstrated that eliminating the risk to reoffend in just one or two sexual offenders out of every 100 treated is enough to cover the costs of treatment. While this analysis is impressive, it does not illustrate the true value of saving future innocent women from suffering at the hands of an effectively treated rapist.

REFERENCES

Abel, G. G., Barlow, D. H., Blanchard, E. B., & Guild, D. (1977). The components of rapists' sexual arousal. *Archives of General Psychiatry, 34*, 894–903.

Abel, G. G., Gore, D. K., Holland, C. L., Camp, N., Becker, J. V., & Rathner, J. (1989). The measurement of the cognitive distortions of child molesters. *Annals of Sex Research, 2*, 135–152.

Abel, G. G., Rouleau, J. L., & Cunningham-Rathner, J. (1986). Sexually aggressive behavior. In W. Curran, A. L. McGarry, & S. A. Shah (Eds.), *Forensic psychiatry and psychology: Perspectives and standards for interdisciplinary practice* (pp. 289–313). Philadelphia: Davis.

Barbaree, H. E. (1990). Stimulus control of sexual arousal: Its role in sexual assault. In W. L. Marshall, D. R. Laws, & H. E. Barbaree (Eds.), *Handbook of sexual assault: Issues, theories, and treatment of the offender* (pp. 115–142). New York: Plenum.

Barbaree, H. E. (1991). Denial and minimization among sex offenders: Assessment and treatment outcome. *Forum on Corrections Research, 3*, 30–33.

Barbaree, H. E., Marshall, W. L., & Lanthier, R. D. (1979). Deviant sexual arousal in rapists. *Behaviour Research and Therapy, 14*, 215–222.

Baxter, D. J., Barbaree, H. E., & Marshall, W. L. (1986). Sexual responses to consenting and forced sex in a large sample of rapists and nonrapists. *Behaviour Research and Therapy, 24*, 513–520.

Bradford, J. M. W. (1990). The antiandrogen and hormonal treatment of sex offenders. In W. L. Marshall, D. R. Laws, & H. E. Barbaree (Eds.), *Handbook of sexual assault: Issues, theories, and treatment of the offender* (pp. 297–310). New York: Plenum.

Bradford, J. M. W., & Pawlak, A. (1993). Double-blind placebo crossover study of cyproterone acetate in the treatment of paraphilias. *Archives of Sexual Behavior, 22*, 383–402.

Bumby, K. M. (1996). Assessing the cognitive distortions of child molesters and rapists: Development and validation of the molest and rape scales. *Sexual Abuse: A Journal of Research and Treatment, 8*, 37–54.

Burt, M. (1980). Cultural myths and supports for rape. *Journal of Personality and Social Psychology, 38*, 217–230.

Check, J. V. (1984). *The hostility towards women scale.* Unpublished doctoral dissertation, University of Manitoba, Winnipeg.

Descutner, C., & Thelen, M. H. (1991). Development and validation of the fear of intimacy scale. *Psychological Assessment: A Journal of Consulting and Clinical Psychology, 3*, 218–225.

Federoff, J. P. (1993). Serotonic drug treatment of deviant sexual interests. *Annals of Sex Research, 6*, 105–121.

Fernandez, Y. M., Anderson, D., & Marshall, W. L. (1997, October). *The relationship between empathy, cognitive distortions and domain specific self-esteem in sexual offenders.* Paper presented at the 16th Annual Research and Treatment Conference of the Association for the Treatment of Sexual Abusers, Arlington, VA.

Fernandez, Y. M., & Marshall, W. L. (1998). *The rapist empathy scale.* Manuscript submitted for publication.

Furby, L., Weinrott, M. R., & Blackshaw, L. (1989). Sex offender recidivism: A review. *Psychological Bulletin, 105*, 3–30.

Garlick, Y., Marshall, W. L., & Thornton, D. (1996). Intimacy deficits and attribution of blame among sexual offenders. *Legal and Criminological Psychology, 1*, 251–258.

Groth, A. N., Burgess, A. W., & Holmstrom, L. L. (1977). Rape: Power, anger, and sexuality. *American Journal of Psychiatry, 134*, 1239–1243.

Hall, G. C. N. (1989). Sexual arousal and arousability in a sexual offender population. *Journal of Abnormal Psychology, 98*, 145–149.

Hanson, R. K. (1997). Invoking sympathy—Assessment and treatment of empathy deficients among sexual offenders. In B. K. Schwartz & H. R. Cellini (Eds.), *The sex offender: New insights, treatment innovations and legal developments* (Vol. II, pp. 6.1–6.7). Kingston, NJ: Civic Research Institute.

Hanson, K., Gizzarelli, R., & Scott, H. (1994). The attitudes of incest offenders: Sexual entitlement and acceptance of sex with children. *Criminal Justice and Behavior, 21*, 187–202.

Hanson, K., & Scott, H. (1995). Assessing perspective taking among sexual offenders, non-sexual criminals and nonoffenders. *Sexual Abuse: A Journal of Research and Treatment, 7*, 259–277.

Hare, R. D. (1991). *Manual for the revised psychopathy checklist*. Toronto, Canada: Multi-Health Systems.

Hudson, S. M., Marshall, W. L., Wales, D., McDonald, E., Bakker, L. W., & McLean, A. (1993). Emotional recognition skills of sex offenders. *Annals of Sex Research, 6*, 199–211.

Hudson, S. M., & Ward, T. (1997). Rape: Psychopathology and theory. In D. R. Laws & W. O'Donohue (Eds.), *Sexual deviance: Theory, assessment, and treatment* (pp. 332–355). New York: Guilford.

Kalichman, S. C. (1991). Psychopathology and personality characteristics of criminal sexual offenders as a function of victim age. *Archives of Sexual Behavior, 20*, 187–197.

Kear-Colwell, J., & Pollack, P. (1997). Motivation or confrontation: Which approach to the child sex offender? *Criminal Justice and Behavior, 24*, 20–33.

Khanna, A., & Marshall, W. L. (1978, November). *A comparison of cognitive and behavioral approaches for the treatment of low self-esteem*. Paper presented the 12th Annual Convention, Association for Advancement of Behavior Therapy, Chicago.

Knight, R. A., Rosenberg, R., & Schneider, B. (1985). Classification of sexual offenders: Perspectives, methods and validation. In A. W. Burgess (Ed.), *Rape and sexual assault: A research handbook* (pp. 222–293). New York: Garland Press.

Koss, M. P., Gidycz, C. A., & Wisniewski, N. (1987). The scope of rape: Incidence and prevalence of sexual aggression and victimization in a national sample of higher education students. *Journal of Consulting and Clinical Psychology, 55*, 162–170.

Koss, M. P., & Harvey, M. R. (1991). *The rape victim: Clinical and community interventions* (2nd ed.). Newbury Park, CA: Sage.

Langevin, R. (1983). *Sexual strands: Understanding and treating sexual anomalies in men*. Hillsdale, NJ: Lawrence Erlbaum.

Laws, D. R., & Marshall, W. L. (1991). Masturbatory reconditioning: An evaluative review. *Advances in Behaviour Research and Therapy, 13*, 13–25.

Lawson, J. S., Marshall, W. L., & McGrath, P. (1979). The social self-esteem inventory. *Educational and Psychological Measurement, 39*, 803–811.

Lipton, D. N., McDonel, E. C., & McFall, R. M. (1987). Heterosocial perception in rapists. *Journal of Consulting and Clinical Psychology, 55*, 17–21.

Malamuth, N. M. (1986). Predictors of naturalistic sexual aggression. *Journal of Personality and Social Psychology, 50*, 953–962.

Malamuth, N. M., Heavey, C. L., & Linz, D. (1993). Predicting men's antisocial behavior against women: The interaction model of sexual aggression. In G. C. N. Hall, R. Hirschman, J. R. Graham, & M. S. Zaragoza (Eds.), *Sexual aggression: Issues in etiology, assessment and treatment* (pp. 63–97). Washington, DC: Taylor & Francis.

Marques, J. K., Day, D. M., Nelson, C., & Miner, M. H. (1989). The sex offender treatment and evaluation project: California's relapse prevention program. In D. R. Laws (Ed.), *Relapse prevention with sex offenders* (pp. 96–104). New York: Guilford.

Marshall, W. L. (1973). The modification of sexual fantasies: A combined treatment approach to the reduction of deviant sexual behavior. *Behaviour Research and Therapy, 11*, 557–564.

Marshall, W. L. (1989). Intimacy, loneliness and sexual offenders. *Behaviour Research and Therapy, 27*, 491–503.

Marshall, W. L. (1992). The social value of treatment for sexual offenders. *Canadian Journal of Human Sexuality*, *1*, 109–114.

Marshall, W. L. (1993). A revised approach to the treatment of men who sexually assault adult females. In G. C. N. Hall, R. Hirschman, J. R. Graham, & M. S. Zaragoza (Eds.), *Sexual aggression: Issues in etiology, assessment and treatment* (pp. 143–165). Bristol, PA: Taylor & Francis.

Marshall, W. L. (1996a). Assessment, treatment, and theorizing about sex offenders: Development over the past 20 years and future directions. *Criminal Justice and Behavior*, *23*, 162–199.

Marshall, W. L. (1996b). The sexual offender: Monster, victim, or everyman. *Sexual Abuse: A Journal of Research and Treatment*, *8*, 317–335.

Marshall, W. L. (1997). The relationship between self-esteem and deviant sexual arousal in nonfamilial child molesters. *Behavior Modification*, *21*, 86–96.

Marshall, W. L., & Anderson, D. (1996). An evaluation of the benefits of relapse prevention programs with sexual offenders. *Sexual Abuse: A Journal of Research and Treatment*, *8*, 209–221.

Marshall, W. L., Anderson, D., & Champagne, F. (1996). The importance of self-esteem in sexual offenders. *Psychology, Crime, and Law*, *3*, 81–106.

Marshall, W. L., Barbaree, H. E., & Fernandez, Y. M. (1995). Some aspects of social competence in sexual offenders. *Sexual Abuse: A Journal of Research and Treatment*, *7*, 113–127.

Marshall, W. L., & Barrett, S. (1990). *Criminal neglect: Why sex offenders go free*. Toronto: Doubleday.

Marshall, W. L., Bryce, P., Hudson, S. M., Ward, T., & Moth, B. (1996). The enhancement of intimacy and the reduction of loneliness among child molesters. *Journal of Family Violence*, *11*, 219–235.

Marshall, W. L., Champagne, F., Sturgeon, C., & Bryce, P. (1997). Increasing the self-esteem of child molesters. *Sexual Abuse: A Journal of Research and Treatment*, *9*, 321–333.

Marshall, W. L., & Christie, M. M. (1982). The enhancement of social self-esteem. *Canadian Counsellor*, *16*, 82–89.

Marshall, W. L., & Eccles, A. (1995). Cognitive-behavioral treatment of sex offenders. In V. M. B. Hasselt & M. Hersen (Eds.), *Sourcebook of psychological treatment manuals for adult disorders* (pp. 295–332). New York: Plenum.

Marshall, W. L., Fernandez, Y. M., Hudson, S. M., & Ward, T. (Eds.) (1998). *Sourcebook of treatment programs for sexual offenders*. New York: Plenum.

Marshall, W. L., & Hall, G. C. N. (1995). The value of the MMPI in deciding forensic issues in accused sexual offenders. *Sexual Abuse: A Journal of Research and Treatment*, *7*, 203–217.

Marshall, W. L., & Hambley, L. S. (1996). Intimacy and loneliness, and their relationship to rape myth acceptance and hostility toward women among rapists. *Journal of Interpersonal Violence*, *11*, 586–592.

Marshall, W. L., Hudson, S. M., Jones, R. L., & Fernandez, Y. M. (1995). Empathy in sex offenders. *Clinical Psychology Review*, *15*, 99–113.

Marshall, W. L., Jones, R. L., Ward, T., Johnston, P., & Barbaree, H. E. (1991). Treatment outcome with sex offenders. *Clinical Psychology Review*, *11*, 465–485.

Marshall, W. L., O'Sullivan, C., & Fernandez, Y. M. (1996). The enhancement of victim empathy among incarcerated child molesters. *Legal and Criminological Psychology*, *1*, 95–102.

Marshall, W. L., & Pithers, W. D. (1994). A reconsideration of treatment outcome with sex offenders. *Criminal Justice and Behavior*, *21*, 10–27.

McGuire, R. J., Carlisle, J. M., & Young, B. G. (1965). Sexual deviations as conditioned behavior: A hypothesis. *Behaviour Research and Therapy*, *2*, 185–190.

Miller, R. S., & Lefcourt, H. M. (1982). The assessment of social intimacy. *Journal of Personality Assessment*, *46*, 514–518.

Miller, W. R., & Rollnick, S. (1991). *Motivational interviewing: Preparing people to change addictive behavior.* New York: Guilford.

Murphy, W. D., & Barbaree, H. E. (1994). *Assessments of sex offenders by measures of erectile response: Psychometric properties and decision-making.* Brandon, VT: Safer Society Press.

Nichols, H. R., & Molinder, I. (1984). *Multiphasic sex inventory manual.* Tacoma, WA: Author.

Overholser, J. C., & Beck, S. (1986). Multimethod assessment of rapists, child molesters, and three control groups on behavioral and psychological measures. *Journal of Consulting and Clinical Psychology, 54,* 682–687.

Pithers, W. D. (1993). Treatment of rapists: Reinterpretation of early outcome data and explanatory constructs to enhance therapeutic efficacy. In G. C. N. Hall, R. Hirschman, J. R. Graham, & M. S. Zaragoza (Eds.), *Sexual aggression: Issues in etiology, assessment, and treatment* (pp. 167–196). Washington, DC: Taylor & Francis.

Pithers, W. D., Beal, L. S., Armstrong, J., & Petty, J. (1989). Identification of risk factors through clinical interviews and analysis of records. In D. R. Laws (Ed.), *Relapse prevention with sex offenders* (pp. 77–87). New York: Guilford.

Pithers, W. D., Martin, G. R., & Cumming, G. F. (1989). Vermont treatment program for sexual aggressors. In D. R. Laws (Ed.), *Relapse prevention with sex offenders* (pp. 292–310). New York: Guilford.

Quinsey, V. L., Chaplin, T. C., & Varney, G. (1981). A comparison of rapists' and non-sex offenders' sexual preferences for mutually consenting sex, rape, and physical abuse of women. *Behavioral Assessment, 3,* 127–135.

Quinsey, V. L., & Earls, C. M. (1990). The modification of sexual preferences. In W. L. Marshall, D. R. Laws, & H. E. Barbaree (Eds.), *Handbook of sexual assault: Issues, theories, and treatment of the offender* (pp. 279–295). New York: Plenum.

Quinsey, V. L., Harris, G. T., Rice, M. E., & Lalumière, M. L. (1993). Assessing treatment efficacy in outcome studies of sex offenders. *Journal of Interpersonal Violence, 8,* 512–523.

Quinsey, V. L., & Lalumière, M. L. (1995). Evolutionary perspectives on sexual offending. *Sexual Abuse: A Journal of Research and Treatment, 1,* 301–315.

Quinsey, V. L., Rice, M. E., & Harris, G. T. (1990). Psychopathy, sexual deviance, and recidivism among sex offenders released from a maximum security institution. *Penetanguishene Research Report 7*(1).

Rathus, S. A. (1973). A 30-item schedule for assessing assertive behavior. *Behavior Therapy, 4,* 398–406.

Russell, D. E. H. (1984). *Sexual exploitation: Rape, child sexual abuse, and workplace harassment.* Newbury Park, CA: Sage.

Russell, D., Peplau, L. A., & Cutrona, C. A. (1980). The revised UCLA loneliness scale. *Journal of Personality and Social Psychology, 39,* 472–480.

Sanday, P. R. (1981). The socio-cultural context of rape: A cross-cultural study. *The Journal of Social Issues, 37,* 5–27.

Schiff, A. F. (1971). Rape in other countries. *Medicine, Science and the Law, 11,* 139–143.

Schlank, A. M., & Shaw, T. (1997). Treating sexual offenders who deny—A review. In B. K. Schwartz & H. R. Cellini (Eds.), *The sex offender: New insights, treatment innovations and legal developments* (Vol. II, pp. 6.1–6.7). Kingston, NJ: Civic Research Institute.

Schwartz, B. K., & Cellini, H. R. (Eds.) (1997). *The sex offender: New insights, treatment innovations and legal developments.* Kingston, NJ: Civic Research Institute.

Segal, Z. V., & Marshall, W. L. (1985). Heterosexual social skills in a population of rapists and child molesters. *Journal of Consulting and Clinical Psychology, 53,* 55–63.

Segal, Z. V., & Stermac, L. E. (1984). A measure of rapists' attitudes towards women. *International Journal of Law and Psychiatry, 7,* 437–440.

Seghorn, T. K., Prentky, R. A., & Boucher, R. J. (1987). Childhood sexual abuse in the lives of sexually aggressive offenders. *Journal of the American Academy of Child and Adolescent Psychiatry, 26,* 262–267.

Selzer, M. L. (1971). The Michigan alcoholism screening test (MAST): The quest for a new diagnostic instrument. *American Journal of Psychiatry, 127,* 1653–1658.

Serin, R. C., Malcolm, P. B., Khanna, A., & Barbaree, H. E. (1994). Psychopathy and deviant sexual arousal in incarcerated sexual offenders. *Journal of Interpersonal Violence, 9,* 3–11.

Seto, M. C., & Barbaree, H. E. (1995). The role of alcohol in sexual aggression. *Clinical Psychology Review, 15,* 545–556.

Skinner, H. A. (1982). The drug abuse screening test. *Addictive Behaviors, 7,* 363–371.

Smallbone, S. W., & Dadds, M. R. (in press). Childhood attachment and adult attachment in incarcerated adult male sex offenders. *Journal of Interpersonal Violence.*

Speilberger, C. D. (1988). *State–trait anger expression inventory: Professional manual research edition.* Odessa, FL: Psychological Assessment Resources.

Stermac, L. E., & Quinsey, V. L. (1985). Social competence among rapists. *Behavioral Assessment, 8,* 171–185.

Thornhill, R., & Thornhill, N. W. (1992). The evolutionary psychology of men's coercive sexuality. *Behavioral and Brain Sciences, 15,* 363–375.

van Dijk, J. J. M., & Mayhew, P. (1992). *Criminal victimization in the industrial world.* The Hague, Netherlands: Directorate for Crime Prevention.

Ward, T., Hudson, S. M., & Siegert, R. J. (1995). A critical comment on Pithers' relapse prevention model. *Sexual Abuse: A Journal of Research and Treatment, 7,* 167–175.

Wormith, J. S., Bradford, J. M. W., Pawlak, A., Borzecki, M., & Zohar, A. (1988). The assessment of deviant sexual arousal as a function of intelligence, instructional set and alcohol ingestion. *Canadian Journal of Psychiatry, 33,* 800–808.

Chapter 11

The Assessment and Treatment of Sexual Offenders Against Children

Tony Ward
University of Melbourne, Melbourne, Australia
Stephen M. Hudson
and
Thomas R. Keenan
University of Canterbury, Christchurch, New Zealand

INTRODUCTION

Sexual offending against children remains a socially significant and complex problem. It is becoming increasingly evident that the psychological and emotional costs to victims and their families are profound, with many victims experiencing major difficulties in adjusting to the demands of adult life (Cole & Putnam, 1992). In addition, the high reoffending rate and financial costs of incarceration underlines the need to both understand, and to treat effectively, men who sexually abuse children. In the past two decades a number of innovations have led to improved treatment of these difficult men (Hudson & Ward, 1997). Factors such as low self-esteem, intimacy deficits, problems empathizing with victims, distorted beliefs, and deviant sexual preferences have all been suggested as causal strands in the genesis of sexual abuse (Marshall, 1996). From a cognitive–behavioural perspective, the problems child molesters present with can be addressed by teaching them more adaptive ways of thinking about children, establishing core social competencies, and increasing their repertoire of coping skills. We suggest that effective treatment needs to

The Essential Handbook of Offender Assessment and Treatment. Edited by C. R. Hollin.
© 2004 John Wiley & Sons Ltd.

be based on an understanding of the variables associated with sexual abuse of children.

The evaluation of treatment outcomes has recently has received considerable attention, particularly since the Furby, Weinrott, and Blackshaw (1989) review of recidivism, which argued that because of profound methodological inadequacies in existing data it was not possible to establish whether treatment reduced recidivism (e.g. Quinsey, Harris, Rice, & Lalumière, 1993). However, the most optimistic evaluators have concluded that despite numerous methodological problems inherent in the best of the existing research, there is evidence that comprehensive cognitive–behavioural programmes, and those that combine antiandrogens with psychological treatment, are associated with ecologically significant reductions in recidivism for treated sex offenders (Hall, 1995; Hudson & Ward, 1997; Marshall, Jones, Ward, Johnston, & Barbaree, 1991; Marshall & Pithers, 1994).

In this chapter we present a model of assessment and treatment for individuals who sexually offend against children. We describe the key components of assessment and treatment and finish with some general comments on future directions. In the description of treatment components we draw upon our experience with the Kia Marama treatment programme for child molesters (Hudson, Marshall, Ward, Johnston, & Jones, 1995).

ASSESSMENT

Effective treatment of child molesters requires a dedicated and systematic assessment period targeting a number of domains, and utilizing a number of methods to collect clinical information. These methods include a clinical interview, the administration of psychological scales, and phallometric testing. It is important to use multiple methods to gather clinically relevant data; relying on just one source of data, for example self-report, is risky (Ward & Haig, 1997). While self-report is a valuable source of information, limitations in cognitive processing and the distorting effects of psychological defences and memory, make it likely that exclusive reliance on this type of data might result in a formulation that bears little resemblance to an individual's real problems. The assessment process should culminate in a clinical formulation (Ward & Haig, 1997) which serves to guide the customization of the programme content to the individual. A comprehensive clinical formulation of sexually aggressive behaviour needs to consider an individual's background, psychological vulnerabilities, current stresses, and the problem behaviour itself.

Comprehensive coverage of the important content areas (as identified in the empirical literature and with clinical experience) will enable the clinical decisions that arise from assessment to be based on the most accurate and scientific information available. These areas include developmental history, social competency, self-regulation, sexual functioning and preferences, beliefs and attitudes towards children and women, capacity for empathy and perception of victim harm, and offence-related information (Barbaree & Seto, 1997; Hudson & Ward, 1997;

Marshall, 1996). The latter category includes degree of denial and cognitive distortions related to the sexual offence, offence antecedents, degree and type of planning, amount of force used to subdue the victim, and emotional states evident throughout the offence process.

The clinical interview is the most common assessment device available to the clinician. However, as noted above, data collected in this fashion, especially from men accused of sexual assault, may be unreliable. This means that collateral information is essential for corroborating or challenging the material obtained during the interview. For example, any records held by the police, including details provided by victims or mental health professionals' reports at the time or during previous arrests, are extremely useful. It is also invaluable in helping formulate interview strategies, as well as predict relevant issues and the excuses given by an offender (Ward, Hudson, Johnston, & Marshall, 1997). The process issues can be divided into those that set the stage for the interview and those designed to manage the interview process itself. Ethical standards require informed consent, which means that the offender, or accused, understands the purpose of the interview and the inevitable limits to confidentiality. Offender disclosure is likely to be enhanced by an honest discussion of the benefits and risks of co-operation.

Denial and the various ways in which offenders minimize their offending are the major problems facing the interviewer (Marshall, 1996); accuracy and completeness is important. An acceptable level of completeness means that while the offender may not fully accept the amount of damage he has done to the victim, he has at least taken physical responsibility for the acts committed. Aggressive confrontation is unlikely to be successful for at least two reasons; namely, these men are skilled at maintaining their privacy, and aggression is likely to increase defensiveness. Overcoming denial depends heavily on the interviewer's ability to demonstrate a genuine awareness and understanding of the offender's situation. Viewing him as a whole person rather than as *the sex offender* is likely to help the process. Reframing disclosure as a fresh beginning can also be helpful. Maximizing retrospective caring about the victim, as in "you may not have thought much about her at the time but it would be great if you were to consider how you could help her now" can also assist the process.

We recommend that all clients undergo phallometric testing to identify the presence or absence of deviant attraction to either children and/or aggressive themes (Earls & Marshall, 1983; Laws & Osborne, 1983). We are aware of the controversy surrounding phallometric assessment (for a discussion of these issues see Hudson & Ward, 1997) and are seeking to develop alternative measures of sexual interest. In essence, the early promise of phallometry to discriminate between offenders and non-offenders has generally not been sustained. For example, exhibitionists are not distinguishable from controls and it has been difficult to distinguish rapists from matched non-offenders, with approximately one-third of both groups demonstrating arousal to rape cues (Hudson & Ward, 1997). However, on the whole child molesters, at least those of the non-familial type, fare a little better, but even here discriminent validity is modest (Barbaree & Marshall, 1989). An additional issue concerns the poor reliability of phallometric assessment, with a seminal study finding that data from 75% of their sample of rapists and non-offenders were unreliable (Barbaree, Baxter, & Marshall, 1989). However, until alternative measures are fully available we believe there to be sufficient utility in this process, at least for child molesters, to justify continuing. We see phallometric testing as an essential component of the assessment process and it should be explicitly covered in the consent form. In our experience, most men accept the therapist's explanation that it is needed to set appropriate treatment goals and to help reduce their risk of reoffending. The link between deviant sexual arousal and offending is also drawn explicitly in the "Understanding Offending" module (see below).

Concerning the selection of psychological scales and tests, we recommend that clinicians select measures that cover the following domains:

1. Sexual attitudes, beliefs, and behaviours, including views of sexual activity between an adult and a child, attitudes and fantasies about various sexual activities, hostile attitudes and acceptance of violence towards women.
2. Emotional functioning, particularly anger, anxiety and depression.
3. Interpersonal competence, particularly issues of self esteem, attachment, intimacy, and loneliness.
4. Personality, using primarily the Millon Clinical Multiaxial Inventory, 2nd Edition (Millon, 1987).

Both the scales and the phallometric assessment are repeated at the completion of treatment. It may also be useful for therapists to complete the Hare Psychopathy Checklist—Revised (Hare, 1991) at the end of treatment, as this instrument can help to formulate an assessment of future risk.

TREATMENT

Overall Structure

The majority of cognitive–behavioural treatment programmes are entirely group-based with individual therapy kept to a minimum, that is, sufficient only to enable a resident to participate in a group. Group treatment is more effective both in terms of use of time in that more men can be dealt with at once, and, we believe, in terms of efficacy in that processes such as credible challenges by other offenders and vicarious learning are not available in individual treatment. In our treatment programme (Hudson et al., 1995) groups are selected on the basis of release dates and currently consist of eight men with one therapist. We suggest that seven core components or modules underlie effective cognitive–behavioural treatment for child molesters. The Kia Marama programme described below incorporates these modules, and runs for 31 weeks with groups meeting for three, two-and-a-half hour sessions per week. Non-therapy time is spent engaged in homework assignments, therapy-related activities, prison work (e.g. kitchen or garden), or at leisure.

Module 1: Norm Building

The primary aim for this module is to establish the rules of conduct that are essential if the group is to function effectively, and to provide an overview of the treatment philosophy, that is the "the big picture". At the first session, the underlying social learning model of human behaviour change is described. The men are told that we do not intend to cure them of their problems, but rather to teach them to control their behaviour by helping them break dysfunctional habits and learn prosocial ways of satisfying their needs. Although each group generates its own set of rules which are in a sense unique to the group, most groups would typically include rules covering confidentiality (prohibiting the discussion of issues raised in group concerning other group members, with people outside the group) and communication procedures (using "I" statements, one person speaking at a time, speaking to each other not about each other, and demonstrating active listening skills). Additional rules may emphasize the importance of accepting responsibility for one's own issues (by facing up to challenges, and by asking questions when something is not understood) and challenging other members constructively and assertively rather than aggressively or colluding.

Module 2: Understanding Offending (Cognitive Restructuring)

Sexually aggressive behaviour is often facilitated and justified by distorted thinking (Ward et al., 1997). In this module the distorted views these offenders so frequently have of their offences are challenged and more accurate and constructive alternative ways of thinking about these issues developed. This process is partially facilitated by encouraging the man to develop a thorough understanding of his offence cycle. We base this process on the descriptive model we have developed regarding the typical offending pathways (Ward, Louden, Hudson, & Marshall, 1995; Ward & Hudson, in press).

In our model child molesters show at least nine discriminable steps in the offence chain. In brief, these are as follows (see Ward et al., 1995). Stage 1 are proximal background factors, such as the offender's perception of his general circumstances and his prevailing mood. Stage 2, distal planning, involves three possibilities: covert planning and chance contact, together with a third route, explicit planning, which may be associated with positive affect. Contributing factors here include the influence of circumstances such as structured contact with the victim, alcohol, victim vulnerability, cognitive distortions, and finally sexual arousal.

Stage 3 involves non-sexual contact with the victim for the purpose of offending. Stage 4 involves the offender re-evaluating his present circumstances and often changing his perception of his relationship with the victim in order to allow offending to occur. There are two major outcome states from this process, i.e. negative and positive affect, both of which involve increasing levels of sexual arousal and a belief that the cause is uncontrollable.

Stage 5, proximal planning, concerns the immediate precursors to the sexual offence and involve behaviours such as getting into bed with the child. Three subcategories were distinguishable: a self-focus, where the offender's needs were paramount; victim focus, where he justifies his offending in terms of caring for the child; and finally a mutual focus or caring relationship with a willing partner. Each of these were associated with different offence styles, with a self-focus being associated with short duration but high intrusiveness, and a mutual focus showing typically longer duration, more perceived reciprocity, and typically less intrusiveness.

Stage 6 is the sexual offence. Stage 7 is the evaluative process occurring in reaction to having committed the offence. Cognitive distortions were evident in the manner in which men appraised their behaviour. A negative evaluation involved feeling guilt or shame and was associated with self-blaming (an abstinence violation effect). While some men who negatively evaluated their behaviour acknowledged that their perceptions of victim willingness were mistaken, they also tended to minimize. Men starting with positive affect typically remained positive. Stage 8, resolutions regarding future behaviour, were largely determined by the affective tone of their post-offence appraisals.

Using a collaborative approach, with help from group members, the man is expected to develop an understanding of how background factors, such as low mood, lifestyle imbalances, sexual difficulties, intimacy difficulties (Hudson & Ward, 1997b; Ward, Hudson, & Marshall, 1996) set the scene for offending. The next two sections of the chain, distal planning and entering the high-risk situation, in which both proximal planning and the offence behaviours occur, are distinguished by the presence of a potential victim (Hudson & Ward, 1996) or being in a situation where the presence of a potential victim is highly probable, for example being in a park at around 3 pm on a school day. The individual's appraisal and emotional response to the initial lapse is carefully described and noted. The final part of the chain involves a description of the types of reactions the man has to having offended, and how these reactions inevitably add to his difficulties and therefore increase the likelihood of the chain continuing. Each man completes this chain during one group session. After receiving feedback from the therapist and other group members he then has a further opportunity to refine his understanding during a further session. The flexibility and scope of our model allows therapists to acknowledge the existence of different offence patterns, and also to look out for changes in mood and cognitions throughout the offence process.

Module 3: Arousal Reconditioning

Inappropriate or deviant sexual arousal to children is hypothesized to be an important factor causing and maintaining sexual offending (Marshall & Barbaree, 1990), and indeed is described as an important part of the problem behaviour process (Ward et al., 1995). Even where there is no phallometric evidence of sexual arousal to children, and this is not uncommon (see Marshall & Eccles, 1991 for a review), our belief is that any extensive pairing of orgasm and children means that it is likely that under circumstances of risk (for example, a negative mood state and the presence of a potential victim) the man will experience deviant sexual arousal.

In terms of the procedures used in this module, there is a limited amount of evidence suggesting that reconditioning strategies can reduce inappropriate sexual arousal in some categories of child molesters (Johnston, Hudson, & Marshall, 1992; Laws & Marshall, 1991). There are three components to this intervention. Covert sensitization comprises the first of these. Each man identifies the process or sequence involved in his most recent or most typical sexual assault and operationalizes this by preparing a personalized fantasy divided into four parts:

1. a neutral scene involving boredom;
2. a scene involving gradual build-up to hands-on contact with a victim, but which ends before sexual contact is actually made;
3. a scene involving detection, arrest, going to jail, humiliation, etc., i.e. negative consequences; and
4. an escape scene involving "coming to his senses" and getting out of the situation, feeling relieved and "very pleased with himself".

Scenes 1 and 2 are repeatedly paired with both scenes 3 and 4. The men are encouraged to activate the escape scene at progressively earlier points in the previous scenes. These are then written on pocket-sized cards and the offender is required to regularly review these behaviour sequences.

The remaining components in this module are designed to decrease deviant sexual arousal, on the one hand, and to strengthen sexual arousal to appropriate images and thoughts on the other. Directed masturbation, where the man is encouraged to become aroused by what ever means is necessary, but once aroused to masturbate to consensual images involving an adult, is designed to pair arousal with thoughts of appropriate sexual activity in order to strengthen these associations. Once the man has ejaculated, and becomes at least relatively refractory to sexual stimulation (Masters & Johnston, 1966), he is asked to carry out the satiation procedures suggested by Marshall (1979). These involve him repeatedly verbalizing components of his deviant sexual fantasies, for at least 20 minutes, whilst in this state of minimal sexual arousal. This pairing of deviant sexual material with both low arousal and arousability is likely to reduce its positive valence.

Module 4: Victim Impact and Empathy

A lack of empathy for their victims, and an inability or refusal to seriously consider the traumatic effects of sexual abuse appear to be common features of sex offenders (Marshall, Hudson, Jones, & Fernandez, 1995). We attempt to enhance each man's understanding of the impact of offending on victims by having the group "brainstorm" immediate effects, post-abuse effects, and long-term consequences (Briere & Runtz, 1993; Cole & Putnam, 1992; Downs, 1993). Any gaps in understanding are filled by the therapist.

Typically, a general deficiency in the capacity to be empathic is seen as facilitating offending, where things that are manifestly harmful are done to others. We doubt this is the case (Marshall et al., 1995) and indeed have evidence (Marshall, 1996) that the deficit is quite selective to the man's own victim, and as such most likely reflects dysfunctional cognitions specifically related to his own offending (Ward et al., 1997). The victim impact material may serve to reinstate offenders' capacity to empathize with potential victims, and reduce the future risk of reoffending.

To enhance this process we have the men engage in several other tasks. They read aloud accounts of sexual abuse and view videotapes of victims describing their experiences. We also have an abuse survivor come in to the group, as a guest speaker; she facilitates a discussion about the impact of abuse, both in general and specifically to her. They then write an "autobiography" from their own victim's perspective. This covers the distress they suffered and the ongoing consequences to having been abused by him. Finally, we have the man role-play both roles between himself and his victim. The group assists in these processes, challenging and suggesting additional material, and provides, along with the therapist, final approval. Marshall (1996) suggests that these procedures produce significant improvements in reported empathic responding specifically focused upon the men's own victims. This work constitutes an excellent beginning but needs to be replicated across other groups.

Module 5: Mood Management

Negative mood states are a frequent precipitating stimulus for the offence chain, usually depression or feelings of rejection, or more rarely anger (Pithers, 1990). Therefore deficiencies in affect regulation are a critical part of the management of risk. However, it is important to keep in mind that positive mood states can also be associated with sexual offending for some individuals (Ward, Hudson, & Keenan, 1998). The men are presented with a cognitive–behavioural model of mood as an overarching framework. They are taught to identify and distinguish between a range of affects including anger, fear, and sadness. They are then asked to identify particular moods that are, for them, especially associated with their offending process and are then taught the physiological, cognitive, and behavioural skills to manage these moods. Cognitive strategies include techniques aimed at challenging or interrupting negative thoughts and include stress inoculation. Behavioural techniques include teaching, and role-playing, effective communication styles for expressing emotions, including assertiveness training, anger management, and conflict resolution techniques. Lastly, problem-solving and time-management strategies are briefly introduced.

Module 6: Relationship Skills

In our clinical and research work we have been struck by the apparent difficulty child molesters have in the area of social competence (Ward et al., 1996). Not only do these difficulties in relating to others result in unmet needs, they also relate to difficulties in regulating affect (Ward et al., 1996). It is therefore of considerable importance to enhance interpersonal functioning. In this module we focus particularly on intimate relationships, first establishing their benefits and then examining ways in which they can be enhanced. The four main areas we focus upon here involve:

- conflict and its resolution;
- the constructive use of shared leisure activities;
- the need to be communicative, supportive and rewarding of each other; and
- finally, intimacy, which is the key issue around which all the others revolve.

We have argued that sex offenders are particularly deficient in their capacity for intimacy and we have provided evidence to support this (Seidman, Marshall, Hudson, & Robertson, 1994) as well as the existence of the related negative emotional states such as loneliness and anger (Hudson & Ward, 1997b).

We pay attention to the relationship style described or exhibited by each man, and identify aspects which may serve to block the development of an intimate relationship. We then examine approaches to relationships which might more effectively serve to develop intimacy. This is completed through the use of brainstorming, role-playing, discussion of prepared handouts, and homework assignments. We also traverse issues relevant to sexuality and sexual dysfunction as part of this module, providing educational material, through handouts and videos, as required to correct misinformation or challenge unhelpful attitudes. We discuss sexuality as an aspect of intimacy, and consider attitudes and behaviours that make for a mutually fulfilling encounter. Two recent studies have provided evidence for the efficacy of self-esteem enhancement (Marshall, Champagne, Sturgeon, & Bryce, 1997) and intimacy skills training with child-molesters (Marshall, Bryce, Hudson, Ward, & Moth, 1996).

Module 7: Relapse Prevention

The overarching framework of the programme is that of a relapse prevention (RP) view of offending, and we introduce RP constructs early in treatment. In this sense the final intervention module of the programme comes as no surprise to the men, and forms a natural extension of the earlier components. The distinction between internal and external management (Pithers, 1990) has utility and we make use of it in structuring this module.

The internal management component involves the man presenting a more refined understanding of his offense chain, and describing the skills he has acquired to manage his risk factors. This approach is based on the assumption that the goal of treatment is to enhance self-monitoring and control over sexually abusive behaviour, rather than to cure the offender. The acquisition of behavioural and cognitive skills and attitudes is designed to enable individuals to meet their needs in more prosocial ways. The emphasis upon understanding the various links in the offense process also encourages attempts to "break the chain" as early as possible. Thus, this module helps the offender to identify the external and internal factors that put him at risk for further sexually abusive behaviour, and to ameliorate these by utilizing appropriate coping responses.

The external management aspect involves the man identifying friends and/or family who are prepared to support him in his goal of avoiding reoffending, and the preparation, and presentation, of his personal statement. This critical component is the bridge between the whole intervention effort and the community in which the offender plans to live. The personal statement articulates the factors or steps in his offending cycle and outlines a plan for both the avoidance of high-risk situations and ways to escape from one if it develops. It also describes the external cues or signs signifying to others that he is at risk for further offending, for example irritable behaviour. This process serves to facilitate good communication between the sex offender and those responsible for his management upon release (community corrections officer), as well as those people who have agreed to assist his self-management process.

Risk Assessment

The assessment of the level of risk for reoffending has become an integral task for treatment providers, particularly where legislators enact "sexual predator" laws (see Anderson, 1992). Hanson and Bussière's (1996) meta-analysis found positive predictive relationships for history of prior sex offences (especially if they exhibited variety), deviant sexual preferences (at least for child molesters), victim profile (interactions between gender and relationship to perpetrator, with offenders with related female children as victims being less likely to reoffend than those with unrelated males as victims), age (younger), and some aspects of developmental adversity (see Chapter 24). This list is quite similar to those variables found by Quinsey, Rice, and Harris (1995) to be related to sexual reoffending in men released from the Oak Ridge facility. It also parallels our own strategies, based on Barbaree's (1991) recommendations, which includes offence variables (length of history, versatility, presence of violence, and victim profile), and personality variables, most notably the Psychopathy Checklist—Revised (Hare, 1991).

CONCLUSIONS

The assessment and treatment of men who sexually offend against children presents many difficulties for clinicians. Only a small proportion of men who behave in sexually abusive ways get to be treated (Hudson & Ward, 1997a). Thus one of the major issues facing treatment providers is what type of client to select for inclusion in their programme. Some authors have argued that entry criteria ought to be set according to who is most likely to benefit from treatment (e.g. Marques, Day, Nelson, & Miner, 1989; Pithers, 1990). Certainly, where the major consequence of a treatment failure is the possibility of the programme being closed down, this strategy confers short-term advantage. An alternative perspective suggests that we ought to treat as wide a range of sex offenders as possible, with as customized an intervention as possible, and assess the results (Hudson & Ward, 1997a). To do otherwise means we are faced with substantial limitations on our ability to generalize from treatment studies. Marshall's more recent suggestions of a tiered approach, where intensive long-term interventions are reserved for those at higher risk of reoffending (Marshall, 1996), provides needed structure to the customization process.

The other area requiring urgent attention is treatment outcome research (Hanson, 1997). The cold facts are that the majority of treatment programmes have not been formally evaluated, and there has been even less attention given to dismantling comprehensive programmes (Barbaree & Seto, 1997). While it appears that effective treatment needs to contain multiple ingredients, it is not clear whether all of the seven components described earlier are essential for good treatment outcome. The second area of concern is the lack of sound evaluation studies. The problem of low base rates of recidivism, and the accompanying issue of statistical power, mean that multi-site studies are essential if we want to establish the efficacy of sex offender treatment. The evidence at this stage is suggestive, but it is still preliminary. We owe it to sexually abused children to do everything we can to improve our ability to treat these difficult men, and to continue to advance the field.

REFERENCES

Anderson, N. W. (Ed.) (1992). Predators and politics: A symposium on Washington's Sexual Violent Predators Statute. *University of Puget Sound Law Review, 15*, 507–987.

Barbaree, H. E. (1991, October). *Assessment of risk in sex offenders*. A workshop presented at the Annual Research and Treatment Meeting of the Association for the Treatment of Sexual Abusers, Fort Worth, TX.

Barbaree, H. E., Baxter, D. J., & Marshall, W. L. (1989). The reliability of the rape index in a sample of rapists and nonrapists. *Violence and Victims, 4*, 299–306.

Barbaree, H. E., & Marshall, W. L. (1989). Erectile response amongst heterosexual child molesters, father–daughter incest offenders, and matched nonoffenders: Five distinct age preference profiles. *Canadian Journal of Behavioral Science, 21*, 70–82.

Barbaree, H. E., & Seto, M. C. (1997). Pedophilia: Assessment and treatment. In D. R. Laws & W. O'Donohue (Eds.), *Sexual deviance: Theory, assessment, and treatment* (pp. 175–193). New York: Guilford.

Briere, J., & Runtz, M. (1993). Childhood sexual abuse: Long-term sequelae and implications for psychological assessment. *Journal of Interpersonal Violence, 8*, 312–330.

Cole, P. M., & Putnam, F. W. (1992). Effects of incest on self and social functioning: A developmental psychopathology perspective. *Journal of Consulting and Clinical Psychology, 60*, 174–184.

Downs, W. R. (1993). Developmental considerations for the effects of childhood sexual abuse. *Journal of Interpersonal Violence, 8*, 331–345.

Earls, C. M., & Marshall, W. L. (1983). The current state of technology in laboratory assessment of sexual arousal patterns. In J. G. Greer & I. R. Stuart (Eds.), *The sexual aggressor: Current perspectives on treatment* (pp. 336–362). New York: Van Nostrand Reinhold.

Furby, L., Weinrott, M. R., & Blackshaw, L. (1989). Sex offender recidivism: A review. *Psychological Bulletin, 105,* 3–30.

Hall, G. C. N. (1995). Sexual offender recidivism revisited: A meta-analysis of treatment studies. *Journal of Consulting and Clinical Psychology, 63,* 802–809.

Hanson, R. K. (1997). How to know what works with sex offenders. *Sexual Abuse: A Journal of Research and Treatment, 9,* 129–145.

Hanson, R. K., & Bussière, M. T. (1996). *Predictors of sexual offender recidivism: A meta-analysis.* Ottawa, Canada: Solicitor General Canada.

Hare, R. D. (1991). *Manual for the Revised Psychopathy Checklist.* Toronto, Canada: Multi-Heath Systems.

Hudson, S. M., Marshall, W. L., Ward, T., Johnston, P. W., & Jones, R. L. (1995). Kia Marama: A cognitive–behavioural program for incarcerated child molesters. *Behaviour Change, 12,* 69–80.

Hudson, S. M., & Ward, T. (1996). Relapse prevention: Future directions. *Sexual Abuse: A Journal of Research and Treatment, 8,* 249–256.

Hudson, S. M., & Ward, T. (1997a). Future directions. In D. R. Laws & W. O'Donohue (Eds.), *Sexual deviance: Theory, assessment, and treatment* (pp. 481–500). New York: Guilford.

Hudson, S. M., & Ward, T. (1997b). Intimacy, loneliness, and attachment style in sex offenders. *Journal of Interpersonal Violence, 12,* 323–339.

Johnston, P. W., Hudson, S. M., & Marshall, W. L. (1992). The effects of masturbatory reconditioning with nonfamilial child molesters. *Behaviour Research and Therapy, 30,* 559–561.

Laws, D. R., & Marshall, W. L. (1991). Masturbatory reconditioning: An evaluative review. *Advances in Behaviour Therapy, 13,* 13–25.

Laws, D. R., & Osborne, C. A. (1983). How to build and operate a behavioural laboratory to evaluate and treat sexual deviance. In J. G. Greer & I. R. Stuart (Eds.), *The sexual aggressor: Current perspectives on treatment* (pp. 293–335). New York: Van Nostrand Reinhold.

Marques, J. K., Day, D. M., Nelson, C., & Miner, M. H. (1989). The Sex Offender Treatment and Evaluation Project: California's relapse prevention program. In D. R. Laws (Ed.), *Relapse prevention with sex offenders.* New York: Guilford.

Marshall, W. L. (1979). Satiation therapy: Changing sexual choice through controlling masturbatory fantasies. *Journal of Behaviour Therapy and Experimental Psychiatry, 1,* 263–271.

Marshall, W. L. (1996). Assessment, treatment, and theorizing about sex offenders. *Criminal Justice and Behavior, 23,* 162–199.

Marshall, W. L., & Barbaree, H. E. (1990). An integrated theory of the etiology of sexual offending. In W. L. Marshall, D. R. Laws, & H. E. Barbaree (Eds.), *Handbook of sexual assault: Issues, theories, and treatment of the offender* (pp. 257–275). New York: Plenum.

Marshall, W. L., Bryce, P., Hudson, S. M., Ward, T., & Moth, B. (1996). The enhancement of intimacy and the reduction of loneliness among child molesters. *Journal of Family Violence, 11,* 219–235.

Marshall, W. L., Champagne, F., Sturgeon, C., & Bryce, P. (1997). Increasing the self-esteem of child molesters. *Sexual Abuse: A Journal of Research and Treatment, 9,* 321–333.

Marshall, W. L., & Eccles, A. (1991). Issues in clinical practice with sex offenders. *Journal of Interpersonal Violence, 6,* 90–96.

Marshall, W. L., Hudson, S. M., Jones, R. J., & Fernandez, Y. M. (1995). Empathy in sex offenders. *Clinical Psychology Review, 15,* 99–113.

Marshall, W. L., Jones, R. L., Ward, T., Johnston, P., & Barbaree, H. E. (1991). Treatment outcome with sex offenders. *Clinical Psychology Review, 11,* 465–485.

Marshall, W. L., & Pithers, W. D. (1994). A reconsideration of treatment outcome with sex offenders. *Criminal Justice and Behavior*, *21*, 10–27.

Masters, W. H., & Johnson, V. E. (1966). *Human sexual response*. Boston, MA: Little, Brown.

Millon, T. (1987). *Manual for the Millon Multiaxial Clinical Inventory* (2nd Ed.). Minneapolis, MN: National Computer Systems.

Pithers, W. D. (1990). Relapse prevention with sexual aggressors: A method for maintaining therapeutic gain and enhancing external supervision. In W. L. Marshall, D. R. Laws, & H. E. Barbaree (Eds.), *Handbook of sexual assault: Issues, theories, and treatment of the offender* (pp. 343–361). New York: Plenum.

Quinsey, V. L., Harris, G. T., Rice, M. E., & Lalumière, M. L. (1993). Assessing treatment efficacy in outcome studies of sex offenders. *Journal of Interpersonal Violence*, *8*, 512–523.

Quinsey, V. L., Rice, M., & Harris, G. T. (1995). Actuarial prediction of sexual recidivism. *Journal of Interpersonal Violence*, *10*, 85–105.

Seidman, B., Marshall, W. L., Hudson, S. M., & Robertson, P. J. (1994). An examination of intimacy and loneliness in sex offenders. *Journal of Interpersonal Violence*, *9*, 518–534.

Ward T., & Haig, B. (1997). Abductive reasoning and clinical assessment. *Australian Psychologist*, *32*, 93–100.

Ward, T., & Hudson, S. M. (in press). Relapse prevention: Conceptual innovations. In D. R. Laws, S. M. Hudson, & T. Ward (Eds.), *Relapse prevention with sex offenders: Reconceptualizations, revisions, innovations* (2nd Ed.). New York: Guilford.

Ward, T., Hudson, S. M., Johnston, L., & Marshall, W. L. (1997). Cognitive distortions in sex offenders: An integrative review. *Clinical Psychology Review*, *17*, 479–507.

Ward, T., Hudson, S. M., & Keenan, T. R. (1998). A self-regulation model of the sexual offense process. *Sexual Abuse: A Journal of Research and Treatment*, *10*, 141–157.

Ward, T., Hudson, S. M., & Marshall, W. L. (1996). Attachment style in sex offenders: A preliminary study. *Journal of Sex Research*, *33*, 17–26.

Ward, T., Louden, K., Hudson, S. M., & Marshall, W. L. (1995). A descriptive model of the offence process. *Journal of Interpersonal Violence*, *10*, 453–473.

Chapter 12

Firesetters

David J. Kolko
*University of Pittsburgh, School of Medicine; Western Psychiatric
Institute and Clinic, Pittsburgh, USA*

SIGNIFICANCE OF THE PROBLEM

Children and youth account for a significant proportion of the fires set in the
United States. On the basis of figures reported by the National Fire Protection
Association (NFPA), children playing with fire committed 98 410 fires that were
reported to US fire departments, causing an estimated 408 civilian deaths, 3130
civilian injuries, and millions of dollars in property damages (see Hall, 1995;
National Fire Protection Association, 1995). Fireplay was the leading cause of
death among preschoolers. Child victims who survive may suffer burn trauma
and its serious medical (e.g. hospitalization) and psychological (e.g. post-
traumatic stress, depression) sequelae (see Cella, Perry, Kulchycky, & Goodwin,
1988; Stoddard, Norman, Murphy, & Beardslee, 1989). Other significant consequences of firesetting include an arrest for arson. In fact, juvenile firesetters
accounted for a majority of the arrests for arson in this country in 1994, making
arson the only crime to have had a higher proportion of juvenile than adult
involvement (US Federal Bureau of Investigations, 1995).

PREVALENCE AND RECIDIVISM

Prevalence rates have been reported in a small number of samples from medium
to large-sized cities. In a large community survey conducted in Rochester,
New York, 38% of the 770 children (ages 6–14 years) surveyed reported ever
having played with fire and 14% reported fireplay since the school year began
(Grolnick, Cole, Laurenitis, & Schwartzman, 1990; Kafry, 1980). Older children
reported the highest percentage of recent fireplay within the past six months

The Essential Handbook of Offender Assessment and Treatment. Edited by C. R. Hollin.
© 2004 John Wiley & Sons Ltd.

(23%). In addition to child age, access to fire-related materials, expectations of no parental response, and fire responsibility predicted the children's involvement in fireplay. A study of 736 children in Lund, Sweden, found that 255 (35%) reported playing with fire "fairly often" and 50 children (7%) played "often or quite often" (Terjestam & Ryden, 1996). Here, too, the number of children who played with fire increased five-fold from grades 1–3 to 7–9. Developmental competence deserves further consideration as a construct that may help to determine the level of a child's involvement with fire, which may be related to variables that reflect both antecedents and consequences of firesetting involvement (e.g. exposure, limited consequences).

Among psychiatric samples, high prevalence rates have been found for firesetting (i.e. an incident of burning with property damages) and matchplay (play with matches or lighters with no damages) in outpatients (19.4%, 24.4%) and inpatients (34.6%, 52.0%), respectively, and for multiple firesetting incidents among inpatients in the metropolitan Pittsburgh area (Kolko & Kazdin, 1988b). Moderate rates of recurrent firesetting have been found among children seen in the fire department (65%; Parrish et al., 1985) or psychiatric centers (23%–58%; Kolko & Kazdin, 1988b; Stewart & Culver, 1982).

A two-year follow-up study of 268 patient and non-patient children (ages 6–13 yrs) used fire history reports to classify cases into one of three mutually exclusive categories in order to determine how many children engaged in firesetting or matchplay only (Kolko & Kazdin, 1995). On the basis of aggregated reports of children and their parents, both patients and non-patients reported high levels of follow-up firesetting (49%, 64%) and matchplay (57%, 76%), though the frequency of each behavior was generally higher for patients than non-patients for both firesetting (M's = 4.2, 1.0) and matchplay (M's = 3.1, 0.9). At initial assessment, there were 50 firesetters (31.3%), 15 matchplayers (9.4%), and 95 non-firesetters (59.4%) in a non-patient sample; similar percentages of firesetters (24.4% or 39), matchplayers only (20.0% or 32), and non-firesetters (55.6% or 89) were found for the follow-up period. In a patient sample, there were 44 firesetters (51.2%), 10 matchplayers only (11.6%), and 32 non-firesetters (37.2%); similar percentages of firesetters (43.3% or 37), matchplayers only (12.8% or 11), and non-firesetters (44.2% or 38) were found for the follow-up period. In each sample, 25 of 50 non-patients (50%) and 26 of 44 patients (59%) were recidivists, whereas 14 of 110 non-patients (13%) and 11 of 42 patients (26%) became late-starters. Such findings highlight the prevalence of firesetting in disturbed and non-disturbed youth, and the continuity of firesetting over time.

Recidivism rates or predictors or subsequent firesetting behavior have been infrequently reported. One prospective study that followed a sample of 138 children for one year showed that 14 of 78 non-firesetters (18%) later had set their first fire, and that 21 of 60 firesetters (35%) had set an additional fire by follow-up (Kolko & Kazdin, 1992). "Late-starting" was associated with limited family sociability, whereas recidivism was associated with child knowledge about combustibles and involvement in fire-related activities, community complaints about fire contact, child hostility, lax discipline, family conflict, and limited parental acceptance, family affiliation, and family organization. A few of these predictors have been identified as correlates of adult arson in other samples (Rice & Harris, 1991). A study of young arsonists receiving forensic evaluations found a recidivism rate of approximately 33% over an average of a seven-year follow-up period (Repo & Virkkunen, 1997).

A more recent study examined fire-specific and general psychosocial measures as predictors of follow-up firesetting and matchplay, separately for patients and non-patients (Kolko & Kazdin, 1995). Early firesetting and matchplay were significant predictors of follow-up fire involvement in both samples. The psychosocial predictors of firesetting that added incremental variance beyond this fire history varied by sample. In the non-patients, two predictors were found (i.e. exposure to fire models, parental psychological control). In the patients, several variables served as predictors (e.g. fire competence, complaints about the child, parental distress, harsh punishment, social service contact). Different predictors in the two samples also were found for matchplay. These findings highlight some of the potential risk factors for later involvement with fire which included, not surprisingly, prior firesetting and matchplay.

DESCRIPTIVE AND CLINICAL CHARACTERISTICS

No specific "profile" of the juvenile firesetter has been identified. In fact, the background and clinical characteristics of firesetting children and youth are quite diverse. Descriptive details of the firesetting incidents and children's motives point to some of the factors that may influence the severity of this problem. Empirical studies have examined group differences between firesetting and non-firesetting samples obtained in different settings, such as community, outpatient, or residential settings.

Studies have examined demographic, diagnostic, and clinical characteristics of firesetting youth. Based on controlled studies, firesetting has been found to be associated with various forms of child dysfunction, such as heightened aggression and social skills deficits (Kolko, Kazdin, & Meyer, 1985). On parent reports, firesetters have been found to exhibit greater covert behavior such as lying, stealing, or running away, than both matchplayers and non-firesetters (Kolko & Kazdin, 1991b). Both firesetters and matchplayers have been found to differ from non-firesetters on other measures of dysfunction (e.g. aggression, externalizing behaviors, impulsivity, emotionality, hostility), but did not differ from one another. It is noteworthy that far fewer differences between firesetters and matchplayers were observed on child than parent self-report measures (e.g. aggression, unassertion, low self-esteem). Heightened aggression and other antisocial behaviors in firesetters have been reported elsewhere (Cole et al., 1986, 1993; Gaynor & Hatcher, 1987; Jacobson, 1985a, 1985b; Kolko et al., 1985; Showers & Pickrell, 1987; Stewart & Culver, 1982). Some studies also have reported a relationship between firesetting and the diagnosis of conduct disorder (see American Psychiatric Association, 1987; see Heath, Hardesty, Goldfine, & Walker, 1985; Kelso &

Stewart, 1986), though others have not (Kolko et al., 1985; Kolko & Kazdin, 1989a, 1989b).

Studies using projective assessments with youth in residential treatment have identified an array of psychological characteristics that were more common among firesetters than non-firesetters (Sakheim, Vigdor, Gordon, & Helprin, 1985; Sakheim & Osborn, 1986). These characteristics include greater problems with sexual excitement, anger at mother and father, rage and fantasies of revenge, sexual conflicts or dysfunction, poor social judgment, difficulty verbalizing anger, and a diagnosis of conduct disorder. The youth's firesetting was viewed as providing the means to exercise power over adults (Sakheim & Osborn, 1994). Similar variables have been found more common in "high-risk" (i.e., deliberate or persistent fires) than "low-risk" (i.e., accidental or occasional fires) residential youth, such as anger and rage, poor judgment, impulsivity, little guilt, animal cruelty, and aggressive conduct disorder (Sakheim, Osborn, & Abrams, 1991). In an inpatient sample, other types of psychopathology that distinguished firesetters from non-firesetters included a greater history of sexual abuse and higher scores on the schizophrenia and mania scales of the MMPI (Moore, Thompson-Pope, & Whited, 1994).

Parental factors have also emerged as correlates of firesetting behavior. For example, parents of firesetters have reported higher levels of personal or relationship problems (e.g. psychiatric distress, marital discord, less child acceptance) and greater difficulties with parenting practices (e.g. less monitoring, discipline, and involvement in prosocial activities) than parents of non-firesetters (Kazdin & Kolko, 1986; Kolko & Kazdin, 1991a). Firesetters have described their parents' child-rearing practices as reflecting greater anxiety induction, lax discipline, and non-enforcement of rules or consequences, with scores for matchplayers generally falling between firesetters and controls. At the family level, firesetters have been found to experience more stressful life events than non-firesetters (Kolko & Kazdin, 1991a). These findings may implicate both deviant parental practices and parental dysfunction in the etiology of firesetting.

The prevalence of psychiatric disorders and criminal recidivism was examined among 45 male arsonists (ages 15–21 years) from Finland who were referred for a forensic evaluation (Repo & Virkkunen, 1997). At intake, almost 65% of the sample had a history of conduct disorder with aggressive features. Alcohol dependence was common, despite the young age of the sample. A six-year follow-up revealed that 73% had repeated general crimes. History of conduct disorder was not significantly related to recidivist firesetting. A related comparison study found that juvenile arsonists had more use of public health services for treatment of psychiatric symptoms, heightened suicidality, and were relieved of their responsibilities for the crime than juvenile crimes of violence (Rasanen, Hirvenoja, Hakko, & Vaisanen, 1995). However, the only difference between delinquents adjudicated for arson or another crime was a greater history of past firesetting in the arson group (Hanson, Mackay-Soroka, Staley, & Poulton, 1994).

These descriptive characteristics provide a general overview of the characteristics of firesetting children and, more recently, adolescents and their family backgrounds. Of course, the precipitants for a child's recent incident of firesetting may or may not be related to any of these documented variables, nor reflect the potential influence of other features, such as the child's interest in or attraction to fire, exposure to fire materials, idiosyncratic motives, and limited fire competence (see Cole et al., 1983, 1986; Kafry, 1980; Kolko & Kazdin, 1989a, 1989b). Also, there is considerable variability in the clinical pictures of firesetting youth, given that the behavior has multiple motives, antecedent conditions, and consequences. Thus, it is important to understand that firesetters may vary significantly in level of personal dysfunction, parental effectiveness, family integrity, and exposure to fire-related factors. We know even less about differences between children who present with varying forms of involvement with fire, such as those who set fires, play with matches, mix chemicals and create bombs, or just smoke. While some research findings have suggested similarities between firesetters and match-players on certain variables, findings indicate group differences on others (see Kolko & Kazdin, 1991a, 1991b).

ASSESSMENT AND EVALUATION

Many of the types of clinical problems shown by firesetting youth or their families have been described in the aforementioned section. Certainly, several individual, family, and environmental factors may contribute to a child's firesetting behavior and may warrant assessment and attention during intervention (see Kolko & Kazdin, 1986). In this section, specific measures for evaluating specific incidents and fire-related risk factors will be examined.

Children's Firesetting Incidents

There are several methods to obtain information regarding children's incidents that have expanded upon the initial screening instruments developed by the FEMA (1979, 1983, 1987). Other important aspects of children's firesetting incidents include the child's intention and social context, personal and environmental reactions, and the consequences or impact of the fire (see Cole et al., 1993). The Fire Incident Analysis for Parents (FIA-P; Kolko & Kazdin, 1991c) is a structured parent interview designed to document parameters of a child's firesetting incident that was based on items from other measures (FEMA, 1979) and the general literature (see Kolko, 1989; Wooden & Berkey, 1984). The FIA-P includes coded responses for several questions. Factor analysis of several items yielded three general motive factors (curiosity, anger, attention/help-seeking) and two other items (accident, peer pressure or destructiveness) designed to understand the presumed reason for the fire.

The FIA-P also evaluated details/characteristics of firesetting incident (e.g. how materials were obtained, site of fire, type of property damage), levels of behavioral and emotional correlates just prior to the fire (e.g. aggression/defiance, depression/withdrawal, rule violations), and consequences following the fire, such as family/disciplinary (e.g. family discipline, child was talked to or counseled by someone outside of the family), financial (e.g. value of damages), medical (i.e. injury, death), legal (e.g. criminal record, removal from home), and social/peer (e.g. peer acceptance, peer rejection/avoidance). This study reported several descriptive details of the children's fires. Other findings comparing children with different firesetting motives showed that heightened curiosity was associated with greater fire involvement out of the house and less costly fire damages, whereas heightened anger was associated with greater aggression/defiance just prior to the fire and peer rejection following the fire.

A parallel study of 95 firesetters described responses to the Fire Incident Analysis for Children which included some of the same items in the FIA-P (FIA-C; Kolko & Kazdin, 1994). The FIA-C consists of 21 questions that identified details/characteristics (e.g. how materials were obtained, site, severity of damages, forethought, planning), primary motives (curiosity/experimentation, anger/revenge/manipulation), consequences from family members and friends (e.g. discipline, attention) and reactions to the incident, and the impact of the incident on future firesetting (e.g. desire to set fire again). Among the study's findings, access to incendiaries, lack of child remorse and parental consequences, and motives of curiosity and fun were reported frequently. Four descriptive characteristics of the fire predicted the overall severity of the child's involvement in fire at follow-up (i.e. fire out of home, acknowledgement of being likely to set another fire, a neutral/positive reaction to the fire, no parental response to the fire). Although the FIA-C and FIA-P provide a quantitative evaluation of the parameters of a firesetting incident, more research is needed to determine how well these measures perform across settings and populations.

Similar descriptive details have been reported in the large Swedish study mentioned earlier (Terjestam & Ryden, 1996). In that study, 9% of the children played with fireworks frequently and 13% played with candles frequently, though the majority of children had set fire to an object (54%); another 43% lit paper, leaves, or grass. Seven percent of the children reported that they had lost control over a fire they had lit. Interestingly, most children reported a motive of wanting to see the fire burn, followed next by being bored and wanting to destroy something, though a high percentage of cases reported that they did not know the reason. Perhaps, then, it is not surprising that 36% of the sample experienced fire as exciting, 60% as nice and cozy, and only 26% as frightful. Finally, the older children in the study did not seem to have a much better understanding of the flammability of different materials than younger children. These data further emphasize the potential role of self-stimulation in firesetting and the need to pay more attention to the types and impact of children's knowledge about fire.

Fire-Related Risk Factors

Turning to other measures, fire-specific and psychosocial factors may increase a child's risk for setting an initial or even a subsequent fire. Drawing upon items in the FEMA (1979, 1983) interviews, we have operationalized certain risk factors in separate interview measures for parents (the Firesetting Risk Inventory or FRI; Kolko & Kazdin, 1989a) and children (Children's Firesetting Inventory or CFI; Kolko & Kazdin, 1989b). The FRI examines several factors specific to fire (e.g. curiosity about fire, involvement in fire-related activities, early experiences with fire, exposure to peer/family models, knowledge of fire safety, fire skill/competence), and more general factors (e.g. positive and negative behavior, frequency and efficacy of harsh punishment). Compared with non-firesetters, parents of firesetters acknowledged significantly higher scores on measures of firesetting contact (e.g. curiosity about fire, involvement in fire-related acts, exposure to peers/family fire models), general child/parent behavior (e.g. negative behavior), and family environment (e.g. use of harsh punishment, less effective mild punishment).

The CFI items were developed to evaluate the children's primary motives, skills, or experiences as potential targets for intervention. Specifically, the following six factors are examined:

- curiosity about fire (e.g. how much do you want to play with fire; how special or magical is fire to you?),
- involvement in fire-related activities (e.g. how many times did you pull a fire alarm?),
- knowledge about things that burn (e.g. will clothes, like a shirt or pair of pants, burn?),
- fire competence (e.g. what steps would you follow to light a fire in a fireplace?),
- exposure to models/materials (e.g. how many of your friends have you seen playing with matches or lighting fire?), and
- supervision/discipline (e.g. how often are you disciplined at home?).

Based on group comparisons, firesetters have shown more curiousity about involvement in fire-related acts, exposure to friends or family who smoke, and, somewhat surprisingly, knowledge of things that burn, although they only tended to show less fire competence (safety skills) on role-plays than non-firesetters.

In sum, several characteristics merit evaluation in cases where children have been implicated in a fire. In the context of understanding the child's behavioral and emotional problems, it is important to evaluate other considerations, some of which are shown in Tables 12.1 and 12.2. These include the presence of psychiatric diagnoses (e.g. attention deficit/hyperactivity disorder, conduct disorder), developmental limitations that reflect poor judgment or contact with reality, medication use, interpersonal or emotional expressiveness difficulties, and involvement with delinquent or deviant peers. Areas of parental or family dysfunction that merit evaluation include parental monitoring and supervision, parental effectiveness, parental drug or alcohol use/abuse, abuse or neglect history, child stimulation, family activities and structure, and the safety of the home environment (see Kolko, 1994).

Table 12.1   Representative clinical characteristics and domains for evaluation

Fire incident and cause/origin report
Fire history
Fire motive and precipitants
Fire consequences and related discipline
Services/community responses
Developmental level/IQ
Psychiatric disorders and history
Child cognitive–behavioral repertoire; affect regulation and expressiveness
Parental functioning and practices
Family environment, functions, and structure
Social supports and activities

Table 12.2   Sample questions for assessment

What happened?
What's the history?
Why fire now?
Does child understand the dangers of fire?
Does child have a learning or psychiatric disorder?
What outside influences make fire exposure and involvement possible?
How does the parent or family contribute to the child's fire problem?
Is there sufficient structure, use of rules, and consequences?
What interactions in the child's environment are stressful?
What threats to the child's safety exist in the environment?

INTERVENTION AND TREATMENT

Overview

Intervention methods may vary in the degree to which they target the child's fire-specific experiences or interest, the child's behavior, or the psychosocial or ecological context in which the fire occurred (Gaynor & Hatcher, 1987; Kolko, 1989, Wooden & Berkey, 1984). This may reflect the fact that fire education is conducted primarily by the fire service, whereas psychological treatment is conducted primarily by mental health practitioners. Programs in the fire department have generally emphasized instruction in fire safety skills, but have expanded to include access to psychosocial interventions, evaluations of child and family characteristics associated with firesetting, and follow-up assessments of outcome (Kolko, 1988). Many of these components have been integrated in novel comprehensive programs.

Fire Safety Skills/Prevention Education

The most common approach to working with the firesetter involves fire safety or prevention education consisting of instruction in various fire safety skills/practices. Information or practice is typically provided in such concepts as recognizing fire, understanding the dangers of fire, making emergency calls or requesting assistance, putting fires out or getting it off of one's clothes (e.g. stop/drop/roll), or other emergency plans or drills. In some cases, training is provided in the appropriate and safe use of fire. Technical manuals that describe interviews for evaluating a child's "risk status" and intervention procedures have been well disseminated (Interviewing and Counseling Juvenile Firesetter Program [ICJF]; Federal Emergency Management Agency [FEMA], 1979, 1983; National Fire Protection Association [NFPA], 1979), although there are few evaluations of their impact on firesetting behavior. Some information has documented improved fire-safety knowledge in trained, relative to control, classroom students (NFPA, 1978). Low recidivism rates have been reported following participation in fire department programs, such as the 6.2% (4/65) figure that was reported using mailings or phone calls over an unspecified time period (Porth, 1996).

Evaluations of various fire evacuation and assistance skills have been conducted with young children (see Jones, Kazdin, & Haney, 1981; Jones, Ollendick, & Shinske, 1989), which have incorporated fear-reduction techniques. For example, Williams and Jones (1989) found improvements in fire emergency responding and less fear of fire following a fire safety skills training group and a combined fire safety/fear reduction group, relative to two control groups. The combined group performed at a higher level at five-month follow-up than the other groups. Elaborative rehearsal strategies have been found to enhance the effects of behavioral rehearsal on acquisition of fire emergency skills and the reduction of fear of fire (Jones, Ollendick, McLaughlin, & Williams, 1989). Children with post-traumatic stress disorder may benefit from the use of these procedures.

A group fire safety/prevention skills training (FSST) program with hospitalized firesetters based on the aforementioned work has been found beneficial relative to individual fire awareness/discussion (FAD; Kolko, Watson, & Faust, 1991). FSST included four sessions devoted to the following content:

1. characteristics and functions of fire (e.g. damages),
2. discriminating objects that are okay or not okay for children to use (e.g. matches are tools),
3. function and use of matches (e.g. return matches if you find them), and
4. personal fire/burn safety (e.g. get help, stop-drop-roll).

Relative to FAD, FSST was associated with significantly less contact with fire-related toys and matches in an analogue play room, and an increase in fire safety knowledge, relative to FAD children. Parent-report measures at six-month follow-up showed that FSST children had engaged less often in firesetting or matchplay than FAD children (16.7% vs. 58.3%). Such findings are encouraging and highlight the need to expand both the skills and scope of this type of intervention.

A similar application of fire safety and prevention education in an inpatient and residential treatment setting made use of the "Smokey the Bear" theme (DeSalvatore & Hornstein, 1991) to train children to understand the fire triangle, hazards, camp fires, and match safety, and to report fires. The program was novel in its efforts to train parents to serve as educators for their children and to encourage family participation in completing fire safety assignments. Only one of 35 children who were followed for one year was found to have set another fire. Although the absence of a control or comparison group makes it difficult to determine the overall effectiveness of the program, the report nonetheless shows that conducting fire safety skills training in controlled settings is viable.

Other recent work has extended the application of fire awareness and prevention training sessions with parents and other adults. Pinsonneault (1996) describes a fire awareness curriculum for foster parents or child protective services workers that includes helpful strategies for identifying the motives of child firesetting and different subgroups of juvenile firesetters. The manual includes brief recommendations for creating a safe environment to minimize a family's risk for another fire, and promote positive relationships, home safety, and discussions of current events involving fire. Numerous practical exercises make this program easily applicable to most circumstances where caregiver participation is a necessary element of intervention.

Another important advance is the integration of multiple approaches or procedures, such as the integration of fire safety materials and psychological procedures. Johnston (1996) has developed an eight-session, group treatment and fire safety education program for younger children with innovative lesson plans that target feelings and behaviors, peer pressure, and identification of appropriate choices in response to challenging interpersonal situations. The inclusion of worksheets and group activities to convey certain fire safety concepts (e.g. understand fire's destructive capability, conduct home fire safety checks, describe fire interventions for the home) is a nice feature of this manual. As is true of many of the program developments in this area, there is still a need to conduct field testing and psychometric evaluations of these manuals and their impact on both firesetting and fire safety.

Psychosocial Intervention and Treatment

Several treatment procedures have been used to enhance the firesetter's prosocial repertoire, parental practices, or family functions. Among the many clinical approaches that are applied in practice, case reports and empirical studies have reported the use of structural and behavioral family therapies (Eisler, 1974; Madanes, 1981; Minuchin, 1974). One of the earliest behavioral procedures reported to be effective was negative practice (repeatedly lighting matches), a technique designed to satiate the child's interest in fire (Holland, 1969; Kolko, 1983; McGrath, Marshall, & Prior, 1979). Perhaps due to the potential controversy about encouraging fireplay in this population, the procedure has been less often reported in recent years. Other behavioral methods, such as the use of contingency management, have been applied both to discourage contact with fire and reinforce positive behaviors or the use of more appropriate materials (Adler, Nunn, Laverick, & Ross, 1988), including the use of stories designed to weaken the child's interest in fire (Stawar, 1976).

The graphing technique has been used at the outset of treatment to represent the personal and environmental context of a fire (Bumpass, Fagelman, & Brix, 1983). This procedure solicits information from the child about the antecedents and consequences of the fire, such as the emotional or cognitive precipitants of the fire (e.g. anger, perception of being unfairly treated). Graphs have been applied during individual and/or family psychotherapy (Bumpass, Brix, & Preston, 1985). The procedure may help to enhance rapport, document the child's responsibility for the fire, and identify potential clinical targets for intervention.

Youth who set fires in response to affective distress have been taught various prosocial, cognitive–behavioral skills to facilitate appropriate expression of anger and emotional arousal (Kolko & Ammerman, 1988; McGrath et al., 1979) and assertive problem-solving behavior (DeSalvatore & Hornstein, 1991). These clinical reports describe multicomponent treatments that target the child's interpersonal repertoire, the functional context of firesetting, and parental use of punishment and reinforcement. Other clinical techniques have been recommended to alter child and family factors related to firesetting, such as the use of communication training and family problem-solving (see Cole et al., 1993; Gaynor & Hatcher, 1987; Kolko, 1989, 1996). For the more serious cases, it seems reasonable to consider applying several procedures during treatment, such as skills training in appropriate behaviors, discussions of the child's motives, the introduction of immediate consequences for both positive and negative behavior, and parental or family monitoring of suspicious behavior that may be associated with firesetting.

Some recent applications have implemented different combinations of cognitive–behavioral and contingency management procedures with psychiatrically referred children and youth, such as home-based reinforcement and response-cost contingencies (Kolko, 1983), graphing of prior incidents and psychological skills training (Kolko & Ammerman, 1988), and fire safety assessment/skills training and parent management training (Cox-Jones, Lubetsky, Fultz, & Kolko, 1990). These interventions were associated with reduced firesetting behavior and improved behavioral adjustment at follow-up. Similarly, diverse psychological services that included cognitive–behavioral assessment information (e.g. functional analysis) and treatment (e.g. social skills, coping and relaxation, assertion training, covert sensitization), in addition to facial surgery, have been found helpful with a young adult (Clare, Murphy, Cox, & Chaplin, 1992). At four-month follow-up, no further firesetting or related behavior had been reported. These clinical reports suggest that there is some benefit to targeting the child's behavioral repertoire and/or environmental contingencies in the home. Moreover, the use of covert sensitization by Clare et al. (1992) highlights the potential for modifying the firesetter's inappropriate attraction to fire which has been targeted in prior reports (see Stawar, 1976). However, all these studies are based on single-case reports or designs. Thus, these psychological procedures have not been evaluated in the context of large-scale, controlled outcome studies.

Among the developments for treating firesetting youth is the articulation of novel assessment methods and conceptualizations of the clinical factors that bear implications for subsequent firesetting and treatment planning. In conjunction with the Oregon Office of State Fire Marshall, a treatment strategies task force has developed a "needs assessment" protocol to assess mental health needs, take an accurate firesetter history, determine precipitating stressors and a firesetter typology, and make appropriate treatment and supervision recommendations (Humphreys & Kopet, 1996). This assessment is designed to suggest potential areas and systems that should be targeted by treatment. For example, the protocol includes suggested interview questions in various domains (e.g. family, social, trauma, mental health, fire) that yield typology scores (e.g. curiosity, delinquent) which allow the evaluator to develop a formulation about case diagnosis, prognosis, and treatment. Practical, clinically oriented questions and assessment guidelines are provided to facilitate application of the protocol.

A related model outlining some of the psychological and environmental factors proposed to influence the likelihood of recidivism has been developed by this task force to promote a more systematic approach to the selection of relevant mental health treatments (Oregon Treatment Strategies Task Force). This model recognizes the importance of understanding the various subtypes of firesetters noted above. Four overlapping cycles or rings are proposed in the model, each representing a domain that may influence a child's and family's behavior:

1.   emotional/cognitive (e.g. thinking errors, believes life is unfair, boredom or anger),
2.   behavioral (e.g. limit testing, power struggles, covert behaviors),
3.   family (e.g. initial response to fire, stressors, ineffective discipline), and
4.   community/social (e.g. special services, institutional conflicts, community resources).

The specific reactions proposed in each domain cycle are examined to determine the likelihood of recidivism and to identify necessary steps to intervention designed to minimize the child's use of fire. For example, specific interventions may target the child (e.g. eliminate negative peer influences, restitution, anger management), family (e.g. communication training, logical discipline, fire safety education), or fire department (e.g. fire education, contract). The model emphasizes how various systems that serve firesetting youth can both help and exacerbate the problem, and demonstrates how solutions to the firesetting problem require a coordinated network of agencies (e.g. school, law enforcement, mental health). The model is exploratory at this point due to the absence of needed information regarding its feasibility in applied settings and psychometric adequacy. For example, it would be useful to determine which of the components of the cycle in each domain are most commonly identified in clinical practice and how easy it is to make changes in these components. Other practical recommendations have been described by members of the Oregon Treatment Task Force to help parents and families address the behavioral and clinical needs of the youthful firesetter. A noteworthy feature of these recommendations is their incorporation of an array of intervention procedures, such as installing smoke alarms, teaching fire safety information and skills, monitoring children's possessions for fire-related materials, encouraging the expression of affective states, establishing structure and consequences in the home, and addressing systemic problems in family therapy (Humphreys, Kopet, & Lajoy, 1994). Humphreys et al. offer several tips to help parents monitor, teach, and manage a child's firesetting, regardless of the level of child or family dysfunction (e.g. remove matches, monitor television habits, discuss consequences in advance, forbid fireplay).

Delinquent firesetters have also been targeted by a group program developed by Campbell and Elliott (1996). The program includes lessons that cover many of the concepts commonly found in cognitive–behavioral treatments, such as communication, assertion, and anger-control, conscience, thinking errors, and relapse prevention plans, as well as how to work with parents. The program is strengthened by the inclusion of discussion questions, homework exercises, and a post-test evaluation. An extension of this work for application to adolescents has incorporated both restitution and fire education components through which the youth completes a community impact report and participates in community service (Clackamas County Juvenile Firesetting Intervention Network, 1996).

Treatment Research and Outcome Studies

As noted earlier, studies that evaluate intervention procedures are rare. One of the few controlled evaluations of alternative approaches to working with children (5–16 years) who were classified as either curiosity and pathological firesetters was conducted in Australia (Adler, Nunn, Northam, Lebnan, & Ross, 1994). Curious and non-dysfunctional firesetters were randomly assigned to either education (fire safety information to child and parents, discussion of fire awareness) or a combined condition (education, satiation, response cost for fires, graphing of fire) with both interventions being conducted by a fire fighter at home, whereas pathological cases were offered psychiatric referral and treatment by a specialist in a children's hospital clinic and then randomized either to the same education alone or combined condition.

The findings revealed a significant reduction in the frequency of firesetting following the intervention but no difference between the home/specialist and education/combined conditions. The overall mean rates of firesetting were 7.1 and 1.5 at each of these two respective time periods. There was also a reduction in the severity of firesetting. Of 80 children considered improved, 59 (42.8%) set no fires during the 12-month post-treatment period and an additional 21 (15.2%) no longer met the referral criterion as they set less than three fires during that period. Home-based (vs. specialist) cases tended to have a higher proportion of improvement (73% vs. 52%) and a lower percentage of dropout (20% vs. 35%). The combined (vs. education only) group also tended to have a higher dropout rate (35% vs. 21%). Although the 28% attrition rate and absence of treatment integrity or child behavior date are limitations, this study is the first controlled outcome study based on these common procedures and it demonstrates that even minimal intervention may be effective in reducing firesetting over a long period of time.

A study in the United States is examining the relative efficacy of fire service and mental health interventions conducted in a "clinic" setting (Kolko, 1996). Firesetting boys, aged 5–13, were randomly assigned to either Fire Safety Education (FSE) conducted by trained firefighters or therapist-delivered cognitive-behavioral treatment (CBT) and compared with cases that were assigned to a brief condition consisting of a Home Visit from a Firefighter (FHV) that was designed to reflect a routine fire service practice. Intervention was designed to be short-term, directed to children and their parents, executed by specialists, and evaluated using multiple measures. FSE involved training in fire safety education principles and tasks (e.g. stop-drop-roll, emergency phone calls, exiting a burning house, declining an invitation to engage in matchplay), whereas CBT involved teaching self-control and problem-solving skills, establishing environmental conditions to encourage prosocial behavior, and altering the motive to use fire. FHV included a brief discussion of fire dangers and firefighting, executing a "no-fire contract", and distributing safety materials (e.g. coloring books). Thus, two intensive programs are being compared with one another and then with a third, minimal contact condition.

Preliminary analyses of outcome data suggest that all three interventions resulted in reductions in child- and parent-reported incidents of firesetting and matchplay. However, both CBT and FSE were associated with even greater improvements than FHV for child-reported firesetting incidents. Only FSE led to improvements in children's fire safety skill. There were few group differences in improvements in child and parent dysfunction. These acute effects will be supplemented with one-year follow-up data. The study will also identify predictors of firesetting recidivism.

Summary of Intervention Procedures

The aforementioned anecdotal, clinical, and limited empirical evidence suggests that there may be some advantage to targeting both fire-specific experiences and skills (e.g. children's involvement with, exposure to, and interest in fire) and the child's behavior and environmental context (e.g. aggression, parental practices). However, the clinical impact of these interventions has been demonstrated with a few, limited empirical studies. Program evaluation and controlled studies of both fire safety education and psychosocial treatment would certainly advance our understanding of interventions for childhood firesetters. An evaluation of the separate and combined effects of these two complementary interventions is warranted because firesetters who set multiple fires may also exhibit significant psychosocial maladjustment, and are often referred for multiple services. The procedures used in these two areas also seem to be quite compatible and may enhance one another's effectiveness.

PROGRAM DEVELOPMENT, ORGANIZATION, AND DISSEMINATION

Collaborative Programs

The National Juvenile Firesetter/Arson Control and Prevention Program (NJF/ACP) of 1987 was sponsored by the Office of Juvenile Justice and Delinquency Prevention (OJJDP) and US Fire Administration (USFA) to "conceptualize, design, develop, and evaluate a variety of community-based approaches to prevent and control juvenile firesetting" (FEMA, 1994, p. 1). The initiative was conducted in different stages (assessment of problem, development of comprehensive approach and training and technical materials, testing and dissemination of materials) and led to the identification of seven components common to effective juvenile firesetter programs (i.e. program management, screening and evaluation, intervention services, referral mechanisms, publicity and outreach, monitoring systems, and developing relationships with juvenile justice), which have been articulated in several guidebooks published by FEMA (1994, FA-145-149). These resources identify various steps to developing a collaborative program.

A large-scale evaluation was conducted of the initial application of the NJF/ACP model for developing fire-department-based programs. As reported by Bourque, Cronin, and Han (1993), this evaluation examined the implementation of a program model in three jurisdictions (Parker, Colorado; Oklahoma City, Oklahoma; West Valley, Utah), tested the effectiveness of the model in controlling firesetting, and suggested modifications to the model and related program materials. Interestingly, about two-thirds of the cases referred to two of the sites were rated as needing a mental health evaluation. In general, the evaluation found that regional evaluations were helpful and that the program guides were useful in developing new programs. Thus, these programs highlight the potential utility of the program guidebooks upon which they were based. However, certain assessed cases were not referred to services. Furthermore, it is not clear whether these programs actually altered the incidence of firesetting following their implementation. Nevertheless, the JFACCP material offers one of the first systematic approaches to the application of field-tested concepts and methods in the organization of multiple services for juvenile firesetters.

Several comprehensive networks of services in different cities were in operation prior to the NJF/ACP initiative but are clearly consistent with its content, such as the combined mental health and fire department program reported in Dallas, Texas (Bumpass et al., 1985). This program is noteworthy for its novel use of the graphing technique, fire safety films, and activities to promote community involvement. Helpful program evaluation data showed before–after improvements for recidivist cases (32% vs. 2%), number of reported juvenile fires reported (204 vs. 141), and fire costs ($1 031 606 vs. $536 102), though these changes were not statistically evaluated. Integrated community-based services also have extended the use of fire department and mental health screening evaluations to select appropriate interventions, incorporated engagement, liaison, and outreach strategies, and provided a range of services that cover school-based curricula, fire education and mental health services, and intensive treatment (Webb, Sakheim, Towns-Miranda, & Wagner, 1990).

Service or Program Networks

Multidisciplinary collaboration in the administration of services for firesetting youth has become an important advance in this area and, in recent years, represents more the rule than the exception. This is due, in part, to the accumulation of evidence suggesting the relevance of fire safety and mental health considerations in understanding the problem of juvenile firesetting, and to the recognition of the roles being played by professionals in the juvenile justice, burn care and other medical, educational, and social service systems. At the same time, there is a strong need to expand the scope and comprehensiveness of intervention programs in this area and level of regional support and resources received by various programs to ensure their long-term viability.

In the last few years several states have developed organized networks of affiliated programs that share common policies and procedures, as reflected in one network's ongoing newsletter (see *The Strike Zone*, Fall, 1997). For example, the Massachusetts Coalition for Juvenile Firesetter Programs represents 12 program sites through the state (e.g. Lowell, Barnstable, West Springfield, River Valley). Staff at each site have received specialty training in various areas (e.g. screening, interviewing, assessment, education, treatment) to serve the various aspects of the firesetting problem. These programs benefit from the participation of experts from multiple disciplines (e.g. fire service, mental health, social services, law enforcement) and include an array of innovative services and resources, such as a weekend "fire school", the use of teachers and firefighter/emergency services technicians as educators, and specialized manuals and audio-visual aids. An interesting development in the State of Massachusetts is the passage of legislation that requires a worker from the Department of Social Services to refer children with a history of either firesetting or sexual offending for a specialized risk-management assessment to identify appropriate treatments and placement options. Coalition members will be participating in the assessment and disposition process with these cases, which, to date, reflects one of the largest collaborative networks established between social services and firesetter programs.

State-wide programs in Oregon have been coordinated by the Office of State Fire Marshall which has developed innovative collaborations and specialized materials (see Juvenile Firesetter Intervention Program's *Hot Issues*, 1998). A newsletter published by the coordinator of these programs disseminates various stories, program descriptions, practical suggestions, and information related to training opportunities and conferences at both the regional and national level. More recently, *The Idea Bank* has developed a web site that provides access to news, announcements, articles, technical resources, and program descriptions throughout the country (Idea Bank, 1997). All these materials are likely to facilitate a discussion of program developments in the field and enhance the quality of care and professional competence in this area.

Of course, there are still many obstacles to developing and maintaining an effective collaborative program in most communities. A task force on juvenile firesetting convened by the NFPA in 1993 reported on several impediments and some potential solutions (NFPA, 1993). To promote greater public and professional awareness of the problem of firesetting, suggestions were made to train juvenile firesetter professionals in community coalition building strategies, educate media professionals, develop fire science information and parent education materials, enlist fire service leaders in juvenile programs, and train mental health professionals in intervention techniques. The need to access existing resources through the establishment of a national clearinghouse that could disseminate information on program descriptions and outcomes also was discussed. Finally, the need to use data effectively was considered important in terms of describing, planning, and revising program components. A follow-up task force meeting identified other needs for the field, including the identification of a "niche" or organization that embraces the juvenile firesetting problem, the need for greater technical assistance to existing programs, and maintenance of communication at a regional and national level (NFPA, 1995).

One of the practical problems in the field reflects the uncertainty about the role of assessment information. A recent study of firesetting youth found that parent ratings on a child behavior checklist were not examined prior to the fire department's referral of the case for services (Pierce & Hardesty, 1997). Significant levels of psychopathology were not found to contribute to the child's future referral for mental health services. Such findings highlight the importance of working collaboratively with mental health practitioners in identifying the most appropriate services for juvenile firesetters.

FUTURE DIRECTIONS

The delivery of services for juvenile firesetters is enriched but also complicated by the inclusion of multiple disciplines and, thus, requires considerable thought to ensure long-term program viability. One practical solution to the development of an efficient and cost-effective approach to the fire problem is to develop "clinical pathways" that specify the order in which specific intervention components are to be implemented based on screening and evaluation information. For example, the most simple procedure (e.g. providing a short brochure on the dangers of fire) may prove useful with a large number of cases referred for services. Some type of informational pack, such as this, may provide tips or suggestions to address a child's interest or initial involvement with fire. Of course, other more intensive and direct procedures may be needed, such as child training in fire safety/prevention skills or parent training in effective child or contingency management techniques. Next, there may be a need to encourage clinical involvement in treatment that focuses on cognitive–behavioral skills, parental counseling, and/or family treatment. Involvement with restitution may be a useful intervention, especially for older firesetters, with or without concurrent juvenile justice involvement. Finally, some children may require hospitalization or residential treatment to address serious forms of psychopathology and family dysfunction. The relative advantage of developing a hierarchy of interventions and their most judicious use merits further conceptual elaboration and empirical evaluation.

As shown in Table 12.3, there are several areas worth examining in research studies. There is a need to understand better the nature of firesetting in children and youth, such as whether there is a continuum of fire behavior that reflects a progression to more serious involvement with fire. For example, fire interest or curiosity may be precursors to matchplay or fireplay, which may stimulate involvement in firesetting. Precipitants of serious firesetting and arson are also important to evaluate. Psychometric evaluation of new fire materials and models, such as the Oregon Cycle of Firesetting Model, is needed to determine their practical utility. We also need to know the relationship between childhood firesetting and adult arson to understand the continuity of this behavior over time. Follow-up studies would help us document the natural history of children's involvement with fire and predictors of recidivism.

In terms of interventions, there is an urgent need to examine the feasibility and efficacy of different interventions, and the overall impact of services at two levels:

1. the individual firesetter, and
2. the community at large.

Whether psychosocial interventions impact upon both firesetting behavior and other behavior problems is also unknown. Likewise, studies should examine the

Table 12.3 Topics for research

Assessment of fire-specific risk factors, including child's attraction to fire
Evaluation of a typology of child motives for firesetting
Outcomes of alternative or comparative interventions
Predictors of program response and follow-up recidivism
Documentation of the effects of preventive programs
Examination of specialized audio-visual materials and curricula

relative utility of fire safety skills training with different groups of children who vary in psychological disturbances in order to determine its generality. The efficacy of both interventions with children who show a heightened attraction to and interest in fire is certainly important to document as few methods have been evaluated in this context. A similar argument could made regarding the need to treat children whose firesetting results in significant avoidance of fire-related stimuli and heightened anxiety. Exposure-based treatments have been effective in such cases (see Jones, Ollendick, McLaughlin et al., 1989). Data collected in community settings could examine both short-term impact and long-term outcome. Finally, it would be of interest to examine the relative benefits of multicomponent interventions that integrate diverse approaches with more simplified interventions that lend themselves to efficient administration, such as films or groups.

Even with advances in intervention, there may be an even greater benefit to the application of primary prevention programs in this area. Prevention programs can be efficiently implemented in multiple naturalistic settings and by a range of community participants (e.g. schools, community centers). In all likelihood, the scope of impact following a media campaign (e.g. public service announcements) designed to reduce exposure to incendiary materials, child matchplay, and other fire-related risk factors may be much greater than those generated by interventions with known firesetters. Effective suppression and prevention of juvenile firesetting will no doubt require advances in scientific knowledge about its etiology and management, the integration of diverse educational and clinical services, and the dedicated efforts of a cadre of community practitioners.

ACKNOWLEDGMENTS

Preparation of this chapter was supported, in part, by a renewal of grant MH-39976 to the author from the National Institute of Mental Health. The author acknowledges the contribution of the staff associated with Project SAFETY (Services Aimed at Fire Education and Training for Youth). Many of the initial background studies reviewed herein were conducted in collaboration with Alan E. Kazdin, Ph.D. Reprint requests can be obtained from David J. Kolko, Director, WPIC/Special Services Unit, Western Psychiatric Institute and Clinic, 3811 O'Hara St., Pittsburgh, PA 15213, USA. E-mail: kolkodj@msx.upmc.edu.

REFERENCES

Adler, R. G., Nunn, R. J., Laverick, J., & Ross, R. (1988, October). *Royal Children's Hospital/Metropolitan Fire Brigade juvenile fire awareness and intervention program: Research and intervention protocol*. Unpublished paper.

Adler, R. G., Nunn, R., Northam, E., Lebnan, V., & Ross, R. (1994). Secondary prevention of childhood firesetting. *Journal of the American Academy of Child and Adolescent Psychiatry*, 33, 1194–1202.

American Psychiatric Association (1987). *Diagnostic and statistical manual of mental disorders-revised* (3rd ed., Rev.). Washington, DC: Author.

Bourque, B. B., Cronin, R. C., & Han, M. (1993, November). *Controlling juvenile fireset-ting: An evaluation of three regional pilot programs*. Final report, submitted to the Office of Juvenile Justice and Delinquency Prevention, Office of Justice Programs, US Depart-ment of Justice. Washington, DC: American Institutes for Research.

Bumpass, E. R., Brix, R. J., & Preston, D. (1985). A community-based program for juve-nile firesetters. *Hospital and Community Psychiatry, 36*, 529–533.

Bumpass, E. R., Fagelman, F. D., & Brix, R. J. (1983). Intervention with children who set fires. *American Journal of Psychotherapy, 37*, 328–345.

Campbell, C., & Elliott, E. J. (1996). Skills building curriculum for juvenile firesetters. Salem, OR: Oregon Office of State Fire Marshal.

Cella, D. F., Perry, S. W., Kulchycky, S., & Goodwin, C. (1988). Stress and coping in rela-tives of burn patients: A longitudinal study. *Hospital and Community Psychiatry, 39*, 159–166.

Clackamas County Juvenile Firesetting Intervention Network (1996). Adolescent fireset-ters: An intervention—A restitution model with fire education emphasis. Salem, OR: Office of State Fire Marshall.

Clare, I. C. H., Murphy, G. H., Cox, D., & Chaplin, E. H. (1992). Assessment and treatment of firesetting: A single-case investigation using a cognitive-behavioral model. *Criminal Behaviour and Mental Health, 2*, 253–268.

Cole, R. E., Grolnick, W. S., McCandrews, M. M., et al. (1986). *Rochester fire-related youth project, progress report, Vol. 2*. Rochester, NY: New York State Office of Fire Preven-tion and Control.

Cole, R. E., Grolnick, W., & Schwartzman, P. (1993). Fire Setting. In R. T. Ammerman, C. Last, & M. Hersen (Eds.), *Handbook of prescriptive treatments for children and adolescents*. Boston, MA: Allyn & Bacon.

Cole, R. E., Laurenitis, L. R., McCandrews, M. M., et al. (1983). *Final report of the 1983 fire-related youth program development project*. Rochester, NY: New York State Office of Fire Prevention and Control.

Cox-Jones, C., Lubetsky, M., Fultz, S. A., & Kolko, D. J. (1990). Inpatient treatment of a young recidivist firesetter. *Journal of the American Academy of Child Psychiatry, 29*, 936–941.

DeSalvatore, G., & Hornstein, R. (1991). Juvenile firesetting: Assessment and treatment in psychiatric hospitalization and residential placement. *Child and Youth Care Forum, 20*, 103–114.

Eisler, R. M. (1974). Crisis intervention in the family of a firesetter. *Psychotherapy: Theory, Research and Practice, 9*, 76–79.

Federal Emergency Management Agency (1979). *Interviewing and counseling juvenile firesetters*. Washington, DC: US Government Printing Office.

Federal Emergency Management Agency (1983). *Juvenile firesetter handbook: Dealing with children ages 7 to 13*. Washington, DC: US Government Printing Office.

Federal Emergency Management Agency (1987). *Juvenile firesetter handbook: Dealing with adolescents ages 14 to 18*. Washington, DC: US Government Printing Office.

Federal Emergency Management Agency (1994). *The national juvenile firesetter/Arson control and prevention program* (Executive summary). Washington, DC: US Fire Administration.

Gaynor, J., & Hatcher, C. (1987). *The psychology of child firesetting: Detection and inter-vention*. New York: Brunner/Mazel.

Grolnick, W. S., Cole, R. E., Laurenitis, L., & Schwartzman, P. I. (1990). Playing with fire: A developmental assessment of children's fire understanding and experience. *Journal of Clinical Child Psychology, 19*, 128–135.

Hall, J. R. (1995, August). *Children playing with fire: U.S. experience, 1980–1993*. Quincy, MA: National Fire Protection Association.

Hanson, M., Mackay-Soroka, S., Staley, S., & Poulton, L. (1994). Delinquent firesetters:

A comparative study of delinquency and firesetting histories. *Canadian Journal of Psychiatry, 39*, 230–232.

Heath, G. A., Hardesty, V. A., Goldfine, P. E., & Walker, A. M. (1985). Diagnosis and childhood firesetting. *Journal of Clinical Psychology, 41*, 571–575.

Holland, C. J. (1969). Elimination by the parents of firesetting behavior in a 7-year old boy. *Behaviour Research & Therapy, 7*, 135–137.

Humphreys, J., Kopet, T., & Lajoy, R. (1994). Clinical considerations in the treatment of juvenile firesetters. *The Behavior Therapist, 17*, 13–15.

Humphreys, J., & Kopet, T. (1996, March). *Manual for juvenile firesetter needs assessment protocol.* Salem, OR: Office of State Fire Marshal.

The Idea Bank (1997). Juvenile firesetter resources. Santa Barbara, CA: The Idea Bank, 1139 Alameda Padre Serra (Info@the ideabank.com).

Jacobson, R. R. (1985a). Child firesetters: A clinical investigation. *Journal of Child Psychology and Psychiatry, 26*, 759–768.

Jacobson, R. R. (1985b). The subclassification of child firesetters. *Journal of Child Psychology and Psychiatry, 26*, 769–775.

Johnston, K. (1996). *A step by step approach to group treatment and fire safety education: An eight session intervention program for child firesetters.* Salem, OR: Office of State Fire Marshal.

Jones, R. T., Kazdin, A. E., & Haney, J. I. (1981). Social validation and training of emergency fire safety skills for potential injury prevention and life saving. *Journal of Applied Behavior Analysis, 14*, 249–260.

Jones, R. T., Ollendick, T. H., McLaughlin, K. J., & Williams, C. E. (1989). Elaborative and behavioral rehearsal in the acquisition of fire emergency skills and the reduction of fear of fire. *Behavior Therapy, 20*, 93–101.

Jones, R. T., Ollendick, T. H., & Shinske, F. K. (1989). The role of behavioral versus cognitive variables in skill acquisition. *Behavior Therapy, 20*, 293–302.

Juvenile Firesetter Intervention Program (1998). *Hot Issues, 8.* Salem, OR: Office of State Fire Marshall.

Kafry, D. (1980). Playing with matches: Children and fire. In D. Canter (Ed.), *Fires and human behavior* (pp. 41–60), Chichester, UK: Wiley.

Kazdin, A. E., & Kolko, D. J. (1986). Parent psychopathology and family functioning among childhood firesetters. *Journal of Abnormal Child Psychology, 14*, 315–329.

Kelso, J., & Stewart, M. A. (1986). Factors which predict the persistence of aggressive conduct disorder. *Journal of Child Psychology and Psychiatry, 27*, 77–86.

Kolko, D. J. (1983). Multicomponent parental treatment of firesetting in a developmentally-disabled boy. *Journal of Behavior Therapy and Experimental Psychiatry, 14*, 349–353.

Kolko, D. J. (1988). Community interventions for childhood firesetters: A comparison of two national programs. *Hospital and Community Psychiatry, 39*, 973–979.

Kolko, D. J. (1989). Fire setting and pyromania. In C. Last & M. Hersen (Eds.), *Handbook of Child Psychiatric Diagnosis* (pp. 443–459). New York: Wiley.

Kolko, D. J. (1994). Conduct Disorder. In M. Hersen, R. T. Ammerman, & L. Sisson (Eds.), *Handbook of aggressive and destructive behavior in psychiatric patients* (pp. 363–394). New York: Plenum.

Kolko, D. J. (1996). Education and counseling for child firesetters: A comparison of skills training programs with standard practice. In E. D. Hibbs & P. S. Jensen (Eds.), *Psychosocial treatments for child and adolescent disorders: Empirically based strategies for clinical practice* (pp. 409–433). Washington, DC: American Psychological Association.

Kolko, D. J., & Ammerman, R. T. (1988). Firesetting. In M. Hersen & C. Last (Eds.), *Child behavior therapy casebook* (pp. 243–262). New York: Plenum.

Kolko, D. J., & Kazdin, A. E. (1986). A conceptualization of firesetting in children and adolescents. *Journal of Abnormal Child Psychology, 14*, 49–62.

Kolko, D. J., & Kazdin, A. E. (1988a). Parent–child correspondence in identification of fire-setting among child psychiatric patients. *Journal of Child Psychology and Psychiatry*, *29*, 175–184.

Kolko, D. J., & Kazdin, A. E. (1988b). Prevalence of firesetting and related behaviors in child psychiatric inpatients. *Journal of Consulting and Clinical Psychology*, *56*, 628–630.

Kolko, D. J., & Kazdin, A. E. (1989a). Assessment of dimensions of childhood firesetting among child psychiatric patients and nonpatients. *Journal of Abnormal Child Psychology*, *17*, 157–176.

Kolko, D. J., & Kazdin, A. E. (1989b). The Children's Firesetting Interview with psychiatrically referred and nonreferred children. *Journal of Abnormal Child Psychology*, *17*, 609–624.

Kolko, D. J., & Kazdin, A. E. (1991a). Matchplay and firesetting in children: Relationship to parent, marital, and family dysfunction. *Journal of Clinical Child Psychology*, *19*, 229–238.

Kolko, D. J., & Kazdin, A. E. (1991b). Aggression and psychopathology in matchplaying and firesetting children: A replication and extension. *Journal of Clinical Child Psychology*, *20*, 191–201.

Kolko, D. J., & Kazdin, A. E. (1991c). Motives of childhood firesetters: Firesetting characteristics and psychological correlates. *Journal of Child Psychology and Psychiatry*, *32*, 535–550.

Kolko, D. J., & Kazdin, A. E. (1992). The emergence and recurrence of child firesetting: A one-year prospective study. *Journal of Abnormal Child Psychology*, *20*, 17–37.

Kolko, D. J., & Kazdin, A. E. (1994). Children's descriptions of their firesetting incidents: Characteristics and relationship to recidivism. *Journal of the American Academy of Child Psychiatry*, *33*, 114–122.

Kolko, D. J., & Kazdin, A. E. (1995). *Two-year follow-up of child firesetters: Late-starting and recidivism.* Poster presented at the Annual Meeting of the Association for the Advancement of Behavior Therapy, Washington, DC.

Kolko, D. J., Kazdin, A. E., & Meyer, E. C. (1985). Aggression and psychopathology in childhood firesetters: Parent and child reports. *Journal of Consulting and Clinical Psychology*, *53*, 377–385.

Kolko, D. J., Watson, S., & Faust, J. (1991). Fire safety/prevention skills training to reduce involvement with fire in young psychiatric inpatients: Preliminary findings. *Behavior Therapy*, *22*, 269–284.

Madanes, C. (1981). *Strategic family therapy.* San Francisco, CA: Jossey-Bass.

McGrath, P., Marshall, P. T., & Prior, K. (1979). A comprehensive treatment program for a firesetting child. *Journal of Behavior Therapy and Experimental Psychiatry*, *10*, 69–72.

Minuchin, S. (1974). *Families and family therapy.* San Francisco, CA: Jossey-Bass.

Moore, J. M., Thompson-Pope, S. K., & Whited, R. M. (1994). MMPI-A profiles of adolescent boys with a history of firesetting. *Journal of Personality Assessment*, *67*, 116–126.

Moos, R. H., Insel, P. M., & Humphrey, B. (1974). *Family work and group environment scales.* Palo Alto, CA: Consulting Psychologists Press.

National Fire Protection Association (1978). *Executive summary report of the Learn Not to Burn Curriculum.* Quincy, MA: Author.

National Fire Protection Association (1979). *Learn Not to Burn Curriculum.* Quincy, MA: Author.

National Fire Protection Association (1993, October). *Report of the NFPA task force on juvenile firesetting* (Inaugural meeting). Norwood, MA: Author.

National Fire Protection Associatio (1995, September). *Report of the NFPA firesetter practitioners' forum.* Braintree, MA: Author.

Oregon Treatment Strategies Task Force (1996). *The cycles of firesetting: An Oregon model.* Salem, OR: Office of State Fire Marshall.

Parrish, J. M., Capriotti, R. M., Warzak, W. J., Handen, B. L., Wells, T. J., Phillipson, S. J., & Porter, C. A. (1985). *Multivariate analysis of juvenile firesetting.* Paper presented at the

Annual Meeting of the Association for the Advancement of Behavior Therapy, Houston, TX.

Pierce, J. L., & Hardesty, V. A. (1997). Non-referral of psychopathological child firesetters to mental health services. *Journal of Clinical Psychology, 53*, 349–350.

Pinsonneault, I. (1996). *Fire awareness: Training for foster parents.* Fall River, MA: F.I.R.E. Solutions.

Porth, D. (1996). A report on the juvenile firesetting problem. *The Portland Report '95.* Portland, OR: Portland Fire Bureau.

Rasanen, P., Hirvenoja, R., Hakko, H., & Vaisanen, E. (1995). A portrait of the juvenile arsonist. *Forensic Science International, 73*, 41–47.

Repo, E., & Virkkunen, M. (1997). Young arsonists: History of conduct disorder, psychiatric diagnoses and criminal recidivism. *Journal of Forensic Psychiatry, 8*, 311–320.

Rice, M. E., & Harris, G. T. (1991). Firesetters admitted to a maximum security psychiatric institution: Offenders and offenses. *Journal of Interpersonal Violence, 6*, 461–475.

Sakheim, G. A., & Osborn, E. (1986). A psychological profile of juvenile firesetters in residential treatment: A replication study. *Child Welfare, 45*, 495–503.

Sakheim, G. A., & Osborn, E. (1994). *Firesetting children: Risk assessment and treatment.* Washington, DC: Child Welfare League of America.

Sakheim, G. A., Osborn, E., & Abrams, D. (1991). Toward a clearer differentiation of high-risk from low-risk fire-setters. *Child Welfare, 45*, 489–503.

Sakheim, G. A., Vigdor, M. G., Gordon, M., & Helprin, L. M. (1985). A psychological profile of juvenile firesetters in residential treatment. *Child Welfare, 44*, 453–476.

Showers, J., & Pickrell, E. P. (1987). Child firesetters: A study of three populations. *Hospital and Community Psychiatry, 38*, 495–501.

Stawar, T. L. (1976). Fable mod: Operantly structured fantasies as an adjunct in the modification of firesetting behavior. *Journal of Behavior Therapy and Experimental Psychiatry, 7*, 285–287.

Stewart, M. A., & Culver, K. W. (1982). Children who set fires: The clinical picture and a follow-up. *British Journal of Psychiatry, 140*, 357–363.

Stoddard, F. J., Norman, D. K., Murphy, J. M., & Beardslee, W. R. (1989). Psychiatric outcome of burned children and adolescents. *Journal of the American Academy of Child and Adolescent Psychiatry, 28*, 589–595.

The Strike Zone (1997, Fall). *Massachusetts coalition for juvenile firesetter programs, 1–8.*

Terjestam, P. Y., & Ryden, O. (1996). Fire-settings as normal behavior: Frequencies and patterns of change in the behavior of 7–16 year old children. *Research report* (pp. 21–147/96). Karlstad, Sweden: Swedish Rescue Services Agency.

US Federal Bureau of Investigation (1995). *Uniform crime reports.* Washington, DC: Author.

Webb, N. B., Sakheim, G. A., Towns-Miranda, L., & Wagner, C. R. (1990). Collaborative treatment of juvenile firesetters: Assessment and outreach. *American Journal of Orthopsychiatry, 60*, 305–310.

Williams, C. E., & Jones, R. (1989). Impact of self-instructions on response maintenance and children's fear of fire. *Journal of Clinical Psychology, 18*, 84–89.

Wooden, W., & Berkey, M. L. (1984). *Children and arson: America's middle class nightmare.* New York: Plenum.

Chapter 13

Assessment and Treatment: Violent Offenders

Devon L. L. Polaschek
Victoria University of Wellington, Wellington, New Zealand
and
Nikki Reynolds
Department of Corrections Psychological Service,
Lambton Quay, Wellington, New Zealand

INTRODUCTION

Violent offending is considered by many to be on the increase. Regardless of whether this is true, violent offenders are an increasing proportion of correctional populations in many parts of the Western world. Non-sexual violence constitutes an extensive and disparate category of human behaviours which, despite its seriousness, has not received the level of attention accorded to sexual offending by clinicians and correctional practitioners. However, interest is growing, especially in the area of treatment provision, although many fundamental research questions remain. The focus of this chapter is generally on violent juvenile and adult male offenders; for convenience the male pronoun will be used throughout. Because of space constraints, readers are referred to more detailed reviews and sources wherever possible.

ASSESSMENT

The aims of treatment-oriented assessment are to develop a sophisticated conceptual model of the offender, his offence characteristics and personal vulnerabilities; to determine which of these are criminogenic, and then to match

The Essential Handbook of Offender Assessment and Treatment, Edited by C. R. Hollin.
© 2004 John Wiley & Sons Ltd.

the offender with a programme that addresses these. Working with violent offenders whether at the assessment or treatment stage poses challenges. Violent offenders often are resistant to fully admitting their offending, to taking responsibility for it, and to committing themselves to behavioural change. Additionally they often bring to assessment an aggressive, hostile, or intimidating interpersonal style. This forms an obstacle to gaining accurate information, challenges rapport building, and can be aversive and stressful for the assessor. Lastly, because few violent offenders are specialists (Reiss & Roth, 1993; Simon, 1997) many have extensive and diverse histories of criminal behaviour. Alongside similar childhood, adolescent, and adult features, these histories render them essentially indistinguishable from frequent offenders (Capaldi & Patterson, 1996; Farrington, 1994), and suggest an underlying criminal propensity that includes the potential for violent behaviour (Farrington, 1994; Reiss & Roth, 1993).

Comprehensive assessment currently relies as much on clinical experience and tradition as it does on the empirical literature, and there is a dearth of standardised assessment measures (Correctional Service of Canada, 1995). Foci are diverse, ranging from early developmental issues to the details of the current offence. The framework used here for organising these foci is the *offence chain* or *problem behaviour process* (Ward, Louden, Hudson, & Marshall, 1995), where assessment topics are structured around the goal of understanding the role of developmental, cognitive, affective, social/contextual, and behavioural factors and interactions as they impinge on the offending concerned, and as each offence sequence unfolds over time (Ward, McCormack, Hudson, & Polaschek, 1997). However, a number of other useful assessment structures exist (see Goldstein & Keller, 1987; Megargee, 1995).

The overall goal of assessment is to develop an individual case formulation for the assessed offender that, regardless of whether treatment is to be provided individually, via a group "package", or a combination of the two, will give a basis for reviewing that individual's progress in treatment and their status at its completion relative to their assessed treatment needs. Empirically derived criminogenic needs assessments for violent offenders are yet to be conducted; assessment is driven largely by clinical practice, theory, and speculation about the relevance to violent offenders of needs assessment with other offender groups (Howells, Watt, Hall, & Baldwin, 1997).

Assessment Methods

Ideally assessment should take place over a number of sessions and include a combination of interview, self-report (e.g. *in vivo* thought sampling), psychometric instruments, interviews with significant others (family, friends, prison and probation staff, psychiatric nurses), response evaluation (Goldstein & Keller, 1987), and behavioural observation. Existing documentation such as previous psychological or psychiatric reports, probation reports, court summaries and sentencing notes, institutional files, and official conviction histories will assist in developing a longitudinal perspective of the individual.

In addition to developing a case formulation, the assessor may simultaneously be involved in "selling" the programme to the participant, where programme participation is not mandatory. Interviewing strategies typically helpful in gaining rapport with offenders, developing a collaborative relationship, and motivating behavioural change, assist with this goal and in improving the quality of self-disclosure by the offender (e.g. McGrath, 1990; Miller & Rollnick, 1991). Issues of cultural and gender appropriateness, and reading level of the client population being assessed need to be considered in making choices about assessors, assessment instruments, and methods that will be used.

Assessment Areas

Essentially areas for assessment include a range of factors found to be common to frequent offenders and a number of issues that are thought to be particularly relevant to violence. Because of the heterogeneity of the violent offender group the list of assessment topics needs to be wide ranging. Clearly in some areas, topics will be directly related to treatment targets, whereas others (e.g. developmental history) may give an indication of the degree of risk or the pervasiveness or entrenchment of a propensity for violent behaviour. The existing literature suggests that the following areas are of potential relevance, but the list is not inclusive. In particular, areas that commonly are included in a general mental health screen (e.g. major psychiatric disorders) may be highly relevant to particular populations but are omitted because of space considerations. Where appropriate psychometric measures exist for a particular area, they are noted. In many areas measurement is in its infancy. Goldstein and Keller (1987) and the Correctional Service of Canada (1995) provide lists of additional suggested measures.

Offender Characteristics

Cognitive Processes and Products

A variety of cognitive or information-processing biases have been implicated in both anger- and violence-proneness. Copello and Tata (1990) found that adult male violent offenders were more likely than non-violent offenders and non-offenders to interpret ambiguous sentences as threatening, similar to the hostile attributional biases found in aggressive children by Dodge and colleagues (e.g. Lochman & Dodge, 1994). Such biases are conceptualised as arising from the influence of established schema (Serin & Kuriychuk, 1994), or behavioural scripts (Huesmann, 1988). Although there is little research, Novaco and Welsh's (1989) suggestions about information-processing mechanisms in the cognitive mediation of anger and aggression may provide a working assessment model. They propose five types of information-processing biases: attentional cueing, perceptual matching, attribution error, false consensus, and anchoring effects, and make suggestions about assessment methodology.

Psychometrically validated measures of cognitive products such as aggressive beliefs are sparse. One such measure is the EXPAGG (Archer & Haigh, 1997a,b). Although instrumental belief scores correlated significantly with scores on the Aggression Questionnaire (Buss & Perry, 1992), they did not significantly differ for violent and non-violent offenders. The expressive beliefs scale appears unrelated to violence use in prisoners. Similar results were found with New Zealand male prisoners (Polaschek & Nichols-Marcy, 2001). More recently, we developed and validated the Criminal Attitudes to Violence Scale with male prisoners (CAVS; Polaschek, Collie, & Walkey, 2003a). CAVS scores were highly correlated with the EXPAGG instrumental scale. The CAVS, but not the EXPAGG, distinguished violent and non-violent offenders. CAVS scores were more highly related to a measure of generally criminal attitudes, and correlated moderately with scores on a statistically-based risk assessment tool. The use of vignettes with coding of responses to probes appears promising (Serin & Kuriychuk, 1994; see also Slaby & Guerra, 1988). One new measure of this type is the Hostile Interpretations Questionnaire (Simourd & Mamuza, 2000).

Impulsivity and Self-Regulation Deficits

Impulsivity can be conceptualised as a cognitive processing deficit (Serin & Kuriychuk, 1994). Self-regulation refers to both self-initiated, well-organised, goal-directed activity and to self-control, particularly restraint, and the ability to delay gratification and tolerate tension when there are significant benefits to doing so (Ward, Hudson, & Keenan, 1998). Most often self-regulatory failure in violent offenders has been viewed simply as a failure to inhibit responding to immediate cues (Serin & Kuriychuk, 1994). Typically such offenders appear to respond violently to the many cues they interpret as provoking (e.g. perceived slights to self-image), without consideration of the costs.

Barratt's (1994) research on impulsiveness suggests that the concept has motoric and cognitive components. Impulsiveness is viewed as being responsible for aggression associated with a "hair-trigger" temper, that results in thoughtless violence, often followed afterwards by guilt and remorse and a resolution not to aggress again, which is not adhered to. However, he notes that two or more types of violence (e.g. impulsive and planned) often occur in the same individual, thus causing confusion for researchers and therapists. A variety of forms of self-regulatory failure not associated with impulsivity may also occur. For example, over a much longer period of time, an individual may brood over a grievance, disrupting internal self-control mechanisms by developing offence-supportive cognitive distortions and escalating anger. Several distinct types of self-regulatory problems have been proposed for sex offending (Ward et al., 1998), and may apply as well to violent offending. Measures of impulsivity currently in use include Barratt's BIS-11 (Barratt, 1994) and Eysenck's I.7 scale (Eysenck & Eysenck, 1977).

Anger and Hostility

Anger is a subjective emotion which while neither necessary nor sufficient for violence to occur, has a causal relationship to violence in that it operates as a mediator of the relationship between subjectively aversive events and behaviour intended to harm (Novaco, 1994). Novaco proposes a conceptual framework for anger with cognitive, behavioural, and physiological domains. The subjective affect of anger results from the highly automatic cognitive labelling of arousal. Violent offenders often appear to overlabel arousal so that their predominant emotional experience is anger.

Anger is often perceived as unpleasant and individuals may undertake a variety of actions to alleviate or avoid it. However, the individual's perceptions of the experience of being angry should be assessed. Some violent offenders find anger very satisfying, and may deliberately expose themselves to situations and cues that will arouse them. Such individuals may have pathways to violence in which by getting angry they are then justified in acting violently. In this sense, exposure to reliably provoking cues can be seen as a form of covert planning on the offender's part.

A variety of aspects of anger can be assessed. Existing scales provide measures of situations that are anger provoking, the extensiveness of anger responding or anger as a trait, how anger is expressed, and the degree to which it is controllable. Novaco's most recent scale (Novaco Anger Scale; 1994) assesses anger across cognitive (attentional focus, suspicion, rumination, and hostile attitude), arousal (intensity, duration, somatic tension, and irritability), and behavioural (impulsive reaction, verbal aggression, physical confrontation, and indirect expression) domains, and also provides an index of anger intensity in various provoking situations.

Other scales with reasonable psychometric properties include the Buss–Durkee Hostility Inventory (Buss & Durkee, 1957), and the State–Trait Anger Expression Inventory (Spielberger, 1988). A new scale recommended by Gendreau, Goggin, and Paparozzi (1996) is the Aggression Questionnaire (Buss & Perry, 1992). Measures of hostility, anger, and aggression may be highly correlated, and there is little evidence that offenders differ from non-offenders on these constructs (Serin & Kuriychuk, 1994). However, the measures are potentially useful in identifying those who do.

Empathy

Empathy deficits can be pervasive and enduring (e.g. in psychopathy) or situation- or affect-specific. Assessment needs to establish which is the case for a particular offender since this will determine the type and extent of intervention required. The four-stage information-processing model suggested by Marshall, Hudson, Jones, and Fernandez (1995) also has assessment implications in that it enables fine-grained analysis of the sources of empathy deficits. The four steps are:

1. recognising the other's emotion;
2. taking their perspective;
3. experiencing a matching or appropriate emotional response from that perspective; and
4. generating a well-formulated behavioural response.

Marshall et al. argue that a precursor deficit to step 1 may be an inability to identify one's own emotional state. This appears common in violent offenders.

There are a number of scales for measuring empathy, including the Interpersonal Reactivity Index (Davis, 1983) and the Hogan empathy scale (Hogan, 1969). Measures of specific victim empathy may also be needed.

Social Competence

Traditional conceptualisations of social skills deficits are being replaced by multi-staged models of social competence. McFall's (1990) information-processing model provides one useful assessment framework. McFall proposes that social competence is a function of the adequacy of social task performance in a particular circumstance, as evident to the individual performer or observers. Social skills are the underlying component processes involved in competent task performance. Three sequential processes are involved:

1. Decoding skills such as correctly perceiving and interpreting incoming information such as social cues.
2. Decision skills as seen in generating possible responses, matching them to the requirements of the situation, choosing the most suitable, checking whether it is behaviourally available, and evaluating its likely outcome relative to other options.
3. Enactment skills such as carrying out the chosen behavioural routine, including smooth performance, monitoring and adjusting to achieve the intended impact (McFall, 1990).

The advantages of using this model are clear; social competence across a wide range of settings will require an extensive behavioural repertoire. Some offenders will have an impoverished range of social behaviours from which to select, while others will have a good range of choices but will fail to utilise an appropriate option because of misperception of others' behavioural intentions or misjudgement about which behaviours will best achieve their goals.

Social Support for Violence

Violent offenders may be socially isolated individuals or have extensive involvement with a supportive peer group. A supportive social context provides plentiful opportunities for (1) developing relationships with potential co-offenders; (2) developing a wider repertoire of violent behaviours with supervised training, rehearsal and practice; and (3) social reinforcement for violence, through gaining peer approval, a sense of belonging, and enhanced status. Even if support in the wider society is limited, significant subcultural pockets exist in many Western countries that support warrior values (McCarthy, 1994), including a code of honour (Nisbett, 1993), physically risky and courageous behaviour, or machismo (Zaitchik & Mosher, 1993). Perhaps the most explicit example is gang membership. Assessment of social support for proviolent and prosocial behaviour needs to consider both how willing the individual is to relinquish subcultural values supporting diverse forms of violence, and the likely accessibility of an attractive non-violent, actively prosocial support network.

Assessment of alcohol and drug use patterns, co-existing psychiatric and personality disorders may also have relevance to the choice of treatment options. General and violent recidivism risk (see Gendreau et al., 1996; Serin, 1995) and readiness to undertake treatment (Serin & Kennedy, 1997) should also be considered in a thorough assessment.

Offence Characteristics

A detailed picture of how the typical or current offence unfolded over time should be constructed with the offender. Interviewing, police and court records, and other file information are essential to this phase. It is important to assess whether there are a variety of offence patterns for an individual offender since diversity seems more typical than does a single repeated pattern. As part of understanding the offence chains of an offender, a full assessment of the range of violent acts committed, the range of victims, the duration of offending, the motives and goals involved should be undertaken. This will identify physical and emotional high-risk situations (Serin & Brown, 1996).

A number of specific foci of enquiry may assist in establishing a clear offence picture. For example, did alcohol or drugs facilitate the offending, or was there a sudden absence of drugs used routinely to manage violence precursors such as anger and boredom? Similarly, did anger feature prominently, and if so at what stages? What relationship did it have to the level of violence used, and to victim resistance? Were there pre-existing violent fantasies? There has been a dearth of research on the role of fantasies or cognitive rehearsal in violent offending, although it is often seen in assessment. Elaborative rumination is thought likely to make overlearned aggressive scripts both more accessible in memory and more generalised (Huesmann, 1988). In adults, general fantasy elaboration may become an established strategy for enhancing emotional well-being, while fantasising in a ruminative way about a particular individual seems clinically to be most often associated with individuals who "hold grudges" and plan revenge, sometimes over very extended periods of time.

As with sexual offending, a number of different types of planning may be discerned in the early portions of the offence chain. Planning may be explicit and elaborate or an offence may at first be presented as impulsive. Closer examination and greater familiarity with the individual's offence style may suggest covert or implicit planning in the early "apparently irrelevant decisions" that help create a situation in which violence is imminent. Lastly, some offenders demonstrate planned opportunism (Pithers, 1993), where they engage in a variety of offending-related high-risk situations on a routine, recreational basis, and can readily respond violently if a suitable situation presents itself. Such violence will appear impulsive on superficial analysis (e.g. getting into fights in bars).

Historically, the motives underlying violent behaviour have been classified into two categories: expressive and instrumental. More recently, multidimensional scaling research suggested four categories of motive: hostile, instrumental, normative, or status-related (Campbell, Muncer, & Bibel, 1985). In reality more than one goal (e.g. hostile and status-related) may be operating simultaneously, and goals and motives may change as the interaction unfolds. In the traditional clinical literature, status-related violence has been given less attention than some argue it deserves (e.g. Indermaur, 1995). Predominant motives may change as the offender's career matures. Indermaur's research on offenders committing acts of violence in the course of property crimes suggests that mixed expressive and instrumental goals are common. Instrumental violence not associated with significant affective arousal (e.g. anger, excitement, fear) may be confined to psychopathic individuals (Cornell et al., 1996; Dempster et al., 1996).

Co-offending is especially common for robbery and street fights (Farrington, 1994) and gang-related crime, but is rarely discussed in the treatment literature. Assessment would include examining the relationship between co-offenders prior to the offence, the relative contribution of each to planning and execution, and how relationship dynamics contributed to the progression of events during the offence. Also of interest is whether the offender persistently recruits younger offenders with whom to commit violent crimes (Farrington, 1994), and whether he has organised or "set up" other offenders to commit violent crimes on his behalf, such as robberies or beatings. In particular, assessment of status-related offending requires analysis of the role of onlookers and co-offenders.

Although there is little evidence of specialisation within types of violent offending, assessment should examine whether offenders target particular victim groups, such as women, men or strangers, the degree of victim injury, the pattern of interaction between victim and offender, and how weapons are used.

Post-offence reactions can range from satisfaction to despair and shock, and enquiry can reveal more information about offence goals and their relationship to actual behaviour as well as whether or not the behaviour is consistent with the offender's personal behavioural standards. Emotional reactions such as remorse and self-disgust, and the resolution to make changes to avoid further violence suggest the existence of some internal constraints against violent behaviour, whereas satisfaction and other positive mood states may suggest that violence is congruent with the offender's self image.

TREATMENT

Recent meta-analyses of offender rehabilitation programmes have done much to refute the contention that "nothing works" and have offered guidance about general principles associated with effective correctional programming. Cullen and Gendreau (1989) confirm in an important review of the literature on correctional rehabilitation, that the most effective theoretical bases for programmes are: social learning theory, cognitive models, skills training, differential association, and behavioural systems including family therapy. Effective intervention components include: anti-criminal modelling, problem-solving, use of community resources, high-quality interpersonal relationships, firm but fair discipline, and relapse prevention/self-efficacy. Non-directive approaches, punishment paradigms, deterrence, and medical model approaches were most often associated with ineffective styles of intervention.

Unlike sexual offending against children, violent offending has not traditionally attracted the funding necessary systematically to develop and evaluate interventions (Blackburn, 1988). Although violent offender programmes currently are proliferating in several countries, especially within North America (J. Bush, personal communication, 18 November 1996; Serin & Brown, 1997), there are few outcome studies to guide the development of these programmes, and methodological problems are frequently found. However, a small group of studies from both the juvenile and adult arenas provides some guidance for treatment programme development. Priority here has been given to studies with higher methodological standards, programmes that appear to be targeting higher-risk rather than low-risk offenders, and those that contain more than one treatment component. Often these programmes are provided in a group or mixed group-and-individual format. For a purely individual case-formulation-based approach to violent offender treatment, see Browne and Howells (1996). Van Voorhis, Cullen, and Applegate (1995) provide guidelines on programme evaluation.

Juvenile Treatment Programmes

A number of secondary and tertiary prevention programmes appear promising with violent or potentially violent youth (see Guerra, Tolan, & Hammond, 1994; Tate, Reppucci, & Mulvey, 1995, for reviews). Goldstein and his colleagues (e.g. Goldstein, 1988) have developed an elaborate behavioural skills curriculum that includes components of anger control, prosocial skills, and prosocial values. Goldstein and Glick (1994) report several evaluations suggesting that Aggression Replacement Training (ART) has the potential to effect positive changes in participants on a number of relevant outcome indices, for a variety of populations and settings, including incarcerated violent youths and adolescent gangs.

A newer approach, the EQUIP programme (Gibbs, Potter, & Goldstein, 1995), integrates a peer-helping group format with cognitive–developmental and social information processing skills adapted from Goldstein's ART and Prepare (Goldstein, 1988) curricula, and Yochelson and Samenow's (1977) work. Seven to nine youths meet daily for 1 to 1.5 hours. The first treatment goal is to develop a prosocial group culture to motivate change. Once this is achieved, the teaching of the EQUIP curriculum commences (Gibbs, Potter, Barriga, & Liau, 1996). An outcome study in which incarcerated juveniles were randomly assigned either to EQUIP or to one of two control groups found significant reductions in self-reported misconduct and staff-reported misconduct in the treated group. General recidivism for the treatment group was 15% at both 6 and 12 months following release; significantly lower than the control groups' 29.7% recidivism at 6 months and 40.5% at 12 months (Leeman, Gibbs, & Fuller, 1993). No data on specific changes in violent behaviour were reported (see Gibbs et al., 1996).

Unlike the adult programme literature, where the offenders themselves tend to be the only direct programme recipients, programmes for youth have better incorporated significant others in treatment delivery. Tate et al. (1995) report preliminary evidence of effectiveness with violent youth for programmes such as Multisystemic Therapy (MST), that include a social–cognitive component and are directed at solving multiple problems across the various contexts in which the youth is embedded; family, peers, school, and neighbourhood.

Henggeler and colleagues have obtained extensive empirical support for MST with serious juvenile offenders. MST is based on social ecology and family systems models and delivers high-quality, individually tailored interventions to youth and their families, at times and places of their choosing (Henggeler, Melton, Brondino, Scherer, & Hanley, 1997; see Henggeler, 1997, for a review). MST has been implemented in four randomised clinical trials with over 300 offenders and their families. Improvements were found in rates of arrest (25–70% reduction) and out of home placement (50–64% reduction). MST has proved equally effective with African–American as with European–American youths.

Programmes for Adult Violent Offenders

The provision of psychological treatment to adult violent offenders predominantly has been limited to clinically unique approaches for individual offenders (Browne & Howells, 1996), or has focused on links between violence and anger (Hollin & Howells, 1989). Particularly vexing has been the absence of an adequate conceptual model to guide theoretically coherent programme development (Howells et al., 1997; Serin & Brown, 1996).

In New Zealand, low intensity anger management (AM) programmes have been offered for over a decade and remain the most common interventions for imprisoned violent offenders, despite few outcome data. A similar trend has been observed in other correctional populations (e.g. Australia: Howells et al., 1997; Canada: Serin & Brown, 1997). These programmes typically are based on Novaco's (1975, 1977) stress inoculation-coping skills approach, perhaps because

Novaco provides an elaborate conceptual framework for anger and aggression (Novaco & Welsh, 1989).

In a recent review of outcome evaluations of AM, Novaco (1997) notes that few involve seriously violent participants, few report on the impact of their programmes on violent behaviour, and reconviction has not been examined. Inadequate descriptions of treatment content and process are common, but many may omit significant treatment targets (e.g. aggression-supportive beliefs; see Guerra & Slaby, 1990) and the level of service, often less than 25 hours, is unlikely to have an impact on all but the lowest risk offenders (Andrews, Bonta, & Hoge, 1990). Furthermore, there is little evidence that anger predicts violent offending (Loza & Loza-Fanous, 1999), or that violent offenders experience anger at pathological levels of frequency or intensity (Serin & Kuriychuk, 1994), rather than simply having developed dysfunctional methods of anger expression. An exclusive anger control focus ignores other common motivational bases for violence (Guerra et al., 1994) such as its normative and status-restorative functions. The observation of a number of writers that this narrow focus on the role of anger in violent offending can be seen to parallel the role ascribed to deviant sexual arousal in sexual offending models a decade ago, is encouraging given the current status of treatment models for sex offenders.

Several approaches show promise with violent offenders. The Cognitive Skills Training (CST) programme comprises 36 two-hour sessions delivered by staff coaches to groups of up to 10 offenders, combining didactic teaching of cognitive skills with group and individual skill practice. Based on the work of Ross and Fabiano (1985), CST deals with a variety of cognitive deficits identified as common to offender populations, including poor interpersonal, decision-making, goal-setting, and general thinking skills. Developed in Canada in the late 1980s, it has been completed by more than 5500 federal offenders in institutional and community settings (Robinson, 1995) and is being implemented internationally.

Robinson (1995) presents outcome data on a sample of 2125 offenders who have been receiving community supervision for at least 12 months following release. Of these, 67.9% were programme completers, 14.2% were drop-outs, and 17.8% were untreated waiting list controls. Within the 12 months, 44.5% of programme completers and 50.1% from the waiting list were readmitted. There were no differences between treated and untreated participants on technical parole violations but there was a 20% reduction in official reconvictions for programme completers. Violent offenders had approximately a 35% reduction in reconviction, except for robbers, whose recidivism rates were unchanged. The programme was most effective with low-risk offenders and Robinson concludes that this is because only relatively high-risk offenders are referred to the programme, so that the lowest risk offenders in the sample are high-risk offenders relative to the remainder of the correctional population. However, an alternative interpretation is that this is a relatively low to medium intensity programme (i.e. apparently 72 hours of programme in total), and thus is not suited to the highest risk offenders (cf. Bush, 1995b).

Another cognition-based programme, for male and female violent offenders, is the Cognitive Self Change (CSC) programme of the Vermont Department of Corrections. First implemented in 1988 (Bush, 1995a), it was developed from the work of Yochelson and Samenow (1977). It targets attitudes, beliefs, and thinking patterns that support violent behaviour. Groups are run by specifically trained prison staff and parole workers and the programme is delivered in three phases; the first two in prison and the third in the community. During Phase I, groups meet twice a week for 8 to 10 weeks, and undertake general programme orientation. In Phase II offenders identify their own high-risk thinking patterns (i.e. thinking associated with past criminal or violent behaviour), learn techniques for controlling and disrupting such thinking, and use what they have learned to develop relapse prevention plans for managing high-risk thinking in the community. Lastly, in Phase III offenders meet twice weekly for a year in maintenance groups after release into the community, and report high-risk situations they have experienced and their strategies for controlling their thinking in these situations (see Bush, 1995b, for details). Recent outcome data suggest significant reductions in parole violation and any rearrest for those who attended the programme for more than six months (Bush, 1995b). Of these, 45.5% had recidivated at three years compared with 76.7% of the untreated group. In an independent evaluation, Henning and Frueh (1996) found that of 55 treated offenders, 50% obtained a new criminal charge in the two years following release, compared with 70.8% of the 141 offenders in the control group. Like CST, this programme's central components are relevant to both violent and non-violent offending, focusing on the cognitive–emotional process leading to rule violation. Data are presented for violent rearrest, but the methodology prohibits drawing firm conclusions because a dichotomous (rearrest/none) measure was used. Since violent offenders are generalists, their first reoffence is likely to be a non-violent one. This will result in underestimation of post-programme violent recidivism.

In New Zealand, both community- and prison-based violent offender rehabilitation programmes appear effective in reducing violent recidivism. In 1987 a residential community-based group programme for violent offenders, the Montgomery House Violence Prevention Project (VPP), was implemented in Hamilton, New Zealand. The VPP consisted of a series of three-month programmes for five to eight offenders on either parole or community supervision for violent convictions. The programme was cognitive–behavioural in content and method, but was embedded in a therapeutic community milieu in which group processes were used to develop mutual trust and skills practice (Dixon & Wikaira, 1988). Because 78% of programme participants were New Zealand Maaori, traditional Maaori customs and protocol were incorporated in the programme process. Participants attended up to 40 hours of structured modular group programming per week, including anger management and altering attitudes to violence, communication, relationship and parenting skills, social problem-solving, alcohol and drug intervention, and tikanga and te reo Maaori (Maaori culture and language) instruction. Forty-six offenders commenced and 33 completed the programme in the first two years. Reconvictions over an average 2.3 years of follow-up were compared with conviction rates for completers in the two years prior to programme admission. Both parolees and community-sentenced participants showed reductions in frequency and seriousness of violent offending (Polaschek & Dixon, 2001). Because of insufficient statistical power, effect size statistics were used to examine recidivism in a long-term (five-year) follow-up with a matched control group. The results found a medium reduction in general reconvictions and a large reduction in violent reconvictions for treated offenders, with insubstantial reductions on both indices for the control group (Dixon & Behrnes, 1996).

The Violence Prevention Unit (VPU), a dedicated 30-bed facility for the cognitive-behavioural rehabilitation of violent prisoners opened in Wellington, New Zealand in 1998. The multi-component, 330-hour programme is delievered over approximately 28 weeks to closed groups of 10 men led by two therapists. After a minimum of 24 months in the community, 63% of treated offenders and 32% of untreated controls had been reconvicted of a violent offence. There was no significant differences in the proportion with subsequent non-violent convictions (Polaschek, Wilson, Townsend, & Daly, 2003b).

Guidelines for Treatment Provision

Treatment of violent offenders should conform to the risk, need, and responsivity principles identified in the rehabilitation literature (Andrews et al., 1990). With low-risk offenders, it may be possible to provide an adequate level of treatment on an individual basis, tailored to violence-related needs identified in assessment. However, provision of low intensity programmes that focus only on anger regulation is unlikely to reduce violence risk in those with an extensive and varied history of violence. For these individuals, it is likely that a more intensive, group treatment programme that contains a variety of treatment methods, and targets affect regulation and violence-related cognitive processes and products, that teaches a range of cognitive and social skills and strategies, and tackles other common correlates such as alcohol and drug abuse will be necessary.

The question of whether offenders in intensive violent offender programmes should be at high risk generally or at high risk of violence remains to be investigated, and depends conceptually on whether a programme is targeting factors relating to all types of offending, or factors hypothesized to be especially relevant to violent offending. Some programmes clearly do both (e.g. CSC, VPP) while others are specifically designed to address violent offending (e.g. Correctional Service of Canada, 1995). Future investigation needs to establish whether these concerns are relevant to reconviction outcomes. Needs assessment research on violent offenders (Howells et al., 1997) would assist in clarifying these issues and in developing more sophisticated conceptual models.

Existing programmes suggest a variety of development options for violent offending-based treatment. Most are cognitive–behavioural and provide a combination of approaches designed to challenge biases in information processing and distorted cognitions, and teach a range of other cognitive and interpersonal skills to manage violence risk. Preliminary interventions to enhance motivation and treatment responsivity and a maintenance or external relapse prevention phase may be added.

There is much work to be done to develop interventions with violent offenders to the level of sophistication of current sex offender programmes. Areas requiring development for this heterogeneous population include: assessment batteries (self-report questionnaires, vignette, and role-play measures) that are both sufficiently robust to assess treatment changes and empirically related to recidivism; comprehensive needs assessments for violent offender populations; risk measures that differentiate between general recidivism and violent recidivism; and lastly, methodologically sophisticated evaluation of programme innovations. Violent offender treatment is entering an exciting era that holds promise in providing a constructive alternative or adjunct to lengthy imprisonment sentences, and in reducing the enormous associated social costs.

REFERENCES

Andrews, D. A., Bonta, J., & Hoge, R. D. (1990). Classification for effective rehabilitation: Rediscovering psychology. *Criminal Justice and Behavior*, *17*, 19–52.

Archer, J., & Haigh, A. (1997a). Beliefs about aggression among male and female prisoners. *Aggressive Behavior*, *23*, 405–415.

Archer, J., & Haigh, A. (1997b). Do beliefs about aggressive feelings and actions predict reported levels of aggression? *British Journal of Social Psychology*, *36*, 83–105.

Barratt, E. S. (1994). Impulsiveness and aggression. In J. Monahan & H. J. Steadman (Eds.), *Violence and mental disorder: Developments in risk assessment* (pp. 21–79). Chicago, IL: University of Chicago.

Blackburn, R. (1988). Cognitive behavioural approaches to understanding and treating aggression. In K. Howells & C. R. Hollin (Eds.), *Clinical approaches to aggression and violence* (pp. 6–23). Leicester, UK: The British Psychological Society.

Browne, K., & Howells, K. (1996). Violent offenders. In C. R. Hollin (Ed.), *Working with offenders: Psychological practice in offender rehabilitation* (pp. 188–210). Chichester, UK: Wiley.

Bush, J. (1995a). *Cognitive self change: A program manual*. Burlington, VA: Vermont Department of Corrections.

Bush, J. (1995b). Teaching self-risk management to violent offenders. In J. McGuire (Ed.), *What works: Reducing reoffending—Guidelines from research and practice* (pp. 139–154). Chichester, UK: Wiley.

Buss, A., & Durkee, A. (1957). An inventory for assessing different kinds of hostility. *Journal of Consulting and Clinical Psychology*, *21*, 342–349.

Buss, A. H., & Perry, M. (1992). The aggression questionnaire. *Journal of Personality and Social Psychology*, *63*, 452–459.

Campbell, A., Muncer, S., & Bibel, D. (1985). Taxonomies of aggressive behavior: A preliminary report. *Aggressive Behavior*, *11*, 217–222.

Capaldi, D. M., & Patterson, G. R. (1996). Can violent offenders be distinguished from frequent offenders: Prediction from childhood to adolescence. *Journal of Research in Crime and Delinquency*, *33*, 206–231.

Copello, A. G., & Tata, P. R. (1990). Violent behaviour and interpretative bias: An experimental study of the resolution of ambiguity in violent offenders. *British Journal of Clinical Psychology, 29*, 417–428.

Cornell, D. G., Warren, J., Hawk, G., Stafford, E., Oram, G., & Pine, D. (1996). Psychopathy in instrumental and reactive violent offenders. *Journal of Consulting and Clinical Psychology, 64*, 783–790.

Correctional Service of Canada (1995). *Persistently violent (nonsexual) offenders: A program proposal* (Report No. R-42). Ottawa, Canada: Author.

Cullen, F. T., & Gendreau, P. (1989). The effectiveness of correctional rehabilitation—reconsidering the "nothing works" debate. In L. Goodstein & D. L. McKenzie (Eds.), *The American prison: Issues in research policy* (pp. 23–44). New York: Plenum.

Davis, M. H. (1983). Measuring individual differences in empathy: Evidence for a multidimensional approach. *Journal of Personality and Social Psychology, 44*, 113–126.

Dempster, R. J., Lyon, D. R., Sullivan, L. E., Hart, S. D., Smiley, W. C., & Mulloy, R. (1996, August). *Psychopathy and instrumental aggression in violent offenders*. Poster session presented at the annual meeting of the American Psychological Association, Ontario, Canada.

Dixon, B. G., & Behrnes, S. (1996). *Violence prevention project reconviction study: Overview of study and findings*. Unpublished report, New Zealand Department of Corrections Psychological Service.

Dixon, B. G., & Wikaira, R. G. (1988, September). *The violence prevention project: Development of residential training programmes for violent offenders*. Poster paper presented at the XXIV International Congress of Psychology, Sydney, Australia.

Eysenck, S., & Eysenck, H. (1977). The place of impulsiveness in a dimensional system of personality description. *British Journal of Social and Clinical Psychology, 16*, 57–68.

Farrington, D. P. (1994). Human development and criminal careers. In M. Maguire, R. Morgan & R. Reiner (Eds.), J. Pepler & K. H. Rubin (Eds.), *The Oxford handbook of criminology* (pp. 511–584). Oxford: Clarendon Press.

Gendreau, P., Goggin, C., & Paparozzi, M. (1996). Principles of effective assessment for community corrections. *Federal Probation, 60*(3), 64–70.

Gibbs, J. C., Potter, G. B., Barriga, A. Q., & Liau, A. K. (1996). Developing the helping skills and prosocial motivation of aggressive adolescents in peer group programs. *Aggression and Violent Behavior, 1*, 283–305.

Gibbs, J. C., Potter, G., & Goldstein, A. P. (1995). *The EQUIP program: Teaching youth to think and act responsibly through a peer-helping approach*. Champaign, IL: Research Press.

Goldstein, A. P. (1988). *The prepare curriculum: Teaching prosocial competencies*. Champaign, IL: Research Press.

Goldstein, A. P., & Glick, B. (1994). *The prosocial gang: Implementing aggression replacement training*. Thousand Oaks, CA: Sage.

Goldstein, A. P., & Keller, H. (1987). *Aggressive behavior: Assessment and intervention*. New York: Pergamon.

Guerra, N. G., & Slaby, R. G. (1990). Cognitive mediators of aggression in adolescent offenders: 2. Intervention. *Developmental Psychology, 26*, 269–277.

Guerra, N. G., Tolan, P. H., & Hammond, W. R. (1994). Prevention and treatment of adolescent violence. In L. D. Eron, J. H. Gentry, & P. Schlegel (Eds.), *Reason to hope: A psychosocial perspective on violence and youth* (pp. 383–403). Washington, DC: American Psychological Association.

Henggeler, S. W. (1997). *Multisystemic therapy with serious juvenile offenders and their families: Program design, implementation and outcomes*. Unpublished manuscript.

Henggeler, S. W., Melton, G. B., Brondino, M. J., Scherer, D. G., & Hanley, J. H. (1997). Multisystemic therapy with violent and chronic juvenile offenders and their families:

The role of treatment fidelity in successful dissemination. *Journal of Consulting and Clinical Psychology*, *65*, 821–833.

Henning, K. R., & Frueh, B. C. (1996). Cognitive–behavioral treatment of incarcerated offenders: An evaluation of the Vermont Department of Corrections' cognitive self-change program. *Criminal Justice and Behavior*, *23*, 523–541.

Hogan, R. (1969). Development of an empathy scale. *Journal of Consulting and Clinical Psychology*, *33*, 307–316.

Hollin, C. R., & Howells, K. (1989). An introduction to concepts, models and techniques. In K. Howells & C. R. Hollin (Eds.), *Clinical approaches to violence* (pp. 3–24). Chichester, UK: Wiley.

Howells, K., Watt, B., Hall, G., & Baldwin, S. (1997). Developing programmes for violent offenders. *Legal and Criminological Psychology*, *2*, 117–128.

Huesmann, L. R. (1988). An information processing model for the development of aggression. *Aggressive Behavior*, *14*, 13–24.

Indermaur, D. (1995). *Violent property crime*. Sydney, Australia: Federation Press.

Leeman, L. W., Gibbs, J. C., & Fuller, D. (1993). Evaluation of a multicomponent group treatment program for juvenile delinquents. *Aggressive Behavior*, *19*, 281–292.

Lochman, J. E., & Dodge, K. A. (1994). Social–cognitive processes of severely violent, moderately aggressive, and nonaggressive boys. *Journal of Consulting and Clinical Psychology*, *62*, 366–374.

Loza, W., & Loza-Fanous, A. (1999). Anger and prediction of violent and nonviolent offenders' recidivism. *Journal of Interpersonal Violence*, *14*, 1014–1029.

Marshall, W. L., Hudson, S. M., Jones, R., & Fernandez, Y. M. (1995). Empathy in sex offenders. *Clinical Psychology Review*, *15*, 99–113.

McCarthy, B. (1994). Warrior values: A socio-historical survey. In J. Archer (Ed.), *Male violence* (pp. 105–120). London: Routledge.

McFall, R. M. (1990). The enhancement of social skills: An information-processing analysis. In W. L. Marshall, D. R. Laws, & H. E. Barbaree (Eds.), *Handbook of sexual assault: Issues, theories, and treatment of the offender* (pp. 311–330). New York: Plenum.

McGrath, R. J. (1990). Assessment of sexual aggressors: Practical clinical interviewing strategies. *Journal of Interpersonal Violence*, *5*, 507–519.

Megargee, E. I. (1995). Assessing and understanding aggressive and violent patients. In J. N. Butcher (Ed.), *Clinical personality assessment: Practical approaches* (pp. 395–409). New York: Oxford University Press.

Miller, W. R., & Rollnick, S. (1991). *Motivational interviewing: Preparing people to change addictive behavior*. New York: Guilford.

Nisbett, R. E. (1993). Violence and U.S. regional culture. *American Psychologist*, *48*, 441–449.

Novaco, R. W. (1975). *Anger control: The development and evaluation of an experimental treatment*. Lexington, MA: D. C. Heath.

Novaco, R. W. (1977). Stress inoculation: A cognitive therapy for anger and its application to a case of depression. *Journal of Consulting and Clinical Psychology*, *45*, 600–608.

Novaco, R. W. (1994). Anger as a risk factor for violence. In J. Monahan & H. J. Steadman (Eds.), *Violence and mental disorder: Developments in risk assessment* (pp. 21–59). Chicago, IL: University of Chicago Press.

Novaco, R. W. (1997). Remediating anger and aggression with violent offenders. *Legal and Criminological Psychology*, *2*, 77–88.

Novaco, R. W., & Welsh, W. N. (1989). Anger disturbances: Cognitive mediation and clinical prescriptions. In K. Howells & C. R. Hollin (Eds.), *Clinical approaches to violence* (pp. 39–60). Chichester, UK: Wiley.

Pithers, W. D. (1993). Treatment of rapists: Reinterpretation of early outcome data and exploratory constructs to enhance therapeutic efficacy. In G. C. N. Hall, R. Hirschman, J. R. Graham, & M. S. Zaragoza (Eds.), *Sexual aggression: Issues in etiology, assessment, and treatment* (pp. 167–196). Washington, DC: Taylor & Francis.

Polaschek, D. L. L., & Dixon, B. G. (2001). The violence prevention project: The development and evaluation of a program for violent offenders. *Psychology, Crime, and Law*, *7*, 1–23.

Polaschek, D. L. L., & Nichols-Marcy, T. (2001). *Beliefs about aggression: A trial of the revised EXPAGG and the Aggression Questionnaire with New Zealand male prisoners and students*. Unpublished manuscript.

Polaschek, D. L. L., Collie, R. M., & Walkey, F. H. (2003a). *Criminal attitudes to violence: Development and preliminary validation of a scale for male prisoners*. Manuscript under review.

Polaschek, D. L. L., Wilson, N., Townsend, M., & Daly, L. (2003b). *Cognitive-behavioral treatment for serious violent offenders: An outcome evaluation of the Violence Prevention Unit*. Manuscript under review.

Reiss, A. J., & Roth, J. A. (Eds.) (1993). *Understanding and preventing violence*. Washington: National Academy.

Robinson, D. (1995). *The impact of cognitive skills training on post-release recidivism among Canadian federal offenders* (Report No. R-41). Ottawa, Canada: Correctional Service of Canada, Correctional Research and Development.

Ross, R. R., & Fabiano, E. A. (1985). *Time to think: A cognitive model of delinquency prevention and offender rehabilitation*. Johnson City, TN: Institute of Social Sciences and Arts.

Serin, R. (1995). Assessment and prediction of violent behaviour in offender populations. In T. A. Leis, L. L. Motiuk, & J. R. P. Ogloff (Eds.), *Forensic psychology: Policy and practice in Corrections* (pp. 69–90). Ontario, Canada: Correctional Service of Canada.

Serin, R., & Brown, S. (1996). Strategies for enhancing the treatment of violent offenders. *Forum on Corrections Research*, *8*(3), 45–48.

Serin, R., & Brown, S. (1997). Treatment programs for offenders with violent histories: A national survey. *Forum on Corrections Research*, *9*(2) (Available at http://198.103. 98.138/crd/forum/e092/e092h.htm).

Serin, R., & Kennedy, S. (1997). *Treatment readiness and responsivity: Contributing to effective correctional programming*. (Report No. R54). Ottawa, Canada: Correctional Service of Canada, Correctional Research and Development. (Available at http://www.csc-scc.gc.ca/crd/reports/r54e.htm).

Serin, R. C., & Kuriychuk, M. (1994). Social and cognitive processing deficits in violent offenders: Implications for treatment. *International Journal of Law and Psychiatry*, *17*, 431–441.

Simon, L. M. J. (1997). Do criminal offenders specialize in crime types? *Applied and Preventative Psychology*, *6*, 35–53.

Simourd, D. J., & Mamuza, J. E. (2000). The Hostile Interpretations Questionnaire: Psychometric properties and construct validity. *Criminal Justice and Behavior*, *27*, 645–663.

Slaby, R. G., & Guerra, N. G. (1988). Cognitive mediators of aggression in adolescent offenders: 1. Assessment. *Developmental Psychology*, *24*, 580–588.

Spielberger, C. D. (1988). *State-trait anger expression inventory: Research edition professional manual*. Odessa, FL: Psychological Assessment Resources.

Tate, D. C., Reppucci, N. D., & Mulvey, E. P. (1995). Violent juvenile delinquents: Treatment effectiveness and implications for future action. *American Psychologist*, *50*, 777–781.

Van Voorhis, P., Cullen, F. T., & Applegate, B. (1995). Evaluating interventions with violent offenders: A guide for practitioners and policymakers. *Federal Probation*, *59*(2), 17–28.

Ward. T., Hudson, S. M., & Keenan, T. (1998). A self-regulation model of the sexual offense process. *Sexual Abuse: A Journal of Research and Treatment*, *10*, 141–157.

Ward, T., Louden, K., Hudson, S. M., & Marshall, W. L. (1995). A descriptive model of the offence chain in child molesters. *Journal of Interpersonal Violence*, *10*, 452–472.

Ward, T., McCormack, J., Hudson, S. M., & Polaschek, D. (1997). Rape: Assessment and treatment. In D. R. Laws & W. O'Donohue (Eds.), *Sexual deviance: Theory, assessment and treatment* (pp. 356–393). New York: Guilford.

Yochelson, S., & Samenow, S. (1977). *The criminal personality, Vol 2: The change process.* New York: Jason Aronsen.

Zaitchik, M. C., & Mosher, D. L. (1993). Criminal justice implications of the macho personality constellation. *Criminal Justice and Behavior, 20,* 227–239.

Chapter 14

Offenders with Major Mental Disorders

Sheilagh Hodgins
Karolinska Institute, Stockholm, Sweden

THE MAJOR MENTAL DISORDERS

The major mental disorders[1] include schizophrenia, major depression, bipolar disorder, delusional disorder, and atypical psychoses. While much is known about the first three of these disorders, knowledge of the latter two continues to elude us. There is relatively good consensus among researchers and clinicians about the diagnoses of schizophrenia and bipolar disorder. The present criteria identify populations of individuals that share a core of symptoms, biological and behavioural characteristics, and outcomes. The current diagnosis of major depression, however, is unsatisfactory; it identifies a population that is heterogeneous as to symptomatology, biological characteristics, and outcome (Hodgins, 1996).

Schizophrenia affects just less than 1% of adult men and women and bipolar disorder approximately 1.6%. While the prevalence of schizophrenia is thought to have remained stable at least since the beginning of the century, there is evidence to suggest that the prevalence of bipolar disorder is increasing among the relatives of those affected. Major depression, according to the most recent and methodologically sound investigations, affects 12.7% of men and 21.3% of women (Kessler et al., 1994), and the prevalence is increasing while the age of onset decreases. Among adolescents, rates as high as 21% have been reported (Klerman & Weissman, 1992; Lewinsohn, Rohde, Seeley, & Fischer, 1993). In most cases, the major mental disorders onset in late adolescence or early adulthood

---

[1] Throughout this chapter the terms major mental disorder and mental illness will be used interchangeably to refer to these five disorders.

The Essential Handbook of Offender Assessment and Treatment. Edited by C. R. Hollin.
© 2004 John Wiley & Sons Ltd.

and are chronic. These disorders inflict unmeasurable suffering on those who are affected and on their family and close friends. They limit all aspects of an individual's functioning. Acute episodes characterized by severe symptoms of psychosis, mania, and/or depression are interspersed with periods in which fewer symptoms are present, but psychosocial functioning remains impaired.[2] These disorders are associated with increased risks for premature death, both from disease and suicide, for certain personality disorders, and for alcohol and drug use disorders (Hodgins, 1996).

PREVALENCE OF CRIMINALITY AMONG PERSONS WITH MAJOR MENTAL DISORDERS

Persons who develop major mental disorders are more likely than persons with no mental disorders to be convicted of criminal offences. Three types of investigations support this conclusion. First, there are studies of birth cohorts followed from pregnancy through adulthood which compare the criminal records of persons who develop major mental disorders and are hospitalized with those of persons with no admission for a major mental disorder. (In these studies, persons with other types of mental disorders and with mental retardation are examined separately.) Five studies of this type using cohorts born between 1944 and 1966 have been conducted and all have obtained similar results (Hodgins, 1998). More of the persons who developed a major mental disorder as compared with those with no disorder were convicted of a crime. The differences between the disordered and non-disordered groups were greater for violent than for non-violent crime, and the associations between mental disorder and criminality and violent criminality were stronger for women than for men.

A second type of investigation which demonstrates that persons who develop major mental disorders are at increased risk for criminal conviction are follow-up studies which compare the criminal activities of persons discharged from inpatient psychiatric wards with those of non-disordered persons living in the same community. Since the middle to late 1960s, studies of persons with major mental disorders living in the community have consistently reported that more of them than their non-disordered neighbours are convicted of crimes. As in the birth cohort studies, the results of most of these investigations indicate that the association between the major mental disorders and violence is stronger than that between the major mental disorders and non-violent crime (Hodgins, 1993).

---

[2] Contrary to popular clinical lore, recent empirical evidence demonstrates that the major affective disorders are recurrent in almost all cases. In addition, psychosocial functioning between the acute episodes is impaired (Coryell et al., 1993; Klerman & Weissman, 1992; Harrow, Goldberg, Grossman, & Meltzer, 1990; Stoll et al., 1993; Tohen, Waternaux, & Tsuang, 1990).

Third, studies conducted in North America find higher prevalence rates for the major mental disorders among convicted offenders than among age and gender matched samples from the general population (Brinded, Stevens, Mulder, Fairley, Malcolm, & Wells, 1999; Brink, Doherty, & Boer, 2001; Brooke, Taylor, Gunn, & Maden, 1996; Hodgins & Côté, 1990). In addition, among unbiased samples of homicide offenders prevalence rates for the major mental disorders far exceed general population rates (Hodgins, 1994a).

FACTORS THAT INFLUENCE THE PREVALENCE OF CRIMINALITY AMONG PERSONS WHO DEVELOP MAJOR MENTAL DISORDERS

Individual Factors

A number of individual and contextual factors have been identified that influence criminality among persons who suffer from major mental disorders. Consider first the individual factors. Evidence suggests that among persons who develop major mental disorders, there is a sub-group who are characterized by antisocial behaviour from a young age throughout their lives (Hodgins, Côté, & Toupin, 1998; Hodgins, 1998). We have hypothesized that this sub-group may be proportionately larger among the mentally ill born since the mid-1940s than among those born previously (Hodgins, 2000). These data have led us to hypothesize that there are two types of persons who develop major mental disorders and who commit crimes. The early-starters are characterized by stable antisocial behaviour across the lifespan. They begin their criminal careers in adolescence, often before the onset of the major mental disorder. The criminality of the early-starters is, we propose, linked to this antisocial personality and lifestyle. By contrast, the late-starters show no evidence of antisocial or aggressive behaviour before the onset of the symptoms of the major mental disorder. Their illegal behaviours are more likely to be the consequence, or at least associated with, the symptoms of the major mental disorder.

A second, individual factor associated with the increased prevalence of criminality among persons who develop major mental disorders is their increased likelihood of aggressive behaviour. A number of studies have found that persons with major mental disorders are more likely than non-disordered persons to behave aggressively towards others (Link, Andrews, & Cullen, 1992; Steadman & Felson, 1984; Swanson, Holzer, Ganju, & Jono, 1990). For example, in samples of persons being discharged from psychiatric wards in three US cities, 35% of the women and 39% of the men reported aggressive behaviour in a two-month period (Steadman et al., 1993). This rate increased by 26% when the reports of collaterals were combined with the subjects' reports (Steadman et al., 1994).

A third individual factor that affects the rate of criminality among those with major mental disorders is the tendency for the late-starters to stay at the scene of the crime and/or to confess to a crime that they have committed (Lapalme, Jöckel, Hodgins, & Müller-Isberner, submitted; Robertson, 1988). Consequently, this sub-group of offenders with major mental disorders would be more likely to be arrested and successfully prosecuted than other offenders.

Another factor that influences the rate of criminality among those who develop major mental disorders is alcohol and drug use. Both disorders (abuse, dependence) and intoxication are associated with an increased risk of illegal behaviour. While the presence or history of an alcohol and/or drug use disorder increases the likelihood of illegal and particularly violent behaviour (Eronen, Tiihonen, & Hakola, 1996), such disorders do not characterize all mentally ill offenders (Lindqvist, 1986), nor are all mentally disordered offenders intoxicated when they commit an offence. Studies have systematically shown that alcohol and drugs are associated with the offending of some, but not all, mentally disordered persons. The ways in which alcohol and drug use increase the likelihood of illegal behaviours, and especially aggressive behaviour, are multiple and complex. This is true both for persons with and without major mental disorders, but those who develop major mental disorders may have a specific vulnerability for abuse/ dependence. Persons with major mental disorders are more likely than non-disordered persons living in the same community to develop alcohol and drug use disorders (Helzer & Przybeck, 1988; Hodgins, 1994b), and more likely to engage in substance abuse as children or young adolescents (Hodgins & Janson, 2002). We have hypothesized that the association between alcohol and drugs and criminality is different for the early and late-start offenders with major mental disorders. Among the early-starters it begins in adolescence and is an integral part of their antisocial life-style. Among the late-starters, abuse and dependence may be less important than intoxication (Hodgins et al., 1998).

Another individual factor that increases the risk of violent behaviour among persons with major mental disorders is the presence of certain types of psychotic symptoms labelled threat-control/override (Link & Stueve, 1994; Swanson, Borum, Swartz, & Monahan, 1996). Like alcohol or drug use, these symptoms constitute a risk factor since they increase the likelihood of violent behaviour, but characterize only some proportion of offenders with major mental disorders at the time of their offence (Tengström, Hodgins, Grann, Långström, & Kullgren, in press). Some studies have suggested that in fact such symptoms are present during the offending of only a small group of offenders with major mental disorders (Hodgins & Janson, 2002).

Contextual Factors

Initially when data began to accumulate showing higher prevalence rates of criminality among persons who develop major mental disorders than those with no disorders, it was often proposed that this was due to discrimination against the mentally ill by police and the judicial system. While one US investigation did find that police were more likely to arrest a mentally ill than a non-mentally ill suspect (Teplin, 1984), all other data suggest that in most countries a great effort is made to divert mentally ill persons from the criminal justice system. Some studies have even found that mentally ill persons are subject to positive discrimination in that their aggressive behaviours lead to prosecution less often than similar behaviours by non-disordered persons (Link et al., 1992; Steadman & Felson, 1984).

While discrimination does not explain the higher rates of criminality among persons who develop major mental disorders, there are societal factors that clearly do influence these rates. Some of these factors are associated with crime among both the disordered and the non-disordered (Hodgins, 1998), while others specifically influence criminality among persons who develop major mental disorders. Existing data suggest that the prevalence of criminality among persons who develop major mental disorders has increased dramatically since the middle to late 1960s (Hodgins & Lalonde, 1999). During this period in most Western industrialized countries mental health policies and practices were drastically changed. Mental health care for the major disorders no longer involved life-time hospitalization in large asylums, but rather short stays in hospital and appointments in outpatient clinics, in many cases limited to evaluations of medications. During this same period, in most countries the criteria for involuntary hospitalization were strengthened and patients were accorded rights to refuse treatment. In retrospect, it seems clear that the implementation of the policy of deinstitutionalizing mental health care and the amendments to laws that were adopted at approximately the same time to limit the legal powers of mental health professionals to impose treatment against the will of a client, have been associated with an increase in the prevalence of criminality among persons who develop major mental disorders. This conclusion suggests that criminality in this population is affected by the quality, type, and intensity of treatment and services that they receive. As will be seen in the latter part of this chapter, this conclusion is further supported by the results of evaluation studies of specialized community treatment programmes for offenders with major mental disorders.

GOALS OF TREATMENT

The primary goal of treatment for persons with major mental disorders is to end, or at least reduce, their suffering. More specifically, the goal is to address and resolve the multiple behavioural, cognitive, and emotional problems that these individuals present in the most humane and least restrictive ways possible. One of the problems that persons with major disorders often present is suicide. Consequently, it is now taken for granted that mental health professionals have a particular responsibility, and in most countries specific legal powers, to prevent suicide. As noted above, another problem that many persons with major mental disorders present is repetitive aggressive behaviour towards others and non-violent criminal activity. In fact, the results of many investigations document rates of aggressive behaviour and criminality that are as high or higher than the rates of suicide. It can be argued, then, that mental health professionals, in addition to their role in treating the symptoms of the major mental disorder, also have a responsibility to evaluate the risks for aggressive behaviour towards others and criminality, and if they are present to intervene to prevent them. Blackburn has put it well:

> ... The rehabilitation "ideal" is aimed at increasing personal effectiveness, of which avoiding further offending is only one component ... this implies that the targets of intervention are those cognitive, emotional and interpersonal disabilities which impede social reintegration. Reduced recidivism is therefore a necessary but not sufficient criterion of the effectiveness of intervention (1996, p. 133).

In order to succeed in meeting these goals, treatment programmes for offenders with major mental disorders must have the following characteristics. First, they must be long-term because major mental disorders are chronic and in most cases involve cognitive, behavioural, and emotional deficits which can be reduced but not eliminated. Second, they must include multiple components because offenders with major disorders present multiple disorders involving both the lack of appropriate skills necessary for autonomous living and the presence of inappropriate behaviours and cognitions. Third, they must be co-ordinated with social services because many of these persons lack the skills to be financially independent and some even lack the skills necessary to eat nutritionally and clothe themselves appropriately for the weather. Fourth, they must include the possibility of legally imposing either inpatient or outpatient care in order to ensure compliance with the various aspects of treatment which are deemed necessary to prevent violence or non-violent criminality (for a more complete discussion, see Hodgins & Müller-Isberner, 2000).

ORGANIZATION AND CO-ORDINATION OF SERVICES

As noted in the previous sections of this chapter, a great deal of evidence has accumulated since the mid-1960s, indicating that many persons who will or who have already developed a major mental disorder are involved in criminal activities. Consequently, the so-called forensic psychiatric populations and traditional psychiatric populations are no longer distinct. For example, in many countries, large proportions of patients with major mental disorders treated in the emergency, inpatient, and outpatient services of general and psychiatric hospitals have a criminal record. In some countries, many such persons are homeless substance abusers whose only contact with services is the use of medical emergency rooms for the treatment of drug overdoses or to detoxify themselves so that a smaller quantity of drug will have a more powerful psychological effect (Côté & Hodgins, 1996).

Regardless of where and when they are first identified, persons with major mental disorders, especially those who have a history of criminal behaviour, present multiple problems requiring treatment and services over many years. In order to successfully limit their suffering, prevent them from committing crimes, and allow them to live under the least restrictive conditions while keeping the costs of hospitalization and incarceration to a minimum, a long-term stable multi-component programme is required which co-ordinates mental health and social services and respects conditions laid out by criminal and civil law. The goals described above can be achieved if a long-term perspective is taken and the mental health professionals responsible for treatment can access different types of services to address the individual client's needs, which will vary over time. While most of the treatment can be effectively and safely provided in the community, in many cases both long-term inpatient care on psychiatric wards with varying degrees of security and short-term rapid hospitalization are necessary.

There are no empirical studies that indicate which types of patients benefit from which type of inpatient care. This is partially due to the fact that in many instances inpatient care is ordered by a criminal court following the commission of a crime. Some jurisdictions provide inpatient care in general hospitals, while others have specialized forensic hospitals with various levels of security (see, for example, the special issue of the *International Journal of Law and Psychiatry, 16* (1/2) 1993 and *23* (5/6) 2000). In some cases, such hospitals exist within a correctional facility. Empirical research has not as yet provided data on the effective use of various types of inpatient settings—general psychiatric wards, high, medium, and low security hospitals (see, for example, Taylor, Maden, & Jones, 1996).

Setting up long-term co-operation between different authorities—health, social, justice—proves difficult in many jurisdictions (see, for example, Petch, 1996; Wormith & McKeague, 1996). Yet, there is a consensus that continuity of treatment is essential (Heilbrun & Griffin, 1993; McGreevy, Steadman, Dvoskin, & Dollard, 1991; Steadman, McCarty & Morrissey, 1989; Wiederanders, Bromley, & Choate, 1997; Wiederanders & Choate, 1994). A model programme set up in Vancouver which illustrates such co-ordination has been described (Corrado, Doherty, & Glackmen, 1989) and evaluated (Wilson, Tien, & Eaves, 1995). In many countries, offenders with major mental disorders are convicted and sentenced to incarceration in correctional facilities where treatment needs to be begun or continued. Models for treatment inside such facilities have been described (Cohen & Dvoskin, 1992; Metzner, 1993). The importance of continuity in the provision of long-term treatment to persons with major mental disorders is demonstrated in the evaluation studies of case management (Brekke, Long, Nesbitt, & Sobel, 1997; Ryan, Sherman, & Bogart, 1997; Wolff et al., 1997).

These investigations have not yet succeeded in identifying programmes that are effective for all sub-groups of persons with major mental disorders, nor in identifying criteria for matching clients to programmes. As in all forms of mental health treatment, some of these programmes have produced positive results, some no results, and others negative results (Ryan et al., 1997).

ASSESSMENT[3]

Identification

Offenders with major mental disorders come into contact with mental health professionals in different ways and at different times in the development of their disorder, depending largely on the laws, policies, and practices of the country or state where they live. Despite these national differences, two situations are common. An individual in an acute episode of psychosis, mania, or depression is brought to the emergency room of a hospital. The immediate concern is to reduce the acute symptoms and protect the individual from harming him/herself. If the individual has committed a violent crime in the previous hours or days, the risk of suicide may be particularly elevated (Hillbrand, Krystal, Sharpe, & Foster, 1994). The other commonly occurring situation that brings offenders with major mental disorders into contact with mental health professionals is arrest and incarceration. In this situation the difficulties are twofold: first, identifying the mentally ill person; second, obtaining adequate and appropriate treatment for him/her. In most countries, mental health professionals do not assess all persons who are arrested. Consequently, it is necessary to develop a cost-effective screening procedure in order to identify those in need of treatment. Such a procedure would be constructed so that initially all new admissions would be assessed by non-clinicians or by questionnaires and only those who were judged to present certain symptoms would undergo a diagnostic interview. The challenge in developing such a screening procedure is to ensure that no one with a serious disorder is missed at the initial stage, and as few as possible of those without such disorders are identified for further assessment. The major mental disorders are especially difficult to identify by non-clinicians. Even the best of the diagnostic instruments designed to be used by lay interviewers in epidemiological investigations fails to identify significant numbers of cases of major mental disorders (Hodgins, 1995). Not surprisingly, then, attempts to develop such screening procedures for use in jails have had varying success (Hart, Roesch, Corrado, & Cox, 1993; Teplin & Swartz, 1989). Even when arrestees with major mental disorders are identified, obtaining appropriate and adequate treatment requires co-operation between criminal justice and mental health authorities and services. Models for such co-operation have been described (Ogloff, Tien, Roesch, & Eaves, 1991; Rowlands, Inch, Rodger, & Soliman, 1996; Solomon & Draine, 1995; Walsh & Bricourt, 1996).

---

[3] Assessment here refers to a mental health assessment and not an assessment requested by a criminal court, for example to determine responsibility for an offence, to identify mitigating circumstances to be considered in sentencing an offender, or to predicting the future risk of criminality.

Three Stages of Assessment

The Primary Disorder

Assessments of individuals suffering from major mental disorders include several steps. Depending on the mental state of the individual and the context in which the assessment is being conducted, these steps may be completed within a few days, weeks, or months. The first step obviously involves accurately diagnosing the major disorder. In most cases this poses no problem for experienced clinicians if they have adequate time to interview and observe the individual in question. However, among persons who suffer from these disorders and who offend there are obstacles to making accurate diagnoses of the primary disorder. The first obstacle to accurately diagnosing the primary disorder is the presence of other disorders. Research has shown that most persons with major mental disorders who commit crimes present several co-morbid disorders (Côté & Hodgins, 1990; Hodgins & Janson, 2002).

A second obstacle to accurately diagnosing the presence of a major mental disorder, particularly among offenders, is their reluctance to acknowledge the presence of symptoms. Males with a well-established antisocial life-style, who have often been part of a criminal sub-culture since adolescence, have an abhorrence of being labelled "crazy" or mentally ill. And in fact, in their world, either a correctional facility or the community, there probably are very real negative consequences associated with such a label, such as physical abuse and being put in isolation cells (Hodgins & Côté, 1991). This refusal to acknowledge the presence of symptoms was well illustrated by findings from a study that a colleague and I conducted in Canada. We promised a representative sample of penitentiary inmates complete confidentiality (except if they represented an immediate threat to themselves or someone else) if they participated in a diagnostic interview. To our astonishment we found that less than half of those who received a diagnosis of a major mental disorder had ever spoken to anyone about their symptoms, despite the fact that the disorder had been present for several years (Hodgins & Côté, 1990).

Paranoid symptoms are another obstacle to accurate diagnosis of persons with major mental disorders who are at risk for crime and for violence. While it has long been thought that paranoid symptoms are associated with violence, very little is known about this association nor about delusional disorder, simply because persons with these symptoms are reticent to talk to either clinicians or researchers. Also, in certain sub-cultures and contexts, for example jails and prisons, it is often difficult for a mental health professional to discern if stories of predators, threats, car chases, listening devices, etc. are true or delusional (Côté, Lesage, Chawky, & Loyer, 1997; Hodgins et al., 1998).

Another obstacle to accurately diagnosing major mental disorders among offenders or persons with a history of antisocial behaviour is that they are often intoxicated when they first come into contact with a mental health professional.

As noted above, alcohol and drug use disorders are more prevalent among those who offend than among those with the same disorders who do not.

Assessment of the immediate risk of harm to self and others must be included at this initial step. However, as this initial assessment usually takes place when the individual is in an acute psychotic, manic, or depressive state, the evaluation is limited to assessing the likelihood of acting out behaviour before medication can reduce the acute symptomatology. It is important to note that the factors associated with aggressive behaviour on an inpatient ward are different from those that influence these behaviours in the community (Davis, 1991; Quinsey & Maguire, 1986).

Co-morbid Disorders and Accompanying Problems

The second step in an assessment involves diagnosing co-morbid disorders and it must wait until the symptoms characterizing the acute episode have been reduced or eliminated. Given current mental health policy and practice in many countries, it is often difficult to hospitalize a person with a major mental disorder long enough to do this. However, it is necessary to accurately identify co-morbid disorders among persons suffering from major mental disorders. Research has shown that accurate diagnoses of alcohol and drug problems (Bryant, Rounsaville, Spitzer, & Williams, 1992), and no doubt personality disorders, can only be made when acute symptoms have been reduced and when detoxification is complete.

This step in the assessment also includes obtaining a detailed history of aggressive and all other illegal behaviours. In taking such a history, it is critical to:

1. distinguish aggressive or violent behaviour from non-violent criminality;
2. document the age when these behaviours first occurred and relate this to the onset of the symptoms of the major disorder;
3. document the situations in which these illegal behaviours occur—for example, when the acute symptoms of the disorder are present, when intoxicated, when disagreeing with another person, when feeling ridiculed or humiliated;
4. document the motives for the behaviour; and
5. document the level of impulsivity associated with these behaviours (Bjørkly, 1997).

It is essential to collect information not only from the individual being assessed but from as many other sources as possible. Family members and friends can be an invaluable source of information on all of these points. Note that in the study reported above, the frequency of aggressive behaviour by patients living in the community increased by 25% when information from a collateral was added to the subject's self-report (Steadman et al., 1994). However, in numerous cases family and friends are reticent to describe the individual's aggressive behaviours, often seeing it as betrayal of a loved one who is ill. Mental health professionals have to take time to meet with these persons and to reassure them that accurate descriptions of their family member's or friend's behaviour is of critical importance for his/her treatment and ultimate welfare. Records of previous mental health assessments, inpatient and outpatient treatment, assessments done for the court, criminal activities, records of both behaviour and academic performance at school, and records of employment can add information which is critical to clarifying the client's reports and planning treatment.

The accuracy and breadth of information collected at this stage in the assessment will determine to a large extent the effectiveness of the treatment programme to be designed for the client and thereby, in some cases, the safety of others. This point is well illustrated by a tragic example which is reminiscent of so many other cases both with respect to the characteristics and history of the patient and the response to him by the mental health and criminal justice systems. Mr Christopher Clunis had suffered from schizophrenia for a number of years. After he stabbed to death another man on a subway platform in London, the North East Thames and South East Thames Regional Health Authorities conducted an inquiry into the treatment and care he had received prior to the murder. In piecing together this man's history, the commission of inquiry found that information concerning incidents of aggressive behaviour, even of incidents that had occurred in the presence of mental health professionals, was not passed on from one treating clinician to the next. While in retrospect a clear pattern emerged of aggressive behaviour increasing in frequency and severity over time, this information was unknown to those responsible for Mr Clunis's care before the murder. Collecting such information is time consuming and sometimes frustrating and difficult. However, it is critical to effectively treating this population and to preventing violent and criminal behaviours among them (Hodgins, 1994a).

Optimal Treatment Conditions

The final step in the assessment involves measuring treatability and identifying what are the optimal conditions for effective treatment for this particular person. For example, most persons who suffer from major mental disorders require medication on a long-term basis. Not only is it necessary to identify the most effective medications for the person, but also to assess the amount and type of supervision that will be required to ensure that the individual continues to take the medication as prescribed, and as well to assess what training the individual requires in order to be able to monitor symptoms and side-effects, to recognize signs indicating the necessity of medical intervention, and if necessary, knowing how to quickly contact the appropriate physician. Medications are only one part of the treatment required by offenders with major mental disorders. It may not be helpful at this stage in the assessment to use a medical model to think about the co-morbid disorders. This would lead, for example, in the case of antisocial personality disorder which will characterize large numbers of such persons, to unwarranted scepticism about even embarking on treatment. A behavioural or behavioural–cognitive approach may be of more use. Such an approach would involve a systematic description of the problems presented by the individual that hinder autonomous living in the community. In addition to these concrete descriptions of the multiple problems that characterize mentally disordered offenders, an evaluation of the individual's capacity to change and to tolerate the different treatments is needed. Many of the possible treatments will involve skills training that requires concentration, memory, a certain level of intelligence, and an ability to tolerate the presence of others. Some of the programmes, for example those designed to end substance abuse, may well require the ability to cope with stressful and frustrating situations and to think abstractly. Most of these programmes will be offered in a group context and require tolerance by each client of the other. Thus, assessments of the problems that need to be addressed by various components of the treatment programme and the personal resources that the individual brings to treatment are essential to ensure that treatment goals are realistic. Furthermore, such information allows the treatment staff to create some success experiences relatively quickly once treatment begins, thereby increasing compliance.

This final step in the assessment involves evaluating the need for supervision in order to ensure that the client follows the treatment programme and does not commit crimes before these interventions have beneficial effects. For the same client, the levels of supervision required for different problems or to ensure compliance with different components of treatment will vary, and will, if treatment is effective, be reduced over time. For example, an individual suffering from schizophrenia who regularly steals money for beer and food when his or her own runs out at the end of the month requires supervision until he/she learns how to manage a monthly income. An individual suffering from bipolar disorder requires supervision to monitor the onset of manic episodes which usually involve paranoid symptoms and are accompanied by aggressive behaviour towards his wife and children. A client with a history of major depression and alcohol abuse requires supervision to prevent binge drinking which in the past has been associated with fighting.

TREATMENT

Offenders with major mental disorders require all of the treatments and services needed by non-offenders who suffer from these disorders, plus additional treatment components which teach them skills for autonomous living and the skills necessary to prevent further aggressive behaviour and/or non-violent criminality. Given the paucity of evaluation studies of such multi-component treatment programmes for this population, the diversity of the clientele, and the broad array of problems that they present, only a brief outline of such programmes and the necessary components will be discussed.

Specialized Inpatient Care

Evaluation studies of inhospital care for offenders with major mental disorders are non-existent. As noted above, no studies have provided information on the types of offenders with major mental disorders who require inhospital treatment with varying levels of security, on the optimal length of inpatient care, and on the components of inpatient care. A major contribution in this direction was made by a group of Canadian researchers (Rice, Harris, Quinsey, & Cyr, 1990). They surveyed the problems presented by the patients in two secure psychiatric hospitals. They then reviewed the empirical literature and identified treatments that directly addressed each type of problem. They concluded that:

> ... Interventions have been developed that are relevant to all of the problem types most commonly exhibited by patients in secure facilities ... the degree to which these treatments have received rigorous evaluations varies but there is at least some encouraging evidence for the efficacy of all of the interventions we recommend (p. 215).

This pioneering study provides a framework and methodology for progress in this area. While the general treatment philosophy presented by Rice and her colleagues has been adopted elsewhere (see, for example, Müller-Isberner, 1993, 1998), evaluation studies are virtually non-existent.

Specialized Community Care

Despite the multiple and complex problems presented by offenders with major mental disorders and the necessity of co-ordinating interventions by mental health, social service, and criminal justice authorities over long periods of time, there is empirical evidence of successful community programmes that prevent recidivism among even high risk cases.[4] In 1993, Heilbrun and Griffin authored a review of studies which had evaluated community-based treatments for insanity acquittees in the United States. While the lengths of the follow-up periods, the combinations of treatment components, social services, and legal contexts varied considerably across studies, the outcomes were generally positive. Similarly, Wiederanders has evaluated services and supervision for insanity acquittees in California (Wiederanders, 1992; Wiederanders & Choate, 1994) and compared them with programmes offered in Oregon and New York State (Wiederanders,

---

[4] A discussion of the appropriate outcome measures for such treatment programmes is beyond the scope of this chapter. However, measures of effectiveness would include assessments of symptoms, levels of psychosocial functioning, quality of life, client's subjective assessment of suffering and of success, and counts of the frequency of suicide attempts, criminal offending, aggressive behaviour towards others, alcohol use, and drug use.

Bromley, & Choate, 1997). Again, the results were positive and demonstrated a crime prevention effect. The programme in Vancouver, referred to above, recruited clients in a correctional facility and compared those admitted to the programme with a group of clients with similar problems and histories who refused admission, for whom there was no place available, or who moved away from the city (Wilson et al., 1995). Another programme in Germany (Müller-Isberner, 1996) and one in Québec (Hodgins, Lapalme, & Toupin, 1999) compared offenders with mental disorders who were treated in a specialized forensic after-care programme and general psychiatry outpatient clinics. Again, the specialized programmes designed for offenders with major mental disorders all demonstrated positive crime prevention effects. Not only are these programmes effective in preventing recidivism, they are highly cost-effective. The community programme in Oregon that has been identified as a model of effectiveness for offenders with major mental disorders (Buckley, 1994) has been estimated to cost 14% that of hospital care (Bigelow, Bloom, & Williams, 1990). The specialized forensic community programme in Germany described above, plus housing provided by the social authorities, is estimated to cost 37% that of inpatient care (Müller-Isberner, personal communication).

As Wiederanders and his colleagues noted (1997), problems of comparability abound in this small but burgeoning outcome literature on treatment of offenders with major mental disorders. Despite this fact, the programmes that have had positive results, share a number of features in common. One, the goals of the programmes are to treat the major mental disorder, the co-morbid disorders that hinder autonomous functioning in the community, and to prevent crime and aggressive behaviour. Two, the programmes are structured, intense, and diversified and include specific components designed to address the multiple problems presented by offenders with major mental disorders. Three, the programmes involve outreach, or what has been referred to as assertive case management. Four, in most cases compliance with the community-based treatment was compulsory. Five, the mental health professionals running the programme had the right to re-hospitalize clients, for short periods, relatively rapidly and easily. As Heilbrun and Griffin (1993) noted, the importance of research in identifying the active and essential components of such programmes cannot be overemphasized. This echoes the conclusion of Rice and her colleagues (1990) with respect to inhospital treatment (Hodgins & Müller-Isberner, 2000).

CONCLUSION

The empirical data available today suggest that much of the criminality and violence perpetrated by persons suffering from major mental disorders could be prevented if policy decisions and the allocation of funds were based on empirical evidence, and programme evaluation was used to continually increase the effectiveness of treatment programmes. Such programmes are long-term and usually involve care both in and out of hospital. Each programme is developed on an individual basis, after extensive assessment of the client, which involves not only interviewing and observing him/her, but also collecting information from family members and friends, other mental health and social service professionals who have treated the client, and if possible records of performance at school, in the military, and at work. Criminal records, both juvenile and adult, are essential. The results of outcome studies available suggest that effective treatment programmes include:

1. components that have been shown to be effective in the treatment of the major mental disorders;
2. components that specifically address the co-morbid disorders or problems in autonomous living presented by most offenders with major mental disorders;
3. varying levels of supervision for different problems;
4. legal obligation for community treatment if compliance is a problem;
5. possibility of involuntary rehospitalization for short periods of time; and
6. adequate social services (income, housing).

The outcome literature on the major mental disorders indicates that such programmes will have a greater likelihood of success if the key staff person organizing the various aspects of the treatment programme and who is in continual contact with the client over the long-term remains stable.

As noted, progress in implementing effective treatment programmes for offenders with major mental disorders will be made only if such programmes are based on empirical data on the effectiveness of the various components of treatment and on knowledge of the major mental disorders and of offenders who suffer from these disorders. All of the interventions described in Chapters 10–16 that have proven to be effective with non-disordered offenders are worth adapting and evaluating with offenders with major mental disorders (Harris & Rice, 1997; Müller-Isberner et al., 2000). Research is urgently needed in order to identify the social services necessary for the various sub-groups of offenders with major mental disorders and ways to provide these services that are acceptable to the clients. For example, men suffering from schizophrenia who have a history of antisocial behaviour from early adolescence are more likely to be homeless than offenders with schizophrenia but no childhood history of antisocial behaviour (Tengström & Hodgins, 2002). They are also more likely to present substance abuse (Mueser, Drake, Alterman, Miles, & Noordsy, 1997). Getting them settled in stable accommodations with an income sufficient for food and clothing may well be a first step to ensuring compliance with the other components of the treatment programme. Civil and criminal laws that support and promote effective treatment under the least restrictive conditions need to be identified. Particularly urgent is the need in several countries for laws providing for compulsory treatment in the community. Finally, factors known to increase criminality among non-disordered persons need to be investigated among persons with major mental disorders, for example the consequences of living in high crime areas where alcohol, drugs, and firearms are readily available.

Several sub-topics within this area have not yet even been addressed. Notable is the absence of descriptions and evaluations of treatment programmes for female offenders with major mental disorders. Another glaring lack of knowledge concerns the parenting skills of offenders with major mental disorders who have children and the effect that both their offending and their mental disorder is having on their children. Finally, while knowledge is available which could be used to implement programmes designed to prevent offending and related problems such as substance abuse among children and adolescents at high risk for the development of major mental disorders, to our knowledge this is not being done.

REFERENCES

Bigelow, D. A., Bloom, J. D., & Williams, M. H. (1990). Costs of managing insanity acquittees under a psychiatric security review board system. *Hospital and Community Psychiatry*, *41*, 613–614.

Bjørkly, S. (1997). Clinical assessment of dangerousness in psychotic patients: Some risk indicators and pitfalls. *Aggression and Violent Behavior*, *2*, 167–178.

Blackburn, R. (1996). Mentally disordered offenders. In C. R. Hollin (Ed.), *Working with offenders: Psychological practice in offender rehabilitation* (pp. 119–149). Chichester, UK: Wiley.

Brekke, J. S., Long, J. D., Nesbitt, N., & Sobel, E. (1997). The impact of service characteristics on functional outcomes from community support programs for persons with schizophrenia: A growth curve analysis. *Journal of Consulting and Clinical Psychology*, *65*, 464–475.

Brinded, P. M. J., Stevens, I., Mulder, R. T., Fairley, N. F., Malcolm, F., & Wells, J. E. (1999). The Christchurch prisons psychiatric epidemiology study: methodology and prevalence rates for psychiatric disorders. *Criminal Behaviour and Mental Health*, *9*, 131–143.

Brink, J. H., Doherty, D., & Boer, A. (2001). Mental disorder in federal offenders: A Canadian prevalence study. *International Journal of Law and Psychiatry*, *24*, 339–356.

Brooke, D., Taylor, C., Gunn, J., & Maden, A. (1996). Point prevalence of mental disorder in unconvicted male prisoners in England and Wales. *British Medical Journal*, *313*, 1524–1527.

Bryant, K. J., Rounsaville, B., Spitzer, R. L., & Williams, J. B. W. (1992). Reliability of dual diagnosis. Substance dependence and psychiatric disorders. *The Journal of Nervous and Mental Disease*, *180*, 251–257.

Buckley, M. C. (1994). A model for management and treatment of insanity acquittees. *Hospital and Community Psychiatry*, *45*, 1127–1131.

Cohen, F., & Dvoskin, J. (1992). Inmates with mental disorders: A guide to law and practice. *Mental and Physical Disability Law Reporter*, *16*, 462–470.

Corrado, R. R., Doherty, D., & Glackman, W. (1989). A demonstration program for chronic recidivists of criminal justice, health, and social service agencies. *International Journal of Law and Psychiatry*, *12*, 211–229.

Coryell, W., Scheftner, W., Keller, M., Endicott, J., Maser, J., & Klerman, G. L. (1993). The enduring psychosocial consequences of mania and depression. *American Journal of Psychiatry*, *150*, 720–727.

Côté, G., & Hodgins, S. (1990). Co-occurring mental disorders among criminal offenders. *Bulletin of American Academy of Psychiatry and the Law*, *18*, 271–281.

Côté, G., & Hodgins, S. (1996). *Problèmes d'alcool, problèmes de drogue et conduite antisociale chez les sujets en demande d'aide psychologique dans une salle d'urgence*. Research report, Conseil Québécois de la Recherche Sociale.

Côté, G., Lesage, A., Chawky, N., & Loyer, M. (1997). Clinical specificity of prison inmates with severe mental disorders: A case control study. *British Journal of Psychiatry, 170,* 571–577.

Davis, S. (1991). Violence by psychiatric inpatients: A review. *Hospital and Community Psychiatry, 42,* 585–590.

Eronen, M., Tiihonen, J., & Hakola, P. (1996). Schizophrenia and homicidal behavior. *Schizophrenia Bulletin, 22,* 83–89.

Gunn, J., Maden, A., & Swinton, M. (1991). Treatment needs of prisoners with psychiatric disorders. *British Medical Journal, 303,* 338–340.

Harris, G. T., & Rice, M. E. (1997). Mentally disordered offenders: What research says about effective service. In C. D. Webster & M. A. Jackson (Eds.), *Impulsivity* (pp. 361–393). New York: Guilford.

Harrow, M., Goldberg, J. F., Grossman, L., & Meltzer, H. (1990). Outcome in manic disorders. *Archives of General Psychiatry, 47,* 665–671.

Hart, S. D., Roesch, R., Corrado, R. R., & Cox, D. N. (1993). The referral decision scale. *Law and Human Behavior, 17,* 611–623.

Heilbrun, K., & Griffin, P. A. (1993). Community-based forensic treatment of insanity acquittees. *International Journal of Law and Psychiatry, 16,* 133–150.

Helzer, J. E., & Przybeck, T. R. (1988). The co-occurrence of alcoholism with other psychiatric disorders in the general population and its impact on treatment. *Journal of Studies on Alcohol, 49,* 219–224.

Hillbrand, M., Krystal, J. H., Sharpe, K. S., & Foster, H. G. (1994) Clinical predictors of self-mutilation in hospitalized forensic patients. *The Journal of Nervous and Mental Disease, 182,* pp. 9–13.

Hodgins, S. (1993). The criminality of mentally disordered persons. In S. Hodgins (Ed.), *Mental disorder and crime* (pp. 1–21). Newbury Park, CA: Sage.

Hodgins, S. (1994a). Schizophrenia and violence: Are new mental health policies needed? *Journal of Forensic Psychiatry, 5,* 473–477.

Hodgins, S. (1994b). Letter to the Editor. *Archives of General Psychiatry, 51,* 71–72.

Hodgins, S. (1995). Assessing mental disorder in the criminal justice system: Feasibility versus clinical accuracy. *International Journal of Law and Psychiatry, 18,* 15–28.

Hodgins, S. (1996). The major mental disorders: New evidence requires new policy and practice. *Canadian Psychology, 37,* 95–111.

Hodgins, S. (1998). Epidemiological investigations of the association between major mental disorders and crime: Methodological limitations and validity of the conclusions. *Social Psychiatry and Epidemiology, 33,* 29–37.

Hodgins, S. (2000). The etiology and development of offending among persons with major mental disorders: Conceptual and methodological issues and some preliminary findings. In S. Hodgins (Ed.), *Violence among the mentally ill: Effective treatments and management strategies* (pp. 89–116). Dordrecht, The Netherlands: Kluwer Academic Publishers.

Hodgins, S., & Côté, G. (1990). The prevalence of mental disorders among penitentiary inmates. *Canada's Mental Health, 38,* 1–5.

Hodgins, S., & Côté, G. (1991). The mental health of penitentiary inmates in isolation. *Canadian Journal of Criminology, 33,* 175–182.

Hodgins, S., Côté, G., & Toupin, J. (1998). Major mental disorders and crime: An etiological hypothesis. In D. Cooke, A. Forth, & R. D. Hare (Eds.), *Psychopathy: Theory, research and implications for society* (pp. 231–256). Dordrecht, The Netherlands: Kluwer.

Hodgins, S., & Janson, C.-G. (2002). *Criminality and violence among the mentally disordered: The Stockholm metropolitan project.* Cambridge, UK: Cambridge University Press.

Hodgins, S., & Lalonde, N. (1999). Major mental disorders and crime: Changes over time?

In P. Cohen, L. Robins, & C. Slomkowski (Eds.), *Where and when: Geographical and historial aspects of psychopathology* (pp. 57–83). Mahwah, NJ: Erlbaum.

Hodgins, S., & Müller-Isberner, R. (2000). *Violence, crime and mentally disordered offenders: Concepts and methods for effective treatment and prevention.* Chichester, UK: Wiley.

Hodgins, S., Lapalme, M., & Toupin, J. (1999). Criminal activities and substance use of patients with major affective disorders and schizophrenia: A two-year follow-up. *Journal of Affective Disorders, 55,* 187–202.

Kessler, R. C., McGonagle, K. A., Zhao, S., Nelson, C. B., Hughes, M., Eshleman, S., Wittchen, H. -U., & Kendler, K. S. (1994). Lifetime and 12-month prevalence of DSM-III-R psychiatric disorders in the United States, *Archives General of Psychiatry, 51,* 8–19.

Klerman, G. L., & Weissman, M. M. (1992). The course, morbidity, and costs of depression. *Archives of General Psychiatry, 49,* 831–834.

Lapalme, M., Jöckel, D., Hodgins, S., & Müller-Isberner (submitted). The management and treatment of offenders with major mental disorders: The role of antisocial personality disorder.

Lewinsohn, P. M., Rohde, P., Seeley, J. R., & Fischer, S. A. (1993). Age-cohort changes in the lifetime occurrence of depression and other mental disorders. *Journal of Abnormal Psychology, 102*(1), 110–120.

Lindqvist, P. (1986). Criminal homicide in Northern Sweden 1970–1981: Alcohol intoxication, alcohol abuse and mental disease. *International Journal of Law and Psychiatry, 8,* 19–37.

Link, B. G., Andrews, H., & Cullen, F. T. (1992). The violent and illegal behaviour of mental patients recondidererd. *American Sociological Review, 57,* 275–292.

Link, B. G., & Stueve, A. (1994). Psychotic symptoms and the violent/illegal behavior of mental patients compared to community control. In J. Monahan & H. Steadman (Eds.), *Violence and mental disorder. Developments in risk assessment* (pp. 137–159). Chicago, IL: University of Chicago Press.

McGreevy, M. A., Steadman, H. J., Dvoskin, J. A., & Dollard, N. (1991). New York State's system of managing insanity acquittees in the community. *Hospital and Community Psychiatry, 42,* 512–517.

Metzner, J. L. (1993). Guidelines for psychiatric services in prisons. *Criminal Behavior and Mental Health, 3,* 252–267.

Mueser, K. T., Drake, R. E., Alterman, A. I., Miles, K. M., & Noordsy, D. L. (1997). Antisocial personality disorder, conduct disorder, and substance abuse in schizophrenia. *Journal of Abnormal Psychology, 106,* 473–477.

Müller-Isberner, R. (1993). Managing insane offenders: The practice of hospital order treatment in the forensic psychiatric hospital. *International Bulletin of Law and Mental Health, 4,* (1 and 2), 28–30.

Müller-Isberner, J. R. (1996). Forensic psychiatric aftercare following hospital order treatment. *International Journal of Law and Psychiatry, 19,* 81–86.

Müller-Isberner, R., Freese, R., Jöckel, D., & Gonzalez Cabeza, S. (2000). Forensic psychiatric assessment and treatment in Germany: Legal framework, recent developments, and current practices. *International Journal of Law and Psychiatry, 23,* 467–480.

Ogloff, J. R. P., Tien, G., Roesch, R., & Eaves, D. (1991). A model for the provision of jail mental health services: An integrative, community-based approach. *The Journal of Mental Health Administration, 18,* 209–222.

Petch, E. (1996). Mentally disordered offenders: Inter-agency working. *The Journal of Forensic Psychiatry, 7,* 376–382.

Quinsey, V. L., & Maguire, A. (1986). Maximum security psychiatric patients: Actuarial and clinical prediction of dangerousness. *Journal of Interpersonal Aggression, 1,* 143–171.

Rice, M. E., Harris, G. T., Quinsey, V. L., & Cyr, M. (1990). Planning treatment programs in secure psychiatric facilities. In D. N. Weisstub (Ed.), *Law and mental health: International perspectives, Vol. 5* (pp. 162–230). New York: Pergamon Press.

Robertson, G. (1988). Arrest patterns among mentally disordered offenders. *British Journal of Psychiatry*, *153*, 313–316.

Rowlands, R., Inch, H., Rodger, W., & Soliman, A. (1996). Diverted to where? What happens to the diverted mentally disordered offender. *Journal of Forensic Psychiatry*, *7*, 284–296.

Ryan, C. S., Sherman, P. S., & Bogart, L. M. (1997). Patterns of services and consumer outcome in an intensive case management program. *Journal of Consulting and Clinical Psychology*, *65*, 485–493.

Solomon, P., & Draine, J. (1995). Issues in serving the forensic client. *Social Work*, *40*, 25–33.

Steadman, H. J., & Felson, R. B. (1984). Self-reports of violence—Ex-mental patients, ex-offenders, and the general population. *Criminology*, *22*, 321–342.

Steadman, H, J., McCarty, D. W., & Morrissey, J. P. (1989). *The mentally ill in jail: Planning for essential services.* New York: Guilford.

Steadman, H. J., Monahan, J., Appelbaum, P. S., Grisso, T., Mulvey, E. P., Roth, L. H., Robbins, P. C., & Classen, D. (1994). Designing a new generation of risk assessment research. In J. Monahan & H. J. Steadman (Eds.), *Violence and mental disorder: Developments in risk assessment* (pp. 297–318). Chicago, IL: The University of Chicago Press.

Steadman, H. J., Monahan, J., Robbins, P. A., Applebaum, P., Grisso, T., Klassen, D., Mulvey, E., & Roth, L. (1993). From dangerousness to risk assessment: Implications for appropriate research strategies. In S. Hodgins (Ed.), *Mental disorder and crime* (pp. 39–62). Newbury Park, CA: Sage.

Stoll, A. L., Tohen, M., Baldessarini, R. J., Goodwin, D. C., Stein, S., Katz, S., Geenens, D., Swinson, R., Goethe, J. W., & Glashan, T. (1993). Shifts in diagnostic frequencies of schizophrenia and major affective disorders at six North American psychiatric hospitals. *American Journal Psychiatry*, *150*, 1668–1673.

Swanson, J. W., Borum, R., Swartz, M., & Monahan, J. (1996). Psychotic symptoms and disorders and the risk of violent behavior in the community. *Criminal Behaviour and Mental Health*, *6*, 309–329.

Swanson, J. W., Holzer, C. E., Ganju, V. K., & Jono, R. T. (1990). Violence and psychiatric disorder in the community: Evidence from the epidemiologic catchment area surveys. *Hospital and Community Psychiatry*, *41*, 761–770.

Taylor, P. J., Maden, A., & Jones, D. (1996). Long-term medium-security hospital units: A service gap of the 1990s? *Criminal Behaviour and Mental Health*, *6*, 213–229.

Tengström, A., & Hodgins, S. (2002). Assessing psychopathic traits among persons with schizophrenia: A way to improve violence risk assessment. In E. Blaauw & L. Sheridan (Eds.), *Psychopaths Current International Perspective* (pp. 81–111). Holland: Elsevier.

Tengström, A., Hodgins, S., Grann, M., Långström, N., & Kullgren, G. (in press). Schizophrenia and criminal offending: The role of psychopathy and substance misuse. *Criminal Justice and Behaviour*.

Teplin, L. (1984). Criminalizing mental disorder: The comparative arrest rate of the mentally ill. *American Psychologist*, *39*, 794–803.

Teplin, L., & Swartz, M. (1989). Screening for severe mental disorder in jails: The development of the referral decision scale. *Law and Human Behavior*, *13*, 1–18.

Tohen, M., Waternaux, C. M., & Tsuang, M. T. (1990). Outcome in mania: A 4-year prospective follow-up of 75 patients utilizing survival analysis. *Archives General of Psychiatry*, *47*, 1106–1111.

Walsh, J., & Bricourt, J. (1996). Improving jail lindages of detainees with mental health agencies: The role of family contact. *Psychiatric Rehabilitation Journal*, *20*, 73–76.

Wiederanders, M. R. (1992). Recidivism of disordered offenders who were conditionally vs. unconditionally released. *Behavioral Sciences and the Law*, *10*, 141–148.

Wiederanders, M. R., Bromley, D. L., & Choate, P. A. (1997). Forensic conditional release programs and outcomes in three states. *International Journal of Law and Psychiatry*, *20*, 249–257.

Wiederanders, M. R., & Choate, P. A. (1994). Beyond recidivism: Measuring community adjustments of conditionally released insanity acquittees. *Psychological Assessment*, *6*, 61–66.

Wilson, D., Tien, G., & Eaves, D. (1995). Increasing the community tenure of mentally disordered offenders: An assertive case management program. *International Journal of Law and Psychiatry*, *18*, 61–69.

Wolff, N., Helminiak, T. W., Morse, G. A., Calsyn, R. J., Klinkenberg, W. D., & Trusty, M. L. (1997). Cost-effectiveness evaluation of three approaches to case management for homeless mentally ill clients. *American Journal of Psychiatry*, *154*, 341–348.

Wormith, J. S., & McKeague, F. (1996). A mental health survey of community correctional clients in Canada. *Criminal Behaviour and Mental Health*, *6*, 49–72.

Chapter 15

Offenders with Personality Disorders

Mary McMurran
Cardiff University, Cardiff, UK

INTRODUCTION

The aim of this chapter is to examine psychiatric approaches to personality disorder. Psychiatric diagnoses have medico-legal significance in that they are the basis on which an offender may be diverted to health services. In England and Wales, for example, an offender may be legally classified as suffering from "psychopathic disorder" under the terms of the Mental Health Act (1983) if he or she is deemed by psychiatrists to meet the definition of suffering from a persistent disorder or disability of mind which results in abnormally aggressive or seriously irresponsible conduct. Offenders legally classified as suffering from "psychopathic disorder" will be referred to as legal psychopaths throughout this chapter. A "persistent disorder or disability of mind" in this context may be taken to mean a personality disorder. As we shall see, there is no personality disorder called psychopathy in the major diagnostic systems, although the issue of psychopathy is clinically important and will be addressed. Provided the personality disorder is deemed treatable, and depending upon the perceived level of risk of harm to self or others, the person legally classified as suffering from "psychopathic disorder" may be detained involuntarily in hospital for treatment or treated in the community by virtue of a compulsory treatment order. Since psychiatric diagnoses of personality disorder can contribute to legal decisions that have significant implications for the disposal and treatment of an offender, the issue of personality disorder warrants examination.

The Essential Handbook of Offender Assessment and Treatment. Edited by C. R. Hollin.
© 2004 John Wiley & Sons Ltd.

PERSONALITY DISORDERS

Psychiatric diagnostic criteria for personality disorders are defined in the *Diagnostic and Statistical Manual of Mental Disorders—IV* (DSM-IV; American Psychiatric Association, 1994) and the *International Classification of Diseases—10* (ICD-10; World Health Organization, 1992). The personality disorders are listed in Table 15.1, along with a brief description of each identifying the most salient features of that disorder. Stone (1993) observes that the personality disorders defined in DSM and ICD are a narrow group compared with the maladaptive

Table 15.1   DSM-IV and ICD-10 personality disorders (adapted from Tyrer, 1992)

DSM-IV	ICD-10
Cluster A	
Paranoid	Paranoid
Distrust and suspiciousness	Sensitivity and suspiciousness
Schizoid	Schizoid
Socially and emotionally detached	Emotionally cold and detached
Schizotypal	No equivalent
Social and interpersonal deficits; cognitive or perceptual distortions	
Cluster B	
Antisocial	Dyssocial
Violation of the rights of others	Callous disregard of others, irresponsibility, and irritability
Borderline	Emotionally unstable
Instability of relationships, self-image and mood	(a) Borderline
	Unclear self-image, and intense, unstable relationships
	(b) Impulsive
	Inability to control anger, quarrelsome, and unpredictable
Histrionic	Histrionic
Excessive emotionality and attention-seeking	Dramatic, egocentric, and manipulative
Narcissistic	No equivalent
Grandiose, lack of empathy, need for admiration	
Cluster C	
Avoidant	Anxious
Socially inhibited, feelings of inadequacy, hypersensitivity	Tense, self-conscious, and hypersensitive
Dependent	Dependent
Clinging and submissive	Subordinates personal needs, and needs constant reassurance
Obsessive–compulsive	Anankastic
Perfectionist and inflexible	Indecisive, pedantic, and rigid

personalities generally recognizable in people at large, and describe conditions that are of interest to clinicians; they do not purport to describe personality in general. Psychological approaches to the study of normal personality traits and maladaptive extremes of these may do better justice to the diversity of human personality and dimensional approaches might be the key to the future (e.g. Costa and Widiger, 1994). At present, however, categorical approaches have more practical relevance and so are the focus of this chapter.

Personality disorder classifications suffer problems with both validity and reliability. Descriptions of personality disorders consist of a mixture of both psychological traits (e.g. impulsivity, anxiety, sensitivity) and behaviour (e.g. self-mutilation, miserliness, law-breaking), leading to doubt as to whether these diagnoses identify "true" personality disorders (i.e. traits) or social deviance (i.e. behaviour). In general, the reliability of clinical diagnosis of personality disorders is only poor to fair, except for those disorders that are primarily described in terms of overt behaviours, antisocial personality disorder diagnosis being particularly reliable (Stone, 1993). Reliance on observable behaviour as a means of identifying a personality disorder may improve the reliability of diagnosis, but introducing operational criteria before the disorder is thoroughly understood may diminish validity.

There are also problems with co-morbidity in that multiple personality disorders are frequently observed in the same person, and personality disorders frequently co-exist with Axis 1 disorders (e.g. psychosis, mood disorders, and substance use disorders). It is quite possible that a person may suffer two conditions at the same time, and co-morbidity may be taken as a measure of the severity of disorder (Tyrer & Johnson, 1996). Co-morbidity of personality disorders may indicate that the descriptive features of several personality disorders overlap and so diagnosticians cannot easily distinguish one from the other. Widiger and Trull (1994), for example, point out that violent behaviour is a defining feature of two of DSM-IV personality disorders (borderline and antisocial), which may explain the high degree of co-morbidity of these two disorders. Co-morbidity of particular groupings of personality disorders is evident, and in DSM-IV they are presented as three clusters—Cluster A: odd or eccentric (paranoid, schizoid, and schizotypal); Cluster B: dramatic or flamboyant (comprising antisocial, borderline, histrionic, and narcissistic); and Cluster C: anxious or fearful (avoidant, dependent, and obsessive–compulsive).

PERSONALITY DISORDERED OFFENDERS

Legal psychopaths are of particular interest to clinicians in that they, in comparison with mentally ill offenders, are more likely to reoffend after discharge from hospital (Bailey & MacCulloch, 1992; Steels et al., 1998). The range of personality disorders that may feature in a group of legal psychopaths is illustrated in a study by Reiss, Grubin, and Meux (1996), where 30 patients in a maximum security psychiatric hospital (a "special" hospital) included those diagnosed as borderline, antisocial, schizoid, narcissistic, schizotypal, and paranoid, many with multiple diagnoses. Similarly, Coid (1992) in a study of male and female patients, all legal psychopaths in special hospitals, and male prisoners held in special units for dangerous or disruptive prisoners found a wide range of DSM-III (American Psychiatric Association, 1980) personality disorders in these groups, with significantly more female patients receiving a diagnosis of borderline personality disorder, and significantly more male prisoners receiving diagnoses of antisocial, narcissistic, paranoid, passive-aggressive, and histrionic disorders (see Table 15.2). A study of female prisoners referred to prison psychiatrists similarly reveal high levels and a broad range of DSM-III-R (American Psychiatric Association, 1987) disorders (Dolan & Mitchell, 1994; see Table 15.2).

Personality disordered offenders may be defined according to the medico-legal definition and disposal but, as the studies by Coid (1992) and Dolan and Mitchell (1994) show, many personality disordered offenders are located within prisons. These personality disordered prisoners may not be involved in treatment by health service personnel because they are deemed untreatable, do not wish to receive treatment, or simply have never been referred to a psychiatrist.

The relationship between personality disorder and offending is complex. Care must be taken to avoid using diagnoses tautologically. For example, persistent aggressive behaviour may lead the clinician to diagnose antisocial personality disorder, and then the diagnosed disorder is simply used to explain aggression, which it plainly does not—the diagnosis merely describes the behaviour. Theoretically driven aetiological studies are important in understanding how a disorder develops, progresses, and remits, and, in the case of offenders, how the disorder relates to particular types of offending (violence, sexual offending, firesetting, and so on).

Table 15.2 Percentage of male and female special hospital patients and male prisoners receiving DSM-III/DSM-III-R personality disorder diagnoses (adapted from Coid, 1992, and Dolan & Mitchell, 1994)

Diagnosis	Female special hospital patients ($n = 93$)	Male special hospital patients ($n = 86$)	Male prisoners ($n = 64$)	Female prisoners ($n = 50$)
Borderline	91	56	55	60
Antisocial	44	38	86	44
Narcissistic	37	45	61	34
Paranoid	46	28	67	52
Passive-aggressive	28	16	50	26
Schizotypal	25	19	30	38
Histrionic	19	13	42	40
Avoidant	36	8	19	32
Dependent	25	20	14	34
Schizoid	11	13	11	28
Compulsive	11	14	5	20
Masochistic	9	4	6	—

Information from such studies is important in determining relevant treatment goals. Some critics would say that a personality disorder diagnosis is of very limited value in identifying treatment goals and that an analysis of the individual's behaviour in historical and current contexts, including cognitive, behavioural, and psychosocial elements, is more productive (Rice & Harris, 1997). This may be true, but research into the aetiology of personality disorders provides information that helps direct the clinician's assessment, as well as revealing implications for prevention and treatment. Biopsychosocial approaches, which look at biologically-based personal characteristics as they interact with the social environment, may hold most promise. Research into antisocial personality disorder, for example, identifies an early history of hyperactivity, impulsivity, and attention problems (Maughan, 1993; Widiger & Trull, 1994). There is evidence that these characteristics may have a biological basis, for example neurochemical or brain dysfunction (Carey & Goldman, 1997; Raine, 1997), but that the resultant antisocial behaviour can best be explained by looking at how biological predispositions interact with the social environment over time.

In summary, the information presented above suggests that all personality types figure in criminal populations, both patients and prisoners, and if professionals intend to offer treatment for personality disordered offenders, then attention should be paid to all diagnoses. An individual approach to problem analysis is the best way to identify treatment needs for any one person, but biopsychosocial research into the aetiology of personality disorders can inform clinical assessment and treatment, as well as provide directions for prevention.

DIAGNOSIS

Psychiatrists may diagnose by clinical interview with reference to the relevant criteria, but there are a number of semi-structured interview schedules to guide the clinician (Van Elzen & Emmelkamp, 1996). These interview schedules present questions matching the diagnostic criteria contained in DSM or ICD and provide scoring systems that identify a diagnosis or otherwise. These schedules are the Structured Clinical Interview for DSM-IV Axis II Personality Disorders (First, Gibbon, Spitzer, Williams, & Benjamin, 1997); the Personality Disorder Examination (Loranger, Susman, Oldham, & Russakoff, 1987); the International Personality Disorder Examination (Loranger et al., 1994); and the Structured Interview for DSM Personality Disorders (Stangl Pfohl, Zimmerman, Bowers, & Corenthal, 1985; Pfohl, Blum, & Zimmerman, 1995). Interview schedules show improved test–retest reliability and inter-rater reliability over clinical diagnosis, yet this is still only moderately good (Zimmerman, 1994). Whilst there is good agreement between interview schedules on continuous scores, diagnostic concordance is moderate, and the match with clinical diagnosis is only fairly good, and so none should be taken as superior (Pilkonis et al., 1995; Van Elzen & Emmelkamp, 1996).

PSYCHOPATHY

Cleckley (1941) defined psychopathy as cluster of personality traits, including lack of guilt, lack of anxiety, inability to learn from punishment, impoverished emotions, inability to form lasting emotional ties, egocentricity, and superficial charm. He argued that these characteristics may be associated with antisocial behaviour, but that this is not necessarily the case. These personality characteristics are captured in the ICD-10 definition of dyssocial personality disorder. Critics of the personality-based approach to diagnosis have argued that it is based too much upon inference and value judgement, and that psychopathy should be operationalized in terms of readily agreed antisocial behaviours (Lilienfeld, 1994). DSM-IV's criteria for antisocial personality disorder are largely behavioural, based upon law-breaking, recklessness, and irresponsibility. Because of the emphasis on antisocial behaviour, a large proportion of criminals meet the criteria for antisocial personality disorder, although they would not meet the criteria for psychopathy as a personality-based disorder.

Hare has incorporated both personality and behaviour in the Psychopathy Checklist—Revised (PCL–R; Hare, 1991). The PCL–R consists of 20 items which are scored from interview, official records, and corroborative checks with significant others. Each item may score absent (0), somewhat applicable (1), or definitely applicable (2), with the resultant range of scores being 0–40. The higher the score, the more psychopathic the individual. Hare recommends a cut-off point of 30 for determining psychopathy, although researchers may use continuous scores or different cut-off points (e.g. Cooke, 1995). The PCL–R is a reliable measure, and two factors may be defined—Factor 1, which measures interpersonal and affective characteristics such as selfishness and callousness, and Factor 2, which measures an antisocial, unstable, and deviant lifestyle (Hare et al., 1990).

A meta-analysis of studies using the PCL–R showed that psychopaths were three times more likely than non-psychopaths to commit further offences and about four times more likely to commit further violent offences (Hemphill, Hare, & Wong, 1998). Correlations between Factor 2 and general recidivism were stronger than for Factor 1, and both factors correlated equally with violent recidivism. Personality disorder diagnoses were not as accurate as PCL–R scores at predicting recidivism. A meta-analysis of treatment outcome indicates that high PCL–R scorers benefit least from psychological therapies (Garrido, Esteban, & Molero, 1996).

TREATMENT OF PERSONALITY DISORDERED OFFENDERS

Offenders with a personality disorder can be legally compelled to participate in treatment only if they are deemed treatable. Decisions about treatability are based upon a number of factors, including the availability of an effective treatment for the identified disorder, the resources currently available to provide an offender with the effective treatment, perceptions of the offender's motivation to change based upon previous engagement in and response to therapy, and the offender's current willingness to engage in the treatment on offer. The first of these issues is the one of primary interest here. Are there effective treatments for personality disorders, and if so what are they?

Where treatment of personality disorder is concerned, there is a fundamental issue of what is to be treated. Should practitioners address the socially deviant behaviour *per se* or the underlying maladaptive personality traits or a combination of the two? Regarding personality disordered offenders in health services, Blackburn (1993) suggests the following position:

> Since it is mental disorder rather than offending which justifies the diversion of mentally disordered offenders to the mental health system, alleviation of the disorder is a necessary outcome criterion, but reduced recidivism will be one indication of successful outcome in the case of personality disorder. Reduced recidivism is therefore a necessary but not sufficient outcome criterion. The primary need is to identify and target the *mediators* of antisocial behaviour, and to establish which treatments influence those mediators (p. 184).

With respect to personality disordered offenders located in the criminal justice system (i.e. prisons or on probation), one may paraphrase Blackburn's statement and argue that since it is crime rather than personality disorder that is the reason that offenders are in the criminal justice system, reduced recidivism will be the indicator of successful outcome, but that this is likely to be achieved by identifying and targeting the mediators of antisocial behaviour. If one accepts both of the above premises (and they are not mutually exclusive), the likely net result would be that treatment programmes for personality disordered offenders in the health services and in the criminal justice system would be indistinguishable, although the ultimate service evaluation criterion might differ between the two settings.

Harris and Rice (1997) suggest that appropriate target outcomes might be a reduction of recidivism, decreases in symptom severity and health service usage, and improvements in community adjustment, quality of life, and general happiness. Direct offence-focused work and the treatment of disorders strongly related to offending (e.g. alcohol and drug use) are clearly relevant but, since other chapters in this book address these specific treatments, they will not be addressed here.

The role of pharmacological treatments for personality disorders is arguably more limited than that of psychosocial interventions, but is nonetheless important to consider. Pharmacological treatments should target specific personality disorder symptoms which are believed to be mediated by neurotransmitter pathologies. Reviews of pharmacological treatments permit the conclusion that symptoms of anger and impulsivity, leading to aggression and violence, can be successfully treated in a number of ways: antidepressants for those who are depressed and irritable, agitated, and impulsive; lithium or anticonvulsants for those with mood lability and impulsivity; low dose antipsychotics for anger and impulsivity related to cognitive–perceptual symptoms; and selective serotonin reuptake inhibitors for the highly anxious and impulsive (Karper & Krystal, 1997; Soloff, 1998). Pharmacological treatments show modest clinical effects, should be used for limited periods, and should not be seen as a cure for personality disorder. They can, however, optimize functioning and minimize disability (Soloff, 1998), and may enhance a person's ability to benefit from psychosocial interventions.

Meta-analyses of what works with offenders in general have revealed that structured, cognitive–behavioural approaches that address criminogenic needs hold most promise in reducing recidivism (Andrews et al., 1990; Lipsey, 1992). Harris and Rice (1997) point out that the same risk factors predict recidivism in mentally disordered and non-mentally disordered offenders alike, therefore the same treatments may be used to address offending behaviour. Most psychosocial treatment approaches for personality disorders are broad-based, addressing interpersonal styles, cognitions, attitudes, beliefs, and emotion control.

Therapeutic communities (TCs) aim to address maladaptive interpersonal styles in a democracy where residents confront each other with the impact of their behaviours. In a study of personality disordered patients referred to a hospital, Copas, O'Brien, Roberts, and Whiteley (1984) found that, at three- and five-year follow-ups, fewer TC participants had further convictions or hospitalizations compared with those assessed but not admitted, and those who stayed in the TC for nine months or longer fared best. In a study of TC participants at the same hospital, Dolan (1997) measured change in symptomatology using the Symptom Checklist 90—Revised (Derogatis, 1975), showing a highly significant reduction in psychological distress. McMurran, Egan, and Ahmadi (1998) examined the criminal recidivism of predominantly personality disordered offenders who had either participated in a hospital-based TC for an average of 17 months or had been rejected after an assessment period averaging two months. At a mean follow-up time of almost five years, there was a significant reduction in crime for the whole sample when comparing pre-admission and post-discharge offences, but there were no significant differences between the two groups in terms of reconvictions, suggesting that the TC intervention had no effect on offending and that personality disordered offenders improved regardless. If an intervention has no effect, then it may be seen at best as a waste of resources and at worst as unethical practice when other more effective interventions could have been used. There is evidence, however, that TCs have done more harm than good with some mentally disordered offenders. Rice, Harris, and Cormier (1992) carried out a retrospective evaluation of a TC in a maximum security institution for mentally disordered offenders, matching the TC participants with comparable assessment-only group. Follow-up at a mean of 10.5 years after discharge showed a modest overall degree of success for the TC (success being no reconviction, revocation of parole, or reincarceration), but those TC participants scoring 25 or more on the PCL–R showed higher rates of recidivism, particularly violent recidivism, than a comparable non-treated group. That is, treatment in a TC made "psychopaths" worse than if they had had no treatment at all. TCs probably have some value in treating personality disordered offenders, but careful attention needs to be paid to who is selected, what is addressed, and how the TC operates (McMurran et al., 1998).

Hughes, Hogue, Hollin, and Champion (1997) describe a structured cognitive–behaviour therapy (CBT) programme for male legal psychopaths who were detained in a maximum security hospital. The programme included a range of groups targeting cognitive, emotional and skills functioning, for example assertiveness, self-esteem, cognitive skills, problem-solving, and emotional awareness, in which patients participated as necessary. Preliminary results on nine patients who have completed the programme show a net overall global positive change on a range of measures relevant to the problems addressed. In this sample there was a significant negative correlation between PCL–R scores and clinical improvement, this relationship being with PCL–R Factor 1 and not Factor 2. These results provide tentative support for CBT with personality disordered offenders who have lower PCL–R Factor 1 scores, in that they lead to clinical improvement, although the effect this has on recidivism remains to be seen.

A unit at Broadmoor Hospital for young male patients, most of whom were legal psychopaths, was based upon a combination of CBT and psychodynamic psychotherapy, run both individually and in groups (Grounds et al., 1987; Reiss et al., 1996). A comparison was made between patients who had undertaken this treatment programme and a matched group from other wards in the hospital. Amongst those discharged into the community, similar numbers in each group committed a further serious offence, but a higher proportion of those treated in the unit showed a good social outcome, and this was predictive of not reoffending.

Dialectical behaviour therapy (DBT) is a broad-based, cognitive–behavioural programme developed specifically to teach those with borderline personality disorders how to regulate their emotions (Linehan, 1993a, 1993b). This treatment is based on the premise that borderline personality disorder is typified by a failure to regulate emotions, which has developed as a result of a biologically-based emotional vulnerability in combination with an invalidating environment, that is where the child's private experiences are denied, contradicted, or punished by significant others (Linehan, 1993a, 1993b). A group skills training programme addressing problem-solving, interpersonal skills, and maladaptive cognitions is conducted in conjunction with individual therapy. Outcome studies with non-offender populations show reduced parasuicidal behaviour, inpatient psychiatric treatment, and anger, and improved social adjustment (Linehan, 1993a). Preliminary results of DBT with female mentally disordered offenders in a secure psychiatric hospital show reduced self-harm, suicidal ideation, depression, and dissociative experiences, along with improved survival and coping beliefs (Low, 1998).

Beck and Freeman (1990) base their cognitive therapy on the notion that cognitive schemas, or controlling beliefs, are the filter through which all incoming information is processed and thus determine affect and behaviour. They see these schemas as the fundamental units of personality. The purpose of therapy is to effect change in these schemas and so influence emotions and behaviour. Evidence for the effectiveness of this approach is limited, but single case studies of patients with borderline ($n = 7$) or antisocial ($n = 5$) personality disorders revealed improvements on targets relevant to each individual, for example anger, irritability, and self-control (Davidson & Tyrer, 1996). Walters (1995a, 1995b, 1996) has identified criminal thinking styles which may be useful to address in cognitive therapy.

CONCLUSION

The treatment of personality disordered offenders, particularly within health services, is a contentious matter. There are ethical objections to "treating" people for violation of social norms (Blackburn, 1992), yet it is clear that this group of offenders, and particularly those with high psychopathy scores, may be responsible for greater amounts of crime, especially violent crime, than mentally ill offenders or non-personality disordered offenders. Ethical admission of personality disordered offenders into health services for treatment requires that mental health professionals can identify the person's disorder, what the goals of treatment are, what treatments are effective, what type of person might benefit from the treatments on offer, and how long the treatment might take. Only when these issues are clarified is it possible for all involved to decide what is the fairest course of action. The vexed question of whether psychopaths, as defined by high PCL–R scores, should be admitted for treatment at all arises from the evidence of poor outcomes in this particular sub-group. Without clear information about what treatments are offered, their goals, and likely effectiveness, the patient is merely detained for the equivalent of respite care and, whilst this may be defensible, the situation should at least be plain to all those involved. Researchers and clinicians working in the field of personality disordered offenders, as in many other clinical areas, are searching for answers to the fundamental question, "What works best with whom under which conditions?" There will never be a simple, one-line answer to this important and socially relevant question.

ACKNOWLEDGMENT

I wish to thank Professor Conor Duggan and Dr Vincent Egan for their help and advice.

REFERENCES

American Psychiatric Association (1980). *Diagnostic and statistical manual of mental disorders* (3rd ed.). Washington, DC: Author.

American Psychiatric Association (1987). *Diagnostic and statistical manual of mental disorders* (3rd ed., Rev.). Washington, DC: Author.

American Psychiatric Association (1994). *Diagnostic and statistical manual of mental disorders* (4th ed.). Washington, DC: Author.

Andrews, D. A., Zinger, I., Hoge, R. D., Bonta, J., Gendreau, P., & Cullen, F. T. (1990). Does correctional treatment work? A clinically relevant and psychologically informed meta-analysis. *Criminology, 28,* 369–404.

Bailey, J., & MacCulloch, M. (1992). Characteristics of 112 cases discharged directly to the community from a new special hospital and some comparisons of performance. *Journal of Forensic Psychiatry, 3,* 91–112.

Beck, A. T., & Freeman, A. (1990). *Cognitive therapy of personality disorders.* New York: Guilford.

Blackburn, R. (1992). Criminal behaviour, personality disorder, and mental illness: The origins of confusion. *Criminal Behaviour and Mental Health, 2,* 66–77.

Blackburn, R. (1993). Clinical programmes with psychopaths. In K. Howells & C. R. Hollin (Eds.), *Clinical approaches to the mentally disordered offender.* Chichester, UK: Wiley.

Carey, G., & Goldman, D. (1997). The genetics of antisocial behavior. In D. M. Stoff, J. Brieling, & J. D. Maser (Eds.), *Handbook of antisocial behavior.* New York: Wiley.

Cleckley, H. (1941). *The mask of sanity.* St Louis, MO: Mosby.

Coid, J. (1992). DSM-III diagnosis in criminal psychopaths: A way forward. *Criminal Behaviour and Mental Health, 2,* 78–79.

Cooke, D. J. (1995). Psychopathic disturbance in the Scottish prison population: The cross-cultural generalisability of the Hare Psychopathy Checklist. *Psychology, Crime, and Law, 2,* 101–108.

Copas, J., O'Brien, M., Roberts, J., & Whiteley, S. (1984). Treatment outcome in personality disorder. *Personality and Individual Differences, 5,* 565–573.

Costa, P. T., & Widiger, T. A. (Eds.) (1994). *Personality disorders and the five factor model of personality.* Washington, DC: American Psychological Association.

Davidson, K. M., & Tyrer, P. (1996). Cognitive therapy for antisocial and borderline personality disorders: Single case study series. *British Journal of Clinical Psychology, 35,* 413–429.

Derogatis, L. R. (1975). *Symptom Checklist 90—Revised.* Minneapolis, MN: National Computer Systems.

Dolan, B. (1997). A community based TC: The Henderson Hospital. In E. Cullen, L. Jones, & R. Woodward (Eds.), *Therapeutic communities for offenders.* Chichester, UK: Wiley.

Dolan, B., & Mitchell, E. (1994). Personality disorder and psychological disturbance of female prisoners: A comparison with women referred for NHS treatment of personality disorder. *Criminal Behaviour and Mental Health, 4,* 130–143.

First, M. B., Gibbon, M., Spitzer, R. L., Williams, J. B. W., & Benjamin, L. S. (1997). *Structured clinical interview for DSM-IV Axis II personality disorders.* Washington, DC.: American Psychiatric Press.

Garrido, V., Esteban, C., & Molero, C. (1996). The effectiveness in the treatment of psychopathy: A meta-analysis. In D. J. Cooke, A. E. Forth, J. Newman, & R. D. Hare (Eds.), *International perspectives on psychopathy. Issues in criminological psychology, No. 24.* Leicester, UK: The British Psychological Society.

Grounds, A. T., Quayle, M. T., France, J., Brett, T., Cox, M., & Hamilton, J. R. (1987). A unit for "psychopathic disorder" patients in Broadmoor Hospital. *Medicine, Science and Law, 27,* 21–31.

Hare, R. D. (1991). *The Hare Psychopathy Checklist—Revised.* Toronto, Canada: Multi-Health Systems.

Hare, R. D., Harpur, T. J., Hakstian, A. R., Forth A. E., Hart, S. D., & Newman, J. P. (1990). The Revised Psychopathy Checklist: Reliability and factor structure. *Psychological Assessment, 2,* 338–341.

Harris, G. T., & Rice, M. E. (1997). Mentally disordered offenders: What research says about effective service. In C. D. Webster & M. A. Jackson (Eds.), *Impulsivity: Theory, assessment and treatment*. New York: Guilford.

Hemphill, J. F., Hare, R. D., & Wong, S. (1998). Psychopathy and recidivism: A review. *Legal and Criminological Psychology, 3*, 139–170.

Hughes, G., Hogue, T., Hollin, C., & Champion, H. (1997). First-stage evaluation of a treatment programme for personality disordered offenders. *Journal of Forensic Psychiatry, 8*, 515–527.

Karper, L. P., & Krystal, J. H. (1997). Pharmacotherapy of violent behaviour. In D. M. Stoff, J. Brieling, & J. D. Maser (Eds.), *Handbook of antisocial behavior*. New York: Wiley.

Lilienfeld, S. O. (1994). Conceptual problems in the assessment of psychopathy. *Clinical Psychology Review, 14*, 17–38.

Linehan, M. M. (1993a). *Cognitive–behavioral treatment of borderline personality disorder*. New York: Guilford.

Linehan, M. M. (1993b). *Skills training manual for treating borderline personality disorder*. New York: Guilford.

Lipsey, M. W. (1992). Juvenile delinquency treatment: A meta-analytic enquiry into the variability of effects. In R. S. Cook, H. Cooper, D. S. Cordray, H. Hartmann, L. V. Hedges, R. J. Light, T. A. Louis, & F. Mosteller (Eds.). *Meta-analysis for explanation* (pp. 83–125). New York: Springer-Verlag.

Loranger, A. W., Sartorius, N., Andreoli, A., Berger, P., Buchheim, P., Channabasavanna, S. M., Coid, B., Dahl, A., Diekstra, R. F. W., Ferguson, B., Jacobsberg, L. B., Mombour, W., Pull, C., Ono, Y., & Regier, D. A. (1994). The international personality disorder examination. *Archives of General Psychiatry, 51*, 215–224.

Loranger, A. W., Susman, V. L., Oldham, J. M., & Russakoff, M. (1987). The personality disorder examination: A preliminary report. *Journal of Personality Disorders*, 11–13.

Low, G. (1998). Treatment of mentally disordered women who self-harm. Paper presented at the III European Congress on Personality Disorders, University of Sheffield, Sheffield, UK.

Maughan, B. (1993). Childhood precursors of aggressive offending in personality disordered adults. In S. Hodgin (Ed.), *Mental disorder and crime*. Newbury Park, CA: Sage.

McMurran, M., Egan, V., & Ahmadi, S. (1998). A retrospective evaluation of a therapeutic community for mentally disordered offenders. *Journal of Forensic Psychiatry, 9*, 103–113.

Pfohl, B., Blum, N., & Zimmerman, M. (1995). *Structured interview for DSM-IV personality disorders (SIDP-IV)*. University of Iowa, Department of Psychiatry.

Pilkonis, P. A., Heape, C. L., Proietti, J. M., Clark, S. W., McDavid, J. D., & Pitts, T. E. (1995). The reliability and validity of two structured diagnostic interviews for personality disorders. *Archives of General Psychiatry, 52*, 1025–1033.

Raine, A. (1997). Antisocial behavior and psychophysiology: A biosocial perspective and a prefrontal dysfunction hypothesis. In D. M. Stoff, J. Brieling, & J. D. Maser (Eds.), *Handbook of antisocial behavior*. New York: Wiley.

Reiss, D., Grubin, D., & Meux, C. (1996). Young "psychopaths" in special hospital: Treatment and outcome. *British Journal of Psychiatry, 168*, 99–104.

Rice, M. E., & Harris, G. T. (1997). The treatment of mentally disordered offenders. *Psychology, Public Policy, and Law, 3*, 126–183.

Rice, M. E., Harris, G. T., & Cormier, C. A. (1992). An evaluation of a maximum security therapeutic community for psychopaths and other mentally disordered offenders. *Law and Human Behavior, 16*, 399–412.

Soloff, P. H. (1998). Symptom-oriented psychopharmacology for personality disorders. *Journal of Practical Psychiatry and Behavioral Health, 4*, 3–11.

Stangl, D., Pfohl, B., Zimmerman, M., Bowers, W., & Corenthal, C. (1985). A structured interview for the DSM-III personality disorders. *Archives of General Psychiatry, 42*, 591–596.

Steels, M., Roney, G., Larkin, E., Jones, P., Croudace, T., & Duggan, C. (1998). Discharged from special hospital under restrictions: A comparison of the fates of psychopaths and the mentally ill. *Criminal Behaviour and Mental Health, 8*, 39–55.

Stone, M. H. (1993). *Abnormal personalities: Within and beyond the realm of treatment.* New York: W.W. Norton.

Tyrer, P. (1992). Flamboyant, erratic, dramatic, borderline, antisocial, sadistic, narcissistic, histrionic and impulsive personality disorders: Who cares which? *Criminal Behaviour and Mental Health, 2*, 95–104.

Tyrer, P., & Johnson, T. (1996). Establishing the severity of personality disorder. *American Journal of Psychiatry, 153*, 1593–1597.

Van Elzen, C. J. M., & Emmelkamp, P. M. G. (1996). The assessment of personality disorders: Implications for cognitive and behavior therapy. *Behavior Research and Therapy, 34*, 655–668.

Walters, G. D. (1995a). The psychological inventory of criminal thinking styles, Part I: Reliability and validity. *Criminal Justice and Behavior, 22*, 307–325.

Walters, G. D. (1995b). The psychological inventory of criminal thinking styles, Part II: Identifying simulated response sets. *Criminal Justice and Behavior, 22*, 437–445.

Walters, G. D. (1996). The psychological inventory of criminal thinking styles, Part III: Predictive validity. *International Journal of Offender Therapy and Comparative Criminology, 40*, 105–112.

Widiger, T. A., & Trull, T. J. (1994). Personality disorders and violence. In J. Monahan & H. J. Steadman (Eds.), *Violence and mental disorder: Developments in risk assessment.* Chicago, IL: University of Chicago Press.

World Health Organisation (1992). *10th revision of the international classification of diseases (ICD-10).* Geneva: WHO.

Zimmerman, M. (1994). Diagnosing personality disorders: A review of issues and research methods. *Archives of General Psychiatry, 51*, 225–245.

Chapter 16

Property Offences

James McGuire
University of Liverpool, Liverpool, UK

INTRODUCTION

Property offences constitute the majority of known illegal acts. In England and Wales, for example, in the year 2000, of the 100 or so categories of notifiable offences, thefts and burglary accounted for well over half of recorded crimes (58%). With fraud and criminal damage added the proportion rose to 83% (Maguire, 2002). This pattern is typical of most countries in which criminal statistics are published. Broadly speaking, the pattern for recorded crime is also reflected in that for total crime as estimated from victim surveys (Kershaw, Chivite-Matthews, Thomas, & Aust, 2001).

What do we understand by "property crime"? This is a collective and somewhat loosely defined category. It is generally distinguished from offences *against the person* and presumed to contain acquisitive crimes such as theft, burglary, fraud, and other acts in which the objective of the perpetrator is to secure by unlawful means goods or money which are another person's property. It is also frequently taken to encompass vandalism in which the aim is to cause damage to property. Yet there remain untidy overlaps with other types of offences. For example, arson is very destructive of property but is understandably regarded as a manifestation of considerable aggression. Robbery, though acquisitive, is a combination of theft and instrumental aggression. Drug trafficking, while primarily an economically-motivated crime, has been studied mainly as an adjunct to investigation of drug abuse itself. For the purpose of the present chapter, attention will be restricted to those criminal offences which involve action by one person to appropriate another individual's possessions by illegal means. Excluded from the chapter will be any discussion of criminal damage (for an excellent overview, see Goldstein, 1996); offences of deception; and embezzlement or other "white-collar" monetary crimes.

The Essential *Handbook of Offender Assessment and Treatment.* Edited by C. R. Hollin.
© 2004 John Wiley & Sons Ltd.

MODELS AND MOTIVATIONS

Most theorizing and planned intervention in relation to property crime has been founded predominantly on sociological, rather than psychologically-based, models of criminal action. To date, however, no clear answers can be given to the question of whether there are any factors which specifically contribute to property as opposed to other types of offences. In traditional criminological research in which patterns of illegal activity were studied in larger social groupings, it was initially hypothesized that property crime emerged in identifiable social-developmental pathways. Thus in Merton's Strain Theory, for example, acquisitive crimes are classed as a form of *innovation* in attempting to resolve the conflict between cultural aims of material success set against restricted opportunities to achieve this through legitimate means. In Cloward and Ohlin's study of subcultural delinquency, a relationship was hypothesized between the existence of patterns of property crime in the surrounding adult environment and the absorption of aspiring delinquents into that culture. Where opportunities for lucrative property crime were available, such activity would flourish. Where this was not the case, alternative patterns of *aggressive* (gang-fighting) or *retreatist* (drug-taking) delinquency would appear instead (Maguire, 1994).

Property crimes by their essence are assumed to be economically motivated. Evidence in support of this proposition comes from several directions. First, Field (1990) analysed trends in crime in England and Wales since 1900 and their relationship to economic indicators. A similar pattern of inter-relationships was found in France, the United States, and Japan. While all forms of crime increased in the long term, the rate of change for property crime was inversely correlated with the overall prosperity of society. Thus during periods when personal consumption declined, the rate of property crime increased; whilst for personal crimes, the reverse was the case. In a revised and more elaborate version of this model, Field (1999) has included other variables, notably the availability of crime opportunities (the numbers of goods available to steal) in the economy, and the proportion of young males aged 15–20 in the population. Second, interviews with offenders have tended, by and large, to confirm the role of economic motives in property crimes. But rates of such crimes also vary in accordance with the numbers and movements of goods in society; and for goods to be stolen they must share certain features, including accessibility, transportability, and demand for them through re-sale outlets (Cohen & Felson, 1979; Felson, 1994). Thus, it has been suggested that the overall level of property crime in society fluctuates in as yet uncharted ways in response to the scale of the market for stolen goods (Sutton, 1993).

Nevertheless, sheer acquisitiveness is not the sole reason for the occurrence of property offences, and in any case that motive itself requires full understanding. The model embodied within economic theory takes material acquisitiveness as a self-evident "given" amongst human motives: there is no pressure to analyse it further. But for a proportion of property offenders, there are established links between law-breaking and substance abuse (Jarvis & Parker, 1989; Walters, 1998). The concept of carefully considered action is unlikely to be applicable here in its pure form. In this connection, other research has indicated that the capacities of those who persistently offend may, in relation to some elements of rational thought and action, be limited or deficient (Ross & Fabiano, 1985). Still other studies have confirmed the view that some offending, especially theft of motor vehicles, is motivated by a quest for excitement or status-seeking amongst peers (e.g. Light, Nee, & Ingham, 1993). Finally, for a small proportion of offenders, criminal acts may fulfil other personal or emotional needs. In relation to several types of crime, then, motives may be very complex; and the balance between them may vary for different age-groups, or even for the same individual at different times.

CRIME PREVENTION

The principal intervention utilized in tackling much property crime, and one that has received considerable official promotion and resourcing, is *crime prevention* (Gilling, 1997; Pease, 2002). This involves a wide range of initiatives; Pease (2002) lists a total of 16 different general techniques. They include situational or "target-hardening" methods (the use of steering column locks on cars; installation of burglar alarms and ensuring their visibility); property identification systems (product coding, serial numbers, licence plates); various forms of surveillance (CCTV; employment of store detectives; park wardens; door staff); "designing out crime" by maximizing inter-visibility of dwellings or improved lighting; and community crime prevention, for example through the introduction of neighbourhood watch schemes, or publicity campaigns ("together we'll crack it"). The cumulative aim of these activities is to reduce the frequency of criminal acts at the point of potential occurrence. Eck (2002) provides a recent, wide-ranging review of their relative effectiveness.

The systematic application of these measures in recent years has been under-pinned by the convergence of two theoretical frameworks. The first is *Routine Activity Theory*, within which the essential ingredients of a "predatory contact offence" (mainly property crimes) are the availability of a suitable target and the absence of capable guardians (Felson, 1994). The intersection of these is the principal focus of study. Discussion of psychological variables is explicitly avoided in order not to distract attention from analysis of the criminal act. The model thus takes for granted the presumption of a "likely offender" but leaves the nature of this unspecified. Cohen and Felson (1979) adduced a great deal of evidence concerning relationships, for example between increasing rates of house burglary and changes in the extent to which houses were left unoccupied by day, as a result of evolving patterns of work and leisure.

The second is the *Rational Choice* perspective. Here the offender is cast in the mould of the calculating and self-interested consumer or decision-maker envisioned within macro-economic theory (Clarke & Felson, 1993). A criminal act is a result of a careful weighing up of relative gains and potential risks. In relation to breaking-and-entering, evidence supporting the view that would-be burglars analyse these components was obtained from several studies. For example, Maguire (1982) showed that houses varied in their degree of victimization as a function of potential for burglary, influenced by aspects of their location (ease of access and escape, visibility from other dwellings, and so on). Interviews with burglars by Bennett and Wright (1984) and by Walsh (1986) furnished further support for this view. Other studies have embraced the concept of "bounded rationality" or reasoned action within a confined frame of reference (e.g. Carroll & Weaver, 1986).

The implementation of situational crime prevention involves an initial stage of *Crime Analysis* (Ekblom, 1988). This analysis is designed to establish features and patterns of crime affecting particular targets, following which a course of action is planned and implemented (Cooper, 1989). In the United Kingdom, the largest-scale departure in this respect has been the *Safer Cities Programme* (Ekblom, Law, & Sutton, 1996). Where crime prevention measures comprised "target-hardening" alone, their impact was fairly marginal; where they were more elaborate and combined with "community mobilization" the outcome was considerably better (Tilley & Webb, 1994). A particularly successful scheme within this field was the *Kirkholt Burglary Project* which combined "situational" and "community" crime prevention methods. Rates of domestic burglary in the targeted area fell by 75% over the duration of that project (Forrester, Frenz, O'Connell, & Pease, 1990). It has been argued that interventions of this kind run the risk of merely "displacing" crime from one area, or one type of offence, to another. Research has shown that the interactions of the types of crime prevention measure taken and a variety of outcome variables are considerably more complex (Tilley, 1995).

The models of crime on which situational prevention is based have made an indispensable contribution to our understanding of criminal events. They do not, however, explicate the nature of the numerous factors which might be at play in contributing to decisions to commit crimes in the first place (the "likely" or "motivated" offender). The question of the relationship between routine-activity, rational-choice, and "dispositional" perspectives on offending has not been resolved. Trasler (1993) has rightly drawn attention to the need for an integrative account within which these perspectives can be fruitfully combined. Probably the most concerted attempt towards integrative theorizing was undertaken by Cohen and Machalek (1988), who applied ideas from evolutionary theory and behavioural ecology to an understanding of 'expropriative' crime, simultaneously incorporating aspects of differential association, social learning, and control theory perspectives.

PSYCHOLOGICAL APPROACHES

Psychological research and theorizing in this field is currently cast in terms of a series of *risk–need* factors which have been empirically demonstrated to be associated with the emergence and potential persistence of patterns of criminality. Recent comprehensive reviews of this research, for example by Andrews and Bonta (1998), Blackburn (1993), or Farrington (2002), have resulted in general accounts which integrate individual and social variables. Their conclusions rest first on evidence which has been obtained with a high degree of consistency from a series of longitudinal studies conducted in many countries. Here, a very wide range of variables has been isolated as being linked with the appearance of juvenile offending and its persistence, where this occurs, into adulthood. Such "risk factors" operate cumulatively, such that the greater the number which are applicable in any given case, the greater the likelihood of offending. Second, meta-analytic reviews of cross-sectional studies examining relationships between individual variables and offence behaviour have identified a set of similar factors. These "criminogenic" factors include: anti-social or pro-criminal attitudes and values; pro-criminal associates; temperamental and personality factors such as impulsivity and egocentrism; limited social, self-control, and problem-solving skills; familial factors including poor parental supervision and discipline practices; and low levels of attainment in educational, vocational, and financial domains (Andrews, 1995).

Assessment

On this basis, it is important to conduct individualized assessment of offenders. This is much more likely to happen when the offence committed is one of a violent or sexual nature. Recent research on the outcomes of work with offenders has emphasized the need for proper assessment and allocation to appropriate services, whatever the type of offence. As a first stage in this, evidence from the meta-analytic reviews virtually dictates that use be made of a validated *risk–needs* assessment instrument. Regrettably, despite the obvious potential value of such measures, the choice remains limited and extensive validation research is required. Several approaches to risk–needs assessment have been reviewed by Bonta (1996). The available inventories generally take into account "static" demographic and historical variables such as an individual's past pattern of offending, together with "dynamic" factors including aspects of present circumstances, current perceived problems, attitudes, and skills.

In a second stage of assessment, selected measures can be introduced to evaluate the extent to which problems in the areas of social skill, self-control, anti-social attitudes, or problem-solving capacities such as alternative or means–end thinking may have influenced the individual's risk of re-offending. This inquiry might be widened to include aspects of an individual's life-style which may be conducive to or supportive of crime, and Walters (1998) has described a number of assessment methods which can be utilized in this area.

Thirdly, to supplement the use of population-based measures, an idiographic approach can be adopted, for example following some of the guidelines provided by McGuire and Priestley (1985). This level of assessment can be carried out within the context of a semi-structured interview and might entail a form of functional analysis with an individual, focused initially on a selected offence (probably the most recent). The circumstances and motivational state of the individual can be explored using, for example, a simple scheme such as the *5WH*; inviting the offender to describe when and where the offence occurred; who was involved and affected by it; what precisely happened; and why in his or her view the events took place. The same procedure is then applied to a series of the individual's offences, with any common patterns being noted: such as criminal associates, links to features of lifestyle, specific life events, or states of mind. Thus for one 15-year-old boy, who had committed a series of car thefts and been involved in a number of high-speed car chases, a relatively focused and concrete beginning (by analysing offence incidents) led to a clarification and understanding of the motives and triggers which maintained his risk of re-offending. Further exploration of attitudes and readiness to change can be undertaken using for example *force field analysis* (compiling parallel lists of reasons for offending versus "going straight"); an *A-B-C* diary of events surrounding the criminal act; and a dysfunctional thoughts record or "thinking report" of cognitions at key decision-points in the offence sequence.

Finally, for more in-depth forensic or psycho-legal assessment where required, an extensive range of standardized psychometric methods can be drawn upon, as outlined by Melton, Petrila, Poythress, and Slobogin (1997). The importance of dynamic variables in risk prediction is illustrated in a study by Zamble and Quinsey (1997) of a sample of 311 high-risk recidivists, approximately one-third of whom had committed a new offence of burglary or theft. The factors identified as preceding their re-offences included ongoing personal problems, dysphoric mood states, life crises, and low levels of coping and self-management skills.

Methods of Intervention

Research findings indicate that the majorities of both juvenile and adult offenders placed on intensive supervision programmes in the community have committed property offences (Bottoms, 1995; Mair, Lloyd, Nee, & Sibbitt, 1995). The differential impact of sentences on rates of recidivism for property crime as opposed to other types of offences is impossible to evaluate as the relevant evidence is simply not available. Evaluation of the outcomes of different sentences *per se* shows negligible differential impact of sentence type (Lloyd, Mair, & Hough, 1994). Probation Centre programmes produce effects which are enormously variable (Mair & Nee, 1992). The principal forms of sentencing "disposal" reserved for serious property offenders do not, in a nutshell, "work" in yielding any discernible effect in reduced recidivism.

Is there any evidence which might indicate the prospect of effective "tertiary prevention" with adjudicated property offenders? Research on criminal careers shows that most offenders are "versatile" or "generalists" who commit a variety of different types of offence (Farrington, 1996). Even in the case of those found guilty of assaults, the majority have only one conviction of this type, the remainder of their records consisting of various other offences (Levi & Maguire, 2002). There is now a large research literature on effective methods for treatment of offenders and reduction of recidivism (Harland, 1996; McGuire, 1995, 2002; Ross, Antonowicz, & Dhaliwal, 1995; Sherman et al., 1997; Sherman, Farrington, Welsh, & MacKenzie, 2002). In the vast majority of the studies subsumed within the published meta-analyses, those participating had committed a variety of offence types. Nevertheless, in two recent though overlapping meta-analytic reviews (Redondo, Sànchez-Meca, & Garrido, 1999, 2002) it was found that the outcome "effect size" for reductions in rates of property offences was lower than that for personal crimes. The number of studies reviewed was, however, relatively small. Overall, therefore, no firm conclusions regarding offence-specific treatments or outcomes are yet permissible. Until further studies appear which focus on offence type as a variable, it can be tentatively suggested that the conclusions drawn from the meta-analytic reviews, and which clarify the respective components of more and less successful interventions, are in principle applicable to property offenders. The best advice which might be given therefore for the design and delivery of systematic intervention with these groups, must be to follow the same guidelines as have been generally extracted from the "what works" treatment–outcome literature. Beyond this, several reports are available of interventions specifically addressed towards reduction of property offences. In the remainder of this chapter, this work will be briefly outlined.

Theft

Stealing can be a conduct problem amongst children prior to the onset of "official" delinquency, and several studies have addressed this issue. Reid and Patterson (1976) reported a series of seven cases of children with high rates of stealing and aggression. These problems were significantly reduced utilizing a parent-directed behaviour modification programme. Stumphauzer (1976) described elimination of stealing in a 12-year-old girl using a combination of self-reinforcement of alternative behaviour and a family-based contingency contract. Henderson (1981) outlined 10 cases of children treated with individually adapted combinations of self-control training, coupled with the involvement of a significant adult. A follow-up of between two and five years revealed that only two of the children had resumed stealing. Finally Hollin (1990) reported on the use of a behaviourally based approach with two brothers, aged 11 and 12, involved in stealing from shops. Assessment included a detailed analysis of the patterns of offending, and self-monitoring of behaviour by the boys. The intervention involved drawing up a set of rules jointly between the boys and their parents, and which were linked to a contingency contract. A one-year follow-up through the parents indicated that the boys' stealing had stopped, though this could not be corroborated from other sources.

However, most existing research on stealing is focused on shoplifting by adults.

Studies show that there are several distinct motives for engaging in shoplifting. They are preeminently economic; but may include an admixture of other factors such as excitement, peer influence, and emotional dysphoria, the balance of which is likely to change over the life span (McGuire, 1997). Here, too, some interventions have entailed the use of behaviourally-based methods. The procedures employed include systematic desensitization (Marzagao, 1972); contingency management (Guidry, 1975); covert sensitization (Gauthier & Pellegrin, 1982; Glover, 1985); self-management training (Aust, 1987); and activity scheduling for an individual with concomitant depressive symptoms (Gudjonsson, 1987). All of these studies entailed single-case designs, and in every instance successful outcomes were reported.

In a contrasting vein, other studies have been carried out using cognitive therapies and allied approaches, or semi-structured counselling. Kolman and Wasserman (1991) planned and delivered group counselling sessions aimed exclusively at women offenders. Solomon and Ray (1984) described a group therapy programme employing methods drawn from Rational Emotive Therapy. A more broadly-based, eclectic approach was adopted by Edwards and Roundtree (1982) integrating methods derived from reality therapy, transactional analysis, assertiveness training, and behaviour modification. MacDevitt and Kedzierzawski (1990) developed a six-session group programme of structured psycho-educational methods. Two studies have been undertaken of diversion programmes for first-offence shoplifters (Casey & Shulman, 1979; Royse & Buck, 1991). The second of these incorporated community service and a series of group sessions utilizing rational behaviour therapy. The outcomes of all of these studies are encouragingly positive, but few employed controlled designs.

Finally, however, Glasscock, Rapoff, and Christophersen (1988) carried out a comparative review of the treatment of convicted shoplifters, and preventive measures in retail outlets, and concluded that the latter would be likely to have a more substantial impact on rates of theft from shops.

Car Crime

The volume of research available on car crime is not large, and falls into two principal categories. The first consists of studies of young offenders involved in car crime, often with an explicit aim of collecting information which might assist crime prevention initiatives. Individuals have been interviewed and asked about their preferences for different models of cars, or which types of security measures are most likely to deter them, combining this interview material with police data on reported crimes (Gow & Peggrem, 1991; McGillivray, 1993; Webb & Laycock, 1992). Other research has emphasized the symbolic importance of cars as objects of general cultural significance (McCaghy, Giordano, & Henson, 1977).

Two studies have delineated the evolution of a "car crime career" (Light et al., 1993; Spencer, 1992). This commences with vehicle-taking as a form of excitement in which at the outset (in the early-to-mid teenage years) entire groups participate. The motivations include the "buzz" or exhilaration of the theft and of fast driving, peer-group expectations, and the possibility of making money, set against an arid background of boredom and a wish to escape from it. In later teenage years, a proportion of those involved in car theft may graduate to vehicle-taking for financial gain, sometimes stealing designated vehicles to order. This change in the balance of motives and proportions of an age-cohort participating has parallels with that suggested for shop theft, and of course reflects the general evidence on age as related to crime.

Second, a variety of initiatives has been taken in attempts to reduce car crime, particularly by focusing upon the needs of those at risk of becoming involved. One such strategy is described by Spencer (1992) who monitored patterns of car theft on an urban housing estate before and after the injection of a new set of local provisions. These included the introduction of community youth workers, and allocation of police officers to school-based crime education work. Following the commencement of these services, there was a decline in recorded vehicle theft on the estate of 27%.

A more commonly favoured option, however, has been the development of specialized interventions for those with convictions for car crime, collectively referred to as "motor projects", generally run by either youth justice services or by the probation service. In the typical case, projects of this type combine a legitimate activity such as go-karting or "banger racing" with a more formal element such as attendance at group sessions. However, formats vary a great deal as do the settings and total amounts of time demanded of the offender (Martin & Webster, 1994). The overall objective is generally one of inculcating positive attitudes towards responsible road use. The formal components of a programme may include: instruction on the laws related to driving; sessions on vehicle maintenance and on road safety; visits to hospitals to meet road-accident victims; discussions with police officers; and offence-focused work on motivations for offending and alternatives to it.

Concerning those projects established for juveniles, very little evaluation work has been carried out. Figures supplied by the National Association of Motor Projects, an informal body with the aim of maintaining contact between staff involved in this work, are quoted by McGillivray (1993). These show that whilst 80% of those sent to prison for car theft re-offended within two years, the corresponding figure for participants in motor projects who continued to attend for a three-month period was 30%.

Regrettably, none of the projects surveyed by Martin and Webster (1994) had been subjected to a properly controlled evaluation. A review of 42 schemes designed to reduce car crime, operating in the period 1989–1993 and using various combinations of structured (usually cognitive-behavioural) interventions with "banger racing" and other types of activity found little encouraging evidence (Sugg, 1998). Other research, however, has indicated that projects of these kinds may have a positive effect. The strongest and most direct evidence comes from evaluation of the *Ilderton Motor Project*, based in London, where a follow-up evaluation has demonstrated significant reductions in re-offending (Wilkinson, 1997). Over a three-year follow-up period, the re-offence rate amongst programme participants was 62%, whilst that amongst a comparison sample was 100%. There was also a significant difference in the proportions receiving custodial sentences (15% as against 46%), though the sample sizes were relatively small. Complementing this, an alternative form of evaluation was employed for the *Turas* project in Belfast (Chapman, 1995; Marks & Cross, 1992). This innovative project involved a programme of activities and the running of sessions for potential and actual joy-riders between 10.00 p.m. and 3.00 a.m., the highest-risk times of day. A sizeable proportion of known joyriders who joined in the programme activities subsequently desisted from stealing cars. During the first year of the project's operation, while the rate of car crime increased by 57% in adjoining police divisions, that in the target area rose by only 4%.

Car crime projects for adults mounted by the West Midlands Probation Service were evaluated by Davies (1993). Those offenders completing projects were compared with non-completers, yielding re-conviction rates of 54% and 100%, respectively. While only 27% of the completers were convicted of another motoring offence within two years, the corresponding figure for non-completers was 61%. This study did not unfortunately contain a genuine control group, therefore there may have been other differences between completers and non-completers which account for the obtained effect.

Evaluative studies of motor projects were reviewed by the Leicestershire Community Projects Trust (1997). The sample sizes in most studies have been relatively small and only one study to date (Ilderton) employed a comparison sample. However, using "benchmark" data such as anticipated rates of re-offending based on prediction studies, it was concluded that there are grounds for optimism concerning the impact of these programmes, both on re-offending itself and on the attitudes towards safe driving of those taking part. This contrasts with the rather disappointing evidence reported in the survey by Sugg (1998).

Burglary

The number of evaluated "tertiary prevention" or treatment programmes which have been directly or exclusively addressed towards burglary offenders is extremely small. Manning (1994) surveyed a number of projects run by probation services which consisted of group programmes with an offence-specific focus on burglary, or involved victim–offender conciliation. However, evaluative follow-up data was available for only one of these initiatives. There was tentative evidence for a group programme based in Lincolnshire, that the burglary recidivism rate over a monitoring period of 21 months was 5%, set alongside a rate of 33% for a comparison custody sample. Wilkinson (1996) conducted a long-term study to compare two probation-based projects in London, one dealing with burglary, the other with car crime. The former, but not the latter, utilized "offence-focused" work within the programme, and was associated with a reduction in recidivism after one year. By a two-year follow-up, however, this effect had disappeared.

Multi-Modal Programmes

Almost all the interventions just described have consisted of a single ingredient; in some instances a behavioural procedure such as contingency contracting, in other cases a community-based initiative involving a programme of legitimate activities. There appear to be no multi-modal programmes specifically designed for property offenders as there are for other selected groups such as those who have committed violent or sexual assaults.

The exception is the *Reasoning and Rehabilitation* programme (Ross & Ross, 1995) which has been employed with a variety of offender groups, in both custodial and community settings, and in several countries. Regrettably, however, results concerning the impact of the programme upon recidivistic property offenders are somewhat inconsistent. Delivery of the programme to a large sample (*n* = 4072) of federal offenders in Canadian prisons produced a significant reduction in offences involving sex, violence, and drugs at 22-month follow-up, but no impact on re-convictions for property offenders (Robinson, 1995; Robinson & Porporino, 2001). Positive results have also been obtained from the use of this programme in prisons in the UK, though outcomes have not yet been differentiated by offence type (Friendship, Blud, Erickson, & Travers, 2002). By contrast in a probation setting in the United Kingdom there was a measurable impact on serious offending, including burglary rates, at one-year follow-up (Knott, 1995). While the overall impact on re-convictions had disappeared by a two-year follow-up, there remained evidence of a reduction in burglary recidivism (Raynor & Vanstone, 1997). Both these findings and that reported by Wilkinson (1996) indicate the possible need for "booster" sessions for programme participants to help maintain any gains made during an intervention.

CONCLUSION

There is evidently a marked need for much more research on the psycho-social factors which contribute to the emergence of the "likely offender" depicted by routine activity and allied theories. Contemporary research on cognitive skills programmes indicates one potentially valuable direction for such efforts; currently ongoing evaluation of probation-based programmes of this type will indicate their relative impact on property re-offending (Hollin et al., 2002). Alongside this, comparatively little is known concerning the most appropriate components of interventions designed for "tertiary prevention" of property offences, and here too much more research is required.

REFERENCES

Andrews, D. A. (1995). The psychology of criminal conduct and effective treatment. In J. McGuire (Ed.), *What works: Reducing reoffending—Guidelines from research and practice.* (pp. 35–62). Chichester, UK: Wiley.

Andrews, D. A., & Bonta, J. (1998). *The psychology of criminal conduct* (2nd edn). Cincinnati, OH: Anderson.

Aust, A. (1987, December). Gaining control of compulsive shop theft. *National Association of Probation Officers' Journal,* 145–146.

Bennett, T., & Wright, R. (1984). *Burglars on burglary: Prevention and the offender.* Aldershot: Gower.

Blackburn, R. (1993). *The psychology of criminal conduct.* Chichester, UK: Wiley.

Bonta, J. (1996). Risk–needs assessment and treatment. In A. T. Harland (Ed.), *Choosing correctional options that work: Defining the demand and evaluating the supply* (pp. 18–32). Thousand Oaks, CA: Sage.

Bottoms, A. E. (1995). *Intensive community supervision for young offenders: Outcomes, process and cost.* Cambridge, UK: Institute of Criminology Publications.

Carroll, J., & Weaver, F. (1986). Shoplifters' perceptions of crime opportunities: A process-tracing study. In D. B. Cornish & R. V. Clarke (Eds.), *The reasoning criminal: Rational choice perspectives on offending* (pp. 19–38). New York: Springer-Verlag.

Casey, L. R., & Shulman, J. L. (1979). Police–Probation shoplifting reduction programme in San José, California: A synergetic approach. *Crime Prevention Review, 6,* 1–9.

Chapman, T. (1995). Creating a culture of change: A case study of a car crime project in Belfast. In J. McGuire (Ed.), *What works: Reducing reoffending—Guidelines from research and practice* (pp. 127–138). Chichester, UK: Wiley.

Clarke, R. V., & Felson, M. (1993). Introduction: Criminology, routine activity and rational choice. In R. V. Clarke & M. Felson, (Eds.), *Routine activity and rational choice. Advances in criminological theory, Vol. 5* (pp. 1–14). New Brunswick; London: Transaction.

Cohen, L. E., & Felson, M. (1979). Social change and crime rate trends: A routine activity approach. *American Sociological Review, 44,* 588–608.

Cohen, L. E., & Machalek, R. (1988). A general theory of expropriative crime: An evolutionary ecological approach. *American Journal of Sociology, 94,* 465–501.

Cooper, B. (1989). *The management and prevention of juvenile crime problems* (Crime Prevention Unit Paper 20). London: Home Office.

Davies, H. (1993). *Evaluation of motor offender projects.* Birmingham, UK: West Midlands Probation Service.

Eck, J. E. (2002). Preventing crime at places. In L. W. Sherman, D. P. Farrington, B. C. Welsh, & D. L. MacKenzie (Eds.), *Evidence-based crime prevention* (pp. 241–294). London and New York, NY: Routledge.

Edwards, D., & Roundtree, G. (1982). Assessment of short-term treatment groups with adjudicated first offender shoplifters. *Journal of Offender Counselling, Services and Rehabilitation, 6,* 8–102.

Ekblom, P. (1988). *Getting the best out of crime analysis* (Crime Prevention Unit Paper 10). London: Home Office.

Ekblom, P., Law, H., & Sutton, M. (1996). *Domestic burglary schemes in the safer cities programme* (Research Findings No. 42). London: Home Office Research and Statistics Directorate.

Farrington, D. P. (1996). The explanation and prevention of youthful offending. In J. D. Hawkins (Ed.), *Delinquency and crime: Current theories.* Cambridge, UK: Cambridge University Press.

Farrington, D. P. (2002). Developmental criminology and risk-focused prevention. In M. Maguire, R. Morgan, & R. Reiner (Eds.), *The Oxford handbook of criminology* (3rd edn) (pp. 657–701). Oxford: Oxford University Press.

Felson, M. (1994). *Crime and everyday life: Insight and implications for society*. Thousand Oaks, CA: Pine Forge Press.

Field, S. (1990). *Trends in crime and their interpretation: A study of recorded crime in post-war England and Wales* (Home Office Research Study 119). London: HMSO.

Field, S. (1999). *Trends in crime revisited*. Home Office Research Study 195. London: Home Office Research, Development and Statistics Directorate.

Forrester, D., Frenz, S., O'Connell, M., & Pease, K. (1990). *The Kirkholt burlary prevention project: Phase II* (Crime Prevention Unit Paper 23). London: Home Office.

Friendship, C., Blud, L., Erikson, M., & Travers, R. (2002). *An evaluation of cognitive-behavioural treatment for prisoners*. Findings 161. London: Home Office Research, Development and Statistics Directorate.

Gauthier, J., & Pellegrin, D. (1982). Management of compulsive shoplifting through covert sensitization. *Journal of Behavior Therapy and Experimental Psychiatry, 13*, 73–75.

Gilling, D. (1997). *Crime prevention: Theory, policy and politics*. London: UCL Press.

Glasscock, S., Rapoff, M., & Christophersen, E. (1988). Behavioral methods to reduce shoplifting. *Journal of Business and Psychology, 2*, 272–278.

Glover, J. H. (1985). A case of kleptomania treated by covert sensitization. *British Journal of Clinical Psychology, 24*, 213–214.

Goldstein, A. P. (1996). *The psychology of vandalism*. New York: Plenum.

Gow, J., & Peggrem, A. (1991). *Car crime culture? A study of motor vehicle theft by juveniles*. Cardiff, UK: Barnardos.

Gudjonsson, G. H. (1987). The significance of depression in the mechanism of "compulsive" shoplifting. *Medicine, Science and the Law, 27*, 171–176.

Guidry, L. S. (1975). Use of a covert punishment contingency in compulsive stealing. *Journal of Behavior Therapy and Experimental Psychiatry, 6*, 169.

Harland, A. T. (Ed.) (1996). *Choosing correctional options that work: Defining the demand and evaluating the supply*. Thousand Oaks, CA: Sage.

Henderson, J. Q. (1981). A behavioral approach to stealing: A proposal for treatment based on ten cases. *Journal of Behavior Therapy and Experimental Psychiatry, 12*, 231–236.

Hollin, C. R. (1990). *Cognitive–behavioral interventions with young offenders*. New York: Pergamon.

Hollin, C. R., McGuire, J., Palmer, E., Bilby, C., Hatcher, R., & Holmes, A. (2002). *Introducing Pathfinder Programmes to the Probation Service*. Home Office Research Study 247. London: Home Office.

Jarvis, G., & Parker, H. (1989). Young heroin users and crime: How do the "new users" finance their habits? *British Journal of Criminology, 29*, 175–185.

Kershaw, C., Chivite-Matthews, N., Thomas, C., & Aust, A. (2001). *The 2001 British Crime Survey: First Results, England and Wales*. Home Office Statistical Bulletin. London: Home Office Research, Development and Statistics Directorate.

Knott, C. (1995). The STOP programme: Reasoning and rehabilitation in a British setting. In J. McGuire (Ed.), *What works: Reducing reoffending—Guidelines from research and practice* (pp. 115–126). Chichester, UK: Wiley.

Kolman, A. S., & Wasserman, C. (1991). Theft groups for women: A cry for help. *Federal Probation, 55*, 48–54.

Leicestershire Community Projects Trust (1997). *Motorvate: An evaluation of its impact on re-offending, self-esteem and attitudes to safety*. Leicester, UK: Author.

Levi, M. (1994). Violent crime. In M. Maguire, R. Morgan, & R. Reiner (Eds.), *The Oxford handbook of criminology* (pp. 295–353). Oxford, UK: Clarendon Press.

Levi, M., & Maguire, M. (2002). Violent crime. In M. Maguire, R. Morgan & R. Reiner (Eds.), *The Oxford handbook of criminology* (3rd edn) (pp. 795–843). Oxford: Oxford University Press.

Light, R., Nee, C., & Ingham, H. (1993). *Car theft: The offender's perspective* (Home Office Research Study 130). London: HMSO.

Lloyd, C., Mair, G., & Hough, M. (1994). *Explaining reconviction rates: A critical analysis* (Home Office Research Study 136). London: HMSO.

MacDevitt, J. W., & Kedzierzawski, G. D. (1990). A structured group format for first offence shoplifters. *International Journal of Offender Therapy and Comparative Criminology, 34,* 155–164.

Maguire, M. (1982). *Burglary in a dwelling: The offence, the offender and the victim.* London: Heinemann.

Maguire, M. (1994). Crime statistics, patterns and trends: Changing perceptions and their implications. In M. Maguire, R. Morgan, & R. Reiner (Eds.), *The Oxford handbook of criminology* (pp. 233–291). Oxford, UK: Clarendon Press.

Maguire, M. (2002). Crime statistics: The "data explosion" and its implications. In M. Maguire, R. Morgan & R. Reiner (Eds.), *The Oxford Handbook of Criminology.* (3rd edn) (pp. 322–375). Oxford: Oxford University Press.

Mair, G., Lloyd, C., Nee, C., & Sibbitt, R. (1995). *Intensive probation in England and Wales: An evaluation* (Home Office Research Study 133). London: HMSO.

Mair, G., & Nee, C. (1992). Day centre reconviction rates. *British Journal of Criminology, 32,* 329–339.

Manning, J. (1994). *A study of burglary victim/offender programmes in the United Kingdom.* Manchester, UK: The Rhodes Foundation.

Marks, J., & Cross, G. (1992). *An evaluation of the Turas project.* Belfast: Centre for Independent Research and Analysis of Crime (CIRAC).

Martin, J. P., & Webster, D. (1994). *Probation motor projects in England and Wales.* Manchester, UK: Home Office.

Marzagao, L. R. (1972). Systematic desensitization treatment of kleptomania. *Journal of Behavior Therapy and Experimental Psychiatry, 3,* 327–328.

McCaghy, G., Giordano, P., & Henson, T. (1977). Auto theft: Offender and offense characteristics. *Criminology, 15,* 367–385.

McGillivray, M. (1993). *Putting the brakes on car crime.* London; The Children's Society; Cardiff: Mid Glamorgan County Council.

McGuire, J. (Ed.) (1995). *What works: Reducing reoffending—Guidelines from research and practice.* Chichester, UK: Wiley.

McGuire, J. (1997). Irrational shoplifting and models of addiction. In J. Hodge, M. McMurran, & C. R. Hollin (Eds.), *Addicted to crime?* (pp. 207–231). Chichester, UK: Wiley.

McGuire, J. (Ed.) (2002). *Offender rehabilitation and treatment: Effective programmes and policies to reduce re-offending.* Chichester: John Wiley & Sons.

McGuire, J., & Priestley, P. (1985). *Offending behaviour: Skills and stratagems for going straight.* London: Batsford.

Melton, G. B., Petrila, J., Poythress, N. G., & Slobogin, C. (Eds.) (1997). *Psychological evaluations for the courts: A handbook for mental health professionals and lawyers.* New York: Guilford.

Pease, K. (2002). Crime reduction. In M. Maguire, R. Morgan, & R. Reiner (Eds.), *The Oxford handbook of criminology.* (3rd edn) (pp. 947–979). Oxford: Oxford University Press.

Raynor, P., & Vanstone, M. (1997). *Straight thinking on probation (STOP): The Mid Glamorgan experiment* (Probation Studies Unit Report No. 4). University of Oxford, Centre for Criminological Research.

Redondo, S., Sànchez-Meca, J., & Garrido, V. (1999). The influence of treatment programmes on the recidivism of juvenile and adult offenders: A European meta-analytic review. *Psychology, Crime, & Law, 5,* 251–278.

Redondo, S., Sánchez-Meca, J., & Garrido, V. (2002). Crime treatment in Europe: A review of outcome studies. In J. McGuire (Ed.) *Offender rehabilitation and treatment: Effective programmes and policies to reduce re-offending* (pp. 113–141). Chichester: John Wiley & Sons.

Reid, J. B., & Patterson, G. R. (1976). The modification of aggression and stealing behavior of boys in the home setting. In E. Ribes-Inesta & A. Bandura (Eds.), *Analysis of delinquency and aggression* (pp. 123–145). Hillsdale, NJ: Erlbaum.

Robinson, D. (1995). *The impact of cognitive skills training on post-release recidivism among Canadian federal offenders.* Ottawa, Canada: Correctional Services of Canada.

Robinson, D., & Porporino, F. J. (2001). Programming in cognitive skills: The reasoning and rehabilitation programme. In C. R. Hollin (Ed.) *Handbook of offender assessment and treatment* (pp. 179–193). Chichester: John Wiley and Sons.

Ross, R. R., Antonowicz, D. H., & Dhaliwal, G. K. (Eds.) (1995). *Going straight: Effective delinquency prevention and offender rehabilitation.* Ottawa, Canada: Air Training and Publications.

Ross, R. R., & Fabiano, E. A. (1985). *Time to think: A cognitive model of delinquency prevention and offender rehabilitation.* Johnson City, TN: Institute of Social Sciences and Arts.

Ross, R. R., & Ross, R. D. (Eds.) (1995). *Thinking straight: The reasoning and rehabilitation programme for delinquency prevention and offender rehabilitation.* Ottawa, Canada: Air Training and Publications.

Royse, D., & Buck, S. A. (1991). Evaluating a diversion program for first offense shoplifters. *Journal of Offender Rehabilitation, 17*, 147–158.

Sherman, L. W., Farrington, D. P., Welsh, B. C., & MacKenzie, D. L. (Eds.) (2002). *Evidence-based crime prevention.* London and New York, NY: Routledge.

Sherman, L. W., Gottfredson, D., MacKenzie, D., Eck, J., Reuter, P., & Bushway, S. (1997). *Preventing crime: What works, what doesn't, what's promising.* Washington, DC: US Department of Justice, Office of Justice Programs.

Solomon, G. S., & Ray, J. B. (1984). Irrational beliefs of shoplifters. *Journal of Clinical Psychology, 40*, 1075–1077.

Spencer, E. (1992). *Car crime and young people on a Sunderland housing estate* (Crime Prevention Unit Series Paper 40). London: Home Office Police Department.

Stumphauzer, J. S. (1976). Elimination of stealing by self-reinforcement of alternative behaviour and family contracting. *Journal of Behavior Therapy and Experimental Psychiatry, 7*, 265–268.

Sugg, D. (1998). *Motor projects in England and Wales: An evaluation.* Research Findings No. 81. London: Home Office Research, Development and Statistics Directorate.

Sutton, M. (1993). From receiving to thieving: The market for stolen goods and the incidence of theft. *Research Bulletin, Home Office Research and Statistics Department, 34*, 3–8.

Tilley, N. (1995). *Thinking about crime prevention performance indicators* (Crime Detection and Prevention Series Paper 57). London: Home Office Police Department.

Tilley, N., & Webb, J. (1994). *Burglary reduction: Findings from safer cities schemes* (Crime Prevention Unit Series Paper 56). London: Home Office Police Department.

Trasler, G. (1993). Conscience, opportunity, rational choice, and crime. In R. V. Clarke & M. Felson, (Eds.), *Routine activity and rational choice. Advances in criminological theory, Vol. 5* (pp. 305–322). London: Transaction.

Walsh, D. (1986). Victim selection procedures among economic criminals: The rational choice perspective. In D. B. Cornish & R. V. Clarke (Eds.), *The reasoning criminal: Rational choice perspectives on offending* (pp. 40–52). New York: Springer-Verlag.

Walters, G. D. (1998). *Changing lives of crime and drugs: Intervening with substance-abusing offenders.* Chichester, UK: Wiley.

Webb, B., & Laycock, G. (1992). *Tackling car crime: The nature and extent of the problem* (Crime Prevention Unit Series Paper 32). London: Home Office Police Department.

Wilkinson, J. (1996). Does offence-focused work reduce offending in the long term? A follow-up of the first ILPS Demonstration Unit 1981–85. In B. Rowson & J. McGuire (Eds.), *What works: Making it happen* (pp. 53–61). Manchester, UK: What Works Group.

Wilkinson, J. (1997). The impact of Ilderton motor project on motor vehicle crime and offending. *British Journal of Criminology*, *37*, 568–581.

Zamble, E., & Quinsey, V. L. (1997). *The criminal recidivism process*. Cambridge, UK: Cambridge University Press.

Epilogue

Clive R. Hollin

I chose the chapters in this *Essential* Handbook in order to produce a text with an explicit focus on working with offenders. At a personal level, it seems to me that there are two fundamental contributions that can be made through working with offenders. The first potential contribution is that it may be possible to lower the likelihood of offenders committing more crimes, thereby reducing victimisation and its attendant suffering. To aim to reduce the psychological and physical pain associated with victimisation is, I'd argue, an entirely laudable professional activity. Second, as anyone who has worked with mainstream offenders knows, a life of crime is generally not a happy life: the longitudinal research shows that many persistent offenders live disrupted lives, marked by family and relationship problems, personal and social disadvantage, and financial hardship (e.g. Farrington, 1995). Further, if anyone thinks there is anything even remotely glamorous about being an offender within the criminal justice system, they should try spending a week in prison to take a reality check. The goal of offering the opportunity to offenders to lead a different type of life seems, to me at least, not a bad thing to aim towards.

While working with offenders may have creditable aims, it is also the case that sustained documented success in reducing offending is remarkably thin on the ground. There are, of course, the widely cited meta-analyses that have given rise to much optimism in the field of offender rehabilitation, clustered in the UK around what has become known as "What Works" (McGuire, 1995, 2002a). While the meta-analyses are not beyond criticism (Hollin, 1999), the "What Works" inspired style of working with offenders is important because it is based on a synthesis of research findings and is therefore firmly adhered to the concept of evidence-based practice. In other words, research evidence is the primary source for the development of practice, both in terms of the style and content of interventions. Again, this particular evidence-based approach raises practice issues

(Hollin, 2002a), but the point is made that there is a clear relationship between practice and empirical research. The clarity of this relationship is, I would suggest, particularly welcome in the field of working with offenders. It is not difficult to find examples of interventions with offenders that are based on someone's pet theory or personal whim, or on some "theory" or style of practice for which there is no empirical support. Indeed, even broadly accepted theory and practice can fall short when placed under scrutiny: for example, the commonly accepted position that penalties, and even harsher penalties, will deter offenders from committing crime fails to find wholly convincing empirical support (Hollin, 2002b; McGuire, 2002b).

The significant contribution made by the chapters in this *Essential* Handbook is that they are all firmly rooted in the empirical literature. While theory is, of course, fundamentally important, it is the reliance on testing theory and practice that is an important hallmark of the scientist–practitioner approach implicit in the work of the current contributors. There are arguments against the scientist–practitioner philosophy (Pilgrim & Treacher, 1992) that are important to consider in developing a full understanding of the field. Nonetheless, it is my view that the bottom line in working with offenders is that it must be possible to show empirically that the interventions lead to a reduction in criminal behaviour. If that reduction can be convincingly and consistently demonstrated over time then perhaps even more fundamental changes in the way society understands and reacts to those who commit offences might be possible. The onus is now on the empiricists to demonstrate the effectiveness of working with offenders: the contributions here show what has been achieved and point to the rich promise of what may be to come in the future.

REFERENCES

Farrington, D. P. (1995). The development of offending and antisocial behaviour from childhood: Key findings from the Cambridge Study in Delinquent Development. *Journal of Child Psychology and Psychiatry*, *36*, 929–964.

Hollin, C. R. (1999). Treatment programmes for offenders: Meta-analysis, "what works", and beyond. *International Journal of Law and Psychiatry*, *22*, 361–372.

Hollin, C. R. (2002a). An overview of offender rehabilitation: Something old, something borrowed, something new. *Australian Psychologist*, *37*, 159–164.

Hollin, C. R. (2002b). Does punishment motivate offenders to change? In M. McMurran (Ed.), *Motivating offenders to change: A guide to enhancing engagement in therapy* (pp. 235–249). Chichester: John Wiley & Sons.

McGuire, J. (Ed.) (1995). *What works: Reducing reoffending*. Chichester: John Wiley & Sons.

McGuire, J. (Ed.) (2002a). *Offender rehabilitation and treatment: Effective programmes and policies to reduce re-offending*. Chichester: John Wiley & Sons.

McGuire, J. (2002b). Criminal sanctions versus psychologically-based interventions with offenders: A comparative empirical analysis. *Psychology, Crime, & Law*, *8*, 183–208.

Pilgrim, D. & Treacher, A. (1992). *Clinical psychology observed*. London: Tavistock/ Routledge.

Index